Aging, Globalization, and Inequality
The New Critical Gerontology

Edited by
Jan Baars, Dale Dannefer,
Chris Phillipson, and Alan Walker

Jon Hendricks, Series Editor
Society and Aging Series

BAYWOOD PUBLISHING COMPANY, INC.
Amityville, New York

Baywood Publishing Company, Inc.
26 Austin Avenue
P. O. Box 337
Amityville, NY 11701
(800) 638-7819
E-mail: baywood@baywood.com
Web site: baywood.com

Library of Congress Catalog Number: 2005053697
ISBN: 0-89503-358-5 (cloth)

Library of Congress Cataloging-in-Publication Data

Aging, globalization, and inequality : the new critical gerontology / [edited by] Jan Baars
    ... [et al.].
        p. cm. -- (Society and aging series)
    Includes bibliographical references and index.
        ISBN 0-89503-358-5 (cloth)
        1. Gerontology. 2. Older people--Social conditions--21st century. 3. Aging--Social aspects. 4. Globalization--Social aspects. 5. Equality. I. Baars, Jan. II. Series

HQ1061.A4274 2005
305.26--dc22   2005053697

Table of Contents

To
the Memory of

Matilda W. Riley
and
John W. Riley, Jr.

Acknowledgments

The editors are grateful to the many people who have made this book possible. We are especially indebted to the contributors, who kept faith with the project over a long period of planning and development. Their enthusiasm and commitment were hugely supportive and instrumental in ensuring the completion of the book. We have been privileged to work with such a fine group of colleagues and friends.

Particular thanks must go to Joe Hendricks, editor of the Baywood's *Society and Aging Series*, who was encouraging and supportive through all stages of preparing this book. Joe has provided inspiration through his own writing, but was also an excellent source of advice and assistance on a number of crucial issues as we put this volume together.

Our sincere gratitude goes to those people who devoted a substantial amount of time to working on the manuscript, especially Lynn Falletta, Sue Humphries, Casey Miklowski, and Rebecca Siders. Their dedication to the project was crucially important, and we are deeply appreciative of the range of skills they have applied to the book. We are also thankful to staff at the Baywood Publishing Company for their support and encouragement. Julie Krempa and Bobbi Olszewski were especially helpful in overseeing production of the book in its final stages.

We are honored to dedicate this volume to Matilda and Jack Riley, who inspired us, as they did so many others, on multiple levels. The story of this project began at the meeting of the International Sociological Association, in Bielefeld in 1994. In the session "Explorations in Critical Gerontology," the Rileys' comments provided special encouragement to all of us. It was at this meeting that the International Sociological Association Research Committee on Ageing (RC11) awarded them life membership for their huge contribution to gerontology and to the work of the Committee in particular.

Matilda Riley's formulation of the multitiered relation of aging and society provides some important elements of the conceptual foundation on which this work is based. Her last book, *Age and Structural Lag,* is subtitled *Society's Failure to Provide Meaningful Roles in Education, Work and Leisure.* Indeed, Matilda was a leader and a role model in seeking to challenge what she termed "society's failures," as a scholar, as mentor, and in developing research and policy agendas nationally and internationally. This is not to say, of course, that Matilda and

Jack agreed with all of the premises or central assumptions of critical theory, or that they would have endorsed all of the arguments set forth in this volume. Yet they understood and modeled an intellectual energy and openness grounded in the recognition that the advance of a subject matter is dialectical, involving not the reproduction of agreement so much as the struggle of ideas in context. Matilda and Jack also provided important encouragement and support to each of us individually, as they did to so many others. And, until the very end of their long lives, they were exemplary models of how to grow into the end of life productively and gracefully. They were pioneers of aging not only as students of age, but also existentially and personally.

Finally, we express our deepest thanks to our families and especially our wives, Carolina Baars, Elaine Dannefer, Jane Phillipson, and Carol Walker, for their immense help over the years and their own commitment to the ideas and themes developed in this volume.

Jan Baars, Dale Dannefer,
Chris Phillipson, and Alan Walker

CHAPTER 1

Introduction:
Critical Perspectives in
Social Gerontology

Jan Baars, Dale Dannefer,
Chris Phillipson, and Alan Walker

This book is the product of our shared conviction that mainstream social gerontology has paid insufficient attention to the degree to which age and aging are
socially constituted (Baars, 1991) and to the ways in which both age and aging
are currently being transformed as a result of the set of social forces surrounding
processes of globalization. The neglect of critical analysis has weakened attempts
to understand the social processes involved in shaping age and the life course
and, consequently, the creation of alternative conceptions and visions about the
future of old age. This failure must itself be linked to general inadequacies of
theory building within gerontology, a deficiency shared across both European and
North American studies of aging (Bengtson & Schaie, 1999; Biggs, Lowenstein,
& Hendricks, 2003; Birren & Bengtson, 1988; Lynott & Lynott, 1996).

Despite its explosive development over the last half-century, social gerontology
has been characterized by an imbalance between the accumulation of data and
the development of theory (Bengtson, Rice, & Johnson, 1999; Hendricks &
Achenbaum, 1999; Riley & Riley, 1994). Researchers interested in aging have
relentlessly collected mountains of data, often driven by narrowly defined,
problem-based questions and with little attention to basic assumptions or larger
theoretical issues. An absence of theoretical development is surely not surprising
for a fairly young enterprise that seeks to capture a complex empirical reality;
especially one that draws from many disciplines, and that is preoccupied with
urgent practical problems (Hagestad & Dannefer, 2001). Yet the lack of attention
to theory has meant that research questions have often been informed by an
uncritical reliance on images and assumptions about aging drawn from popular
culture or from traditions and paradigms of theory that are considered outdated

within the broader discourses of behavioral and social theory. When such assumptions are used to guide the formulation of research questions and research designs, the result can be what has been termed "dust-bowl empiricism" (Birren, 1988), unintended reductionisms or other fallacies that misspecify the level of analysis and, therefore, missed opportunities to pursue the most revealing aspects of the subject matter in question (Hendricks, 1999).

Yet without question, several major gerontological paradigms of the late 20th century have contributed fundamental insights to inform theoretical development. These include, for example, the principles underlying cohort analysis and the interplay of demographic and economic forces, which in turn reflect the importance of history and social structure. These paradigms have included age stratification (Riley, Johnson, & Foner, 1972), life-course theory (Elder, 1974), life-span development (Baltes, 1987), and the first paradigmatic source of critical gerontology, political economy (Estes, 1979; Minkler & Estes, 1999; Phillipson, 1982; Walker, 1980, 1981).

Although these important traditions of thought have contributed organizing principles that have become classic in their influence upon both theoretical and methodological questions, with the exception of political economy approaches they do not claim to provide specific theoretical guidance. Instead, they provide some bedrock elements that must be included in any adequate theory, such as the importance of cohort flow and cohort succession, the tension between agency and structure, and the complexities involved in the articulation of individual and social change.

Moreover, almost all of these approaches have been appropriately criticized for their lack of attention to the actual experience of aging. By definition, such approaches give little attention to interpretive phenomena, such as the rich and complex fields of experience, consciousness, and action (Gubrium, 1993). As human phenomena, both age and aging are, by definition, experiences that are laden with meaning, and it is now understood that the dynamics surrounding the interpretation of events can have powerful effects on health and physiology (Ryff & Marshall, 1999). Yet many research traditions focused at the individual level are also problematic. First, some popular conventional approaches, such as exchange theory (Bernheim, Schleifer, & Summers, 1985; see Bengtson, Parrott, & Burgess, 1997), rational choice theory (Cromwell, Olson, & Avary, 1991), or socioemotional selectivity theory (e.g., Carstensen, Fung, & Charles, 2003), deal with meaning only in within narrowly formulated terms.

Second is research in the psychodynamic and psychoanalytic traditions. Much of this work deals more directly with experience and meaning, psychodynamic and psychoanalytic traditions. Much of this work deals with experience and meaning, but with a universalizing impulse that forces data into prefigured categories and patterns. Such approaches include Tornstam's (1996) exploration of gerotrans-cendence as a form of personal integration and Levinson's (1994) theories of adult development. Such approaches do justice neither to the complexities of data on the one side nor to the range of outcomes found under diverse social conditions on the other (Dannefer, 1984; Morss, 1995).

In response to such approaches, a third set of analyses have sought to make the diversity of experience and the contingency and uncertainty of meaning—phenomena that are closely allied with the theme of social change—into integral parts of theory. These include narrative approaches (Gubrium, 1993), work in the "risk society" tradition (Beck, 1992; O'Rand, 2000) and the related "postmodern" or "poststructural" accounts (Gilleard & Higgs, 2000; Gubrium & Holstein, 2002). These approaches seek to draw on humanistic and critical elements in social theory that have rightly been viewed as missing from the mainstream contemporary discourse in social gerontology (Cole, 1993).

Thus, in contrast to the traditional lament of a dearth of theory, social gerontology is now courted by numerous theoretical suitors. Despite the valuable and often provocative insights generated by each of these perspectives, our shared conviction is that none of these approaches, taken alone, provides an adequate paradigm or conceptual basis for theorizing aging.

This is the case, even though some of these approaches have effectively identified the limitations of others. For example, the discovery of cohort analysis (Riley et al., 1972; Ryder, 1965; Schaie, 1965) and cross-cultural studies of physiological, psychological, and social aspects of development and aging (e.g., Fry, 1999; Rogoff, 2003) revealed that individuals who live under different conditions develop and "age differently" (e.g., Maddox, 1987; Rowe & Kahn 1998). More than that, however, "age stratification" (Riley & Riley, 1994) and related traditions made clear that age is a feature not just of individuals, but of social organization. Age is used politically and bureaucratically as a principle of social organization and social control. Age is also a feature of culture, carrying the force of meaning and power back into the minds and bodies of citizens. When such forces are recognized, it becomes clear that age-related outcomes are, thus, not mere consequences of organismic aging, but of complex interrelations that combine social structural, cultural, and interactional processes.

In this situation, it becomes clear that it is indeed a premature closure of inquiry to accept the widely popular assumption that chronological age reflects natural, organismic changes that can therefore be the basis for the search for a general theory of human aging (Baars, 1997, 2000). This is a form of naturalization and, as with most instances of naturalization, it is also ideological because it hides from view the role of political power in structuring age-related outcomes. As a familiar example, consider the reasoning used by those working in the tradition of disengagement theory (Cumming & Henry, 1961). It is a curious logic that discovers that individuals post-65 are socially disengaged and decides that this is indicative of human nature, while ignoring the fact that their study population lived under a social regime in which age-graded retirement was a social institution. Such analyses always, and necessarily, eclipse the role of institutional power, assuming that it is nothing but an accommodation to the natural inclinations of the body. Because it deflects attention away from the importance of social and political forces, naturalization can serve as a form of *legitimation* of a social order. Indeed, it can be a particularly strong form of legitimation since it renders social forces and their explanatory potentials completely invisible. One notable feature of such models is the absence of attention to the importance of power in social relationships, or power differentials between individual and society. In this model, individuals are assumed to be largely predetermined and fixed in their nature, characteristics, and developmental possibilities; the roles of power, private interest, and ideology are eclipsed or sidelined (Dannefer, 1984, 1999).

While the importance of social forces in the constitution of aging can be glimpsed through cohort and cross-cultural studies, these approaches by themselves do not provide an analysis of the actual face-to-face processes through which both individual selves and cultural meanings are constituted and sustained. Such mechanisms have been described by work in the interactionist (Kuypers & Bengtson, 1984) and constructivist (Gubrium & Holstein, 2002; Gubrium & Wallace, 1990) traditions of sociology. In addition, the related meaning-focused analyses of other scholars from several disciplines (e.g., Cole, 1993; Kenyon, Birren, & Schroots, 1991; Marshall & Tindale, 1978; Moody, 1996). Some of this work demonstrated the potentials of analyzing micro-interaction and self-processes, and in so doing offered an implicit and occasionally explicit critique of quantitatively based approaches. Some would claim that such perspectives are, paradoxically, the most rigorous in their methodology and in their approach to empirical data, even though they are typically nonquantitative. The first task of science, Herbert Blumer proposed, is "to respect the nature of its subject matter" (1969, p. 44).

Such approaches thus stand as powerful critics of both the psychologistic and the conventional quantitatively oriented social science. Yet these approaches themselves are characterized by at least two important problems. The highly descriptive microfocus, welcome as it is, entails a risk of microfication (Hagestad & Dannefer, 2001). This has two sources. First, work in the constructivist and humanistic traditions typically *substitutes* microsocial or narrative analysis for macroanalysis, rather than seeking to conjoin the micro and macro. This practice ignores the degree to which microprocesses are shaped by macrolevel forces that are beyond the control and often beyond the sphere of knowledge of the experienced realities of everyday life. Second, related to the first, is the neglect of the centrally important reality of power. Key to understanding both individual aging and the development of age, as a property of social systems is a recognition of the centrality of power. Power is at work in determining, for example, which ideologies of age become accepted within popular or scientific discourse and which individuals have the best odds to "age successfully."

An adequate understanding of human aging requires the contributions of all the various approaches described above, despite their limitations. It requires a recognition of the importance of cohort analysis, cross-cultural and historical analysis, and it requires serious attention to processes of meaning construction and self-constitution at the microlevel of face-to-face interaction.

We share the conviction that it also requires more. It requires a recognition of how social forces operate at the macrolevel to shape the microlevel of everyday experience; of how legitimating ideologies are enacted at that microlevel to reproduce the larger institutional patterns or are occasionally resisted in ways that challenge and transform the larger institutional patterns. Such analyses make explicit the need to attend to connections between micro and macro and to the reality that power is always at play in those interrelationships and in the ongoing processes that occur at both micro- and macrolevels. These assertions represent some of the key insights of critical theory, the second paradigmatic source of critical gerontology. They are built upon contributions of other theoretical efforts in social gerontology, but go significantly beyond them.

DEVELOPING CRITICAL GERONTOLOGY

These key principles of critical gerontology are informed and enriched by foundational work in the related fields of the sociology of aging (e.g., Riley et al., 1972), the demography (Ryder, 1965; Uhlenberg, 1978), anthropology (Fry, 1999; Keith, 1982; Sokolovsky, 1990), and political economy of aging (Minkler & Estes, 1984; Phillipson & Walker, 1986). Taken together, these bodies of work have made unmistakable the fundamental importance of the social in understanding human aging. As result of this work, an opening was created for analyses that begin to comprehend aging in terms that include power, ideology, and stratification, and the expanding global reach of such forces. This book is devoted to a detailed assessment of work in this tradition. Its development can be traced to symposia exploring aspects of critical gerontology, organized at conferences in Europe and the United States in the late 1990s. The editors have brought together a range of papers first presented at these events, as well as commissioning new contributions to provide a detailed overview of current work in the broad area of critical gerontology.

This book is divided into three sections, each of which deals with key issues and concerns behind the development of critical gerontology. Each section reflects a number of forces driving debates within the discipline. First, from the mid-1990s onwards, social and political science started to analyze the impact of globalization, notably in terms of the changing role of the nation-state, the accelerated movement of people across the globe, and the rise of transnational organizations and agencies (Urry, 2000). In general terms, debates about globalization have focused on issues such as the ecological crisis, the power of multinational corporations, problems of debt repayment, and related concerns. All of these affect the lives of older people to a substantial degree. Yet as a group they have been treated as marginal to critiques of globalization and related forms of structural change. But the paradox for older as well as younger generations is that the macrolevel has become more rather than less important as a factor influencing daily life. Indeed, one might argue that while social theory in gerontology has retreated from the analysis of social institutions, the phenomenon of globalization (as ideology and process, and struggles around both) has transformed the terms of the debate. Even in the case of political economy perspectives, which continue to focus on structural issues, globalization has re-ordered the concepts typically used by researchers. Ideas associated with society, the state, gender, social class, and ethnicity have retained their importance; but their collective and individual meaning is substantially different in the context of the influence of global actors and institutions (Bauman, 1998). We see it as an important task of this book to take forward the analysis of globalization in the field of aging. All three sections of the book cover this area in different ways and at complementary levels of analysis.

A second influence running throughout the book concerns the various strands connected with the socially constructed nature of later life. This was an early theme in critical gerontology, with a variety of researchers exploring the extent to which social, biomedical, cultural, and economic forms contributed to the identity and status of older people (Minkler & Estes, 1991). In an early development of this approach, Estes (1979) summarized the "social construction of reality perspective" in old age as follows:

> The experience of old age is dependent in large part upon how others react to the aged; that is, social context and cultural meanings are important. Meanings are crucial in influencing how growing old is experienced by the aging in any given society: these meanings are shaped through interaction of the aged with the individuals, organizations, and institutions that comprise the social context. Social context, however, incorporates not only situational events and interactional opportunities but also structural constraints that limit the range of possible interaction and the degree of understanding, reinforcing certain lines of action while barring others. (p. 14)

The idea of aging as a "social construction" is taken forward in a variety of ways in all of the chapters: from the standpoint of political economy on the one side, to that of bio-medicalization on the other. A further concern of many of the contributors (notably in Section 2) is the examination of various discourses associated with the concept of age: first, in ideas about "functional age"; second, in attempts to reverse aging associated with the rise of the anti-aging industry; third, in the dominance of biological models in ordering debates about the nature of disease in later life.

A third major dimension of this book concerns debates about the nature of inequality in later life. This has been an explicit theme of research focusing on the impact of cumulative advantage and disadvantage over the life course, further reinforced by studies on the theme of social and cultural diversity in old age. Biggs and Daatland (2004) summarize this area of work as follows:

That there are more older adults around than at any time in history is now well known. It is less well understood that, as the population ages, it becomes more diverse. In part, this is because individuals have had time to develop a more integrated and particular sense of self; in other words, who they believe themselves to be. Additionally, we are exposed to many more cultural pathways than preceding generations, making life appear richer and with substantially more options than has traditionally been the case. Diversity is also a consequence, however, of cumulative inequalities that have been accrued across a lifetime and now accentuate difference in later life. Each of these trends contributes to a widening variety of experiences of aging in contemporary societies—for good or bad. (p. 1)

Section 3 of the book explores the issue of inequality in greater depth, with contributors exploring aspects of cumulative advantage/disadvantage at local, national, and global levels, drawing on a mix of quantitative and qualitative data.

SECTION 1:
Dimensions of Critical Gerontology

In Chapter 2, Jan Baars clears the ground for macrolevel theorizing in critical gerontology by dissecting the most common global descriptions of the changes taking place in contemporary society: late modern society, risk society, neo-modernism (neoliberalism), antimodernism, and postmodernism. He proposes instead "reflexive modernization" as a more appropriate term to characterize the present stage of development, which is a form of modernity and is aware both of its own limitations and trying to confront its pressing problems. He distances this idea from that of Beck's (1992) theory of reflexivity chiefly because, like Giddens' (1999) parallel theory, it leads to the individualization of social inequality and its rejection as a primary subject of research and policy. Baars argues for a fundamental reassessment of three key modernist ideas: responsible individual fulfillment, solidarity, and human dignity. The chapter ends with a call for a combination of structural and narrative scientific approaches, each with its unique contribution, into a research agenda focused on the social distribution of risks as life chances across the life course.

In Chapter 3, Chris Phillipson maintains the macrosocial focus by considering the challenges raised by the growth of globalization. He argues that globalization has precluded a distinctive stage in the history of aging by creating tensions between policies promoted by nation-states in response to demographic change and those formulated by global actors and institutions. In effect, the locus of power with regard to welfare is being shifted from local and national arenas to global ones. The chapter examines how globalization has challenged the essentially national accounts of critical gerontology and demanded an increasingly broader compass. Specifically, it considers three ways in which the "radical" view of globalization may be applied to understanding aging and older people:

its ideological influence on the social construction of aging; the particular construction of aging as a new form of risk; and its role as a driver of global inequalities in aging. The chapter concludes by calling for a new politics of old age that attempts to unite diverse networks of power and action, including feminism, black and ethnic minority groups, and transnational movements.

Alan Walker starts Chapter 4 with a retrospective review of the political economy strand of critical gerontology and continues with a focus on the relationship between social policy and aging. Walker charts the changing social construction of the relationship between old age and the welfare state over the second half of the last century. He takes issue with the criticism of a structural myopia in political economy analyses and argues that agency is not neglected. The political economy of aging was developed to rebut the previously simplistic, mainly functionalist, accounts that characterized aging as either an inevitable period of decline or as a stage of human development separate from the rest of the life course. By placing the spotlight on the social structure, it emphasized sources of inequality in old age and that remains a major aspect of its legacy. The chapter uses the "cultures of aging" thesis to illustrate the shortcomings of microsociological perspectives when compared to structural ones and, especially, highlights their acquiescence in the growth of inequality and the individualization of risk. The final part of the chapter draws on recent European theorizing on social quality to show how *both* structure and agency may interact across the life course and to emphasize the crucial role of the welfare state in enabling individual and collective agency.

In Chapter 5, Carroll Estes provides a critical feminist perspective on the issue of women's vulnerability and dependency through the life course. The first part of her chapter explores the role of the state in influencing the life chances of older women, a theme she examines in the context of various feminist theories of state and class relations. The chapter goes on to provide an analysis of the role of ideology in the construction of gender relations, especially in relation to patriarchy and the role of neoconservatism in the struggle to subjugate women. Estes brings these themes together in her discussion of globalization, with a particular focus on the rise of neoliberal, market-based policies, which reduce protection for women in vital health and social policy arenas.

In Chapter 6, Dale Dannefer considers some of the dynamics involved in the application of critical theory to gerontology. He suggests ways in which critical ideas have sometimes been co-opted by gerontology. He also argues that in less obvious ways, the ready application of critical theory to gerontology has been an occasion for those working in the critical tradition to avoid the profound and existential issues of human development, human aging, and human mortality that are ultimately generated by the topic of age—a reciprocal co-optation. The latter, involving coming to terms with morbidity and mortality even after ameliorative efforts have been applied, is the greater challenge for critical theory, and Dannefer suggests a possible avenue for beginning to confront that challenge.

SECTION 2:
Critical Dimensions of Medicalization:
Aging and Health as Cultural Products

Chapter 7 follows as Stephen Katz builds upon earlier research that has looked at the genealogy of concepts used in the discipline of social gerontology. In this chapter, he asks why the term "functional age" and its correlate, "functional health," have become widespread within studies of aging. He provides a valuable historical survey of this cluster of ideas, highlighting milestones in both theoretical debates and empirical surveys. Katz draws the conclusion that the move from "chronological" to "functional" notions of age may be seen as signaling the need to establish measurable states of being, reinforced through neoliberal health mandates around self-care and independence. He concludes that critical gerontology faces the important task of questioning the extent to which "functionality" has emerged as a dominant way of understanding the aging process.

In Chapter 8, Neil King and Toni Calasanti examine the competing discourses provided by critical gerontology and the anti-aging industry on the theme of empowering older people. The former focuses on reframing dependency in old age as a social construction, underpinned by the social relations of capitalism and the market economy; the latter placing emphasis on activity and consumerism, with the possibility of older people reversing age-related dysfunctions and disorders. The authors observe how both approaches are located in the political economy of the Global North, this often accompanied by a failure to acknowledge the stark inequalities experienced by those in the Global South. In the second half of the chapter, Calasanti and King provide a detailed analysis of debates on the theme of empowerment, noting connections between critical gerontology and the anti-aging model, while pointing to fresh areas of debate in which each will need to engage.

In Chapter 9, Kathryn Douthit picks up the medicalization strand in the social construction debate, applying this to the field of psychiatry and its treatment of dementia of the Alzheimer's type. Her critique focuses on the uncritical acceptance (within and beyond the psychiatric establishment) of biopsychiatry and its privileging of time-efficient, instrumental therapies. Douthit illustrates this through a detailed analysis of the *Diagnostic and Statistical Manual of Mental Disorders* (*DSM*), confirming the extent to which medical/biological approaches have become embedded within psychiatry. She goes on to consider the impact of biomedicalization on approaches to

Alzheimer's disease, pointing to the failure to acknowledge the loss of self-esteem, the impact of anxiety and depression, and the need for support among such patients.

SECTION 3:
Age and Inequality: Local, National, and Global Dynamics

In Chapter 10, Larry Polivka and Charles F. Longino, Jr. examine what they term as "the emerging postmodern culture of aging." The chapter begins with a discussion of the decline in traditional values and certainties along with the growth of new forms of individual autonomy and reflexivity. Then, among a range of postmodern analyses, they emphasize the significance of the neoliberal version that favors privatization of the welfare state. Polivka and Longino contrast the neoliberal "cultures of aging" thesis—that most older people are now affluent and that an even greater majority will be so in the future—with evidence about the socioeconomic status of retirees in the United States. For example, more than two-thirds of all retirees depend on Social Security for at least 50% of their income, 75% for women and 77% for minority ethnic groups. With regard to the next generation of older people, the evidence suggests that most retirees over the next 30 years will not be substantially better off than their parents. The final section of the chapter considers whether there is an alternative to the neoliberal path toward a viable postmodern old age. The answer, they argue, lies in a new narrative for social policy that stresses empowerment and is designed to create both security and freedom. Reflecting the political economy strand of critical gerontology, the authors reject privatization, given the substantial risks when applied to the field of social welfare.

Chapters 11 and 12 expand on the theme, anticipated in some of the earlier chapters, of cumulative advantage/disadvantage (Crystal & Shea, 2002; Dannefer, 2003). In Chapter 11, Stephen Crystal combines a newly elaborated cumulative advantage model with disablement theory to explore the interaction between health status and economic resources over the life course. He makes the case for the importance of midlife for understanding the precursors to late-life economic and health status. He points out that the consequences of differences in socioeconomic status in health become more marked in midlife following decades of exposure to differential stresses and risks. Crystal goes on to provide an analysis of the factors shaping later-life inequality. He concludes by laying out a conceptual model for understanding health inequality, disablement, and cumulate advantage over the life course.

In Chapter 12, Linda M. Burton and Keith E. Whitfield explore another dimension to the cumulative advantage/disadvantage theme, focusing on the health experiences of low-income families. They explore the extent to which lifetime poverty affects a range of social, psychological, and economic domains, with profound consequences for physical and mental health status. The authors report findings from a pioneering longitudinal, ethnographic study of multigenerational families, exploring two main questions: first, how is "cumulative disadvantage" experienced in daily life? Second, how are these disadvantages evidenced in family comorbidity? They emphasize a number of important findings for future research and policy, drawing out the high incidence of chronic physical and mental health problems experienced by mothers and their children. They note the cumulative effects of the early onset of certain diseases that lead on to chronic morbidity in middle and later life.

In Chapter 13, Sandra Torres returns directly to the theme of globalization, but focuses on its implications for studies of culture, migration, and aging. She is especially concerned with applying some of the concepts from the globalization debate to aging members of minority groups. Torres emphasizes the growth in the number of international migrants and the emergence of what has been termed "transnational communities." The chapter examines the implications of transnationalism for understanding both the nature of the migrant experience and the policies that need to be developed on their behalf. Torres also brings out the contradictory nature of globalization as an economic and social process. Drawing parallels with an earlier debate on gerontology around modernization theory, she highlights both the inequalities and the potential benefits that migration can bring for some groups.

Chapter 14 concludes this book with John A. Vincent's broad overview of demographic change. He employs macrocritical theory in order to understand population movements. The chapter opens with a summary of political-economy theories of population and a critique of their limited macrolevel vision and failure to account for rapid technological change. The main part of the chapter concentrates on pension-fund capitalism as a political economy that, in the last two decades of the 20th century, has become a central component of global capital markets. Drawing on the literature on "grey capitalism," the chapter demonstrates the enormous power wielded by its institutions in a largely private, undemocratic way. Vincent describes the ways that the ideology of pension-fund capitalism are reflected in the policies of a range of global organizations and agencies. He concludes with a detailed assessment of the basis for a political-economy perspective regarding demography and the operation of pension funds.

REFERENCES

Baltes, P. B. (1987). Theoretical propositions of life-span development psychology: On the dynamics of growth and decline. *Developmental Psychology, 23,* 611-626.

Baars, J. (1991). The challenge of critical gerontology: The problem of social constitution. *Journal of Aging Studies, 5,* 219-243.

Baars, J. (1997). Concepts of time and narrative temporality in the study of aging. *Journal of Aging Studies, 11,* 283-296.

Baars, J. (2000). Time, age, and autonomy. *European Journal of Social Quality, 2*, 9-27.

Bauman, Z. (1998). *Globalization*. Oxford: Polity Press.

Beck, U. (1992). *Risk society*. London: Sage Books.

Bengtson, V. L., Parrott, T., & Burgess, E. (1997). Theory, explanation and a third generation of theoretical developments in social gerontology. *Journal of Gerontology, 52b*, S72-88.

Bengtson, V. L., & Schaie, K. W. (Eds.). (1999). *Handbook of theories of aging*. New York: Springer Publishing.

Bengtson, V. L., Rice, C. J., & Johnson, M. (1999). Are theories of aging important? Models and explanations in gerontology at the turn of the century. In V. L Bengtson & K. W. S. Schaie (Eds.), *Handbook of theories of aging* (pp. 3-20). New York: Springer Publishing.

Bernheim, B. D., Shleifer, A., & Summers, L. H. (1985). The strategic bequest motive. *Journal of Political Economy, 93*, 1045-1076.

Biggs, S., Lowenstein, A., & Hendricks, J. (2003). The need for theory in gerontology. In S. Biggs, A. Lowenstein, & J. Hendricks (Eds.), *The need for theory: Critical approaches to social gerontology* (pp. 1-14). Amityville, NY: Baywood.

Biggs, S., & Daatland, S. (2004). Ageing and diversity: A critical introduction. In S. Biggs & S. Daatland (Eds.), *Ageing and diversity: Multiple pathways and cultural migrations* (pp. 1-12). Bristol: Policy Press.

Birren, J. E. (1988). A contribution to the theory of the psychology of aging: A counterpart of development. In J. E. Birren & V. L. Bengtson (Eds.), *Emergent theories of aging* (pp. 153-174). New York: Springer Publishing.

Blumer, H. (1969). *Symbolic interactionism: Perspective and method*. Berkeley: University of California Press.

Carstensen, L. L., Fung, H., & Charles, S. (2003). Socioemotional selectivity theory and the regulation of emotion in the second half of life. *Motivation and Emotion, 27*, 103-123.

Cole, T. R. (1993). The prophecy of senescence: G. Stanley Hall and the reconstruction of old age in twentieth century America. In W. K. Schaie & W. A. Achenbaum (Eds.), *Societal impact on aging: Historical perspectives* (pp. 165-181). New York: Springer.

Cromwell, P. F., Olson, J. N., & Avary, D. W. (1991). *Breaking and entering: An ethnographic analysis of burglary*. Newbury Park, CA: Sage.

Crystal, S., & Shea, D. (2002). Prospects for retirement resources in an aging society. *Annual Review of Gerontology and Geriatrics 22*, 271-281.

Cumming, E., & Henry, W. E. (1961). *Growing old: The process of disengagement*. New York: Basic Books.

Dannefer, D. (1984). Adult development and social theory: A paradigmatic reappraisal. *American Sociological Review, 49*(1), 100-116 .

Dannefer, D. (1999). Neoteny, naturalization, and other constituents of human development. In C. D. Ryff & V. W. Marshall (Eds.), *The self and society in aging processes* (pp. 67-93). New York: Springer Publishing.

Dannefer, D. (2003). Cumulative advantage/disadvantage and the life course: Cross-fertilizing age and social science theory. *Journal of Gerontology, 58b*, S327-S337.

Elder, G. H. (1974). *Children of the Great Depression*. Chicago: University of Chicago Press.

Estes, C. L. (1979). Toward a sociology of political gerontology. *Sociological Symposium, 26,* Spring, 1-25.

Fry, C. L. (1999). Anthropological theories of age and aging. In V. L. Bengtson & K. W. Schaie (Eds.), *Handbook of theories on aging* (pp. 271-286). New York: Springer Publishing.

Giddens, A. (1999). *Globalization.* BBC Reith Lectures, number 1, www.lse.ac.uk/Giddens/lectures.htm.

Gilleard, C., & Higgs, P. (2000). *Cultures of ageing: Self, citizen, and the body.* London: Prentice Hall.

Gubrium, J. F. (1993). Voice and context in a new gerontology. In T. Cole, W. A. Achenbaum, P. Jakobi, & R. Kastenbaum (Eds.), *Voices and visions of aging: Toward a critical gerontology.* New York: Springer.

Gubrium, J. F., & Holstein, J. A. (2002). Going concerns and their bodies. *Cultural Gerontology,* 191-206.

Gubrium, J. F., & Wallace, J. B. (1990). Who theorizes age? *Ageing and Society, 10*(2), 131-149.

Hagestad, G., & Dannefer, D. (2001). Concepts and theories of aging: Beyond microfication in social science approaches. In R. Binstock & L. George (Eds.), *Handbook of aging and the social sciences* (5th ed., pp. 3-21). San Diego: Academic Press.

Hendricks, J. (1999). Practical consciousness, social class, and self-concept: A view from sociology. In C. D. Ryff & V. W. Marshall (Eds.), *The self and society in aging processes* (pp. 187-222). New York: Springer Publishing.

Hendricks, J., & Achenbaum, W. A. (1999). Historical development of theories of aging. In V. L. Bengtson & K. W. Schaie (Eds.), *Handbook of theories of aging* (pp. 21-39). New York: Springer Publishing.

Keith, J. (1982). *Old people as people: Social and cultural influences on aging and old age.* Boston: Little Brown.

Kenyon, G. M., Birren, J. E., & Schroots, J. F. (1991). *Metaphors of aging in science and the humanities.* New York: Springer Publishing.

Kuypers, J. A., & Bengtson, V. L. (1984). Perspectives on the older family. In W. H. Quinn & G. A. Houghston (Eds.), *Independent aging: Family and social systems perspectives* (pp. 3-19). Rockville, MD: Aspen Systems.

Levinson, J. D. (1994). *The seasons of a woman's life.* New York: Knopf.

Lynott, R. J., & Lynott, P. P. (1996). Tracing the course of theoretical development in the sociology of aging. *The Gerontologist, 36*(6), 749-760.

Marshall, V. (1996). The state of theory in aging and the social sciences. In R. Binstock & L. George (Eds.), *Handbook of aging and the social sciences* (pp. 12-30). San Francisco: Academic Press.

Marshall, V., & Tindale, J. A. (1978). Notes for a radical gerontology. *International Journal of Aging and Human Development, 9*(2), 163-175.

Maddox, G. L. (1987). Aging differently. *The Gerontologist, 27*(5), 557-564.

Minkler, M., & Estes, C. L. (Eds.). (1984). *Readings in the political economy of aging.* Amityville, NY: Baywood.

Minkler, M., & Estes, C. (Eds.). (1999). *Critical gerontology: Perspectives from political and moral Economy.* Amityville, NY: Baywood.

Moody, H. R. (1996). Critical theory and critical gerontology. In G. L. Maddox (Ed.), *The encyclopedia of aging* (2nd ed., pp. 244-245). New York: Springer Publishing.

Morss, J. (1995). *Growing critical: Alternatives to developmental psychology.* New York: Routledge.

Neugarten, B., & Neurgarten, D. (1986). Changing meanings of age in the ageing society. In A. Pifer, & L. Bronte (Eds.), *Our ageing society: Paradox and promise* (pp. 33-52). New York: Norton.

O'Rand, A. M. (2000). Risk, rationality, and modernity: Social policy and the aging self. In K. W. Schaie (Ed.), *Social structures and aging* (pp. 225-249). New York: Springer Publishing.

O'Rand, A. (2002). Cumulative advantage theory in life course research. In S. Crystal & D. O'Shea (Eds.), *Economic outcomes in later life: Annual review of gerontology and geriatrics* (Vol. 22, pp. 14-30). New York: Springer Publishing.

Phillipson, C. (1982). *Capitalism and the construction of old age.* London: Macmillan.

Phillipson, C., & Walker, A. (1986). *Ageing and social policy: A critical assessment.* Aldershot: Gower.

Riley, M. W. (1987). On the significance of age in sociology. *American Sociological Review, 52,* 1-14.

Riley, M. W., & Riley, J. W. Jr. (1993). Connections: Kin and cohort. In V. L. Bengtson & W. A. Achenbaum (Eds.), *The changing contract across generations* (pp. 169–190). New York: Aldine De Gruyter.

Riley, M. W., & Riley, J. W. Jr. (1994). Structural lag. In M. W. Riley, R. L. Kahn, & A. Foner (Eds.), *Age and structural lag* (pp. 15-36). New York: Wiley.

Riley, M. W., Johnson, M., & Foner, A. (1972). *Aging and society, Vol. 3: A sociology of age.* New York: Russell Sage.

Rogoff, B. (2003). *The cultural nature of human development.* New York: Oxford University Press.

Rowe, J. W., & Kahn, R. L. (1998). *Successful aging.* New York: Pantheon Books.

Ryder, N. (1965). The cohort as a concept in the study of social change. *American Sociological Review, 30,* 843-861.

Ryff, C., & Marhsall, V. (Eds.). (1999). *The self and society in aging processes.* New York: Springer Publishing.

Schaie, K. W. (1965). A general model for the study of development problems. *Psychological Bulletin, 64,* 92-107.

Sokolvsky, J. (Ed.). (1990). *The cultural context of aging: Worldwide perspectives.* New York: Bergin and Garvey.

Tornstam, L. (1996). Gerotranscendence: A theory about maturing into old age. *Ageing and Identity, 1*(1), 37-50.

Uhlenberg, P. (1978). Changing configurations of the life course. In T. K. Hareven (Ed.), *Transitions* (pp. 65-98). New York: Academic Press.

Urry, J. (2000). *Sociology beyond societies.* London: Routledge.

Walker, A. (1980). The social creation of poverty and dependency in old age. *Journal of Social Policy, 9,* 49-75.

Walker, A. (1981) Towards a political economy of old age. *Ageing and Society, 1*(1), 73-94.

SECTION 1

Dimensions of
Critical Gerontology

Beyond Neomodernism, Antimodernism, and Postmodernism: Basic Categories for Contemporary Critical Gerontology

Jan Baars

Macrotheorizing in studies of aging is quite rare. Although references to an "aging society" are frequent, they are mostly not elaborated theoretically. The "aging society" is, however, not a society composed only of home care, nursing homes, or gerontological laboratories. Nor is it just the abstract world of demographic figures and their extrapolations. The issues that are referred to with the metaphor "aging society" are part of and influenced by a historical reality, which goes through rapid changes at an increasingly interconnected macrolevel. The transition to an "aging society" is, at the same time, a transition to a globalizing world of ICT (Information and Communication Technology) networks and biotechnology. Such changes may, to an important degree, *situate* and *qualify* what happens at a more local or communal level. Although the presence of more older people will change the societies they live in, technical, political, and cultural developments in these societies are equally influential in shaping *their* lives.

References to the macrolevel of society using terms such as "late-modern society, risk society," "neomodernism" ("neoliberalism"), or "postmodernism" are used with increasing frequency in gerontological studies. Typically, this occurs without the necessary elaboration or digestion of the debates that are taking place about these issues. Their relevance for social gerontology is therefore not fully clarified. This chapter presents a systematic effort to analyze these concepts and their implications for social gerontology. In this discussion, a perspective unfolds in which these basic categories or approaches are assessed in a way that does not promise an escape from modernity, but emphasizes the need to readdress and reinterpret basic modernist ideals which have been both fought for and ideologically misused: *responsible individual fulfillment, solidarity,* and *human dignity.* This perspective makes it possible to point to the crucial contributions of gerontological studies to macrotheorizing, as these may show how important societal structures are in shaping both positive and negative life chances; as gerontologists can show the build-up and full consequences of such structures during long lives.

In the next section, I will review in some detail these contours of contemporary society. This will be followed by two sections that provide a critical analysis of modernity. Finally, I will identify how this analysis of modernity points to the need for a critical gerontology and its implications for gerontology more generally.

DESCRIPTIONS AND EVALUATIONS OF
CONTEMPORARY SOCIETY

In trying to summarize the most important characteristics that emerge from the efforts of contemporary social theory to get a clear picture of present society, it becomes clear that we can only hope to get hold of contemporary *dynamics*. The self-destructive or self-innovative unrest that is typical for modernity has become a daily reality. Proclaiming change, innovation, and newness has become a normal ingredient of everyday functioning for organizations of all sorts, making it hardly possible to paint a static picture. A theoretical approach can only hope to be adequate if it succeeds in providing a useful characterization of the most important societal dynamics, which can guide further exploration and yet be open enough to be corrected by them or to question ambivalent findings.

Most contemporary societal self-descriptions begin with the theme of *globalization*: a society which is still dominated by the goals of economic and technological progress, but has been revolutionized by new possibilities for the movement of capital and of the means of production, as well as new forms of electronic communication and networking, leading to increasing global interdependencies. As Castells (1996) puts it: "a technological revolution, centered around information technologies, is reshaping, at accelerated pace, the material basis of society" (p. 1ff.). Digitalized information, images, capital, and people move around the world faster and faster. These developments lead to many new problems and questions. Most comments focus on the major challenges facing democratic control in and by nation-states. New global (e.g., ecological) risks, international crime and international mobility of capital undermine the effectiveness of legal regulation and control by nation states, questioning their sovereignty. The present situation is, however, characterized by many important ambivalences.

First, on the one hand, the nation-states appear indeed no longer capable of regulating many important processes that take place within their own territories. On the other hand, they often use this observation in a *pars pro toto* fashion: it is partially true, but also ideologically misused to evade or reduce responsibilities that should be assumed by the nation-states, such as taking care of intergenerational solidarity (Walker & Deacon, 2003).

Second, to counteract the new weakness of the nation-states, several international configurations are emerging that try to get a grasp of processes that evade national sovereignty. They are as different as bilateral and multilateral connections between nation states, the World Bank, the International Monetary Fund (IMF), and the World Trade Organization (WTO) notably. An ambivalence that arises here is that most of the dominant nation-states claim to be governed democratically, but operate through the structures of the international configurations that lack democratic legitimacy, as democracy is still based on national structures and traditions. In this undemocratic vacuum, politics are developed that go much further than compensating the nation-states for their weakness as a result of globalization. Not only can they undermine the potential weakness of the nation-state, but they can also offer the national governments an easy excuse to legitimize certain actions or regulations that might be accepted reluctantly or not accepted at all by their own democratic institutions (Walker, 1990, 2004).

Third, international mobility leads to multicultural societies in which people with different backgrounds learn to appreciate each other; but it also leads to a stronger appeal to nationalist sentiments. Democratic institutions are put to the test as they are committed to a discursive solution of conflicts, civil rights, and citizenship, regardless of ethnic origin (Habermas, 1997). Migrating workers or asylum seekers and their families will inevitably age and develop ambivalent patterns of integration and disintegration, both with the new country of residence and their origins. Multicultural aging emerges as a complicated result of international migration (Gardner, 1995, 2002; Phillipson, Ahmed, & Latimer, 2003).

Fourth, there is a rapidly growing worldwide distribution of Western products and images which has many different effects, but does not simply lead to a "McDonaldization" of the world (Appadurai, 1996; Featherstone, Lasch, & Robertson, 1995; Robertson, 1992). Its influences do not merely result in Westernization or Americanization, but lead to dynamic innovative interactions in which local cultures redefine themselves with new language and symbols: "If a global cultural system is emerging, it is filled with ironies and resistances, sometimes camouflaged as passivity and a bottomless appetite in the Asian world for things Western" (Appadurai, 1996, p. 29). In other words, globalization produces "glocalization" (Robertson, 1992). As local cultures have never been grounded in natural (inborn) qualities, there is a continuing *historical* articulation of local cultures, taking place under intensified confrontation with plural global influences. This continuing importance of locality is also relevant for the different directions societies may take in the globalization process.

As for the Western societies, we can speak of "late-modern societies" (not late moder*nism*), to emphasize that they are gradually moving away from their national identities that developed in the context of modern Western history.

They will have to establish new identities in the interfering processes of globalization and glocalization, during which time a crucial question will be in what way and to what degree they will succeed in realizing some important principles that have been developed during the modernization process, such as human dignity, freedom, and the struggle against gross forms of social inequality or exclusion.

Contemporary Societal Self-Evaluations

Or have we already entered a universe in which these elements or principles have been transcended or have become meaningless? Can we call our world *postmodern;* and what could be meant by that? Luhmann (2000) offers the following comments:

> Were we to care for realities, we would not see any sharp break between a modern and a postmodern society. For centuries we have had a monetary economy and we still have it. We also had, for centuries now, a state-oriented political system, and we still have it. . . . We have positivistic legal systems, unified by constitutions. . . . We do scientific research as before, although now more conscious of risks and other unpleasant consequences. And we send, wherever possible our children to schools, using up the best years of their lives to prepare them for an unknown future. Our whole life depends on technologies, today more than ever, and again we see more problems, but no clear break with the past, no transition from a modern to a postmodern society. (p. 35)

The discussion about modernism and postmodernism is, however, mainly a discussion about how to *evaluate* contemporary developments, especially what to expect from the further development of practical forms of reason (democracy, technology, organization, and so on); the most solid ground that enlightened people have learned to trust in the past centuries (Kunneman, 2002). In the last decades, there have been many contributions to such evaluations at a societal level that can roughly be distinguished in three main positions.

The first could be called neomodernism, which puts all its trust in the innovative furthering of the productive sources of modernity: rationally guided economic and technological growth. Sometimes this position is superficially legitimized by the neoliberal identification of "freedom" and a "free world' with a free *market*, without much doubt about the costs of this equation in terms of inequality or ecological damage.

The second position could be called *antimodernism*, as its diagnosis aims mainly at criticizing modernity for its hopeless illusions and points the way back to a supposedly solid and unquestionable foundation that should be found in a specific tradition. This may vary from traditional Marxism, to Eastern wisdom, conservative Christianity, or the Sharia. Some forms of ecological fundamentalism also belong to this category.

Finally, the third position could be called (or calls itself) postmodernism. This could be characterized as the disillusioned counterpart of neomodernism. It does not believe in the promises or hopes of the neo-modernists, but cannot be positioned under antimodernism, as it refuses to believe in any unquestionable foundation.

In my opinion, a contemporary critical social theory has more in common with postmodernism than with the other two positions because of its *latent* critical potential. The heterogeneous theoretical configuration of postmodernism (including poststructuralism) gained intellectual momentum in the 1970s and 1980s as a way to reflect on the *débacle* of Marxist revolutionary thought. Most of its leading authors, such as Jean-Francois Lyotard, Jacques Derrida, and Andre Glucksmann, were active Marxists before they became disillusioned postmodernists. The postmodern reflection of the Marxist critique of society, which was predominant during the 1960s, made it clear that the Marxists tried to criticize capitalist modernity, but held on to one of its most predominant ideas. This is the idea that history has an *immanent* force and direction, which humans can rationally understand and actively partake in so that they can appreciate their actions, not only as a fulfillment of history's meaning, but also as a personal self-realization. This basic idea gave Marxist scholars in the social sciences, philosophy, and history a firm conviction about the way they should take a stand, and evaluate their position and the actual historical situation. It gave them the possibilities for a solid and comprehensive "Diagnosis of our Time," to quote Karl Mannheim's (1943) great title.

The modernist idea that history shows an immanent force and direction that can be rationally understood and implemented in subjective action has been left behind in postmodernism. The fundamental opposition that negatively unites this otherwise rather heterogeneous work of philosophers like Lyotard, Foucault, and Derrida is directed against the Hegelian idea that history harbors a meaningful direction or end that can be rationally and systematically understood; an idea which had been turned into a historically grounded political program by Marx. In this respect, the postmodernists repeated the dramatic transition that Theodor Adorno, but especially Max Horkheimer, made toward the end of the 1930s, as they moved away from a Marxist vision of history, under the lasting impression of the Stalinist regime (Baars, 1987). In their *Dialectic of Enlightenment,* written during the Second World War, we find already the typical reactualizing of Nietzschean motives, such as the interdependency of reason and power, which is also characteristic of the postmodernist position. They also emphasized the loss of the unity of rationality, morality, and historical development and were consequently criticized by the more traditional Marxists for not being able to identify, let alone *mobilize,* a "revolutionary subject."

Whereas postmodernism could be seen as a reactualization of Nietzsche, critical theorists like Karl-Otto Apel and Jürgen Habermas, have also discarded the Hegelian heritage of Marxism and have returned to the more formal position of Kant. According to Habermas (1968), modernity must derive all meaning from itself, without being able to rely on any authority outside it. But he tries to establish a new universal (although modestly called *quasi*-transcendental) foundation of rationality and justice through the concept of communicative action and theoretical and practical discourses. The rational foundation for this endeavor, however, is a rather formal and *procedural* discursive rationality.

The postmodernists appear to be right in the sense that we cannot rely any more on a rational comprehensive understanding of the meaning or *telos* of history; but they have often made problematizing into an aporetical style that is explicitly intended to lead nowhere; from rightly criticizing massive utopian programs to atopian disorientation. But we cannot leave the world and are consequently always already involved in it, which makes a certain level of responsibility inevitable. Even Derrida's pleas to dismiss the idea that language and, therefore, rationality could offer the possibilities to understand anything clearly or communicate any understanding unequivocally, presupposes that this message comes across. The postmodern emphasis on differences and heterogeneity can easily become an academic cult, which does not clarify, but occludes, the most important issues and, consequentially, puts *aesthetic* categories in the place of *ethical* considerations; a theoretical movement that is paralleled in postmodern social theories where important differences in life *chances* are just presented as different life*styles*.

Postmodern thinkers may contribute to the unmasking of inadequate understandings of modernity, but offer little with regard to thinking and acting responsibly in the situations we are living in. I suggest, therefore, to leave the pseudo-apocalyptic terminology that has emerged in the expressions postmodernity, posthistory, poststructuralism, posthumanism, and so on. The term *reflexive* modernization appears to be a more adequate general term to characterize our present situation in an *evaluative* sense. Interpreting postmodern criticism from the perspective of reflexive modernization allows us to understand postmodernist criticism as ways of criticizing absolutist pretensions of massive modernization. Reflexive modernization is a form of modernity, which is responsibly aware of and confronted with its own limitations, but tries to find better ways of dealing with problems that we cannot avoid or look away from. As I am using the same concept, this leads to a discussion of Beck's theory of reflexive modernization.

REFLEXIVE MODERNIZATION IN CRITICAL PERSPECTIVE

In *Risk Society: Towards a New Modernity* (1992), but especially in his later work (Beck, 1994), Ulrich Beck aims at an analysis of typical changes that occur as the process of modernization enters its reflexivity. In order to give a critical perspective on this theory, I shall present an alternative vision of the process of modernization, which is differentiated in three phases: early, massive, and reflexive modernization. The reasons behind this differentiation are twofold. First, the distinction between *massive* and *reflexive* modernization offers a perspective in which we can appreciate the strengths and shortcomings of postmodernism. Secondly, the origin of modernity in *early* modernization puts Beck's theorem of "individualization" in a broader perspective, showing its limitations, especially with regard to his perspective on social inequality.

Early, Massive, and Reflexive Modernization

Modernization is defined by Beck (1992) as follows:

> Modernization means surges of technological rationalization and changes in work and organization, but beyond that it includes more: the change in societal characteristics and normal biographies, changes of lifestyle and forms of love, change in the structure of power and influence, in the forms of political repression and participation, in view of reality and in norms of knowledge. In social science's understanding of modernity, the plough, the steam locomotive and the microchip are visible indicators of a much deeper process, which comprises and reshapes the entire social structure. Ultimately the *sources of certainty* on which life feeds are changed. (p. 50)

Modernity in this broad sense can be characterized primarily as a process of modernization, which does not have a specific positive goal, but must rather be regarded as a movement "away from"—away from still existing, but as out-dated and "traditional" experienced forms of life or ideas. This movement "away from" was characterized centuries ago by an expression that can be regarded as a traditional proverb of the spirit of modernity: "The air of the city makes one free," dating back to the earliest forms of modernity, when the cities in 12th century France offered freedom from feudal authorities (e.g., Le Goff, 1980). Of course, the freedom that the modern city offered was by no means unconditional, but it was freedom from traditional forms of domination.

This early modernity of the European cities liberated the markets from feudal restrictions and liberated adult males from larger, premodern family structures so that they could have their own families. They could, in principle, all be a classical *pater familias* on a smaller scale, dominate the other members of the modern nuclear family, and be the only one to work outside the house and to really count in the world. Individualization announces itself as an important ingredient in the modernization process, although in a limited form that can be seen as a modernized version of a much older patriarchal tradition. The liberation and individualization of the male head of the nuclear family, ruling over his wife and children, continued into the 1960s until it fell prey to further modernization.

Beck's characterization of present society as a *Risk Society* takes place, however, in the context of an historical perspective in which the individualization, which already characterized early modernization, does not play an important role. To give *reflexive* modernization its specific status in his theory, the earlier phase of modernization is constructed by Beck as its preparation: the structural overthrow of a traditional society, rooted in feudal and rural relationships, through a rationalistic debunking of traditional prejudice and dogmas. The way to the future was paved by instrumental applications of rationality in the forms of efficient organization and productive technology, which promised to lead to prosperity for all. I prefer to see this as a phase that came after *early* modernization and suggest it be called *massive* modernization. This phase of the modernization process was certainly reflected upon intensely, but these reflections led to a strengthening of the rational and moral eminence of the modernization process. To demonstrate this inherent connection between rationality and morality repre- sented Kant's highest pride and ambition, a connection, which was reaffirmed and strengthened in Hegel's philosophy of history. In this historical form, it was reinterpreted by Marx, who turned this proclaimed Hegelian unity of historical moral rationality against the limitations that were posed by the societal structures, in order to free the full productive potential and actually realize the rational *and* moral goal of history. Marxism represented only a specific version of massive modernization, according to which society would be organized as the best possible world on the foundation of rational knowledge and its technological application. This is basically a continuation of the program of the Enlightenment as the intellectual movement that would establish a perfect rational world, freed from the errors of tradition, at the basis of a unity of rationality and morality.

Although there have been early voices opposing this process, especially of authors such as Schopenhauer and Nietzsche, who are preferably reread by the late 20th-century postmodernists, the intellectual mainstream that accompanied industrial modernization was a testimony to its undoubted massivity. In this sense, both extremes, Marx *and* his bourgeois opponents, believed in the his- torical mission of progressive industrial development. This massive phase of the modernization process got stuck as it only *modernized traditional forms of domination* and resulted in life forms that resisted further change. It got stuck, and subsequently overthrown, as the dynamics of modernization have not come to a standstill. Modernization enters its reflexive phase when the industrial society itself becomes critically interrogated—and subsequently changed—by a further implementation of its own modern principles and predominant among these is individualization.

Structures change because people begin to act differently. At such moments, deviating people tend to be seen by the representatives of the challenged structures as (too) individualist; put otherwise, the structures are suffering from individual- ization. Throughout modernity, every major change was a modernization of earlier modernizations and, from its earliest phases, the many shifts in the modernization process have been dismissed as processes of individualization. This also puts Beck's theorem of individualization in some perspective. MacPherson (1964) referred to a *tradition* of "possessive individualism" when he discusses the work of of the 17th-century philosopher Thomas Hobbes. Marx worried about the uprooting of workers by modern production forces; Durkheim, who can hardly be called a Marxist, interpreted the change of mechanical to organic solidarity as an increase of individualism; Weber was again opposed to Marx as well as to Durkheim, but he too emphasized the consequences of a process of rationalization that had thrown the individual back on itself. In a report of the research he did among late 19th-century agricultural workers, Max Weber (1984) concluded in 1892 that they showed a "sharp individualism," wanting to break away from the patriarchal community into a proletariat without a *Fatherland*. Finally, Tönnies (1887) worried about the loss of solidarity in the transition of the *Gemeinschaft* to the individualistic *Gesellschaft*; and one could go on adding to this list.

Beck's individualization is nothing more than a further development of the early modern emancipation, which was limited to the liberation of male heads of the family who continued to dominate Western societies into the 1960s, until the baby-boom generation, and especially their feminist part, revolted against this pattern. Women contested the modernized patriarchal tradition, claiming the *effectuation* of universal rights that had been a legacy of modernity for a long time. At the same time, the specific articulation of these universal rights has become one of the centers of a globalized clash between cultural traditions, making clear that theories of modernization have their own ethnocentric limitations. But for Western societies, this process had many implications for both men and women as they were "freed" from many coordinates that were orienting life: family, profession, religion, uncritical belief in science and rational progress. This results in a different, more radical individualization as each person must answer the most important questions of life for him- or herself, without being able to rely on pregiven roles, answers, or respected authorities.

As a result of these changes, not only patriarchal hierarchies and morals, but also many less traditional institutions and organizations have lost their appeal: Catholic, Protestant, Socialist, and Humanist alike. In this conflict, the representatives of the traditions that were dominant until the late 1960s tend to see only the egoism and denial of the traditional values that have guided their communities for such a long time. Throughout Europe, we hear especially the complaints of the Christian Democrats who are defending (very different interpretations of) Christianity, trying to unite their internally clashing forces to keep something of their previous dominance alive. Equally, traditional socialists complain about the loss of solidarity as they understood it, and finally we hear the complaints of the conservatives who see traditional hierarchies and traditional interpretations of decency and obedience vanish. The cause of these complaints is often, as in Beck's theory, something supposedly "new" which is called *individualization*.

The Individualization of the Social

Beck's problems with the concept of individualization become obvious when he refers to individualization as *homogenization* and to a *standardization* of individualization. I propose that the basic problem Beck tries to analyze and articulate in his theory of reflexive individualization, culminating in his characterization of individuals as "architects of their own life" is a *moral uprooting*. The loss of a unity of rationality and morality, the loss of the conviction that what is rational is also good, is the essence of Beck's reflexive modernization.

Concerning the theory of individualization, a problem arises when the *moral* condition of individualization, meaning that everybody has to make his or her own decisions, without being able to rely on outside authorities, becomes mixed up with an empirical interpretation, implying that every individual is actually free in making decisions. An analogous problem occurs in Giddens' work (1991, 1992) when he identifies actor and agency: the moral evaluation that every individual must decide for himself or herself, because there is no outside authority to rely on, is misunderstood in an empirical way as if each individual is in fact the agent of his or her life. Although we can learn from many studies—sociology owes its existence mainly to this situation—that individual behavior is in many ways influenced, restricted or pre-programmed by societal structures and agencies, this societal structuring cannot fully enter the diagnosis of Beck and Giddens, although it is mentioned occasionally.

The different models of the welfare states, which could be seen as projects that were far from perfect, but that tried to realize systems of solidarity that could be regarded as both favorable for productivity and morally responsible in relation to social problems, have not been updated in order to become more adequate to face the new challenges of globalization, but have proclaimed to be definitively lost, as an unwarranted and unfounded unity of rationality and morality. The paradox is that the pretensions of a more superior unity of rationality and morality return in the idea of a "free" market that is home to the *homo economicus*, whose rationality is unfounded, but frees the way to prosperity for those who "deserve" it. The fact of being prosperous is, within this logic, at the same time proof of its moral justification and an example for all.

This historical transition to a situation in which the market serves as both a rational and moral medium of progress has been shared by people who have witnessed the gradual decay of the welfare states of Western Europe (Guillemard, 1986) as well as by those who were suddenly freed from state socialism (Ferge, 1997). Of course, the individual *homo economicus* can only function as a tiny part of an overwhelming economic system that tends to dominate all other social relations. In this sense, the individualization is only a phenomenon at the surface, serving as an ideology for those who justify their unsocial policies by referring to "the individual" with his presumably autonomous preferences and choices. This "individualization of the social", to use Zsuzsa Ferge's term, has many important consequences, the most predominant of which is the eclipse of social inequality.

The Eclipse of Social Inequality

The individualization of the social manifests itself clearly in the eclipse of *social* inequality, which is announced in Beck's work as the "individualization of social inequality" (Beck, 1992). Here too, the distinction between *massive* versus *reflexive* modernization can throw some light on the meaning of Beck's diagnosis. It makes sense to criticize massive Marxist programs that made social inequality the fundamental "class" dimension of society from which not only its present situation, but also its history and future development, should be clearly understood. In its classical form, inequality between the classes (related to the means of production) was seen as the cause of all other social problems. Consequentially, by taking away this cause, social *equality* should be established, organizing society in such a way that would have been shown in the absolutized understanding of history, in which rationality and morality are pretended to be intimately unified.

Contemporary criticism of absolutized, massive programs for the rational creation of a perfect world, free from social inequality and other mishaps, can easily be accepted and even strongly underlined as their historical manifestations have led to social disasters. But to conclude from this that social inequality or social exclusion would have to disappear from the list of important subjects of inquiry and policy is quite another matter. Yet this eclipse of social inequality can be observed in the work of many important social theorists who are devoted to the development of a critical analysis of contemporary society.

We can see it not only in the work of Beck but also in the work of Habermas and, with some nuance, in the work of Giddens. In Habermas' critical diagnosis of our time, which follows his exposition of *The Theory of Communicative Action* (1987), problems of social inequality, which gave rise to the postwar welfare states, are theoretically approached as problems of the *distribution of compensations* by the welfare states. As a consequence of his thesis of the colonization of the life world, this compensatory distribution is suspect and partly for good reasons. But the result is that problems of social inequality in terms of material reproduction and, especially *unequal life chances,* with their many different 'causes, are neglected in favor of conflicts that arise in the domain of cultural reproduction: "The issue is not primarily one of compensations that the welfare state can provide, but of defending and restoring endangered ways of life. In short, the new conflicts are not ignited by distribution problems but questions having to do with the grammar of forms of life" (Habermas, 1987, p. 392).

Giddens' diagnosis of our time shows the same basic tendency. In his view, *emancipatory* politics, with their primary imperatives of justice, equality, participation, and a focus on *life chances,* must be left behind for so called life politics. This is defined as follows: "Life politics concerns political issues which flow from processes of self-actualisation in post-traditional contexts, where globalising influences intrude deeply into the reflexive project of the self, and conversely where processes of self-realisation influence global strategies" (Giddens, 1992, p. 214). He criticizes Habermas for clinging to an old idea of trying to develop a framework for emancipatory politics in terms of a theory of communication. However, in his further elaboration of the relation between emancipatory politics and life politics, Giddens admits that this is more complex than what he suggested earlier as a consequence of his theoretical exposition in *Modernity and Self-Identity*.[1]

LATE MODERNITY—AN IMMANENT CRITIQUE

In spite of many differences and ambivalences that characterize the present, it remains possible and even necessary to articulate critical analyses of a more general (macro) type, to give context and orientation to more specific interpretations, although in a more modest way than approaches that assume to have the forceful truth of history on their side. Such a modest approach does not mean that the criteria or ideas that can guide a critique must be abstractly constructed without any respect for traditions. On the contrary, the leading ideas of critical interpretations can often be taken from the traditions of the societies concerned, but not in a *traditionalist* way, assuming that all was better in the past. The proposed method is rather an immanent critique that takes principles as criteria for criticism and orientation that are *embodied*, although not adequately, in the tradition and institutions of the society that is subjected to the critical interpretation.

The Western societies, which are usually referred to with the concept of late modernity, face the challenge of continuing in an adequate way the most important principles that have been brought forward by their traditions. Even if they have been realized inadequately or only used ideologically, without taking them seriously, they form an important part of their characteristic heritage and can be used as criteria to guide critical interpretations. Of course, the orienting principles are not in any way self-evident, beyond doubt or important because they are traditional. They must be reflectively selected for their significance in addressing *contemporary* problems.

To give a well-argued account of this complex problematic, which would do some justice to the many differences between Canada, the United States, and the countries of Western Europe or the larger European Union, is far beyond the

---

[1] "Thus far, emancipatory politics has been described as though it were merely the preparation for the emergence of life politics. The relation between emancipatory and life politics is, of course, more complicated than such a view would suggest" (Giddens, 1992, p. 228). As could be shown more extensively, Giddens mixes up two distinctly different phases in Habermas' work. He criticizes Habermas for something he was trying to develop in *Knowledge and Human Interests* (1968), but actually abandoned by the time he wrote *The Theory of Communicative Action* (1987).

ambitions of this chapter. It must suffice to mention briefly some principles that even though they are still worth striving for, have, in different forms, inspired social movements of the past.

A first idea is the liberation of the individual in the sense of a *responsible self-fulfillment*, an idea that has been cherished by the liberal tradition. The realization of the idea need not necessarily be opposed—as in complaints about individualization—to the second basic idea, which has been characteristic of the socialist tradition: *solidarity*. The development of individuals is not opposed to, but *presupposes* solidarity and a mutual acknowledgment that citizens are in many ways dependent on each other. This basic idea and ideal of solidarity has been something many modernist movements have been fighting for and implies a criticism of social inequality or exclusion in the sense of gross differences in life chances. Finally, the modern tradition has articulated in many ways a third critical idea: *human dignity*. This seemingly abstract idea has become urgently important again. Although human beings share an existence that is fundamentally fragile and never free from the dangers of suffering and becoming dependent on others, it may seem that some forms of revolutionary genetic engineering might fundamentally change the human condition. Even if this would be the case, the fundamental respect for human dignity must be reinterpreted and reestablished.

These three principles appear to present the most important challenges for a critical reflexive gerontology and serve as points of orientation for a critical approach to late modernity, in which these ideas have to be reinterpreted and revitalized. (See also Alan Walker, in this volume, about the articulation of Social Quality for the E.U.). Although the critical ideas may have been developed during modern history in an absolutist or otherwise distorted form, the critique of these distortions should not lead to abandoning them completely with the false argument that contemporary globalization would make them outdated. Generally, there are different paths that societies may (and do) take in the globalization process, as has been shown by Scharpf and Schmidt (2000), Scharpf (1999), and Sykes, Palier, and Prior (2001). It seems inevitable that globalization takes place in the form of glocalization as each region or nation-state will also guard, articulate, and emphasize its own specific identity and not disappear in an anonymous mist of globalization.

The three critical ideas that were referred to allow a criticism of contemporary dominant models of neomodernism or neoliberalism that overemphasize and exploit the limited contribution that a market economy may have in terms of a flexible satisfaction of needs and an adequate distribution of resources to enhance productivity. In the following, I shall argue that one of the basic strategies of the neomodernist project to dominate late modern society is a *flexibly marketed colonization*, which transforms and threatens individualization, social relations, organized care, and human dignity in specific ways. At the same time, I shall try to clarify the helpless opposition, which is characteristic for *anti*modernism (including reactionary or fundamentalist positions) and *post*modernism, and point to the possibly crucial contribution of gerontological work.

Flexibly Marketed Colonization

The concept of a flexibly marketed colonization shows some affinity with Habermas' concept of a colonization of the life world (1987). It refers to the process in which flexible marketing exceeds its relative meaning and functions as a strategy to exercise and extend power. As in the more classical forms of colonization, its centers are still centers of power, which try to dominate the domains that interest them, although they are no longer only or even primarily nation-states. These former agents of the colonization process have to share their power and are typically losing their grip on the most important global players of the new forms of colonization. The colonization of foreign markets has become, however, just one possibility as the colonizing energy also turns inward, to the rich populations of the Western world, as they possess the material riches the colonizers are after. A continuity with historical forms of colonization is, however, that it is carried forward by the forceful, productive combination of natural science, technology, and profit-oriented enterprise that has been developed during the modernization process.

One of the premises of this critical concept is, however, that colonization is not just a one-sided, overpowering domination: colonization allows for counteraction, but tries to change the preconditions under which social life takes place, in order to put it to productive use. Theoretical and practical forms of anticolonization remain possible, but can, paradoxically, often be seen as essential for these new forms of colonization as they try to keep the systems flexible enough to incorporate rebellion or deviation in their operations as innovation. An important question remains whether these counteracting processes succeed in somehow maintaining their *nonidentity* or are absorbed and exploited for a further sophistication of the colonization process. Ambivalence rather than clear-cut dichotomies are typical for this flexibly marketed colonization.

Flexibly Marketed Social Relations

One of the main points of the postmodern and poststructuralist criticisms of neo-Marxist theories of society was their assumption of a total societal system that could be turned around and guarantee freedom and affluence for all. The alternatives that were proposed emphasized the flexibility, ambiguity, and differentiation of structures and processes. Deleuze and Guattari (1980), for instance, developed the idea of a "rhizome," an invisible and underground network of offshoots that, unlike the tree that reduces the multiple into one, is flexible, and its parts can even continue independently if broken. Basic to such approaches is the idea that societal systems are never closed, but always leaking; there is always something that flees and escapes the system and is not yet controlled.

In the last two decades, these ideas were absorbed and used to innovate the systems. Postmodern constructions emphasizing flexibility, creativity, and potentials have been integrated as a mode of accelerating the dynamics of the system, resulting in a neomodern reinterpretation of the leftist criticism of capitalism (Ray & Sayer, 1999). Instead of hierarchic bureaucratic organizations that were typical of the postwar time until the early seventies, more flexible, marketlike structures were introduced into the organization to allow more personal space for the autonomy and potential of the workers. Through rotation of tasks, lifelong learning, and marketable self-presentation, workers become strategically operating managers of their own career and life course. Postmodern, aesthetically inspired images of social relations as open networks that are able to expand without limits and that integrate new nodes, became appropriate paradigms for an innovation-based capitalist economy, which decentralized concentration, resulting in endless rhizomatic deconstruction and reconstruction. The danger is that more solidarity-oriented forms, such as collectively negotiated wages, job security, and trade union membership are becoming residual and discarded as traditional. This changes the potential to provide for the needs of old age: those who cannot compete effectively during the relatively few years in which the capital must be earned and partially invested for the future will encounter material hardship while aging.

The strategies of a flexibly marketed colonization operate more by exclusion than through control. As too much energy would be lost in total control, the aim of colonization is to stimulate the colonized to act in ways that are beneficial for the colonizing system by rewarding such behavior. Besides the people who are worth stimulating, there are the categories of people who are irrelevant because they cannot be put to productive use or have ceased to do so, like older people.

Flexibly Marketed Lifestyles

Although there have never been watertight walls between them, there is an increasing de-differentiation of culture and material production that has led to new phenomena (Crook, Pakulski, & Waters, 1992). The production for contemporary markets in the richer parts of the world is not primarily oriented toward satisfying material needs, such as needs for protective clothing, food, shelter, or transportation. It aims, rather, at a culturalized and branded mixture designed to satisfy many needs at the same time. That culture has lost a certain autonomy, and some of its internal differentiations, such as *high* versus *popular* culture, does not make it less, but more important as it pervades all domains of life in the form of typical lifestyles. The classical distinction between *use* value and *exchange* value has lost its hold; the consumption of material objects can no longer be separated clearly from the consumption of lifestyle related images. Moreover, the production of images as such (movie, TV, the Internet, and so on) has increased dramatically, and their consumption has become of major economic and political importance, granting enormous influence and power to large corporations like AOL, Time Warner, Disney, and Bertelsmann.

Consumption goods are cast as images offering a certain identity, be it of the Armani, Benetton, Camel, or Nike type. This does not lead to a standardization that is connected with static forms of stratification, but to a dynamic differentiation that no longer addresses the desire to keep up with the Joneses, but to be *different* from them. The subtle machinery of these branded differences of lifestyles is kept going by an integration of the revolt against consumerist conformity by rebellious young talent, which is absorbed and used as a way to innovate the supply of consumption goods through talent scouting and trend watching. Baudelaire's (1964) observation, 150 years ago, of the rise of the 19th-century dandy, who aesthetically designs and invents himself and his life, has turned out to be an early announcement of this phenomenon that has become integrated in the dynamics of the markets.

In the last decades, the further development of individualization, *getting away* from traditional community and family structures, was also made possible by the growing material resources flowing since the 1950s and 1960s, also to others than the male heads of the family. This emancipatory move has been partially absorbed and manipulated by the commerciality of the market that designs the lifestyles of teenagers, young dynamic career builders, and other possible *clientele* and typically emphasizes the independence and successfulness of the buyers of its most advanced products.

But manipulation does not appear to cover the whole story. The involvement in the dynamic market can also be regarded as a more "authentic" impulse of freedom, as Charles Taylor (1989) has emphasized, as it also makes it possible to explore and shape how people want to live. Also, the marketing of information in a broad sense helps people to get answers to many new and changing questions that confront them, where traditional values offer no convincing answers or have to be reinterpreted to be able to point to possible answers (Giddens, 1992).

Marketed lifestyles are related to phases of life and consequently, also to aging (e.g., Gilleard & Higgs, 2000). The lifestyle of the aged, but vital, adventurous, and young-at-heart is increasingly marketed, casting for the successful cosmopolitan man or woman, who can appreciate and afford quality. The dynamic market responds flexibly to spending power and offers the elderly who can afford this opportunities to break away from what they see as traditional, outdated roles and self-presentations of the elderly. To be able to participate in these privileged activities and situations, a level of material and cultural resources is needed that illustrates that lifestyle, consumption, and life chances are systematically interconnected.

Flexibly Marketed Service and Care

The present orientation in care appears to be dominated by market-oriented management, which aims at a restructuring of solidarity using the dynamics of the market. As a result of this, many traditional forms of "care" are supplanted by market-regulated forms of "service." Many organizations specializing in care for the elderly eagerly show how they also can operate in market terms and develop models of care that are preferably presented as both more cost-effective and qualitatively better. The criteria of such new models of service are often articulated by determining more or less precise "time-budgets," in order to achieve specific goals that are presented explicitly to the clients. The dynamics of the market that assert themselves as the components of this "contractual care" are ideally a clearly stated organizational service. Such service should be rendered in a precise amount of time, approximating individual needs—be it the repair of a hip fracture or putting somebody's socks on—in the managerial terms of the organization. The market-oriented individual has to articulate his or her need in the established terms of an organization, which may offer something that might satisfy this need; the client then gets this service within a clearly limited time span and pays the required amount of money in return, asserting his or her autonomy. This general model, which seems to embody the ambition of many care managers, could be called a "pitstop model of service," which may be adequate in terms of maintenance and repair, but not for care, especially long-term care.

This is not to deny that there is a certain gain in freedom that is indeed expressed in terms of autonomy in much gerontological research (Baars, 2000). This reflects the experience that the individual does not want to be dependent on axiological structures such as we find typically in traditional institutions. The individual can determine what she or he wants, without being bothered by values of traditional habits that are of no interest for this individual. He or she just receives the service as required, pays the money, and leaves. The combination of advanced technology and market mechanisms has resulted in a premium on the accelerating effectiveness of health services. The autonomy of the market, based on articulated needs and contractual reciprocity, presupposes the ability and readiness to assert one's autonomy and opt out.

The uncritical embrace of these developments is characteristic for *neo*modernism. What this consumption-oriented service misses may become clearer when we compare it with the ethics of care as they are articulated by Berenice Fisher (e.g., Abel & Nelson, 1990), Gilligan (1977), or Tronto (1992). The presupposed market model of two contractual parties who agree on a service to be delivered or go elsewhere is, however, a source of problems for those persons who are really dependent on care and cannot afford to roam the market for better offers. Efficiently organized service is not an adequate model for care, especially not for long-term care. Moreover, market orientations do not build or support mutual solidarity. That is often rightly put forward by the representatives of more traditional forms of solidarity. But the antimodernists fail to acknowledge that the traditional forms of solidarity were often bought at the expense of excluding whoever did not accord with the norms or values of the particular community. These particularistic tendencies and other weaknesses have been repeatedly and typically criticized by the *post*modernists, who, however, have not been able to point to alternative ways of living together. The antimodernists, as advocates of traditional forms of solidarity, rightly point their finger at this, but fail to inspire those who are not attracted to their particular brand of traditional values. They welcome the freedom that the market offers and join the neomodernists, which causes the representatives of traditional orientations to call even more loudly for a reawakening of traditional values.

Human Dignity and a Flexibly Marketed Colonization of Life

In the last few years, we have witnessed an accelerating increase in activities in the domains of biotechnology, cybertechnology, and nanotechnology. The media are filled with the sensational, excited, worried, or disoriented comments about phenomena such as DNA, RNA, cloning, xenotransplantation, genomics, and so on. After the biotechnological creation of Dolly, the new Eve of sheep, we have been able to see many other marketed creatures, ranging from the transgenic mouse Oncomouse, the first patented animal in the world, designed and marketed for cancer research, to more ordinary generations of genetically modified bulls and cows to produce better steaks (Best & Kellner, 2001; Haraway, 1997; Vandenberghe, 2002). And, of course, there is a more or less hidden race to produce the first cloned baby.

These developments may imply, for gerontology, a fundamentally new approach to aging as its technologically advanced branches will proceed from traditional "receptive" modes such as description and analysis to more active modes of technological design. This challenging and precarious gerontological situation, which is characterized by unforeseeable consequences, can easily be extended and exaggerated into a fundamentally new technological horizon. In these visions, every living being might be characterized as a specific variation of a general DNA text, a "hypertext" of life in which every form of life is reduced to bits and digits, explored by computer programs that simulate the evolution of life, opening the door to endlessly expandable informatics of life (Haraway, 1991; Hayles, 1999). Consequently, in these technofantasies, there would be no naturally occurring genome that cannot be experimentally (re)designed, culminating in the objectification of life in *cyborgs* (cybernetic organisms). (For analysis of the related issues raised by the anti-aging industry, see King & Calasanti, this volume.)

All these possible or impossible but certainly unforeseeable developments can easily lead to fantastic excursions into realms of doom or bliss. Even to statements that such qualifications are still too "anthropocentric" to be able to grasp the newness of the emerging technological world. For the most advanced technosectarians, such as transhumanists and extropianists, the reality is that our 1400cc brain cannot cope with the complexities of the technological world, which would imply that we must try to control our evolution by trusting ourselves to cybertechnology, downloading the contents of our brain into more complex computers, which are supposedly better equipped to deal with the accelerating realities.

These projections can easily be seen as continuations of modern philosophy's preoccupation with subjective consciousness. The Cartesian search for the immutable laws of a rational consciousness, which becomes, from a position of splendid isolation, confronted with an *outside* reality, has been transformed into a search for the technological structure of the human brain as the origin of an artificial intelligence that would lead far beyond imaginable horizons. This is the moment for a resurrection of massive modernist dreams, before they were, in a Hegelian fashion, attached to historical processes. This antihistorical mode of thinking is more typical for the early Enlightenment that counted on reason to decipher the ultimate codes of nature, building on Galileo's thesis that the hidden text of nature would be written in the language of mathematics. Presently, nature is supposed to be written in the text of genetic codes, and its discovery has become connected with the same promises of safety from illness, decay, and death through efficient control over nature that already inspired Descartes' work. Technology appears to get ready to play the role of a supreme creator whose ways may again be a mystery to man. In combination with expanding markets, this leads to exalted neomodernist dreams.

The extreme positions in these debates may easily be neutralized, but there are nevertheless serious problems confronting us. What have been the major responses to these neomodernist projections?

The postmodern reflection of these developments has disappointingly little to offer. In its perspective, the worried questions about *human dignity* are seen as inspired by outdated modernist ideas that merely limit the possible forms identity may assume. As human beings become what they can be, thanks to technology, there can, according to Deleuze and Guattari (1980), no longer be any opposition between human and machines. The whole idea of alienation would be hopelessly old-fashioned and essentialist: when there is no clear essence of humanity, this cannot be alienated or damaged. Here, cybertechnocratic dreams praise the neo-Nietzschean death of Man, which was proclaimed by postmodernists and poststructuralists like Foucault, who concluded his well-known work *The Order of Things* (1973), by stating that Man disappears like a face playfully drawn in the sand of a beach. What can be regarded as *human*, is in other words nothing more than the result of discursive formations. Horkheimer and Adorno (1979) have grasped this process already in their *Dialectics of Enlightenment* by showing that in terms of an uncritically absolutized domination over nature, "man" can only be an anthropomorphic illusion.

A flat rejection of contemporary or future technologies, as brought forward by the antimodernist position is, however, not a realistic option because technological devices have already entered human bodies. Simple external aids, such as glasses, hearing devices, and crutches have been followed by implantations, such as pacemakers, artificial (parts of) organs, and artificial hips and other joints. In many situations of treatment and care, the human body is connected to machines that take over many bodily functions. It is likely that in the near future, not only many more forms of transplantation and implantation will be practiced, but all kinds of artificial intelligence, bio- and gene technology will invade our bodies. It is also likely that we will learn to know and accept many devices that nowadays may seem unacceptable, as we know from history that dissection of corpses and, much more recently, transplantation of hearts or artificial insemination have ceased to be unacceptable to most people.

One important part of a possible answer to the almost overwhelming perspectives of recent biotechnological perspectives is to point out that this technology is *socially* constituted (Baars, 1991) and should not be treated as a self-creating myth. These technological developments require enormous investments and are driven by markets that are also targeting the aging populations of the Western societies. They thrive on the pseudoexistential fears of the overaffluent part of the world that are angered by the fact that they cannot buy or considerably prolong their own existence. That this is not possible should not be interpreted as a technological imperfection, but as the dignity of the (inter)human condition (Baars, 2002).

There may be a fundamental ambivalence we cannot get rid of. But the aging population of the next decades will especially be confronted with these developments, either as objects of experiment or as consumers of new forms of technology or as donors of organs. Is the gerontological community ready to handle or fundamentally discuss these new responsibilities, or will they leave them to the investors? There are many questions that urgently need to be debated. I give some examples that can easily be elaborated:

- To the degree that the development, production, and purchase of technological prosthetic devices in a broad sense will be governed by market forces, they will, consequentially, become available only to those clients who can afford them. There are inevitable effects on insurance schemes as some devices will be very expensive. Living longer and staying mobile may become even more dependent on income and capital than before.
- Even if the personal effects for health and well-being would be unequivocally positive, the person with an implanted device, such as a pacemaker, becomes *bodily* connected to a market beyond his or her control. This leads to a whole complex set of questions concerning the protection of personal interests regarding such dependencies.
- The medical success of technological prostheses may enforce the present preference for quick medical repair and maintenance instead of care, especially long-term care.

- What are the implications for gerontological contributions to these developments? Are we losing all control as soon as knowledge becomes implemented and market forces take over; forces that are notoriously difficult to control through nationally based political regulations? How can responsibility still be possible (e.g., Habermas, 2001)?
- What does this all imply for our ideas about human dignity? Will the human body be seen even more predominantly as a machine?

These questions with all their ambivalent implications may be difficult to answer, but if we don't even take them seriously, we give ourselves up to a myth of cyborgtechnocracy, behind which operate mainly the market mechanisms of globalization.

CRITICAL GERONTOLOGY BEYOND NEOMODERNISM, ANTIMODERNISM, AND POSTMODERNISM

The contemporary debate about general societal developments and their desired orientation is dominated by three main positions that should be transcended by reflecting on the positive and negative elements of each of them, in the light of modern principles that are still worth considering: *responsible individual fulfillment, solidarity,* and *human dignity.*

Neomodernism (or neoliberalism) has become a dominant orientation that emphasizes the dynamic qualities of the market and appear to function, in many respects, better than bureaucratic alternatives that have been tried in the socialist experiments. This dynamic and flexible character of the market tends, however, to become idealized as the *only* societal form of integration or regulation that counts. In this form, it represents a "colonization" that defies the freedom that is marketed by the mass media, culminating in the equating of a *free market* with a *free world*. The critique of colonization that I have proposed focuses on situations or social domains in which market forces and marketing models are dominant where they should not be: for instance, when quality of care is defined in market terms, when intergenerational solidarity is seen only in terms of capital returns, when education is seen only in terms of investing in future income, or when citizens are taken seriously insofar as they can take care of themselves.

The antimodernists are clearly dissatisfied with this neomodernist domination of the market and appeal to community values, traditional forms of solidarity, and care. They rightly worry about many private vices that they cannot, like Mandeville and Adam Smith, see as public virtues. But they often presuppose and absolutize specific normative or religious orientations that tend to exclude each other; consequentially they have difficulties in accepting the multicultural society and the fact that many people develop personal preferences, for instance, in their sexual conduct, which is unacceptable in their world views. Politically, they often end up supporting the neomodernists in a common appeal to "personal responsibility," which is alternatively and ambiguously interpreted in a moral sense and in an economic sense, so that personal responsibility can suddenly mean that everybody has to take care for their own material well-being in old age, preferably through investments they cannot control.

The postmodern position represents the second helpless criticism of neo-modernism. Its representatives emphasize, with good reasons, the importance of respecting differences. But their analysis of society has been so strongly colored by the criticism of absolutist political programs, that they content themselves with respecting singularity or mere differences in lifestyles. In that way, they lose sight of social inequality or exclusion that refers to major differences in life chances: differences that should not be respected, but thoroughly questioned because they are likely to cause many problems in present life and in the future life course of the people concerned and in those of their offspring. The problem of social inequality or social inclusion/exclusion refers to structurally constituted *decisive* differences in life chances, which cannot be explained away by referring to individual differences such as talents, but have to be explained by analyzing social processes and structures without advocating collectivist models in which singularity or differences should be banished. One important contribution of gerontologically interested scholars could be to show how decisive differences in life chances are built up and produce their detrimental effects over the life course.

The Crucial Importance of Critical Gerontology

To untangle these factors, there should be a gerontological cooperation between several disciplines. Such a cooperation requires that structural approaches are conducted besides and in close contact with more interpretive or narrative approaches as both have their own contributions to make.

The importance of *narrative* approaches to aging is that through them we can learn more about the personal meaning of aging in certain situations than is possible through standardized empirical surveys. The emphasis on narrative as a method, moreover, has valuable normative aspects as their subjects are approached respectfully as persons with "expert" single or double knowledge about their own lives and experiences (Baars, 1997). This does not legitimate a simple empiricism of storytelling, but poses complex questions as implicit theories and models of narrativity shape the ways in which the experiences of the persons concerned are articulated and organized (Baars, 2003). Moreover, narrativity does not justify ways of living or actions, nor can it serve to justify specific circumstances; this would potentially be a repressive use of narratives. Listening to the story of somebody who has suffered under miserable conditions but dealt with them magnificently does not justify the miserable circumstances or make them less problematic.

One of the tasks of the structurally oriented paradigms would be to analyze the structural production of problematic situations, referred to above as social inequality or social inclusion/exclusion in a life course perspective: for instance, mechanisms that allocate different life chances to different categories of people *during* the life course, from childhood to old age; or mechanisms that produce structural advantage or disadvantage of institutionalized *phases* of the life course, where the period after gainful activity is as particularly vulnerable as it is economically residual and may be seen as only of importance in terms of spending capacity or as an expensive burden of care (Walker, 1981, 1990).

Dannefer (2003) has articulated the paradigm of cumulative advantage and disadvantage over the life course with reference to many investigations that have highlighted the phenomenon of social inequality as decisive differences in socially constituted life chances that are built up and accumulate their negative effects over the life course (see also Burton & Whitfield and Crystal in this volume). Other examples can readily be found, such as the "feminization" of poverty in old age, which is reasonably well-documented (although not given adequate attention) and cannot seriously be explained by referring to the individual talents or insufficient efforts of the women concerned. It is rather a result of the cooperation of different factors, such as gender specific education, labor market dynamics, and pension systems (Walker & Maltby, 1997). The German BASE (Berlin Aging Study) project also presents ample documentation about the effect of social inequality into very high ages (Baltes & Mayer, 1999). Finally, evidence about the effects of various forms of social inequality, such as poverty, social exclusion, minorities, and unemployment over the life course can be found in research on social determinants of health (Marmot & Wilkinson, 1999; see also Leisering & Leibfried, 1999).

The structural approach cannot deduct from its analysis how specific circumstances are experienced by the persons living through them; here a narrative approach has a better chance. But the narrative perspective cannot clarify how the circumstances that are shown in the narratives as generating problems are produced and how they can be structurally improved. Both paradigms have their own indispensable value.

The earlier criticism of Beck's *Risk Society* and its individualization of social inequality can be followed by critical research: exploring the social distribution of risks as life chances from a life-course perspective might result in the critical reconstruction of several different life-course trajectories that typically accumulate positive and negative life chances. There is still a case for social inequality and exclusion as certain societal mechanisms show their effects in different life chances for categories or groups of individuals without implying that these differences originate from differences between such individuals. Not all differences in the late-modern society are differences of lifestyles that should be accepted and valued in their own dignity. Some differences are less easily acceptable. We can say this without claiming that everybody should be equal.

Finally, it must be emphasized that the exploration of these issues is not something on the periphery of orthodox social gerontology. If it wants to contribute to the complex issue of understanding aging, its specific task would be to slowly disentangle processes of aging from the negative effects of social factors on people over a long period of time. The understanding of the effects of major differences in life chances over the life course, as referred to in the updated concept of social inequality, leads to a better understanding of the social constitution of aging (Baars, 1991; Walker, 1981), which goes beyond the old Ciceronian saying that "old age is sickness of itself."

ACKNOWLEDGMENTS

I want to thank my fellow editors for their intellectual solidarity and especially Alan Walker for his clarifying comments on an earlier draft of this text.

REFERENCES

Abel, E., & Nelson, M. (Eds.). (1990). *Circles of care: Work and identity in women's lives.* New York: SUNY Press.

Appadurai, A. (1996). *Modernity at large: Cultural dimensions of globalization.* Minneapolis: University of Minnesota Press.

Baudelaire, C. (1964). *The painter of modern life and other essays.* London: Phaidon.

Baars, J. (1987). *De mythe van de totale beheersing. Adorno, Horkheimer en de dialektiek van de Vooruitgang* [The myth of total domination: Adorno, Horkheimer and the dialectics of progress]. Amsterdam: SUA.

Baars, J. (1991). The challenge of critical gerontology: The problem of social constitution. *Journal of Aging Studies, 5,* 219-243.

Baars, J. (1997). Concepts of time and narrative temporality in the study of aging. *Journal of Aging Studies, 11,* 283-296.

Baars, J. (2000). Time, age and autonomy. *European Journal of Social Quality, 2,* 9-27.

Baars, J. (2002). *Ouder worden en de fragiliteit van de intermenselijke conditie* [Aging and the vulnerability of the interhuman condition]. Utrecht: University for Humanistics.

Baars, J. (2003). *Tell me your life. Questioning narrativity.* Unpublished manuscript.

Baltes, P., & Mayer, K. U. (1999). *The Berlin aging study: Aging from 70 to 100.* New York: Cambridge University Press.

Beck, U. (1992). *Risk society: Towards a new modernity.* London: Sage.

Beck, U. (1994). *Reflexive modernization: Politics, tradition and aesthetics in the modern social order.* Cambridge: Polity Press.

Best, S., & Kellner, D. (2001). *The postmodern adventure: Science, technology and cultural studies at the third millennium.* London: Routledge.

Castells, M. (1996). *The rise of the network society.* Oxford: Basic Blackwell.

Crook, S., Pakulski, J., & Waters, M. (1992). *Postmodernization: Change in advanced societies.* London: Sage.

Dannefer, D. (2003). Cumulative advantage/disadvantage and the life course: Cross-fertilizing age and social science theory. *Journal of Gerontology, 58B,* S327-S337.

Deleuze, G., & Guattari, F. (1980). *Mille plateaux: Capitalisme et schizophrénie 2* [A thousand plateaus: Capitalism and schizophrenia]. Paris: Minuit.

Featherstone, M., Lasch, S., & Robertson, R. (Eds.). (1995). *Global modernities.* London: Sage.

Ferge, S. (1997). A Central European perspective on the social quality of Europe. In W. Beck, L. van der Maesen, & A. Walker (Eds.), *The social quality of Europe.* The Hague: Kluwer.

Foucault, M. (1973). *The order of things: An archeology of the human sciences.* London: Tavistock Publications.

Gardner, K. (1995). *Global migrants, local lives.* Oxford: Clarendon Press.

Gardner, K. (2002). *Age, narrative, and migration.* Oxford: Berg.

Giddens, A. (1991). *The consequences of modernity.* Cambridge, Polity Press.

Giddens, A (1992). *Modernity and self-identity: Self and society in a late modern age.* Cambridge: Polity Press.

Gilleard, C., & Higgs, P. (2000*).* *Cultures of aging: Self, citizen, and the body.* Harlow: Pearson.

Gilligan, C. (1977). *In a different voice: Psychological theory and women's development.* Cambridge: Harvard University Press.

Guillemard, A.-M. (1986). *Le déclin du social* [The decline of the social]. Paris: PUF.

Habermas, J. (1968). *Knowledge and human interests.* Boston: Beacon Press.

Habermas, J. (1987). *The theory of communicative action* (2 vols.). Cambridge: Polity.

Habermas, J. (1997). *Die Einbeziehung des Anderen: Studien zur politischen Theorie* [The inclusion of the other: Studies in political theory]. Frankfurt/Main: Suhrkamp.

Habermas, J. (2001). *Die Zukunft der menschlichen Natur: Auf dem weg zu einer liberalen Eugenik?* [The future of human race]. Frankfurt/Main: Suhrkamp.

Haraway, D. (1991). *Simians, cyborgs and women: The reinvention of nature.* New York: Routledge.

Haraway, D. (1997*).* *Modest_Witness@Second_Millenium. FemaleMan©_Meets_ Oncomouse™.* London: Routledge.

Hardt, M., & Negri, A. (2000). *Empire.* Cambridge, MA: Harvard University Press.

Harvey, D. (1989). *The condition of postmodernity: An inquiry into the origins of cultural change.* Oxford: Blackwell.

Hayles, C. (1999). *How we became posthuman. Virtual bodies in cybernetics, literature and informatics.* Chicago: University of Chicago Press.

Horkheimer, M., & Adorno, T. W. (1979). *Dialectics of enlightenment.* London: Verso.

Jameson, F. (1991). *Postmodernism or, the cultural logic of late capitalism.* London: Verso.

Kunneman, H. (2002). Humanistics and the future of the human sciences. In A. Halsema & D. van Houten (Eds.), *Empowering humanity* (pp. 13-36). Utrecht: De Tijdstroom.

Le Goff, J. (1980). *Time, work and culture in the Middle Ages.* Chicago: University of Chicago Press.

Leisering, L., & Leibfried, S. (1999). *Time and poverty in Western welfare states.* Cambridge University Press.

Luhmann, N. (2000). Why does society describe itself as post-modern? In W. Rasch (Ed.), *Observing complexity: Systems theory and postmodernity.* Minneapolis: University of Minnesota Press.

MacPherson, C. B. (1964). *The political theory of possessive individualism: Hobbes to Locke.* Oxford: Oxford University Press.

Marmot, M., & Wilkinsion, R. G. (Eds.). (1999). *Social determinants of health.* Oxford University Press.

Mannheim, K. (1943). *Diagnosis of our time.* London: Kegan Paul.

Phillipson, C., Ahmed, N., & Latimer, J. (2003). *Women in transition:? The experiences of Bangladeshi women living in Tower Hamlets.* Bristol: Policy Press.

Ray, L., & Sayer, A. (Eds.). (1999). *Culture and economy after the cultural turn.* London: Sage.

Robertson, R. (1992). *Globalization: Social theory and global culture.* London: Sage.

Scharpf, F. (1999). *Welfare and work in the open economy.* Oxford University Press.

Scharpf, F., & Schmidt, V. (Eds.). (2000). *Welfare and work in open economies.* Oxford University Press.

Sykes, R., Palier, B., & Prior, P. (Eds.). (2001). *Globalization and the European welfare states: Challenges and change.* Basingstoke: Palgrave.

Taylor, C. (1989). *Sources of the self: The making of the modern identity.* Cambridge: Harvard University Press.

Tönnies, M. (1887). *Gemeinschaft und gesellschaft.* Darmstadt: WBG.

Tronto, J. (1992). *Moral boundaries: A political argument for an ethic of care.* New York: Routledge.

Vandenberghe, F. (2002). *Posthumanism, or the cultural logic of global capitalism.* Unpublished manuscript.

Walker, A. (1981). Towards a political economy of old age. *Ageing and Society, 1*(1), 40-55.

Walker, A. (1990). The economic "burden" of ageing and its prospect of intergenerational conflict. *Ageing and Society, 10*(4), 377-396.

Walker, A. (2004, November 21). *Towards an international political economy of aging.* Paper presented to the Gerontological Society of America.

Walker, A., & Deacon, B. (2003). Economic globalization and policies on aging. *Journal of Societal and Social Policy, 2,* 1-18.

Walker, A., & Maltby, T. (1997). *Ageing Europe.* Buckingham: Open University Press.

Weber, M. (1984). *Die Lage der Landarbeiter im Ostelbischen Deutschland.* [The situation of German agricultural workers east of the Elbe]. Tübingen: Mohr.

CHAPTER 3

Aging and Globalization: Issues for Critical Gerontology and Political Economy

Chris Phillipson

The aim of this chapter is to consider some of the challenges raised by the growth of globalization alongside the consolidation of population aging.[1] Debates around the theme of globalization were highly influential in many areas of the social sciences during the 1990s, notably in sociology and political science (Held, McGrew, Goldblatt, & Perraton, 1999). Subsequently, this work was to expand out with extensive discussions in social policy (George & Wilding, 2002; Mishra, 1999; Yeates, 2001), and more recently, within social gerontology (Estes & Phillipson, 2002; Vincent, 2003b; Walker & Deacon, 2003). However, it might be argued that much work remains to be done exploring the full impact of globalizing processes both on older people and on the social institutions through which they are supported.

In general terms, globalization has produced a distinctive stage in the history of aging, with tensions between nation-state-based policies concerning demographic change and those formulated by global actors and institutions. Social aging can no longer be viewed solely as a national problem or issue, but one that affects individuals, groups, and communities across the globe (see further, Torres in this volume). Local and national interpretations of aging had substance where nation-states (at least in the developed world) claimed some control over the construction of welfare policies. They also carried force where social policies were being designed with the aim or aspiration of leveling inequalities and where citizenship was still predominantly a national issue. The changes affecting

[1] The arguments in this chapter have been developed at a number of conferences, in particular, at those organized by the Gerontological Society of America. I am grateful for the helpful comments and suggestions of participants at these events, as well as to the coeditors of this volume.

all of these areas, largely set in motion by different aspects of globalization, are generating significant implications for work in the field of gerontology (O'Rand, 2000).

To consider these developments, this chapter will first, link debates around globalization to concerns within critical gerontology; second, review changes introduced by globalization and their impact on the development of economic and social policy; third, assess the implications of these changes for the organization of the welfare state; fourth, identify new agendas for social gerontology introduced by globalization.

CRITICAL GERONTOLOGY AND GLOBALIZATION

Social theory in gerontology brings together a variety of intellectual streams, reflecting in large measure shifts in sociological perspectives over the last 50 years. Over the past decade, one particular strand, critical gerontology, was especially prominent, although this approach itself follows a number of paths, reflecting contributions from feminism, the humanities, and political economy (Arber, Davidson, & Ginn, 2003; Cole, Achenbaum, Jakobi, & Kastenbaum, 1993; Minkler & Estes, 1999). Central to the approach taken by critical geron-tology is the idea of aging as a socially constructed experience and process (Vincent, 2003a). With respect to political economy, this is seen as a reflection of the role of elements such as the state and economy in the social construction of old age. The interaction between these areas is viewed as creating significant inequalities in the experience of growing old, especially in relation to living standards, life expectancy, and expectations of daily living. The task of political economy thus becomes that of developing a critical analysis of processes that lead to empowerment and control for some older people, while creating dependency and powerlessness for others.

The first phase of critical gerontology, spanning over the period from 1980 to the late 1990s, was built around the application of a range of disciplinary perspectives (e.g., Marxist, conflict theory, psychoanalytic perspectives, theories of the state, the Frankfurt School) to problems of inequality and exploitation affecting older people within individual nation-states.[2] Problems associated with what Townsend (1981) defined as "structured dependency," to take one example, were linked to forms of welfare organization, these viewed as contributing to the experience of alienation and poverty in old age (Phillipson, 1982; Walker, 1981). The strength of this approach, as well as that from historical and socio-logical work outside critical gerontology, in part arose from its linkage to clearly defined national settings, this contributing to a narrative that combined a nation's history with that of the emergence of older people as a social group. Examples of

---

[2] The development of critical gerontology is discussed in Estes, Biggs, and Phillipson, 2003.

this work include Fischer's (1977) *Growing Old in America*, Cole's (1992) *The Journey of Life*, Graebner's (1980) *A History of Retirement*, Achenbaum's (1978) *Old Age in the New Land*, and Thane's (2000) *Old Age in English History*.

This historical research was complemented by work exploring the nature of citizenship, with particular emphasis on the contribution of T. H. Marshall (1992). The main focus of Marshall's work concerned exploring links between the nation-state on the one hand, and citizenship on the other. In this tradition, as Delanty (2000) notes, citizenship was viewed as "the internal or domestic face of nationality" (p. 51). In the case of old age, the provision of care and support was viewed as an example of the way in which the state sought to modify class-based inequalities operating within national borders. Critical gerontology was, in part, a response to the perceived limitations of these policies and, in particular, their construction of older people as "passive dependents" (Estes, 1979). In the case of political economy, an important element in this work was exploring the role of the state in regulating and reproducing different life chances through the life course, with the social production of inequalities in old age a significant outcome of this process (Dannefer, 2003b; Estes & Associates, 2001).

By the end of the 1990s, the need to extend approaches beyond the nation-state had become apparent. Pressures on welfare states were increasingly global rather than national in scope (Dannefer, 2003a). The *globalization* of capital itself had a destabilizing effect in many spheres, most notably on the organization of work and welfare (Beck, 2000). Anthony Giddens (1999) describes two views on globalization: those of the "skeptics" who view globalization as a myth, not altogether different from earlier transformational changes in society; and those of the "radicals" who view globalization as real and with consequences that are largely indifferent to national borders. Giddens himself takes the view of the "radicals," noting that globalization is revolutionary on multiple economic, political, cultural, and societal levels. He argues that globalization is characterized by a complex set of forces, embodied by contradictory, oppositional processes that pull away power and influence from the local and nation-state level while also creating new pressures for local autonomy and cultural identity.

The approach taken in this chapter is broadly in support of the radical view. Responses and solutions to aging issues need to be addressed in a global as much as a national context. John Urry's (2000) analysis of the "new mobilities" affecting the twenty-first century and Castells' (1996, 2004) focus on the role of networks rather than countries, providing the architecture for the global economy, come to the same conclusion in highlighting the various pressures facing nation-states. Increasingly, national sovereignty is influenced, to a greater or lesser degree, by transnational organizations and communities of different kinds. Older people themselves experience a range of global, national, regional, and local forces that influence the construction of later life. To explore this issue, this chapter examines the implications of the radical view of globalization for a political economy of aging, focusing, in particular, on key developments in global social and economic policy over the past ten years.

GLOBALIZATION AND THE RECONSTRUCTION OF AGING

How might the radical view of globalization be applied to understanding issues and policies affecting older people? Three aspects of globalization need to be examined here: first, its influence on the ideological terrain around which aging is constructed; second, its construction of aging as a new form of "risk"; third, its role in creating global inequalities in aging.

The impact of globalization on ideologies relating to aging was one of the most obvious developments that took place over the course of the 1990s. The key issue concerned the move from debates that focused on aging as a burden for national economies to perspectives that viewed population aging as a worldwide problem. The report of the World Bank (1994) *Averting the Old Age Crisis* was a crucial document in this regard, but more recent contributions have included those from the Central Intelligence Agency (2001) and documents such as *The Global Retirement Crisis*, produced by the Washington-based Center for Strategic and International Studies (Jackson, 2002). There is insufficient space in this chapter to deal with the particular arguments raised by these papers (see, however, the discussions in Blackburn, 2002; Stiglitz, 2003; Vincent, 2003b), but the general point raised concerns what amounted to a "politicization of aging" generated by the intensification of global ties. This development arose from at least three factors. The growth of neoliberalism is one obvious dimension, this propagating hostility toward collective provision by the state or, at the very least, a view that private provision was inherently superior to that provided by the public sector[3] (Walker & Deacon, 2003; Yeates, 2001). But politicization was also reflected in the way in which globalization produced greater awareness about the relative economic position of one nation-state compared with another. George and Wilding (2002, p. 58) make the point here that: "Globalization has created an economic and political climate in which national states become more conscious of the taxes they levy and their potential economic implications." Neoliberal ideology feeds and justifies these "concerns." Finally, the ideological debate was also promoted through key supranational bodies, such as the OECD, the WTO, the World Bank, and the IMF, along with transnational corporations (notably pharmaceutical companies), all of which contributed to a distinctive worldview about the framing of policies for old age.[4]

---

[3] See Stiglitz (2003) for a general discussion on this question.

[4] Though the lack of interest in the problems facing older people in developing countries is still of concern, particularly in the context of the profound impact of HIV-AIDS on sub-Saharan Africa. See Knodel, Watkins, and VanLandingham (2002) for an important report on this issue.

Globalization has also played an influential role in the production of new forms of risk associated with the privatization of social policy. Growing older seems to have become *more* secure, with longer life expectancy, rising levels of economic well-being (Disney & Whitehouse, 2002), and enhanced life styles in old age. Set against this, the pressures associated with the *achievement* of security are themselves generating fresh anxieties among older people as well as younger cohorts. Risks once carried by social institutions have now been displaced onto the shoulders of individuals and/or their families (Bauman, 2000; O'Rand, 2000). Dannefer (2000) summarizes this process in the following way:

> . . . corporate and state uncertainties are transferred to citizens—protecting large institutions while exposing individuals to possible catastrophe in the domains of health care and personal finances, justified to the public by the claim that the pensioner can do better on his or her own, and that Social Security can do better diversified into equity markets. (p. 270)

More generally, Stiglitz (2003) argues that risk has been turned into "a way of life" through a combination of changes in the labor market (with the erosion of jobs for life) and reliance on private pension arrangements—these subject to the volatility of the global stock market (Blackburn, 2002; Minns, 2001; see Vincent in this volume).

Finally, globalization—both through the spread of worldwide communications and via the power of global organizations—has elevated aging to an issue that transcends individual societies or states. Gerontology, for much of the twentieth century, was preoccupied with issues affecting older people in advanced capitalist societies (Dannefer, 2003a). Indeed, theories such as disengagement and modernization theory took the view that the western model of aging would ultimately be diffused across all cultures of the world (Fennell, Phillipson, & Evers, 1988). Globalization has provided a fundamental challenge to vestiges of this approach. Global interests may indeed continue to be subject to U.S. hegemony and/or Western imperialism in various guises, but globalization also illustrates the emergence of new social and political forms at international, national, regional, and local levels (Held & McGrew, 2002). Cerny & Evans (2004) make this point in the following way:

> The central paradox of globalization, the displacement of a crucial range of economic, social and political activities from the national arena to a cross-cutting global/transnational/domestic structured field of action, is that rather than creating one economy or one polity, it also divides, fragments and polarizes. Convergence and divergence are two sides of the same process. Globalization remains a discourse of contestation that reflects national and regional antagonisms and struggles. (p. 63)

But the globalization of communications has introduced a further dimension into the understanding of demographic change. Thompson (2000) has explored the processes involved in the appropriation of globalized media products as follows:

I want to suggest that the appropriation of globalized symbolic materials involves what I shall describe as the *accentuation of symbolic distancing from the spatial-temporal contexts of everyday life.* [author's emphasis]. The appropriation of symbolic materials enables individuals to take some distance from the conditions of their day-to-day lives—not literally but symbolically, imaginatively, vicariously. Individuals are able to gain some conception, however partial, of ways of life and life conditions that differ significantly from their own. They are able to gain some conception of regions of the world that are far removed from their own locales. (p. 212)

The process described by Thompson is transforming aging at various levels. Global communications sharpened awareness in the 1990s of the suffering of older people in zones of conflict, notably in the former Eastern bloc countries and in sub-Saharan Africa.[5] But from another perspective, it also generated ideas about the new lifestyles that might be possible to develop in middle and older age. Older people in developed countries became aware of the possibilities of travel, migration, and the potential benefits of global tourism. Bauman (1998, p. 78) observes that "spiritually at least we are all travelers." During the past ten years, this been put into practice by a minority of wealthier retirees, even though many of their contemporaries remained tied to localities experiencing the costs associated with global change (Scharf, Phillipson, Smith, & Kingston, 2002). Such examples confirm the way in which globalization has been radical in its transformation of aging with, to paraphrase Beck (1992), few social groups or societies immune to its effects. The next section of this chapter examines the way in which these changes have been institutionalized within social policy itself.

INSECURITY AND GLOBAL AGING

The impact of globalization on aging can be best understood in terms of a "destabilizing" force, one that disturbs and reconfigures conventional narratives about the meaning of growing old. Hitherto, images and policies about aging were built around ideas of "containment," "stasis," and "dependency." For much of the twentieth century, older people were viewed as a static population ("immobile" or "disengaged"), constrained within a narrow range of cultural as well as geographical spaces. They were also regarded—in formulations expressed on the left as well as the right of social policy—as a group locked into different forms of dependency. From the left, this was attributed to the impact of means testing and "passive" forms of community care (Townsend, 1981); from the right, through what was viewed as a form of collectivism that weakened individual self-control and responsibility (Murray, 1994).

---

[5] Linos's (2001) paper "How Can International Organizations Shape National Welfare States" provides a valuable exploration of this question.

From both perspectives, however, institutions associated with the welfare state were viewed as crucial to maintaining and controlling the lives of older people. The steady growth in the proportion of elderly people in the population was, at least until the 1980s, managed in western societies through the emergence of retirement on the one side and the construction of the welfare state on the other. These institutions created the social, economic, and moral space within which growing numbers of people were supported (Phillipson, 1998). To use the formulation developed by Manuel Castells (2004), they served to create "a legitimizing identity" for old age: the domination of older people at one level, but a legitimation for *being* an older person at another—welfare as a "reward" for a lifetime of labor and service.

Cerny (1997) takes the view that this traditional model of the welfare state has now been replaced by what he calls "the competition state." In this formulation: "Social policy is less concerned with civilizing and softening the outcomes of the free market and more with sustaining and sharpening competitiveness" (George & Wilding, 2002, p. 61). Castells (2004) relates this restructuring of welfare to the globalization of production and investments.

> In an economy whose core markets for capital, goods and services are increasingly integrated on a global scale, there seems to be little room for vastly different welfare states, with relatively similar levels of labor productivity and production quality. Only a global social contract (reducing the gap, without necessarily equalizing social and working conditions), linked to international tariff agreements, could avoid the demise of the most generous welfare states. Yet because in the newly liberalized, networked, global economy such a far-reaching social contract is unlikely, welfare states are being downsized to the lowest common denominator. . . . (p. 314)

In a context of rapid globalization, the welfare state no longer represents a meaningful boundary sustaining the lives of elderly citizens. Older people are creating new types of spaces (Andrews & Phillips, 2005; Bernard, Bartlam, Biggs, & Sim, 2003) and identities in the process. Following writers such as Beck (1992) and Giddens (1991), this may also be seen to reflect trends toward individualization, or what is viewed as the "progressive loss of tradition and social bonds as a means of structuring the life course and forming personal identity" (Lupton, 1999, p. 4). Globalization creates a mobile form of aging: less controlled by the ideology of welfare on the one side, more differentiated and fragmented on the other. The new attachments range from urban ghettos, care homes, and seaside bungalows to specialist retirement communities and "second homes." The meaning of old age is thus reconstructed through a diffuse range of spaces—re-creating new forms of security for some but issues of insecurity and exclusion for groups, such as older women, minority ethnic elders, and blue-collar workers.

Zygmunt Bauman (1996) makes the point that finding secure and predictable spaces is a major challenge in a globalized world. The erosion of boundaries can represent an opportunity for some older people; for others unpredictability and uncertainty. Bauman (1996) theorizes this as follows:

> . . . the boundaries which tend to be simultaneously most strongly desired and most acutely missed are those of a rightful and secure place in society, of a space unquestionably one's own, where one can plan one's life with the minimum of interference, play one's role in a game in which the rules do not change overnight and without notice, and reasonably hope for the better. . . . It is the widespread characteristic of men and women in our type of society that they live perpetually with the "identity problem" unresolved. They suffer, one might say, from a chronic absence of resources with which they could build a truly solid and lasting identity, anchor and stop it drifting. (p. 26)

The radical view of globalization thus suggests a major reconstruction of traditional and stereotypical models of aging. Older people join those from other age groups in living what Beck and Beck-Gernsheim (2002, p. 26) refer to as an "experimental life" in which the usual forms of social integration are abandoned or subject to critical scrutiny. But the questions that arise from this are: what new types of security need to be identified in a globalized world? What forms of legitimacy are now available to older people? How might insecurity be addressed at the level of organization and politics? The next section of this chapter starts to address some of these questions.

GLOBALIZATION, SOCIAL GERONTOLOGY, AND THE NEW POLITICS OF AGING

The argument of this chapter is that globalization raises major issues both for the discipline of gerontology and for understanding the lives of older people. This section illustrates this by exploring the impact of global aging at three different levels: the organization of the life course; the development of social policy; political engagement with global organizations.

On the first of these, an important issue concerns the transformation in the organization of the life course (Dannefer, 2003a). For much of its history, social gerontology—at least in its focus on older people in western societies—was built around the idea of the progressive emergence of an orderly life course developed through phases of education, work, and retirement (Riley & Riley, 1994). Globalization, however, poses a challenge to this notion of a normal biography constructed around a linear model of the life course. The causal elements include: the impact of detraditionalization; the increase in the magnitude and intensity of risks through the life course; the collapse of lifetime jobs (hastened by the globalization of finance and the mobility of capital); and increased rates of human migration (albeit only a return to the levels of population movement in the late nineteenth century).

The challenge for studies in aging lies in acknowledging the way in which the life course may, as a result of the above processes, assume a "nonlinear" shape, with features of so-called normal aging occurring earlier or later in life depending upon a particular sequence of biographical events (Hoerder, 2001). By extension, an additional issue concerns greater variability in respect of images and definitions of aging. In the context of accelerated movement of populations, interlaced with powerful global networks, ideas about the meaning of old age, when old age begins, and normative behaviors for later life, will demonstrate greater variation within any one society than has historically been the case. Dannefer (2003a) summarizes the implication of what he terms the "global geography of the life course" as follows:

> Viewed in global perspective, it is clear that [the traditional] life course pattern is not at all typical for much of the human population. Quite different patterns are found in the "Majority World"—the poorer and less developed countries where most of the people inhabiting the earth live. . . . If the life course area is to encompass the full range of human diversity and human possibility, these diverse patterns cannot be ignored. Many "alternative" life course configurations are also strongly institutionalized. Such established patterns can be observed in spite of the high population turnover of countries that have not undergone the demographic transition—witnessing powerfully to the fact that the life course is indeed a social institution that transcends, and yet encases, the biographies of individuals. In some cases, such patterns are well entrenched, and are clearly older than the "the three boxes" of the "modern" life course with which the term institutionalization has been equated. (p. 649)

The second area of concern relates to global governance in the context of aging societies. This theme introduces us to the contradictory effects of globalization on everyday life. The problems have been well-rehearsed, notably as regards pressures to restrain taxation and public spending, the punitive conditions attached to debt repayments, and the rise of chronic social problems within civil society. Ramesh Mishra (1999) summarizes these aspects as follows:

> The main problem [appears to be] that those conditions and social forces which made *national* welfare states possible, e.g. the existence of a state with legitimate authority for rule-making and rule-enforcement, electoral competition and representative government, strong industrial action and protest movements threatening the economic and social stability of nations, nationalism and nation-building imperatives are unavailable at the international-level. Moreover, globalization is disempowering citizens within the nation-state as far as social rights are concerned, without providing them with any leverage globally. At the same time, trans-national corporations and the global marketplace have been empowered, hugely, through financial deregulation and capital mobility. (p. 130)

But the contrary trends are also important and require analysis in the framing and development of social theory and social policy in relation to aging. Deacon (2000; see also Walker & Deacon, 2003) has noted the emergence of what he views as a "new politics of global social responsibility." He observes that

> Orthodox economic liberalism and inhumane structural adjustment appear to be giving way to a concern on the part of the [World Bank] and the IMF with the social consequences of globalization. International development assistance is concerned to focus upon social development. United Nations agencies are increasingly troubled by the negative social consequences of globalization ... [there is a shift away] from a politics of liberalism to a global politics of social concern. (p. 13)

In any event, the impact of policies at a nation-state level will almost certainly be affected and potentially reduced in many instances by transnational organizations. George and Wilding (2002) make the point here that

> [National policies] will fail unless complemented and underpinned by parallel policies at the global level. When national welfare states came into being and flourished in the 1940s, 1950s and 1960s there were few social problems that had ramifications beyond the reach of individual nation-states. States could be sovereign in their social policies. Half a century later, national self-sufficiency in social policy is no longer a realistic option. In an increasing number of areas, action at the national level has to be complemented and supplemented by action at a supranational level. (p. 187)

This last development may bring some advantages to older people. In the European context, avoidance by successive U.K. governments of age-discrimination legislation has been challenged by a European Union directive outlawing discrimination in the workplace on grounds of age, race, disability, or sexual orientation. Similarly, national legislation following the European Convention on Human Rights also has the potential to be used to challenge age discrimination in areas such as service provision and employment, as well as fundamental issues relating to the right to life, the right not to be subject to inhumane treatment, and the right to a fair hearing. Such examples illustrate the way in which international law may be used to challenge discrimination against older people. They further highlight the need for new approaches to theorizing about age that can integrate the continuing power and influence of the nation-state, with the countervailing powers of global institutions.[6]

Third, it will be especially important, given the pressures associated with globalization, to engage older people and their organizations with the debate launched by national governments and IGOs about the future of pension provision and health and social care services. Thus far, older people and their representative

---

[6] Wade (2004) reviews recent data in this area; see Firebaugh (2003) for evidence that while inequality within nations is increasing, that between countries has decreased.

organizations can claim only limited influence on the major debates about population aging launched by the World Bank and similar organizations (Estes & Phillipson, 2002). The case that needs to be made is for an "age-sensitive" globalization in which older people have greater influence in key international fora. Relevant aspects might include:

- auditing the activities of key IGOs with respect to their activities on aging issues
- building an age dimension into development policies and strategies
- promoting aging organizations as major players alongside existing multi-lateral agencies
- strengthening the age dimension in human rights legislation
- encouraging older people's organizations to play a prominent role in the network of groups and fora that are comprised in global civil society

This is an important agenda, but one that is being only partially addressed in the United Nations, the World Health Organization (WHO), and related bodies. This is illustrated by the Madrid International Plan of Action on Ageing (MIPAA), which arose from the Second World Assembly on Ageing (held in Madrid in April 2002). Sidorenko and Walker (2004) note that the idea of a "Society for All Ages" is a guiding theme in the Plan and that this is seen to embrace

> . . . human rights; a secure old age (including the eradication of poverty); the empowerment of older people; individual development, self-fulfillment and well-being throughout life; gender equality among older people; inter-generational inter-dependence, solidarity and reciprocity; health care, support and social protection for older people; partnership between all major stake-holders in the implementation process; scientific research and expertise; and the situation of ageing indigenous people and migrants. (p. 152)

The authors further suggest that the ultimate goal of MIPAA is to "improve the quality of life of older people on the basis of security, dignity and participation, while at the same time promoting measures to reconcile aging and development, and sustaining supportive formal . . . and informal . . . systems of individual well-being" (Sidorenko & Walker, 2004, p. 156). Although such a goal provides a strong platform for developing a new agenda for population aging, the need to engage with growing income inequality must also be confronted. Wade (2001) summarizes data indicating that incomes across the globe became markedly more unequal in the period from the late 1980s to the early 1990s. He reports one study that found the share of world income going to the poorest 10% of the world's population falling by over a quarter, whereas the share of the richest 10% rose by 8%. More generally, Wade (2004) suggests that globalization, as it currently operates, is increasing inequality within as well as between countries. Such inequalities are creating new forms of exclusion, notably for women, the working class, and minority ethnic groups (see footnote 6). Developments such as these require more positive action from bodies such as the United Nations and WHO. The concern of these organizations to encourage the empowerment of older people and to achieve what has been defined as "active ageing" (World Health Organization, 2001), will surely fail unless national and global inequalities are tackled in a systematic way—notably those that reduce the life chance of those older people living in less-developed countries and the poorer communities of the developed world. Moreover, bodies such as the UN and the WHO will need to confront the power of IGOs, such as the IMF and World Bank, to impose social policies that result in drastic cuts in expenditure on services for groups such as older people (Barlow & Clarke, 2001; Estes & Phillipson, 2002). This has been a particular feature of economic programs directed at Latin American and East European countries and is in direct conflict with the aspirations of the Madrid plan to build a secure and dignified old age across the global community.

CONCLUSION:
BUILDING A NEW POLITICS OF OLD AGE

Attempts to improve the quality of life in old age will almost certainly be frustrated unless there is also a new politics of old age that recognizes the changed realities resulting from the collapse of the welfare state (Vincent, Patterson, & Wale, 2001). Despite their inadequacies, welfare institutions provided an essential framework for supporting older people. They produced as well a space around which a defensive politics of aging could be developed. But the movement of old age beyond this space raises the issue of exploring the basis for different types of political action and identity formation in later life. From a more general standpoint, Castells (2004, p. 7) suggests new forms of identity are likely to emerge given the impact of globalization on weakening/delegitimizing traditional sources of authority. He identifies first, *resistance identities* that build "trenches of resistance and survival on the basis of principles different from, or opposed to, those permeating the institutions of society"; second, *project identities* that seek to construct an identity in a way that redefines the position of a group in society and, by so doing, "seek the transformation of overall social structure."

O'Rand (2000) explores the challenges to the aging self within the context of the "risk culture" associated with the privatization of welfare, arguing that the rapid spread of individualized pensions and similar developments in health are pushing individuals to become "more self-reflexive and calculating in the planning and control of their lives." At the same time, she makes the point that

> . . . the unequal distributions of information, resources, and power do not translate into greater freedom for individuals. Rather, individuals respond to newer choices based on their diverse social locations, past experiences, limited vantage points, and value preferences. The future is more uncertain in many respects and elicits a general response of risk-aversion and a retreat in many ways to the more familiar. (p. 245)

The approach taken by Castells (2004) and O'Rand (2000) may be especially relevant in the context of the attitudes adopted by new cohorts of older people and changing ideologies about old age. The contribution of feminism, the views of particular black and minority ethnic groups, the problems facing the socially excluded, and the more critical perspective of an aging baby-boom generation, are likely to produce distinctive networks of power and political action. To these must be added possibilities for political activity at a global level in the context of transnational movements and the struggle against the arbitrary power exerted by multinational corporations and IGOs (Klein, 2000; Sklair, 2002; Stiglitz, 2003). These elements should produce a reflexive politics with the potential for greater influence by individuals both on the structures supporting old age and on ideas concerning the meaning of later life. At the same time, political organization will be highly differentiated, from groups of affluent baby boomers concerned with transforming stereotypes of aging, to groups of the socially excluded building defensive identities in the face of financial impoverishment on the one side and the experience of environmental degradation on the other.

Much of this political engagement will continue to operate within nation-states, which will maintain their role in initiating and shaping social and economic policies of relevance to older people. But the impact of global aging as a discourse, and globalization as a political process, will be fundamental. Globalization will undoubtedly be highly contradictory in its impact. On the one hand, it can challenge unjust or inadequate national laws and policies; it can promote new political alliances; and it can sharpen awareness of problems and issues that are transnational and cross-cultural in scope. On the other hand, globalization greatly extends the power of multinational organizations; it has created powerful IGOs in which the influence of consumer groups is relatively weak; and it can undermine the policies of nation-states in vital areas such as pensions and public provision for health and social care. How these diverse influences will affect the lives of older people will be a crucial issue for gerontology to address. The question of globalization should certainly become central to advancing research in the political economy of aging in the next phase of its development.

REFERENCES

Achenbaum, A. (1978). *Old age in the new land.* Baltimore: Johns Hopkins.

Andrews, G., & Phillips, D. (Eds.). (2005). *Ageing and place: Perspectives, policy and practice.* London: Routledge.

Arber, S., Davidson, K., & Ginn, J. (2003). *Gender and ageing.* Buckingham: Open University Press.

Barlow, M., & Clarke, T. (2001). *Global showdown.* Ontario: Stoddart.

Bauman, Z. (1996). *Postmodernity and its discontents.* Oxford: Blackwell.

Bauman, Z. (2000). *Liquid modernity.* Cambridge: Polity Press.

Beck, U. (1992). *The risk society.* London: Sage Books.

Beck, U. (2000). *The brave new world of work.* Cambridge: Polity Press.

Beck, U., & Beck-Gernsheim, E. (2002). *Individualization.* London: Sage Books.
Bernard, M., Bartlam, B., Biggs, S., & Sim, J. (2003). *New lifestyles in old age: Health, identity and well-being in Berryhill Retirement Village.* Bristol: Policy Press.
Blackburn, R. (2002). *Banking on death.* London: Verso Books.
Castells, M. (1996). *The rise of the network society.* Oxford: Blackwell.
Castells, M. (2004). *The power of identity* (2nd ed.). Oxford: Blackwell.
Cerny, P. G. (1997). Paradoxes of the competition state: The dynamics of political globalization. *Government and Opposition, 32*(2), 251-274.
Cerny, P. G., & Evans, M. (2004). Globalization and public policy under new labour. *Policy Studies, 25*(1), 51-65.
Central Intelligence Agency. (2001). *Long term global demographic trends: Re-shaping the geo-political landscape.* Retrieved November 3, 2004 from http://www.odci.gov/cia/reports/index/html.
Cole, T. (1992). *The journey of life.* Cambridge: Cambridge University Press.
Cole, T. R., Achenbaum, W. A., Jakobi, P. L., & Kastenbaum, R. (1993). *Voices and visions of aging: Toward a critical gerontology.* New York: Springer Publishing.
Dannefer, D. (2000). Bringing risk back in: The regulation of the self in the postmodern state. In K. W. Schaie & J. Hendricks (Eds.), *The evolution of the aging self: The societal impact on the aging process* (pp. 269-280). New York: Springer Publishing.
Dannefer, D. (2003a). Toward a global geography of the life course. In J. Mortimer & M. Shanahan (Eds.), *Handbook of the life course* (pp. 647-659). New York: Kluwer Academic/Plenum Publishers.
Dannefer, D. (2003b). Cumulative advantage/disadvantage and the life course: Cross-fertilizing age and social science theory. *Journal of Gerontology, 58B*(6), S327-S337.
Deacon, B. (2000). *Globalization and social policy. The threat to equitable welfare.* (Occasional Paper no. 5). Retrieved October 2, 2004 from http://www.org.unrisd Globalism and Social Policy Programme (GASPP), UNRISD.
Delanty, G. (2000). *Citizenship in a global age.* Buckingham: Open University Press.
Disney, R., & Whitehouse, E. (2002). The economic well-being of older people in international perspective: A critical review. In S. Crystal & D. Shea (Eds.), *Economic outcomes in later life: Public policy, health and cumulative advantage* (pp. 59-94). New York: Springer Publishing.
Estes, C. (1979). *The aging enterprise.* San Francisco: Jossey-Bass.
Estes, C., & Associates. (2001). *Social policy and aging.* Thousand Oaks: Sage.
Estes, C., & Phillipson, C. (2002). The globalization of capital, the welfare state and old age policy. *International Journal of Health Services, 32*(2), 279-297.
Estes, C., Biggs, S., & Phillipson, C. (2003). *Social theory, social policy and ageing: A critical introduction.* Buckingham: Open University Press.
Fennell, G., Phillipson, C., & Evers, H. (1988). *The sociology of old age.* Milton Keynes: Open University Press.
Firebaugh, G. (2003). *The geography of global income inequality.* London: Harvard University Press.
Fischer, D. J. (1977). *Growing old in America.* New York: Oxford University Press.
George, V., & Wilding, P. (2002). *Globalization and human welfare.* London: Palgrave.
Giddens, A. (1991). *Modernity and self-identity.* Cambridge: Polity Press.
Giddens, A. (1999). *Globalization.* Reith Lecture No.1. BBC Online Network. Retrieved November 12, 2004 from www.lse.ac.uk/Giddens/lectures.htm.

Graebner, W. (1980). *A history of retirement.* New Haven, CT: Yale University Press.

Held, D., McGrew, A., Goldblatt, D., & Perraton, J. (1999). *Global transformations.* Oxford: Polity Press.

Held, D., & McGrew, A. (2002). *Governing globalization: Power, authority and global governance.* Cambridge: Polity Press.

Hoerder, D. (2001). Reconstructing life courses: A historical perspective on migrant experiences. In V. Marshall, W. Heinz, H. Kruger, & A. Verma (Eds.), *Reconstructing work and the life course.* Toronto: University of Toronto Press.

Jackson, R. (2002). *The global retirement crisis.* Washington: Citigroup/CSIS.

Katz, S. (n.d.). *Spaces of age and the gerontology of mobility: The elder-scapes of Charlotte County, Florida* (mimeo).

Klein, N. (2000). *No logo: Taking aim at the brand bullies.* London: Flamingo Books.

Knodel, J., Watkins, S., & VanLandingham, M. (2002). *AIDS and older persons: An international perspective* (PSC Research Report No. 02-495). University of Michigan: Population Studies Center.

Linos, K. (2001). How can international organizations shape national welfare states? Evidence from compliance with EU directives (Working Paper No. 17). Harvard University: Centre for European Studies.

Lupton, D. (1999). *Risk and sociocultural theory.* Cambridge: Cambridge University Press.

Marshall, T. H. (1992). *Citizenship and social class.* London: Pluto.

Minkler, M., & Estes, C. (Eds.). (1999). *Critical gerontology: Perspectives from political and moral economy* (2nd ed.). Amityville, NY: Baywood.

Minns, R. (2001). *The cold war in welfare: Stock markets versus pensions.* London: Verso.

Mishra, R. (1999). *Globalization and the welfare state.* Cheltenham: Edward Elgar.

Murray, C. (1994) *Underclass: The crisis deepens.* London: IEA Health and Welfare Unit/Sunday Times.

O'Rand, A. M. (2000). Risk, rationality, and modernity: Social policy and the aging self. In K. W. Schaie (Ed.), *Social structures and aging* (pp. 225-249). New York: Springer Publishing.

Phillipson, C. (1982). *Capitalism and the construction of old age.* London: Macmillan.

Phillipson, C. (1998). *Reconstructing old age.* London: Sage.

Riley, M. W., & Riley, J. W, Jr. (1994). Age integration and the lives of older people. *The Gerontologist, 34*(1): 110-115.

Scharf, T., Phillipson C., Smith A. E., & Kingston P. (2002). *Growing older in socially deprived areas: Social exclusion in later life.* London: Help the Aged.

Sklair, L. (2002). *Globalization: Capitalism and its alternatives.* Oxford: Oxford University Press.

Sidorenko, A., & Walker, A. (2004). The Madrid International Plan of Action on Ageing: From conception to implementation. *Ageing and Society, 24*(2), 147-166.

Stiglitz, J. (2003). *The roaring nineties.* London: Penguin Books.

Thane, P. (2000). *Old age in English history: Past experiences, present issues.* Oxford University Press.

Thompson, J. B. (2000). The globalization of communication. In D. Held & A. McGrew (Eds.), *The global transformations reader.* Cambridge: Polity Press.

Townsend, P. (1981). The structured dependency of the elderly: The creation of policy in the twentieth century. *Aging and Society, 1*(1), 5-28.

Urry, J. (2000). *Sociology beyond societies.* London: Routledge.

Vincent, J. A., Patterson, G., & Wale, K. (2001). *Older citizens and political processes in Britain.* Aldershot: Ashgate Publishing.

Vincent, J. (2003a). *Old age.* London: Routledge.

Vincent, J. (2003b). *New forms of global political economy and ageing societies.* Paper presented at the European Association Conference, Ageing in Europe: Challenges for Globalization for Ageing Societies, Murcia, Spain.

Wade, R. (2001, April 28). Winners and losers. *The Economist,* pp. 93-97.

Wade, R. (2004). On the causes of increasing world poverty and inequality, or why the Matthew Effect prevails. *New Political Economy, 9*(2), 163-188.

Walker, A. (1981). Towards a political economy of old age. *Ageing and Society, 1*(1), 73-94.

Walker, A., & Deacon, B. (2003). Economic globalization and policies on aging. *Journal of Societal and Social Policy, 2*(2), 1-18.

World Bank. (1994). *Averting the old age crisis.* Oxford: Oxford University Press.

World Health Organization. (2001). *Health and ageing: A discussion paper.* Geneva: WHO.

Yeates, N. (2001). *Globalization and social policy.* London: Sage.

CHAPTER 4

Reexamining the Political Economy of Aging: Understanding the Structure/Agency Tension

Alan Walker

The main purposes of this chapter are to review the political economy of aging thesis and to outline a theoretical perspective in which the commonly (and falsely) dichotomized relationship between structure and agency may be understood as a creative tension. One of the impetuses for looking back over past work is the emergence of a narrow cultural critique of aging in which the structured dependency and political economy theses are caricatured as implying that older people are the mere pawns of policy (Gilleard & Higgs, 2000). More positively, the prospective aspect of the chapter arises from a current European endeavor aimed at providing a new set of autonomous social standards as an alternative to the dominance of economic issues in the policy process. Key questions are whether or not the political economy approach—born under modernism—still has relevance for the way we interpret aging in the late-modern, postindustrial period characterized by globalization and new forms of risk. And can the structure/agency debate, that has consumed so much intellectual effort, be used to productive effect in understanding old age? This account involves revisiting the relationship between old age and the welfare state because the new culture of aging perspective, and the risk society analysis on which it is based, have major implications for the welfare state. Also, the discourse on old age and the welfare state is particularly strong in Europe, my intellectual and cultural reference point.

ORIGINS

In any discipline, a mainstream or orthodoxy develops that is often conservative and rarely self-critical. Such dominant paradigms can become inward looking and stultifying, preventing a reappraisal of concepts, ideas, and approaches, as well as limiting a subject's scope and ability to analyze fundamental socio-economic changes. So it was in the field of social gerontology in the late 1970s where a new critical paradigm began to take shape. Scholars in France, Great Britain, and the United States, working in parallel and fortuitously touching base together at the World Congress of Sociology in Uppsala in 1978, produced, in 1979 and 1980, the elements of this new paradigm, initially labeled the social construction of aging or structured dependency, and later the political economy of aging and, still later, critical gerontology (Estes, 1979; Guillemard, 1980; Walker, 1978). The same transformation in the study of youth and childhood that followed more than a decade later has been labeled the "new sociology of childhood" (James, Jenks, & Prout, 1998).

The main thrust of the early work on political economy was against the dominant benign functionalist theories in social gerontology that implied that features of aging in advanced industrial societies were somehow natural or inevitable. For example, poverty was accepted too readily and uncritically as a "fact" of old age to which older people had to adjust. The dominant liberal-pluralist framework of social gerontology had, hitherto, paid very little attention to the different impact of aging, especially along class, gender, and ethnic lines (Phillipson, 1982; Townsend, 1981; Walker, 1980, 1981).

Not surprisingly, therefore, the thesis emphasized economic and material dependency and exclusion, and argued that they are not an inevitable fact of aging but, in part, the result of conscious thought and action in the twentieth century. Thus it is not chronological age, as such, that is the main determinant of economic dependency, but the socially constructed relationships between, principally, age and the labor market and age and the welfare state. This analysis had the effect of diverting the gerontological gaze away from the problems of old age and individual adjustment to features of the aging process, towards structural constraints and sources of inclusion or exclusion such as pension policies, retirement policies, age discrimination, and so on. It emphasized struc-tural inequalities between different groups of older people and focused on two key, but then neglected, aspects of the aging process: cumulative life-course advantages and disadvantages between different groups and the consequences of economic dependency on the state. (Cumulative advantage/disadvantage is an important theme of this book; see Chapters 3, 6, 11, and 12.) It was seen by the scientific community as a radical departure and has provided the basis of an enormous flow of research in this field.

This is not to suggest that the thesis is without criticism, but I will return to that. First I want to emphasize the relationship between old age and the welfare state in order to explain the potential impact of the risk-society analysis and to counterbalance the tendency, particularly in North America, to emphasize two other narratives of age—the biomedical and biology of aging, on the one hand, and on the other, lifestyle and consumerist culture in old age. In contrast, the discourse on the relationship between old age and the welfare state has been stronger in Europe.

OLD AGE AND THE WELFARE STATE

Older people are closely connected to the welfare state: all European welfare states either had their origins in provision for old age or their arrival in fully fledged form was marked by the introduction of a pension system. In other words, old age was acknowledged collectively as a risk status from the early part of the last century. But it was with the advent of the postwar welfare state that both the risk of old age and the definition of old age itself became institutionalized. Regardless of the particular variant of European welfare state (Beveridge, Bismarck, or hybrid) the risk associated with old age has always been regarded as a legitimate one with few of the sanctions attached to it compared with provision for people of working age. Today, of course, older people are the largest beneficiaries of welfare states, and pensions are the largest item of social expenditure. They are also the biggest users of health and social care services.

The relationship between old age and the welfare state has not been a static one, and it is when we examine its dynamics that we can see the critical role of social policy and social institutions in structuring and restructuring the life course and the meaning of old age. Economic dependency and exclusion have been socially constructed primarily by institutions such as the labor market and the welfare state. Elsewhere, I have distinguished three distinct phases in the postwar European evolution of social policy with regard to older people that are summarized here (Walker, 1999; see also Phillipson, 1998 for a similar periodization).

Old Age as a Social Problem: 1940s-Early 1970s

In the years following the Second World War, aging became identified as a social problem. National pension systems were put in place and/or consolidated during this period, and social expenditure rose rapidly in what proved to be the golden age of the welfare state. Of course the origins of social policy in the field of pensions predates this period by more than 50 years: Bismarck's system of worker insurance in Germany in 1889, the first old age pensions in the United Kingdom in 1908 and in France in 1910. However, universal coverage was achieved in this period, and there is no mistaking the proliferation of social policy measures. In the period 1960 to 1975, the increase in pension expenditure in the Organisation for Economic Cooperation and Development (OECD) countries accounted, on average, for one-quarter of the rise in the share of public expenditure in GDP. In France it was more than one-third, Germany just under one-fifth and, in the United Kingdom, around one-seventh (OECD, 1988, p. 21). This reinforces the conclusion of Pampel, Williamson, and Stryker (1990) that there are "multiple paths to higher pension spending" (p. 547).

The main goals of public policy in this period were to provide for income security in old age and, in doing so, to ensure the efficient transition of older workers from employment to retirement. The early postwar period was one of full employment; indeed in the early 1950s in the United Kingdom, a National Advisory Committee on the Employment of Older Men and Women was formed to encourage older people to remain in the labor market (Phillipson, 1982). While full employment lasted, there was some resistance to the assumptions of neoclassical economics and scientific management theories concerning declining productivity in older age (Taylor, 1947). Thus the main focus of public policy was on those that had left the labor market. This focus was determined largely by economic management and policy because this group was, in effect, defined as "externalities" by the macroeconomic policy system. Public pensions were regarded as an appropriate way of socializing the costs of retirement as well as assisting industry to rejuvenate the workforce (Graebner, 1980). This was an important element of the postwar settlement between Keynesian economics and Beveridge-style (i.e., liberal) social policy: it was intended that economic growth would generate sufficient resources for universal pension provision.

The establishment of public pension systems and, more importantly, their accompanying retirement conditions encouraged the rapid spread of fixed age retirement. Thus, in policy terms, old age came to be uniquely associated with retirement ages. In other words, old age was objectified at retirement age (Graebner, 1980; Townsend, 1981; Walker, 1980). What are the consequences of the institutionalization of age-related retirement? There are five key points.

In the first place, the economic dependency of older people on the state was enlarged substantially. One hundred years ago in the United Kingdom, two-thirds of the male population aged 65 and over were economically active (in employment or seeking it); today it is only 7%. Older people were not helpless pawns in this social definition of old age. On the contrary, individually and collectively, workers called for retirement and public pensions. But the creation of a fixed-age barrier in European pension systems led to widespread economic exclusion. As we shall see, in the second half of the twentieth century, large numbers of older workers opted for retirement before the fixed-age barrier, a choice that has become more widely available as pensions have risen in value.

Second, age-barrier retirement has been the main wellspring of age discrimination in employment, social security, and in wider social relations (Bytheway, 1995; McEwan, 1990). It has not been the sole cause of age discrimination, but it has encouraged the view that, past a certain age, an individual's economic and social worth is diminished.

Third, as a corollary to retirement, it has been accepted that the income needs of older people are lower than those of the "economically active." Typically, public pensions are set at rates below and sometimes considerably below average earnings and, even when occupational pensions are included and idealized projections are made, some leading EU countries still have quite low replacement ratios: 69% in Germany and 64% in the United Kingdom for example (Walker, Guillemard, & Alber, 1993).

Fourth, age-barrier retirement and these foregoing factors have encouraged the view that older people are not just a social problem but an economic burden as well. Thus, in this early postwar phase, there were occasional warnings, for example from the UN in 1954, about the "burden" of population aging (Walker, 1990). This approach to aging is best exemplified in the old-age dependency ratio that crudely expresses a ratio between those over pension age and younger adults and thereby objectifies the assumption that economic dependency must be associated with aging. Such calculations are ubiquitous in European policy discourse in this field, despite their many flaws.

Fifth, with regard to health and social services policy and practice, it was this first phase that saw the major expansion of these services and their profes-sionalization. Since policy makers had come to regard older people as largely dependent and passive objects, it is not surprising that the professional and institutional structures of the health and social services also tended to reflect this view: for example, forms of education and training that encouraged professionals to regard themselves as experts operating autonomously. Thus the expansion of health and social services in this period was a two-sided coin: it enhanced the welfare of older people, but it was delivered in ways that reinforced their social and physical dependency and powerlessness. The professionalization of old age in the health and social services, therefore, is an important component of age segregation.

Old Age as the Solution to One Economic Problem and the Cause of Another: Mid 1970s-Late 1980s

There occurred a transitional phase that stretched from the origins of the fiscal crises in the mid-1970s to the late 1980s. During this relatively short space of time, the social meaning of aging was reconstructed along two dimensions.

First there was a massive fall in male economic activity in later life throughout the E.U. and, indeed, all industrial countries with the exceptions of Sweden and Japan (Kohli, Rein, Guillemard, & van Gunsteren, 1991). The decline in activity is most marked among those aged 65 and over and those aged 60–64, but is also clear in the age group 55–59. In most E.U. countries, working after the age of 65 has been eradicated. The position of older women is harder to disentangle from the cohort effect of rising rates of participation among younger women, but it does appear that a similar decline has taken place (Walker et al., 1993).

The main factors explaining this decline in Europe are demand related, particu-larly the collapse of employment in the mid-1970s and early 1980s. Research on early retirement following redundancy in the Sheffield steel industry shows two distinct paths being followed. On the one hand, there were those who, faced with redundancy, chose early retirement as a preferable option to unemployment while, on the other, there were those who were effectively coerced into it by a hostile labor market. Thus, early retirement was, for the first group, a welcome release from employment and, for the second group, a refuge from a hostile labor market. The key explanatory factors in this social division were age (proximity to pension age) and income level (Westergaard, Noble, & Walker, 1989). A key feature of the demand-side causation of the rise of early retirement was public policy. During this period, there was a proliferation of employment and pension measures designed to encourage early retirement. Examples include the Job Release Scheme in the United Kingdom and preretirement benefits in Denmark and Germany (Walker et al., 1993).

During this transitional phase, the growth of early retirement reconstructed old age from a simple age-related status with a single lower entry point into a much broader category that stretches from around age 50 to death. This has necessitated the widespread functional separation of the third (50–74) and fourth (75+) ages, the young-old and old-old, a distinction that first appeared in France in the 1960s. It has also meant, as Guillemard (1993) has shown, that public pension systems are no longer the key regulators of retirement. The traditional pattern of labor-force exit at pension age has become a minority one—for example, in Germany (former FDR) and the United Kingdom only around one-third of male entrants to the public pension system come directly from employment. In other words, compensation for the risk associated with old age has been detached from the functional commencement of old age and potential economic dependence.

Another important consequence of the unchecked growth of early retirement from the labor force is that it has reinforced the devaluation of older people in the labor market. The downward redefinition of aging has had consequences for the ways that employers perceive older workers and in turn the chances they offer them for reemployment. Indeed, there is a large body of evidence in different E.U. countries to show that third-agers are frequently discriminated against with regard to job recruitment, promotions, and training (Drury, 1993, 1997; Walker, 1997). This is despite the fact that age is not a good proxy for the ability to work and learn; therefore discrimination is not only unjust but wasteful of economic capacity and potential. Anecdotal evidence suggests that anti-age discrimination legislation in the United States is a factor in the higher employment rate among older U.S. citizens compared to their non-U.S. counterparts.

The only E.U.-wide survey evidence on this topic comes from 1992 (Walker, 1993). We asked the general public in each country whether or not older workers are discriminated against with regard to job recruitment and other aspects of employment. A remarkably high proportion—four out of five for the E.U. as a whole—said that such discrimination *does* exist with regard to recruitment. Moreover, there was hardly any difference based on the age of respondents—all age groups believe that discrimination takes place against older workers (Walker, 1993).

During this second phase, the social meaning of aging was transformed from its long association with pension ages to labor market criteria such as employability. Public policy, particularly in the employment sphere, was one of the main engines driving this change. But while encouraging early retirement was seen as a solution to unemployment (though the policy does not seem to have been very effective), aging also came to be seen as an economic problem in its own right. From the late 1970s onward, there has been mounting concern on the part of national governments about the economic consequences of population aging. Forward projections of dependency ratios have been used to paint a pessimistic picture of the socioeconomic implications of aging. Sometimes these border on the alarmist, as these quotations show.

> Under existing regulations the evolution of public pension schemes is likely to put a heavy and increasing burden on the working population in coming decades. Such a financial strain may put inter-generational solidarity—a concept on which all public retirement provisions are based—at risk. (OECD, 1988)

> If no action is taken to deal with the incipient crisis of population aging, then it seems certain that western societies will experience major social and economic dislocation, and they may experience this relatively soon. (Johnson, Conrad, & Thomson, 1989)

The question as to why international agencies and European governments should adopt an avowedly pessimistic stance toward the societal implications of population aging takes us beyond the scope of this chapter. What it illustrates is that neoclassical assumptions about the "burden" of aging held sway in national and international policy arenas (Walker, 1990). In other words, the implicit theory of old age that dominated public policy in this period was an extremely pessimistic economic one, the precursor of neoliberal globalization.

THE LATE 1980s ONWARDS: THE INDIVIDUALIZATION OF RISK AND WELFARE

The transition from the second to the third phase of aging policy development was marked by the termination, starting in the late 1980s, of some of the main mechanisms for early retirement. One of the first E.U. countries to act was France, in 1986, when early retirement contracts were abolished. Soon after, similar actions were taken in Belgium, Germany, and the United Kingdom, and now every E.U. country has followed suit. However, the early retirement trend has developed its own momentum; it has become institutionalized in the labor market for the reasons outlined above. Although the transition has happened, European societies are only just on the threshold of this third phase and, therefore, the future of aging and public policy is a now matter of speculation. However, although there are contraindications, a likely scenario—the individualization of risk—is becoming clear in outline at least.

The underlying assumption of this scenario is that old age constitutes a "burden" to society and, therefore, national governments have to attempt to reduce its economic cost in the form of pensions as well as health and social services. There is no doubt that in several leading E.U. countries, the costs of pensions and long-term care is a major political issue. Most of them have already taken action to limit costs. In the pensions field, the most favored policy is an increase in retirement ages. For example, over the next decade, Germany and the United Kingdom are increasing their retirement ages. But in Sweden and especially Italy, there have been substantial revisions to the pension formulae themselves, in both cases to introduce an element of prefunding into those systems.

These sorts of pension reforms are in line with the policies of the key architects of the neoliberal response to globalization—the World Bank, the IMF and the WTO—all of which are promoting a reduction in state provision and a larger role for personal responsibility (Estes & Phillipson, 2002; Walker & Deacon, 2003). In the EU, this approach has not been taken very far, except in one country, the United Kingdom, where the Thatcher pension reforms reconstructed pension provision away from the state and into private prefunded schemes. This is not the place to explore the detail of this remarkable story in the history of social insurance, but its impact has been dramatic. In particular, two forms of risk have been enlarged. First, because of the reduction in state pension provision, the risks of future deprivation and poverty among some groups of people in retirement have been increased. Second, the switch from public to private provision for those of working age has increased the precariousness of their future pension income. Many part-time female workers, in particular, will be unable to make sufficient contributions to fund a pension above the minimum state one. This is a unique story in the E.U., but all other Member States are exploring the potential of private prefunded pensions, and some are encouraging their growth.

The individualization and privatization of pensions is part of a more general trend towards the "individualization of the social" (Ferge, 1997), whereby states are expecting individuals and families to take responsibility for risks that were previously collectivized. This trend is not strong in Western Europe at the moment, except in the United Kingdom, but in Central and Eastern Europe, driven by the World Bank, it has been deep and widespread (as it has in the Southern Hemisphere). Leaving aside these transition states, ten of which joined the E.U. on May 1, 2004, why is it taking place in the established welfare states?

Globalization figures prominently in arguments for welfare state reform, particularly under the Transatlantic Consensus, which holds that growing inequality is an inevitable feature of globalization and that social costs must be minimized (Walker, 2002). However, in practice, there is little evidence of the impact of globalization and plenty of counterevidence that the European welfare states compete well internationally (Gough, 1997). Nonetheless, it does seem that the fear of global competition, again stoked by international economic agencies, is driving some of the policy agenda, except in a few clear instances; it is hard to distinguish it from a general political concern about the effects of direct taxation at elections. In the E.U., this is linked with the economic criteria for monetary union that have imposed some strict limits on public spending.

Second, there are undoubtedly pressures on several European pension systems, and population aging is commonly seen as the culprit. However, it is not population aging alone that is the problem but its combination with the European culture of early exit. Thus, over the last 50 years, life expectancy has increased by around 10 years while labor force participation, particularly among older male workers (60–64), has dropped from close to 80% to 30%. Now only just over one-third of 55–64-year-olds are economically active. This age/employment paradox is the main problem, and it is one that is amenable to policy.

Third, it is argued that social insurance systems created at the beginning of the century cannot be relevant to today's labor market and life course; the late-modern life course is incompatible with the modernist or industrial welfare state. This, again, lacks evidence but is taking on the status of a truism. Arguably, a system of risk pooling is even more relevant today than 50 or 100 years ago. Insecurity in the labor market is at its 50 year peak and may become more so. The late-modern working life is characterized by insecurity for a majority and gross insecurity for up to 40% of the working population, mainly women. This makes it less and less likely that they will be able to build up the necessary capital to fund a private personal pension. Employers in the United Kingdom are reducing their commitments to occupational pensions, by delaying entry and changing from defined benefit to defined contribution schemes, and some are taking money out of their schemes, and increasing numbers are closing them to new employees.

Finally, there is the largely theoretical argument advanced by the gurus of late modernity or postmodernity and their acolytes. This runs along the lines that, as the structures of modernity crumble, this opens up new opportunities for agency and that, in a future era when everyone follows a different life-course pattern, standardized social institutions cannot possibly respond sensitively to individual needs. In short, such arguments reinforce the case for the individualization of the social, although there are many variants in these arguments, and some of them seek to reconstruct welfare states in more responsive forms.

The risk society thesis of Beck (1992) and Giddens (1994) takes a very specific line on the nature of late modernity. Their thesis, in a nutshell, is that risks that were calculable under industrial society become incalculable and unpredictable in the risk society. The implications for the welfare state (and its major user groups) are momentous: if you want to survive in a global market, where risk is also globalized, you have to change the basic foundations of modernity: social security, the nation state, and so on.

The risk theorists put a heavy emphasis on ecological, scientific, and techno-logical risks. Their analysis of the welfare state rests on a functionalist argument that it must be reconstructed in the face of the new, globalized basis of risk. They see the welfare state as a system designed to respond to "external" risks (unemployment, retirement) or "accidents of fate" in Giddens' terms. But, the new form of "manufactured risk" makes obsolete the institutions designed to deal with external risks. According to Giddens, ". . . in an era of manufactured risk—the welfare state cannot continue on in the form in which it developed in the post 1945 settlement," and "The crisis of the welfare state is not purely fiscal, it is a crisis of risk management in a society dominated by a new type of risk" (1994, p. 24).

Unfortunately, there is very little or no evidence for this contention with regard to the welfare state. It is undeniable that citizens face new technological and ecological risks, and that many of these are global. But at the same time, many of the existing risks continue, and there is evidence that welfare states are able to accommodate newly emerging ones. In fact when the changing nature of risk in Western Europe is considered, it can be seen how important it is to ensure that the welfare state continues to pool risks and also that it begins to prevent them. Boscoe and Chassard have highlighted four main developments (1999, p. 48):

- a reduction in the financial risk associated with old age but with a new risk of becoming unemployable after 50
- the emergence of a new risk associated with longevity—long-term care
- a change in the nature of the labor market and unemployment so that, for the unemployed, it is not just a matter of geographical mobility to find work but also skills mobility to remain employable
- new forms of insecure work with no or very low workers' rights to social protection

It is obvious that these new forms of risk all have major direct or indirect implications for old age. Equally obviously the new risks are borne unequally by class, gender, race, and ethnicity, and so on. They also emphasize a fundamental flaw in the risk society analysis: the welfare state was designed to pool risks, to share the social costs of economic progress, and to support accumulation; not just to respond to "external risks." Indeed, in the E.U. at least, the indications are that social protection systems are responding to the changing nature of risk, for example, by changing policies toward those over 50 and by introducing support for long-term care. Nonetheless the danger exists that this process of adaptation, and with it, the underlying collectivization of risk, will be rejected in some countries in favor of the individualization of risk. This would be perverse, even in the risk-society analyst's own terms, because individuals are already at the mercy of a wide range of new risks and should not be needlessly exposed to others. It would undermine the mature welfare states of Western Europe and relocate old age squarely back into the risk market. It is not inevitable that this will happen, but it could if policy makers continue to encourage pessimism about both old age and the welfare state and if neoliberalism remains the dominant response to economic globalization.

POLITICAL ECONOMY REVISITED

This brings this short history of critical social gerontology, aging, and social policy full circle. Political economy and the structured dependency theses were never posed in deterministic or purely utilitarian terms that portrayed older people as helpless pawns in a capitalist conspiracy. They were intended to illuminate the structural features of the aging process—social class, gender, ethnicity, race, and so on—and the role of social and economic policies precisely in order to counterbalance the previous overconcentration on individual adjustment and situational factors. Nonetheless, the main recurring criticism of the thesis is that it neglects agency (the ability of individuals to act within, engage with, and change social structures) (Archer, 2000; Barnes, 2000; Weber, 1968). It has been indicated already that this is factually incorrect, and also, it is rather ironic because the thesis originated as a critique of the implicit pessimism of acquiescent functionalism, which assumes that everyone over retirement age is a dependent burden, and which fails to recognize that many of the features associated with old age have their origins in social structures and processes beyond their immediate control, but are amenable to collective political action. The social construction of old age showed that in important respects the risks associated with aging differ between social groups—class/occupation, gender, race, and so on—and that these differences are determined to a large extent prior to old age, and that this core message is as true today as it was nearly three decades ago. The trajectories of individual aging are determined by the interaction between social actors (who are also unique genetic and anatomical creations) and social structures, but in conditions of relative power and powerlessness.

Nonetheless the concept of structured dependency and political economy have suggested to some gerontologists a view of action as overdetermined by external forces. This is not the way it was intended, and it is important to realize the limitations of the structural metaphor when "structures" are created by the actions and thoughts of people (Giddens, 1998; Weber, 1968). It is equally important to understand that agency may be exercised by not acting; for example, in refusing to claim a means-tested social security benefit, an issue that figured significantly in the early U.K. versions of the political economy thesis. However this thesis was said to limit the scope for individuals to construct their own meanings and destinies. This in turn led to interactionist and ethnographic approaches emphasizing agency in terms of the construction of social relations through everyday encounters. Unfortunately, microsociological gerontological perspectives have ignored the constraints of structure (out went the baby with the bathwater) and therefore have unnecessarily diverted attention from the sources of inequality in old age.

The latest addition to the gerontological literature that follows this path in overestimating agency is the "cultures of aging" thesis advanced by Gilleard and Higgs (2000). While this analysis properly directs attention to the importance of aging as a cultural phenomenon and points the way to research on anti-aging technologies and the "staying young" culture, in trying to suggest that political economy insights are no longer relevant and have been replaced by a "culture of personal identity," its authors commit the very sin that they criticize the political economists for: one-sidedness. Unfortunately, in this case, there is no evidence to support the argument that old age has been transformed into one characterized by enhanced status and "agentic" power, even among those in their third age.

The cultures of aging argument may be criticized on numerous grounds, but that is not the purpose here (Walker, 2002). Its relevance for this discussion is that it purveys the false choice between agency and identity on the one hand and structural determination on the other (Gilleard & Higgs, 2000, p. 12). Political economy (which is wrongly conflated with structured dependency) is caricatured as suggesting that aging is something that happens to people, while cultural explanations see aging as something that individuals have to engage with (p. 13).

> Whatever heuristic value it once possessed, structured dependency theory and the "political economy" approach no longer provide a satisfactory under- standing of aging and old age. Postwork lives have become richer and more complex. Not only has this approach failed to acknowledge the agency that individuals exercise in retirement, but it has signally failed to recognize the diversity of the social processes and structure that shape the choices available to people in later life. (Gilleard & Higgs, 2000, p. 193)

As noted previously, the political economy thesis highlighted the neglected but critical role of policy; it did not suggest that policy explains everything. The quotation above fails to recognize that there are two key elements in the political economy of aging. One is the structural impact of social and economic roles and statuses prior to retirement, and the other is the impact of retirement itself. This cultural critique focuses only on the second. It rightly observes growing affluence in Western society and a diminution in the impact of retirement on some groups, opening up new opportunities. However, in overemphasizing the potential for agency, the extent of the changes that have taken place and the degree of freedom enjoyed by third agers are also overestimated. For example, Table 1 emphasizes the continuing differences in income between older men and women in Britain. Of course, how people respond individually to their own aging is a legitimate and vital aspect of microsociological analysis. Such research can reveal important narratives about how different older people negotiate old age to construct a life of quality and how creative they are in doing so (Kellaher, Peace, & Holland, 2004): similarly, with the variations in the exercise of agency by older people in different ethnic and cultural groups (Moriarty & Butt, 2004; Nazroo, Bejekal, Blane, & Grewal, 2004; Wray, 2003). Furthermore, it is an empirical

Table 1. Personal Weekly Income
(£ sterling before tax) of Men and Women 65+,
Britain

	Mean	Median
All men	190	140
All women	98	77
Single	132	112
Widowed	122	100
Divorced/separated	124	89
Married	72	45

Source: Ginn (2003) from GHS 1998.

question whether dependency on the state for pensions, on the one hand, or, on the other, dependency on the agents of "grey capitalism" controlling the private pension funds represent fundamentally different experiences (Blackburn, 2002). A serious problem arises, however, when it is suggested that the equally necessary structural analyses are no longer relevant because of factors such as increased diversity. Leaving aside the fact that the political economy perspective was responsible for highlighting diversity in old age, in terms of structural inequalities, the evidence of continuing structural divisions based on class, age, gender, disability, race, and ethnicity, demand, in both scientific and moral terms, continued analyses.

On the policy front, the optimism of the cultural thesis concerning the new aging leads to a completely uncritical perspective. This entails the wholesale acceptance of the risk society thesis, as articulated by Giddens (1994, 1998): that the crumbling of the structures of modernity opens up new opportunities for agency and that, in a future era when everyone follows a different life-course pattern, standardized social institutions cannot possibly respond sensitively to individual needs. In short, as emphasized earlier, such arguments reinforce the case for the individualization of risk.

THEORIZING THE SOCIAL

The cultural critique of the political economy of aging is inadequate in terms of both evidence and theory. Moreover, it requires the detachment of scientific research from engagement with policy issues that have a huge impact on older people's lives, such as the choice between public and private pensions. The uncritical acceptance of the policy prescriptions of the risk society analysis unwittingly condones the neoliberal perspective on globalization that leads down a path of state residualization—in pensions, health and social care—and the individualization of the social. For more than two decades the political economy of aging perspective has provided a counterargument to privatization by demonstrating over and over again the unequal impact of such policies on different groups of older people and the cumulative disadvantage that can accrue from such policies toward young and middle-aged people. But when the dominant global policy perspective focuses on the inevitability of inequality, with some even celebrating it as "diversity," this perspective is in danger of becoming sidelined as a worthy academic theory, but one that is increasingly irrelevant to the real world.

Of course this marginalization is not peculiar to social gerontology; it is part of the wider struggle that the sociologically based social sciences have been losing with the economic one since the breakup of political economy and, especially over the last 50 years, as the economic has become preeminent in the policy field. The core problem is that the social, for example, in social policy, lacks the coherent theory and clear policy prescriptions of the economic world. It is this conclusion and the commitment to contribute to the creation of an authentic, independent rationale for social action and social policy that have led to a new European endeavor that may have something to contribute to a better understanding of the tension between agency and structure in the field of gerontology.

Over the past decade, the concept of "social quality" has been created in Europe as the starting point for a new approach to policy based on a balance between economic and social development. The immediate European pressures behind this work need not concern us here, but part of the case for a new approach was the threat posed to the E.U.'s welfare states by the Transatlantic Consensus on economic globalization (Beck, van der Maesen, Thomése, & Walker, 2001; Beck, van der Maesen, & Walker, 1997; Walker, 1999).

Social quality is defined as "the extent to which individuals are able to participate in the social and economic life of their communities under conditions that enhance their well-being and individual potential." That is, the extent to which the quality of social life promotes participation and personal development. In order to achieve an acceptable level of social quality, it is hypothesized that four conditions have to be fulfilled.

First, people have to have access to *socioeconomic security*, whether from employment or social security, in order to protect them from poverty and other forms of material deprivation. Socioeconomic security in the E.U. requires good-quality paid employment and social protection to guarantee living standards and access to resources: income, education, healthcare, social services, environment, public health, personal safety, and so on.

Second, people have to experience *social inclusion* in, or minimum levels of social exclusion from, key social and economic institutions such as the labor market. Social inclusion concerns citizenship. This may be a wide and all-embracing national or European citizenship or "exclusive" with large numbers of outcasts and quasicitizens (denied citizenship completely or partially by means of discrimination).

Third, people should be able to live in communities and societies characterized by *social cohesion*. Social cohesion refers to the glue that holds together communities and societies. It is vital for both social development and individual self-realization. The contemporary discussion of cohesion often centers on the much narrower and ill-defined concept of social capital, but its legacy stretches back, via Durkheim, to embrace solidarity, shared norms and values. Reference to social cohesion does not mean that traditional forms of solidarity must be preserved at all costs but rather, it requires a recognition of the changing social structure (e.g., family structure) and the need to renew those that continue to underpin social cohesion, such as intergenerational solidarity, and to find new forms to take the place of those that are weakening or that are not appropriate to altered social circumstances such as the growth of multiculturalism.

Fourth, there must be *social empowerment* in order for people to be able to fully participate in the face of rapid socioeconomic change. Social empowerment means enabling and supporting citizens to control their own lives and to take advantage of opportunities. It means increasing the range of human choice. Therefore, it goes far beyond participation in the political system to a focus on the individual's potential capacity (knowledge, skills, experience, and so on) and how far this can be realized. This is not a matter of individual will, but one concerning the role of social relationships and structures in enabling or preventing autonomy.

These four components can be represented diagrammatically in a two-dimensional model (Figure 1). On the one hand, there is the distinction between the macro- and micro-levels, between structure and agency in sociological terms, while on the other, there is the horizontal relationship between the formal and the informal, between institutions and organizations and communities, groups, and individuals. The vertical axis represents the tension between societal processes (including global ones) and individual biographies. The horizontal axis represents the tension between institutional processes and individual actions (between, in Lockwood's terms, system integration and social integration or, in Habermas' terms, between the system and the life world).

The foregoing is by way of necessary background, and a large European project is currently formulating indicators of these four conditional factors. It was soon realized that the search for a rationale for social policy was too restricting and, instead, what was required was a scientific framework that establishes whether the *social* component of social quality is an authentic entity in its own right and, if it is, that would enable conclusions to be developed about its quality. It is the failure to pursue this endeavor that has left social policy trapped in a limited domain defined by economists as non-economic (Donzelot, 1979; Walker, 1984). Classical economists defined society's problems as "social" rather than "economic" and social policy has been working within that straightjacket ever since.

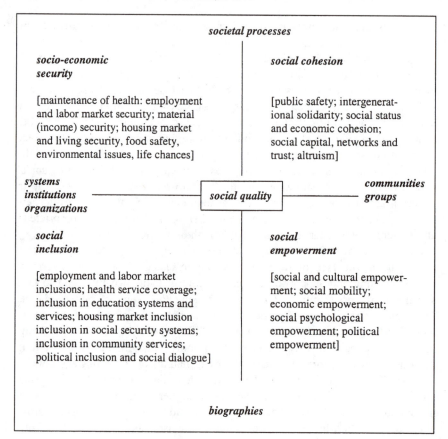

Figure 1. The conditions for social quality.

The heart of what is social, it is argued, is the self-realization of individuals, as social beings, in the context of the formation of collective identities. Thus "the social" is the outcome of constantly changing processes through which individuals realize themselves as interacting social beings. Rather than being atomized economic agents, we argue, from Honneth (1994), that a person's self-realization depends on social recognition. The processes whereby we all achieve self-realization, to a greater or lesser extent, are partly historically determined and partly determined by the agents themselves (structure and praxis).

According to this theory, first of all, as previously stated, the social world is realized in the interaction (and interdependence) between the self-realization of individual people as social beings and the formation of collective identities. This is called the *construction* of "the social." Second, four basic conditions determine the opportunities open for social relations to develop in the direction of social quality. People must have the capability to interact (empowerment); the institutional and structural context must be accessible to them (inclusion); they must have access to the necessary material and other resources that facilitate interaction (socioeconomic security); and the necessary collectively accepted values and norms that enable community building (cohesion). This refers to the *opportunities* or conditions for social quality. Of course there may be substantial variations between individuals on one or all of these conditions. Third, the actual nature, content, and structure of what is the social quality component of human relations are a function of the relationship between two axes (Figure 2). Again the horizontal axis represents the tension between systems, institutions, and organizations, as well as communities and groups. The vertical axis mirrors the tension between social processes and biographical ones. These twin tensions create the dynamic that influences both self-realization and the formation of collective identities and that transform social actors into ones capable of social quality. This refers to the *constitution* of competence for social quality.

Given the two sets of tensions that are in permanent confrontation, it is argued that social quality is realized by the dynamic between the world of systems and the world of human praxis within the context of the relationship between the two axes. On the horizontal axis, we see the contrast between rationality and subjectivity, between demos on the left and ethnos on the right. So, on the left side we are concerned with the relationship between the individual and the world of systems and institutions, in short with capacity for *social participation*. On the

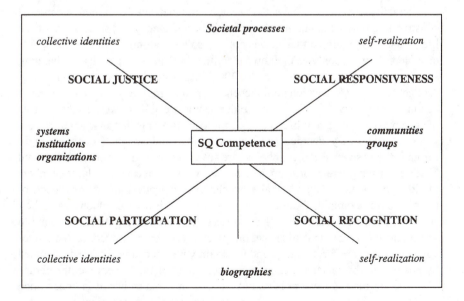

Figure 2. The constitution of competence for social quality.

right side, there are relations between individuals and social groups and communities in the negotiation of everyday life. Access and belonging in these relationships concern *social recognition and appreciation.* The vertical axis represents the worlds of societal and biographical developments and, within them are embedded values, norms, principles, rights, conventions, and so on. The left side of the axis concerns the *social justice* while the right side indicates *social responsiveness.* These four constitutional factors are derived normatively from the social quality approach (Beck et al., 2001).

STRUCTURE AND AGENCY ACROSS THE LIFE COURSE

The relevance of this discussion of the theoretical basis of the social is that it provides a methodology for understanding the constant tension between structure and agency in everyday life, including over the life course, and thereby, a way to reconcile the critiques that political economy overemphasizes structure (Gilleard & Higgs, 2000) and that life course and some cultural perspectives overemphasize agency (Dannefer & Uhlenberg, 1999). Moreover, the conceptual approach to the social outlined here defines the relationship between social structures and human agency while retaining the distinctiveness of both. This contrasts with Elias' (1978) work on figuration and Giddens' (1984) theory of structuration in which the two are constitutionally enmeshed. In practice, they are two sides of the same coin (Layder, 1994).

In practical terms, we have the basis, if not yet a fully honed theoretical construction, to understand the interaction between agency and structure over the life course. Older people themselves are not isolated, atomized individual agents or subjects focusing only on their own identities, but interacting with and changing social structures. In fact, as Barnes (2000) has argued, social life consists of "collective agency" in which nonindependent people routinely affect each other's actions. As reflexive social subjects, older people are able to exercise the choices of agency concerning their lifestyles and approach to aging, just as when they were younger adults they decided (within constraints) on careers, housing, family formation, and so on. But these choices are always exercised within immediate and historical structural relations and, depending on structural category, large numbers of older people are not able to make any choices whatsoever about key aspects of their lives, for example, about the age they retire, their level of income, and their access to long-term health care. Nonetheless, how they negotiate and respond to aging and the values that older people place on different aspects of their lives varies across a very broad range and is certainly not mechanically predetermined by position in the social structure. At earlier stages of the life course, the choice of a pension plan, for example, is not an open one, but rather, it is constrained by structures such as class, gender, and race (mainly by their influence on occupation) and by factors such as income and health (Ginn, 2003). (A thorough, interdisciplinary account would also include genetic factors and their interaction with social ones, see Chapter 7). Forgoing occupation and income altogether or taking part-time employment to care for an older relative or child will also have a bearing on the choices available (Evandrou & Glaser, 2003, 2004). In other words, agency is embedded within structure. As individuals pursue identity and self-realization, they must interact with others and in doing so, they will sometimes have to compromise or simply conform to formal or informal rules, sometimes be able to exercise choice or resist constraints, and sometimes encounter good or bad luck. The ways that they exercise this agency are diverse, for example, between ethnic and religious groups (Torres, 1999; Wray, 2003), as are the meanings given to autonomy and the values that they place in individual as opposed to collective action. The key question that requires further investigation is what problems are structurally induced for older people, problems that are inevitable and must be responded to by them in their own individual or collective ways? This points to the negative aspects of social action where agency is constrained, sometimes severely, and an individual is on the receiving end with no freedom to influence another individual or institution, only the ability to frame their response. In situations of abuse or extreme social exclusion, even this latter autonomy is limited. It also reminds us of the point made earlier that the choice not to do something is a legitimate exercise of agency.

CONCLUSION

This brings me back to the welfare state and the role of social policy. Risk pooling and collective support should enable people to make choices and limit the structural constraints on them. Thus the roles of the welfare state should be to promote choice and flexibility and to empower people to negotiate their way through the changing life course. Public structures and constitutions should enable, not inhibit, individual and collective agency. Moreover, the welfare state should not be seen as the alternative to agency because down that route lies the individualization of the social, based on the false assumptions that the market is the only source of choice and that human beings are merely individual economic agents.

ACKNOWLEDGMENTS

I am very grateful to Jan Baars and Dale Dannefer for their helpful comments on a draft of this chapter and to Wolfgang Beck and Laurent van der Maesen for their intellectual inspiration.

REFERENCES

Archer, M. (2000). *Being human: The problem of agency*. Cambridge: CUP.

Barnes, B. (2000). *Understanding aging: Social theory and responsible action.* Camden: Sage.

Beck, U. (1992). *The risk society.* Camden: Sage.

Beck, W., van der Maesen, L., & Walker, A. (Eds.). (1997). *The social quality of Europe.* The Hague: Kluwer International.

Beck, W., van der Maesen, L., Thomése, F., & Walker, A. (Eds.). (2001). *Social quality: A vision for Europe.* The Hague: Kluwer International.

Blackburn, R. (2002). *Banking on death.* London: Verso.

Boscoe, A., & Chassard, Y. (1999). A shift in the paradigm: Surveying the European Union discourse on welfare and work. In M. Heikkila (Ed.), *Linking welfare and work* (pp. 43-58). Dublin: European Foundation.

Bytheway, B. (1995). *Ageism.* Buckingham: OU Press.

Dannefer, D., & Uhlenberg, P. (1999). Paths of the life course: A typology. In V. Bengtson, & W. Schaie (Eds.), *Handbook of theories of ageing* (pp. 306-326). New York: Springer Publishing.

Donzelot, J. (1979). *The policing of families.* London: Hutchinson.

Drury, E. (Ed.). (1993). *Age discrimination against older workers in the European community.* London: Eurolink Age.

Drury, E. (Ed.). (1997). *Public policies to assess older workers.* Brussels: Eurolink Age.

Elias, N. (1978). *What is sociology?* London: Hutchinson.

Estes, C. (1979). *The aging enterprise.* San Francisco: Jossey-Bass.

Estes, C., & Phillipson, C. (2002). The globalization of capital, the welfare state and old age policy. *International Journal of Health Services, 32*(2), 279-297.

Evandrou, M., & Glaser, K. (2003). *Family work and quality of life: Changing economic and social roles (GO Findings 5).* Sheffield: Growing Older Programme, University of Sheffield.

Evandrou, M., & Glaser, K. (2004). Family, work and quality of life: Changing economic and social roles through the lifecourse. *Ageing and Society, 24*(5), 771-792.

Ferge, Z. (1997). A central European perspective on the social quality of Europe. In W. Beck, L. van Der Maesen, & A. Walker (Eds.), *The social quality of Europe* (pp. 165-181). The Hague: Kluwer International.

Giddens, A. (1984). *The constitution of society.* Cambridge: Printing Press.

Giddens, A. (1994). *Beyond left and right.* Cambridge: Polity Press.

Giddens, A. (1998). *The third way.* Cambridge: Polity Press.

Gilleard, C., & Higgs, P. (2000). *Cultures of aging.* Harlow: Prentice Hall.

Ginn, J. (2003). *Women, work, and pensions.* Cambridge: Policy Press.

Gough, I. (1997). Social aspects of the European model and its consequences. In W. Beck, L. van Der Maesen, & A. Walker (Eds.), *The social quality of Europe* (pp. 89-108). The Hague: Kluwer International.

Graebner, W. (1980). *A history of retirement.* New Haven: Yale University Press.

Guillemard, A. M. (1980). *La vieillesse et l'etat* [Old age and the state]. Paris: Presses Universitaires de France.

Guillemard, A. M. (1993). Older workers and the labour market. In A. Walker, J. Alber, & A. M. Guillemard (Eds.), *Older people in Europe: Social and economic policies.* Brussels: DG V, Commission of the European Communities.

Honneth, A. (1994). Die soziale dynamik von missachtung [The structural dynamic of disdain]. *Leviathan, 1,* 90.

James, A., Jenks, C., & Prout, A. (1998). *Theorising childhood.* Oxford: Polity Press.

Johnson, P., Conrad, C., & Thomson, D. (Eds.). (1989). *Workers versus pensioners: Intergenerational justice in an ageing world.* Manchester: Manchester University Press.

Kellaher, L., Peace, S., & Holland, C. (2004). Environment, identity and old age—Quality of life or a life of quality? In A. Walker & C. Hagan Hennessy (Eds.), *Growing older: Quality of life in old age.* Maidenhead: OUP.

Kohli, M., Rein, M., Guillemard, A. M., & van Gunsteren, H. (Eds.). (1991). *Time for retirement: Comparative studies of early exit from the labour force.* Cambridge: Cambridge University Press.

Layder, D. (1994). *Understanding social theory.* London: Sage.

McEwan, E. (Ed.). (1990). *Age: The unrecognised discrimination.* London: ACE Books.

Moriarty, J., & Butt, J. (2004). Inequalities in quality of life among older people from different ethnic groups. *Ageing and Society, 24*(5), 729-754.

Nazroo, J., Bajekal, M., Blane, D., & Grewal, I. (2004). Ethnic Inequalities. In A. Walker & C. Hagan Hennessy (Eds.), *Growing older: Quality of life in old age* (pp. 35-59). Maidenhead: Open University Press.

OECD. (1988). *Reforming public pensions.* Paris: OECD.

Pampel, F., Williamson, J., & Stryker, R. (1990). Class context and pension response to demographic structure in advanced industrial democracies. *Social Problems, 37*(4), 535-550.

Phillipson, C. (1982). *Capitalism and the construction of old age.* London: Macmillan.

Phillipson, C. (1998). *Reconstructing old age.* London: Sage.

Taylor, F. W. (1947). *Scientific management.* New York: Harper.

Torres, S. (1999). A culturally-relevant theoretical framework for the study of successful aging. *Ageing and Society, 19,* 35-51.

Townsend, P. (1981). The structured dependency of the elderly: The creation of social policy in the twentieth century. *Ageing and Society, 1*(1), 5-28.

Walker, A. (1978, July). *The social construction of old age.* Paper presented to the World Congress of Sociology, Uppsala.

Walker A. (1980). The social creation of poverty and dependency in old age. *Journal of Social Policy, 9*(1), 49-75.

Walker, A. (1981). Towards a political economy of old age. *Ageing and Society, 1*(1), 73-94.

Walker, A. (1984). *Social planning.* Oxford: Blackwell.

Walker, A. (1990). The economic "burden" of aging and the prospect of intergenerational conflict. *Ageing and Society, 10*(4), 377-396.

Walker, A. (1993). *Age and attitudes—Main results from a Eurobarometer survey.* Brussels: Commission of the European Communities.

Walker, A., Guillemard, A. M., & Alber, J. (1993). *Older people in Europe: Social and economic policies.* Brussels: Commission of the European Communities.

Walker, A. (1997). *Combatting age barriers in employment.* Luxembourg: Office for the Official Publications of the European Communities.

Walker, A. (1999). Public policy and theories of aging: Constructing and reconstructing old age. In V. Bengtson & K. Schaie (Eds.), *Handbook of theories of aging* (pp. 361-378). New York: Springer Publishing.

Walker, A. (2002, September). *Cultures of ageing—A critique.* Paper presented to the British Society of Gerontology Annual Conference, Birmingham.

Walker, A., & Deacon, B. (2003). Economic globalization and policies on aging. *Journal of Societal and Social Policy, 2*(2), 1-18.

Weber, M. (1968). *Economy and society.* New York: Bedminster Press.

Westergaard, J., Noble, I., & Walker, A. (1989). *After redundancy.* Oxford: Polity Press.

Wray, S. (2003). Women growing older: Agency, ethnicity and culture. *Sociology, 37*(3), 511-527.

CHAPTER 5

Critical Feminist Perspectives, Aging, and Social Policy*

Carroll Estes

A goal of the feminist political economy of aging is to understand how the dominant social institutions render older women vulnerable and dependent throughout their life course (Estes, 1982, 1991a, 2004; Estes, Biggs, & Phillipson, 2003). An important consideration is how state policies define, individualize, and commodify the problems of aging (e.g., as individual problems and personal private responsibility for the purchase of services sold for profit) (Estes, 1979), and how these processes are ideologically and practically consistent with state roles and activities that advance the interests of capital accumulation and the legitimation of patriarchal and capitalist social relations.

Four premises undergird our approach (Estes, 2004; Estes, Biggs, & Phillipson, 2003). The first is that the experiences and situation of women across the lifespan are socially constructed (Estes, 1979, 1991a). In particular, the predicament of older women is profoundly shaped by the division of labor and power between men and women, the institutional configurations (family, labor market, and state), and the normative proscriptions that are embodied and enacted through men's and women's social roles and responsibilities and the societal rewards that attend them.

The second premise, flowing from the first, is that the lived experiences and problems of older women are not solely, or even largely, the product of individual behavior and decisions. The individual "choices" and "preferences" (in economist's terms) that are available to females and other socially disadvantaged groups are, in many respects, highly constrained if not illusory. They are more

---

*Portions of this chapter are drawn from "Women, Ageing and Inequality: A Feminist Perspective." In M. Johnson (Ed.), *Cambridge Handbook of Age and Ageing*. Cambridge, UK: Cambridge University Press; and Estes, C. L., S. Biggs, and C. Phillipson. *Social Theory, Social Policy and Ageing: A Critical Introduction*. London: Open University Press.

ideological market rhetoric than reality. For women, constraining forces reside in "gender regimes" (Connell, 1987) that are embedded and inscribed in the capitalist *state,* the *market* and the *family.* Gender regimes are pivotal in understanding how both old age and old-age policy are constructed in ways that maintain and reproduce the relatively disadvantaged social, political, and economic status of older women and particularly older women of color. In both the national and global context, these regimes operate through a sex/gender system (Rubin, 1984) (sometimes called patriarchy), the economic system, and the state (Dickinson & Russell, 1986; Estes, 2001; Orloff, 1993). Key problems are the social production, social control, and management of gender-based and age-based dependency (Estes, 2000) through gender regimes (Connell, 1987).

The third premise is that the disadvantages of women are cumulative across the lifespan (Crystal & Shea, 2002; Dannefer, 2003). Cumulative advantage theory posits that systematic processes result in the selection and allocation of individuals on the basis of status and performance, predicting more stratified fortunes in old age than at earlier phases of the life course (O'Rand, 2002; see also Burton & Whitfield, and Crystal & Phillipson, this volume). Minority elderly women experience more inequalities and disadvantages today than they did 65 years ago, with institutional effects arising from 1) normative schedules of achievement (e.g., age-graded timing of major life transitions, including job-market entrance and exit, schooling, and family formation); 2) their organizational/institutional time clocks of advancement (e.g., tenure, promotion, employee benefit eligibility, and forced or voluntary retirement schedules); and 3) community opportunity structures (e.g., employment and wage opportunities, housing and neighborhood quality, educational nourishment resources, and healthcare access). The cumulative effects are also understood in terms of three pathways or interlocking trajectories of life course capital (human capital, social capital, and personal capital) (O'Rand, 2002, p. 20).

The fourth premise is that the feminization of poverty is inextricably linked to the complex and interlocking oppressions of race, ethnicity, class, sexuality, and nation that produce the marginalization of older women (Collins, 1991, 2000; Dressel, 1988; see Burton & Whitfield, this volume). As Patricia Hill Collins notes, these are "interrelated axes of social structure" and not "just separate features of existence." Our approach acknowledges and incorporates the critique of essentialist thinking that is said to characterize mainstream (most often white and Western) feminist writings that simplify, ignore, or homogenize the diversity and intersectionality of gender, sex, sexuality, race, ethnicity, class, age, *and* nation.

While there are definitive variations in approaches within the West (Esping-Andersen, 1990), U.S. and British scholars portray their welfare states as distinctly gendered and raced (Acker, 1988; Orloff, 1993; Omi & Winant, 1994; Pateman, 1989; Quadagno, 1994; Williams, 1996). In many European welfare regimes (e.g., Germany, Italy, France, and Ireland), laws support the authority of the husband, although policies vary and are contradictory. Even the Scandinavian welfare states of Norway, Sweden, and Denmark depend on gender-biased, unpaid labor of women, raising questions about the "woman friendliness" of these states (Leira, 1993; Siim, 1993).

This highlights the "contradictory character of welfare states" (O'Connor, Orloff, & Shaver, 1999, pp. 2-3) describing the two faces of the state: 1) the "woman friendliness" of the state (Hernes, 1987) opening political participation, and recognizing and improving women's situation; and 2) the other, *less-friendly side of the state*: the Social Security, long-term care, and the social safety net provision systems that reward citizens engaging in paid labor at the expense of those in unpaid caregiving; workplace policies that ignore worker's caregiving work; laws that impede reproductive choice and provide little protection against male violence (O'Connor et al., 1999; Pateman, 1989). Current U.S. policy proposals affirm the Bush Administration's view of women's dependency as being either on a man or on the state. President Bush proposes to allocate $400 million of state funds to encourage the marriage of single mothers on welfare. This is a curious departure for a conservative advocate of less government intervention, yet it is consistent with the patriarchal policy leanings of the conservative Christian coalition that helped elect President Bush.

CRITICAL FEMINIST EPISTEMOLOGY

A feminist perspective on aging and old age policy requires critical reflexivity and a feminist epistemology (Collins, 1991; Harding, 1996; Smith, 1990). Scholars engaged in the gerontological imagination and the production of knowledge about aging (Estes, 1979, 1991a, 2001; Estes, Binney, & Culbertson, 1992) are compelled to work outside the frame of "patriarchal thought" (Lerner, 1986, p. 228). This means "accepting . . . our [women's] knowledge as valid" and exhibiting "intellectual courage" in pushing beyond mainstream and masculinist social science frameworks and methods (Lerner, 1986, p. 228). Feminist stand-point theory and feminist epistemology "enable one to appropriate and redefine objectivity" (Harding, 1996, p. 134), which is crucial because:

> Culture's best beliefs—what it calls knowledge—are socially situated. The distinctive features of women's situation in a gender-stratified society are being used as resources in the new feminist research. It is these distinctive resources, . . . not used by conventional researchers, that enable feminism to produce empirically more accurate descriptions and theoretically richer explanations than does conventional research. (Harding, 1996, p. 119)

> Women's perspective comes from everyday life. . . . The perspective from women's everyday activity is scientifically preferable to the perspective available only from the "ruling" activities of men in the dominant groups. (Harding, 1996, p. 128)

Critical feminist epistemology is consistent with Dorothy Smith's (1990) critique of male power and "relations of ruling" that are embedded in objectified and alienated knowledge of social science. Smith's proposal is for "an alternative sociology, from the standpoint of women, [that] makes the everyday world problematic" (Smith, 1990, p. 27).

THE GENDERED STATE AND AGING

The study of the state is central to the understanding of old age and the life chances of older women, given that the state has the power to: (a) allocate and distribute scarce resources to ensure the survival and growth of the economy, (b) mediate between the different needs and demands across different social groups (gender, race, ethnicity, class, and age), and (c) ameliorate social conditions that could threaten the existing order (Estes, 1991a).

Women are linked to the state by three types of status that form a complex and dynamic interrelationship: as citizens with political rights, as clients and consumers of welfare state services, and as employees in the state sector (Estes, Gerard, Zones, & Swan, 1984; Hernes, 1987; Jones & Estes, 1997; Sassoon, 1987). These roles are neither inclusive nor mutually exclusive. Women's different roles have corresponding institutional structures that mediate between them as individuals and society: the family, the state, and the market. In old age, women's status as clients or consumers (beneficiaries) of government programs is particularly significant because, with age, women's dependency on the state increases (see later discussion).

Feminist Theories of the State

Joan Acker contends that theories of the state and of social class that do not explicitly and adequately address the subordination of women and the "privileging of men" fail as comprehensive frameworks for understanding social phenomena (Acker, 1988). She further argues that class is produced through gendered processes structured by production and distribution. Distribution, in particular, is vitally affected by (a) the dominance of market relations as the basis of distribution; and (b) the indifference of the economic system to the reproduction of the working-class and the demands of working class daily life (Acker, 1988), for which responsibility is born by women.

Acker (1992) asks to what extent the overall institutional structure of the state has "been formed by and through gender."

> How are men's interests and masculinity . . . intertwined in the creation and maintenance of particular institutions, and how have the subordination and exclusion of women been built into ordinary institutional functioning? (p. 568)

Utilizing the concept of "gendered institutions," Acker (1992) contends that

> Gender is a dimension of domination and discrimination [that is] neither obviously discrete nor structurally analogous [to social class and race]. Class relations do not function in the same way as gender relations; race relations are still another matter. All of these come together in cross-cutting ways. . . . Gender is present in the processes, practices, images and ideologies and distributions of power in the various sectors of social life. (pp. 566-567)

Quadagno also faults class and state theory for their inattention to the role of state policy in mediating race relations and for their blindness to "a defining feature of social provision: its organization around gender" (p. 14). Connell argues that the power of the state extends beyond the distribution of resources to the formation and reformation of social patterns. Indeed, the state does more than regulate institutions and relations like marriage and motherhood; it manages them. The state actually *constitutes* "the social categories of the gender order," as "patriarchy is both constructed and contested through the state" (Connell, 1987).

"State masculinism" is a concept introduced by Wendy Brown, who argues that female subjects are produced by the state through 1) reproduction and the regulation of pornography; and 2) women's dependence on the state for survival. Four features of "state masculinism" are identified:

1. *Juridicial-Legislative*—the formal and constitutional rights in which civil society is seen as a masculine right in relation to the natural and prepolitical place of women and the family.
2. *Capitalist*—the defined property rights and the possibilities for active involvement in wealth accumulation.
3. *Prerogative*—the [state's] legitimate monopoly of force and violence.
4. *Bureaucratic*—expressed through the institution of the state and its discourse, as discipline, presented as a neutral means of power. This makes it especially potent in shaping the lives of female clients of the state.

Each of these features of the state has implications for women and old-age policy. Reflecting the juridicial-legislative state role, the caregiving role of women is assumed as the natural and prepolitical place for females. Under the state's role *vis-a-vis* capitalism, property rights and the ability to accumulate wealth are limited by the impaired ability of women to actively access paid employment as a result of their substantial caregiving responsibilities and sexism in the workplace (Ferree & Hall, 1996; Orloff, 1993). In the state's prerogative role, violence, hate crimes against women, and state control of reproductive options each profoundly shape women's opportunities for participation and livelihood in the society. In the state's bureaucratic role, older women, as clients of welfare and other state assistance programs, must deal with demeaning and unequal power relations with state agents of social control.

PATRIARCHY AND THE SEX/GENDER SYSTEM

Carol Pateman describes "the patriarchal welfare state" in which "since the early 20th Century, welfare policies have reached across from public to private and have helped uphold a patriarchal structure of family life" (Pateman, 1989, p. 183). Some have criticized theories of patriarchy for giving insufficient attention to social class and to ideology and for being too deterministic and functionalist by assuming the state is the modern instrument of patriarchal relations (Lorber, 1998). Others contend that the concept of patriarchy is valid and appropriate because of its emphasis on power (Mutari, 2001) and human agency (Ortner, 1996). Wiegersma (1991) defines patriarchy as "more than a form of male-dominant family structure. It is also an independent, political-economic system of production" (p. 174).

Supporting this view, Ciscel and Heath (2001) aver that "patriarchy is irrepressible" in that

> a new form of patriarchy has arisen with women primarily performing gendered labor in the service sector of the capitalist marketplace, and the unpaid domestic labor of the home. The face of patriarchy is now that of the virtual male, where patriarchal rules and values are transmitted through the media, at home, at work, and in leisure activities. (p. 407)

Women are left with whatever the market has not usurped as profitable— "the creation of the web of relationships." This

> freedom from the unfettered expansion of markets in reality represents another form of oppression, confining women and their families to lives of market supporting activities. (Ciscel & Heath, 2001, p. 408)

Bonnie Fox (1988, p. 177) argues that both social structure and "gendered subjectivity/ideology" are more important than patriarchy in "explaining women's oppression" (for more on ideology, see later section). Gayle Rubin (1984) proposes an alternative concept, the "sex/gender system," to denote the "empirically oppressive ways in which sexual worlds have been organized" (p. 33) and in which the evolution of kinship structures and marriage rituals have established "the traffic in women" (p. 38). This "traffic" occurs without granting women access to the networks of power, money, and culture because "kinship and marriage systems are always parts of total social systems and are always tied to economic and political arrangements" (p. 56). These arrangements form the basis of the "political economy of sex."

Social Reproduction

Social reproduction is a concept that embraces the *work* of both producing the members of society as educated, healthy, knowledgeable, and productive human beings and the *work* of setting up conditions by which such production of individuals and society may continue to be reproduced across generations and time (Estes & Binney, 1990).

Acker (2000, p. 49) cites a major lacuna in feminist work as the dearth of conceptual attention to the social and economic contributions of domestic labor. As Brush observes, "The question of what counts as work is related to who does it (men "labor," women "love") and where (in the formal labor market, in the underground economy, or in the "domestic" realm)" (Brush, 2000, p. 179).

Ginn, Street, and Arber (2001, p. 20) note that a key component of the relationship between the labor market and the household is women's paid and unpaid work.

> Traditional gender ideology—the assumption that women are financially supported by men in the male breadwinner/female career model of the gender contract (Lewis, 1992 as quoted in Ginn et al., 2001)—bolsters exclusionary employment practices.

Feminists critique traditional Marxist views of reproduction, which have "privileged" relations of production that men do through paid work and "ignore . . . much of the process by which people and their labor power are reproduced" (Himmelweit, 1983, p. 419). This is the reproduction work that women do that is seen as informal, unpaid, invisible, and devalued. Reproduction takes place on two levels: "the reproduction of labor power both on a daily and generational sense; and human and biological reproduction" (Himmelweit, 1983, p. 419). The blindness toward reproductive work and its lack of recognition (devaluation) in public policy explains and justifies the continuing treatment of women's and men's relations in the family (the division of caregiving and household work) as private and beyond the scope of state intervention (O'Connor et al., 1999, p. 3).

When attention is given to reproductive relations in the context of the two major old-age policy arenas of retirement income and long-term care, the gendered division of labor, the lack of women's equal access to the labor market, and the unpaid informal work of women throughout the life course must be placed squarely at the center of analysis. The vital import of social reproduction in old age is illustrated by the significant, unpaid caring labor which, for women, has lifelong cumulative (and negative) consequences (Balbo, 1982; Binney, Estes, & Humphers, 1993; Estes & Zulman, 2004; Finch & Groves, 1983). For example, under current U.S. Social Security policy, the decision to ignore the contributions of reproductive relations as part of economic activity results in "zeroes" (zero dollar contributions toward Social Security) for a woman's years out of the labor market to give care to children and elders. The assumption of women's "free" reproductive relations and its categorization as "nonwork" is a "Care Penalty" (Folbre, 2001) that signals much about the economic vulnerability of older women in the United States (Estes & Binney, 1990) inasmuch as it is a core assumption of old-age policy in both Social Security and long-term care policy.

Thus, a central dynamic concerning old age and the gendered state is the contradiction between the *needs* of women throughout the life course and the *organization of work* (particularly capitalist modes of production and social reproduction) and its modes of *distribution* (Acker, 1988). Focus on the role of the state in the relations of distribution "conceptualizes class in a way to include unpaid, mostly female workers and others outside the paid labor force" (Acker, 2000, p. 49).

Feminist Perspectives on Old Age and the State

A key point is that women's dependency has shifted 1) from the man to the state (Brown, 1995), and 2) from the family to the state (Dickinson & Russell, 1986; Estes, 1991a, 1998a, 1998b; Orloff, 1993). The problem has now become that "Instead of private patriarchy dependent on a husband, women are subject to public patriarchy of a paternalistic state" (Lorber, 1998, p. 44). This situation renders older women highly vulnerable to state welfare policies that are subject to politically charged, uncertain, and partisan conflicts, which may result in erratic, radical, and regressive policies with regard to the treatment of women. For the large majority of older women who are dependent on the state, there is a triple threat of welfare reform and the threatened privatization initiatives under Social Security and Medicare.

Feminist perspectives on the state and old-age policy have addressed 1) the life course and cumulative consequences of the gendered wage and the family wage in producing the economic vulnerability of older women; 2) how older women's fate in the welfare state is predicated upon her marital status, her husband's work history, and how social policy is built around the traditional model of the autonomous nuclear family; and 3) the two tiers of social policy that divide women by race and class: means-tested social assistance and social insurance (Estes, 2001; Harrington Meyer, 1990, 1996). As noted earlier, a central critique is the omission of policy compensation for free reproductive labor under the dominant U.S. policy model and the associated care penalties and gender inequities.

To summarize, old-age income provisions in the U.S. state are gendered in three key ways: 1) retirement income is linked to waged labor, which is itself gendered; 2) nonwaged reproductive labor, performed predominantly by women, is not recognized or counted under state policy as labor; and 3) retirement policy is based on a model of family status as married with male breadwinner (and with marital status as permanent rather than transient). Thus, retirement income programs (Social Security, private and personal pensions) "produce a gendered distribution of old age income" (Harrington Meyer, 1996, p. 551). Insofar as benefits are higher for married than nonmarried persons and for dependent spouses than nondependent spouses and single individuals (who are more likely to be women than men), state policy sustains the subordination of women by imposing a normative and preferential view of a particular family form with a male bread-winner and a dependent wife (Pascall, 1986) that is inherently disadvantageous to the majority of older women (the majority of whom are not married, especially among women of color and the very old).

The degree of dependency of older women upon the state grows with age, widowhood, divorce, retirement, and the associated declines in their economic and health status. The increasing probability and negative results of all of these events pose a serious threat for all women, and particularly for nonwhites (both women and men), the less educated, and the poor and near-poor. Current U.S. state policy does little to redress the multiple lifetime jeopardies of gender, race, ethnicity, and lower social class. Since welfare reform in the mid-1990s, the burdens of women of all generations have increased, including those of older women (Estes et al., 2006 [in press]). Older women who are mothers of adult children on welfare may find themselves in a new form of indentured servitude, this time through the caregiving requirements of their grandchildren as their adult children seek or undertake formal work outside the home. Such care will be provided without cash assistance in many instances, including when the adult child was or is a substance abuser (disqualified from welfare). Thus, welfare reform has augmented the burdens of women's childbearing and caregiving across the life cycle, extracting an unknown cost across all female generations (young to old).

FEMINIST ECONOMICS

The developing field of feminist economics contributes to the study of gender and old-age policy, where scholars are challenging and reformulating the work of classical "liberal" economists such as Adam Smith and "the failure of neoclassical economics to accurately analyze (or even recognize) the role of the market in creating intractable inequalities in power relations within the family" (Cisel & Heath, 2001, p. 408, citing Bergmann, 1995). Gillian Hewitson's *Feminist Economics* (1999) brings feminist poststructuralism to economics in her critique of neoclassical economics (e.g., abstract individualism and theory of individual optimizing behavior) for distorting the experience of women in its production of gender meanings and sexed bodies.

In the past three decades, the *Review of Radical Political Economics* has published special issues on women, commencing in 1972 with *The Political Economy of Women* (Mutari, 2001). The "problem" of the treatment (or lack thereof) of reproductive labor is considered, as are the strengths and limitations of the works of Marx, Engels, and other scholars from feminist perspectives on capitalism, patriarchy, class, ideology, and classical economics. The journal *Feminist Economics,* produced by the International Federation of Feminist Economists, is in Volume 11 (2005). Feminist principles of economics include (a) nonmarket activities and the household conceptualized as loci of economic activity; (b) gender, race, and ethnicity seen as important concepts; (c) emphasis on cooperation and caring (not just competition); (d) power relationships conceptualized as an important force in the economy; and (e) government action understood as potentially improving (rather than impeding) market outcomes (Schneider & Shackelford, 2001).

MacArthur Awardee economist Nancy Folbre (2001) challenges Adam Smith's classical theory that "The Invisible Hand" of the market promotes selfish behavior that benefits all. Instead, she posits that

> The invisible hand of the market depends upon the invisible heart of care. Markets cannot function effectively outside the framework of families and communities built on values of love, obligation, and reciprocity. . . . The invisible hand is about achievement. The invisible heart is about care for others. The hand and the heart are interdependent, but they are also in conflict. The only way to balance them successfully is to find fair ways of rewarding those who care for other people. This is not a problem that economists or business people take seriously. (p. xvi, p. 4)

A woman's dilemma is that they "know they can benefit economically by becoming achievers rather than caregivers" (Folbre, 2001, p. 4). Folbre's perspective is directly relevant to multiple dimensions of the problems of women under old age policy as exemplified in Social Security and long-term care policy, which will only be exacerbated by the privatization initiatives that are gaining strength in the United States.

THEORIES OF MASCULINE DOMINATION

There is a growing body of relevant work on theories of masculinity. French sociologist Pierre Bourdieu in *Masculine Domination* (2001) speaks to the social practices of a society that are so dominant that they are hardly perceived. Masculine domination is "a form of symbolic violence, a kind of gentle invisible pervasive violence that is experienced through the everyday practices of social life." Robert Connell advances the concept of *hegemonic masculinity,* referring to the gender practices of everyday life that "embod[y] the currently accepted answer to the problem of the legitimacy of patriarchy which guarantees (or is taken to guarantee) the dominant position of men and the subordination of women" (Connell, 1995, p. 77). In his threefold model of the structure of gender relations, which he calls "gender regimes," Connell distinguishes between the relations of labor, power, and cathexis or emotional attachment (Connell, 1987, pp. 90-118). The *structure of labor* (labor market) is such that men gain material advantage, which he labels the "patriarchal dividend" (Connell, 1996, pp. 161-162). The *structure of power* is one in which men also control the means of institutionalized power—the state and the army. The *structure of cathexis* is controlled by men through the institution of the family and male superiority and violence therein, rather than reciprocity and intimacy (Connell, 1996, p. 163). More recently,

Connell has added a fourth category to his earlier work on the structure of gender relations. The *structure of symbolism* signals that "gender subordination may be reproduced through linguistic practices such as addressing women by titles that define them through their marital relationships to men" (Connell, 2000, pp. 26, 42-43, 150-155).

Ideology

Ideology is used by all political regimes to justify their position and impose their political will on others. The contest for ideological hegemony is about achieving and maintaining power through the means of the production and control of ideas. In the feminist political economy perspective, "the value systems, normative orientations, moral codes, and belief systems of . . . society . . . are . . . connected [both] to the larger process of class rule and domination" (Knuttila, 1996, p. 164), as well as the processes of gender rule and domination (Bourdieu, 2001; Connell, 1996, 2000).

The strength of the New Right's ideological political assault on all domestic government programs and especially entitlements is the most successful and enduring element of the Reagan legacy (Estes, 1991b). The twin ideologies of neoliberalism and neoconservatism have been deployed in the political struggles to radically transform the Social Security and Medicare programs in the United States from government-defined benefits to market-dependent programs. The policy shift to privatization is generally treated by politicians and the media as gender neutral, but the outcomes of privatization would decidedly NOT be gender neutral.

According to Barrett (1988), gender is an ideology that is created and re-created through social practices (Mutari, 2001, p. 389).

> Ideology is a generic term for the processes by which meaning is produced, challenged, reproduced, transformed. . . . Ideology is embedded historically in materialist practice. (Barrett, 1988, pp. 97-98)

Sen (1980, p. 77) speaks of "patriarchal ideology" in arguing that "gender analysis takes ideology seriously as a determining force" (as quoted in Mutari, 2001, p. 389). The *gender ideology* and the ideology of familism and separate public and private spheres remain a powerful force bolstering both ideologies of neoliberalism and neoconservatism.

Neoliberal ideology argues for a "minimalist state" and is hostile toward anything that may impede the "natural superiority" of the market (Levitas, 1986). *Neoconservative ideology* has contributed to rekindling a war on women, laying the affective base for a return to traditional patriarchal family structures and norms. For older women, the accompanying resurgence in women's subjugation is likely to be manifested by *increased demands on women for more unpaid reproductive work* with no recognition or compensation in state policy for its economic contribution either toward reducing the state costs of long-term care or the individual loss of retirement income (e.g., through Social Security). Nevertheless, the growing proportion of women who live outside of matrimony, those who are widowed, divorced, or never married who experience poverty rates two to three times higher than married women, are severely penalized and controlled.

Ideologies structure beliefs and limit a vision of alternative futures to those with the most power to shape the reigning ideology (Therborn, 1978). A necessary condition of acquiescence and resignation to policy "choices" that economic and policy elites proffer (such as the privatization of public entitlement of Social Security) is whether or not alternative regimes or strategies are even conceivable. The most successful ideologies are distinguished by their remarkable capacity to shape public consciousness. Successful neoliberalist ideology limits the vision of the "possible" to inherently promarket solutions, and neoconservative ideology limits solutions to those that impose benefits (discipline) to the market and the traditional (patriarchal) family structure, accompanied by a "profoundly pessimistic view of the possibilities of change" (Therborn, 1980, p. 98). This pessimism is promoted through the construction of the crises of social security, the family, the economy, and globalization.

The "welfare state cleansing" (Estes, 2001) from the 1990s to the present through welfare reform and pressures for privatization in the United States, directly and personally are likely to generate substantial and negative effects across the life span of women. *A major significant limitation on old-age policy is that the dominant power group, composed of white males, does not equally share with women the benefits of the longevity revolution.*

There is almost no U.S. public discourse about the existence of positive elements of intergenerational relationships and the significant exchanges (monetary and nonmonetary) that occur across gender, time, and the generations. This is surprising, given the stability in the positive opinion polling concerning support for old-age programs in the United States such as Social Security and Medicare. However, not surprisingly, a distinctly male perspective is reflected among the proponents of "generational accounting" that ignores caregiving within and across the generations and all noneconomic exchanges as well as monetary exchanges that exist between generations that are outside the labor market.

GLOBALIZATION, INEQUALITY, AND OLDER WOMEN

Connell observes that, in the West, the gender order centers on a single structural fact, "the global dominance of men over women" (Connell, 1987, p. 183). The concepts of masculine domination (Bourdieu, 2001) and hegemonic masculinity are unrecognized but significant threads in the fabric of old-age policies, with direct links to the perilous state of most older women.

Hotly contested struggles around sexism, racism, and social class accompany global capitalism and its attendant (and largely negative) potential outcomes for women of all ages around the world (Mittelman & Tambre, 2000; Moghadam, 2000). Rarely has this work linked these struggles to age and aging.

Our contention is that *globalization is being used to advance a new form of ageism through the socially constructed socio-demographic crisis of an aging world* (Estes & Phillipson, 2002; see also Phillipson & Walker chapters, this volume). This "apocalyptic demography" (Robertson, 1999) is being advanced by the World Bank and the International Monetary Fund (IMF) among other financial interests as a symbolic weapon in support of their privatization agendas (Estes & Phillipson, 2002).

Among the *most significant effects of globalization on older women is the reduction in the state role with regard to the economic and health security of the people.* Globalization, marginalization, and gender form an interconnected matrix that "shape[s] patterns of poverty [and] other distributional outcomes" (Mittelman & Tambre, 2000, p. 88) that are particularly disadvantageous to women.

> Central to the chain of relationships are the varied ways in which economic globalization marginalizes large numbers of people by reducing public spending on social services and de-links economic reform from social policy. This type of marginalization manifests a gendered dimension inasmuch as women constitute those principally affected by it. (Mittelman & Tambre, 2000, p. 75)

Neoliberal market-based globalization and ideology are layered on top of preexisting "rigid hierarchies of patriarchy [that] work to impoverish women." Markets further ingrain and deepen "poverty on a gendered basis" (Mittelman & Tambre, 2000, p. 76).

> The twin ideologies of gender and globalization separately and in combination exacerbate the inequalities of an already-stacked deck against women, as both women's work and hardship are dramatically increased—with women pressed to take on the lowest paying jobs while continuing to care for their children, families, and elders. (Mittelman & Tambre, 2000, p. 76)

The ideology of globalization (Estes, 2001; Mittelman & Tambre, 2000) injures women, as state "functions in the realm of social services [shift] from the state to women" (Mittelman & Tambre, 2000, p. 76) with reductions in the safety net for women and children (e.g., welfare reform in the United States). The loss of state protections for subsistence activities in developing countries where women's economic participation is so restricted is disastrous. This "gendered marginalization" includes 1) the widening of self-regulating markets and the privatization of farming land for cash crops that add new problems of food insecurity; 2) the added personal costs of the privatization of public health services; and 3) reductions in state spending on vital services, including education/teachers and local transportation (Mittelman & Tambre, 2000, pp. 83-84).

With the globalization of capital and demographic aging, there are serious threats to public pension provisions and services, rights to health and social care, and the meaning of citizenship across the life course. Privatization schemes are highly problematic for all peoples, especially for women and for older persons (Estes & Phillipson, 2002). Vast profit incentives exist for multinational financial and insurance institutions to obtain "global custody" (*Financial Times,* 2001) of the world's pensions and health insurance programs. Their success is dependent upon the extent to which these private-sector financial corporations can succeed in snuffing out or limiting public-sector provision. Negative outcomes are already evident: first, in India where "the World Bank mandated privatization of health care has priced medical treatment out of the reach of the poor in places where health care was once government run and free" (Women's Edge Coalition, 2003); and second, in Chile, where there is Social Security privatization.

> The new privately managed pension system in Chile has increased gender inequalities. Women are worse off than they were under the old pay-as-you-go system of Social Security. . . . Women's longer life expectancy, earlier retirement age, lower rates of labor-force participation, lower salaries, and other disadvantages in the labor market are directly affecting their accumulation of funds in individual retirement accounts, leading to lower pensions, especially for poorer women. (Arenas de Mesa & Montecinos, 1999, p. 3)

Given that women provide most of the world's work of child and long-term care without financial remuneration and at great economic, physical, and psychological hardship (Estes & Zulman, 2004), the continuing and deepening themes and patterns of privatization that are instituted globally will further jeopardize women through unpaid "overwork" over their lifetimes and with predictably deleterious health and economic consequences.

Key issues concern the extent to which women of all generations and all older persons will be a major (or even minor) voice in the new global economy and efforts to reshape the institution of old age and retirement that are occurring across different nation-states (Estes & Phillipson, 2002). This is part of a larger question of globalization—the influence of politics in constructing the present and the future (Sassoon, 2001). Globalization as a process is both a historical transition, opening new "spaces" and an opportunity for the development and testing of political power and strategy involving the balance between consent and coercion.

Eastern European and Third World women are networking in their struggles for making "women's rights as human rights" a defining principle of citizenship under globalization through collaborations such as Women's EDGE, the Association for Women in Development, the Center for Economic Justice, the InterAction/Commission on the Advancement of Women, and the Open Society Institute's Network Women's Program. The Soros-funded Network has targeted the problems of "Democracy with a male face," the "silencing of women's voices," and the disparities between rights and practices occurring since the fall of communism in Central and Eastern Europe and the former Soviet Union. Women's absence at the leadership level in emerging democracies diminishes reform efforts in economic, social, and legal systems.

> Enduring gender biases have contributed to the failure to revise outdated employment laws, modify health care fees to ensure equal access for women, and adopt enforcement laws on gender-based violence. (Network Women's Program, 2002)

This decline in women's political participation and new relegation to traditional women's work has given rise to the conviction that "Democracy without women is no democracy" (the slogan of the first independent Women's Forum in 1991) and the understanding of women's rights as human rights.

Although the mobilization of globalization opponents exists in human rights, ecology, women's rights, race and ethnic justice, and the worker rights, the cautionary words of Kuumba (2001, p. 91) merit attention: "patriarchies and sexist notions [are] . . . major impediments to the mobilization of women into gender-integrated movements."

Thus far, older people and women of all ages have been largely absent from influential debates such as those initiated by the World Bank (against pay-as-you-go pensions) or the WTO (for the commercialization of care services). The major players in these debates have either been governments (from rich countries) wishing to deregulate state provision, or corporations wanting to expand into lucrative areas of profit. But it is also the case that older people (and their organizations) have been marginalized in the various forums that are now raising concerns about globalization, despite Walker and Maltby's (1997) observation that there is as an upsurge of political activity among pensioners in a number of countries (Estes, Biggs, & Phillipson, 2003). A starting point, therefore, must be the linkage of organizations representing women and those representing older people with the larger organizations and forums working toward a global agenda on social issues. Political organization and the formulation of policies that will have an impact on key transnational bodies are major tasks ahead.

Unless women around the world accelerate their struggles, there is serious danger of the eclipse of women's rights and the further immiseration of women as a defining outcome of globalization. The struggle is to ensure that developing and developed states recognize the essential contributions of women to social reproduction via state policy that fully supports the interdependency between and among generations through women's care work.

Navarro (2000) argues that it is erroneous to accept the social construction of reality that globalization is *inevitably* antithetical to social rights and a progressive welfare state with full employment. Instead, he argues that those working on behalf of human rights must insist that nation-states do not shrink from their commitments to social and human rights, full employment, and a safety net for all peoples.

GENDER AND SOCIAL MOVEMENTS

The enormous gender stakes in the current Social Security privatization struggle (Estes, 2004) and in other key old-age policy arenas, such as Medicare and long-term care in the United States, highlight the importance of gender and social movement research to understand factors that constrain or promote insurgency (Kuumba, 2001, p. 140). Scholarship toward a "systematic theory of gender and social movements" (Taylor, 1999) includes work on the 1) creation of gender hierarchies in organizational practices, 2) role of gender stratification in the emergence of social movements, 3) collective identities within which gender is fused, and 4) processes of resistance and challenge to oppressive gender relations. Work is developing on the macro-, meso-, and microlevels of analysis (Kuumba, 2001, p. 93), and a synthesis is proposed of "old competing theoretical dichotomies—objective/structural *versus* subjective/ideological factors to recognize dialectical relations between these levels of social struggle" (Kuumba, 2001, p. 93). It has been argued that women are

> more often willing to take a radical stance and to push further in demands, since they . . . had more to gain and less to lose from capitulating to the power structures. (Kuumba, 2001, p. 81)

A significant issue concerns whether "women and men have different complaints or interpretations of a given situation [and] How . . . grievances that motivate individuals to join resistance struggles differ by gender" (Kuumba, 2001, p. 81). In old-age policy, struggles around Social Security privatization, women's unpaid labor, burden in long-term care, and women's complaints should be fertile ground for social movement development. Understanding why this has not been the case will be informative for the development of the field of study of women and old-age movements.

As this chapter illustrates, insightful and influential feminist scholarship is growing in economics, sociology, philosophy, anthropology, and political science, among other disciplines. Voice is being given to erudite and blistering intellectual critiques that are often accompanied by calls for profound social change. Yet the reality is that there is little state old-age policy action and nascent, if any, grassroots feminist social-movement activity building on the critiques. Estes (2001) calls this "the missing feminist revolution" in social policy and aging.

This perplexing circumstance underscores the import of engaging the study of gender and social movements along lines proposed by Kuumba (2001). From a critical theoretical perspective, questions concern structural power and agency: Who has material, cultural, and political resources? Who has autonomy to enter the labor market? Who has the power to set the terms of pay or no pay for the labor provided? These questions necessitate a feminist epistemology that considers the social construction of "knowledges" and consciousness that shape the current gendered old-age policy and the likelihood of feminist social movement responses in opposition to it or in support of it.

REFERENCES

Acker, J. (1988). Class, gender, and the relations of distribution. *Signs, 13*(3), 473-493.

Acker, J. (1992). Gendered institutions—From sex roles to gendered institutions. *Contemporary Sociology, 21*, 565-569.

Acker, J. (2000). Rewriting class, race, and gender: Problems in feminist rethinking. In M. M. Ferree, J. Lorber, & B. B. Hess (Eds.), *Revisioning gender* (pp. 44-69). Walnut Creek, CA: Rowman & Littlefield Publishers.

Arenas de Mesa, A., & Montecinos, V. (1999). The privatization of social security and women's Welfare: Gender effects of Chilean reform. *Latin American Research Review, 34*(3), 7-38.

Balbo, L. (1982). The servicing work of women and the capitalist state. *Political Power & Social Theory, 3*, 251-270.

Barrett, M. (1988). *Women's oppression today: The marxist/feminist encounter.* London: Verso.

Binney, E. A., Estes, C. L., & Humphers, S. E. (1993). Informalization and community care. In C. L. Estes, J. H. Swan, & Associates (Eds.), *The long term care crisis: Elders trapped in the no-care zone* (pp. 155-170). Newbury Park, CA: Sage Publications, Inc.

Bourdieu, P. (2001). *Masculine domination.* Stanford, CA: Stanford University Press.

Brown, W. (1995). *States of injury: Power and freedom in late modernity.* New Jersey: Princeton University Press.

Brush, L. (2000). Gender, work, who cares?! Production, reproduction, deindustrialization, and business as usual. In M. M. Ferree, J. Lorber, & B. B. Hess (Eds.), *Revisioning gender* (pp. 161-189). Walnut Creek, CA: A Division of Rowman & Littlefield Publishers.

Ciscel, D. H., & Heath, J. A. (2001). To market, to market: Imperial capitalism's destruction of social capital and the family. *Review of Radical Political Economics, 33*(4), 401-414.

Collins, P. H. (1991). *Black feminist thought: Knowledge, consciousness, and the politics of empowerment.* New York: Routledge.

Collins, P. H. (2000). *Black feminist thought: Knowledge, consciousness, and the politics of empowerment* (2nd ed.). New York: Routledge.

Connell, R. W. (1987). *Gender and power: Society, the person, and sexual politics.* Stanford, CA: Stanford University Press.

Connell, R. W. (1995). *Masculinities.* Sydney: Allen & Unwin.

Connell, R. W. (1996). *Politics of changing men.* Sydney: Allen & Unwin.

Connell, R. W. (2000). *The men and the boys.* Sydney: Allen & Unwin.

Crystal, S., & Shea, D. (2002). Prospects for retirement resources in an aging society. *Annual Review of Gerontology and Geriatrics, 22*, 271-281.

Dannefer, D. (2003). Cumulative advantage/disadvantage and the life course: Cross fertilizing age and social science theory. *Journal of Gerontology, 58B*(6), S327-S337.

Dickinson, J., & Russell, B. (1986). *Family, economy & state: The social reproduction process under capitalism.* New York: St. Martin's Press.

Dressel, P. L. (1988). Gender, race, and class: beyond the feminization of poverty in later life. *Gerontologist, 28*(2), 177-180.

Esping-Andersen, G. (1990). *The three worlds of welfare capitalism.* Cambridge: Polity Press.

Estes, C. L. (1979). *The aging enterprise.* San Francisco: Jossey-Bass Publishers.

Estes, C. L. (1982). Austerity and aging in the United-States—1980 and beyond. *International Journal of Health Services, 12*(4), 573-584.

Estes, C. L. (1991a). The new political economy of aging: Introduction and critique. In M. Minkler & C. L. Estes (Eds.), *Critical perspectives on aging: The political and moral economy of growing old* (pp. 19-36). Amityville, NY: Baywood.

Estes, C. L. (1991b). The Reagan legacy: Privatization, the welfare state, and aging in the 1990's. In J. Myles & J. S. Quadagno (Eds.), *States, labor markets, and the future of old age policy* (pp. 59-83). Philadelphia: Temple University Press.

Estes, C. L. (1998a). *Older women and the welfare state, keynote address.* Conference on Autonomy and Aging, Kingstin University, Kingstin-on-Thames, UK.

Estes, C. L. (1998b). *Patriarchy and the welfare state revisited: The state, gender and aging.* The World Congress of Sociology, Montreal, Canada.

Estes, C. L. (2000). From gender to the political economy of ageing. *The European Journal of Social Quality, 2*(1), 28-46.

Estes, C. L. (Ed.). (2001). *Social policy and aging: A critical perspective.* Thousand Oaks, CA: Sage.

Estes, C. L. (2004). Social security privatization and older women: A feminist political economy perspective. *Journal of Aging Studies, 18*, 9-26.

Estes, C. L., Biggs, S., & Phillipson, C. (2003). *Social theory, social policy and ageing: A critical introduction.* Milton Keynes, UK: Open University Press.

Estes, C. L., & Binney, E.A. (1990). *Older women and the state.* San Francisco, UCSF Institute of Health and Aging.

Estes, C. L., Binney, E. A., & Culbertson, R. A. (1992). The gerontological imagination: Social influences on the development of gerontology, 1945-present. *International Journal of Aging and Human Development, 35*(1), 49-65.

Estes, C. L., Gerard, L., Zones, J. S., & Swan, J. (1984). *Political economy, health, and aging.* Boston: Little Brown.

Estes, C. L., Goldberg, S. C., Wellin, C., Shostak, S., Beard, R., & Linkins, K. (2006 [in press]). Implications of welfare reform on the elderly: A case study of provider, advocate and consumer perspectives. *Journal of Aging and Social Policy, 18*(1).

Estes, C. L., & Phillipson, C. (2002). The globalization of capital, the welfare state, and old age policy. *International Journal of Health Services, 32*(2), 279-297.

Estes, C. L., & Zulman, D. L. (2004). Informalization of long term caregiving: A gender lens. In H. C. Estes & C. L. Estes (Eds.), *Health policy* (4th ed., pp. 147-156). Boston: Jones and Bartlett.

Ferree, M. M., & Hall, E. J. (1996). Rethinking stratification from a feminist perspective: Gender, race & class in mainstream textbooks. *American Sociological Review, 61*, 929-950.

Financial Times. (2001). New York: F.T. Publications, Inc.

Finch, J., & Groves, D. (1983). *A labour of love: Women, work and caring.* London: Routledge and Kegan Paul.

Folbre, N. (2001). *The invisible heart: Economics and family values.* New York: New York Press.

Fox, B. (Ed.). (1988). *Family bonds and gender divisions: Readings in the sociology of the family.* Toronto: Canadian Scholars' Press.

Ginn, J. D., Street, D., & Arber, S. (Eds.). (2001). *Women, work, and pensions: International issues and prospects.* Buckingham: Open University Press.

Harding, S. (1996). Standpoint epistemology (a feminist version): How social disadvantage creates epistemic advantage. In S. P. Turner (Ed.), *Social theory and sociology: The classics and beyond* (pp. 146-160). Cambridge, MA: Blackwell Publishing.

Harrington Meyer, M. (1990). Family status and poverty among older women: The gendered distribution of retirement income in the US. *Social Problems, 37*(4), 551-563.

Harrington Meyer, M. (1996). Making claims as workers or wives: The distribution of social security benefits. *American Sociological Review, 61*(3), 449-465.

Hernes, H. M. (1987). *Welfare state and woman power: Essays in state feminism.* Oxford: Oxford University Press.

Hewitson, G. (1999). *Feminist economics: Interrogating the masculinity of rational man.* Cheltenham, UK: Edwin Elgar.

Himmelweit, S. (1983). Reproduction. T. Bottomore. *Dictionary of Marxist thought* (pp. 417-419). Cambridge: Harvard University Press.

Jones, V. Y., & Estes, C. L. (1997). Older women: Income, retirement, and health. In S.B. Ruzek, V. L. Olesen, & A. E. Clarke (Eds.), *Women's health: Complexities and differences* (pp. 425-445). Columbus: Ohio State University Press.

Knuttila, M. (1996). *Introducing sociology: A critical perspective.* New York: Oxford University Press.

Kuumba, M. B. (2001). *Gender and social movements.* Walnut Creek, CA: Alta Mira Press.

Leira, A. (1993). The 'woman-friendly' welfare state? The case of Norway and Sweden. In J. Lewis (Ed.), *Women and social policies in Europe: Work, family, and the state* (pp. 49-71). Aldershot Hants, UK: Edward Elgar Publishing.

Lerner, G. (1986). *The creation of patriarchy.* New York: Oxford University Press.

Levitas, R. (Ed.). (1986). *The ideology of the new right.* Cambridge, MA: Polity Press.

Lorber, J. (1998). *Gender inequality: Feminist theories and politics.* Los Angeles: Roxbury Publishing Company.

Mittelman, J. H., & Tambe, A. (2000). Global poverty and gender. In J. H. Mittleman (Ed.), *The globalization syndrome* (pp. 74-89). New Jersey: Princeton University Press.

Moghadam, V. M. (2000). Gender and the global economy. In M. M. Ferree, J. Lorber, & B. B. Hess (Eds.), *Revisioning gender* (pp. 128-160). Walnut Creek, CA: Division of Rowman & Littlefield Publishing.

Mutari, E. (2001). . . . "As broad as our life experience": Visions of feminist political economy, 1972-1991. *Review of Radical Political Economics, 33*(4), 379-399.

Navarro, V. (2000). Are pro-welfare state and full employment policies possible in the era of globalization? *International Journal of Health Services, 30*(2), 231-251.

Network Women's Program. (2002). *Bending the bow.* New York: Open Society Institute.

O'Connor, J. S., Orloff, A. S., & Shaver, S. (1999). *States, markets, families: Gender, liberalism and social policy in Australia, Canada, Great Britain and the United States.* Cambridge University Press.

Omi, M., & Winant, H. (1994). *Racial formation in the United States: From the 1960s to the 1990s*. New York: Routledge.

O'Rand, A. (2002). Cumulative advantage theory in life course research. *Annual Review of Gerontology and Geriatrics, 22*, 14-30.

Orloff, A. S. (1993). Gender and the social rights of citizenship: The comparative analysis of gender relations and welfare states. *American Sociological Review, 58*(3), 303-329.

Ortner, S. B. (1996). *Making gender: The politics and erotics of culture*. Boston: Beacon Press.

Pascall, G. (1986). *Social policy: A feminist analysis*. New York: Tavistock Publications.

Pateman, C. (1989). *The disorder of women: Democracy, feminism, and political theory*. Stanford, CA: Stanford University Press.

Quadagno, J. S. (1994). *The color of welfare: How racism undermined the war on poverty*. New York: Oxford University Press.

Robertson, A. (1999). Beyond apocalyptic demography: Toward a moral economy of interdependence. In M. Minkler & C. L. Estes (Eds.), *Critical gerontology: Perspectives from political and moral economy* (pp. 75-90). Amityville, NY: Baywood.

Rubin, G. (1984). The traffic in women. In A. M. Jaggar & P. S. Rothenberg (Eds.), *Feminist frameworks: Alternative accounts of the relations between women and men* (pp. 155-171). New York: McGraw-Hill.

Sassoon, A. S. (1987). *Women and the state: The shifting boundaries of public and private*. London: Hutchinson.

Sassoon, A. S. (2001). The space for politics: Globalization, hegemony, and passive revolution. *New Political Economy, 6*(1), 5-17.

Schneider, G., & Shackelford, J. (2001). Proposed feminist responses to standards and lists of economic principles. *Feminist Economics, 7*(2), 77-89.

Sen, G. (1980). The sexual division of labor and the working-class family: Towards a conceptual synthesis of class relations and the subordination of women. *Review of Radical Political Economics, 12*(2), 76-86.

Siim, B. (1993). The gendered Scandinavian welfare states: The interplay between women's roles as mothers, workers and citizens of Denmark. In J. Lewis (Ed.), *Women and social policies in Europe: Work, family and the state* (pp. 25-48). Aldershot Hants, UK: Edward Elgar Publishing.

Smith, D. (1990). *The conceptual practices of power: A feminist sociology of knowledge*. Boston: Northeastern University Press.

Taylor, V. (1999). Guest editor's introduction—Special issue on gender and social movements—Part 2. *Gender & Society, 13*(1), 5-7.

Therborn, G. (1978). *What does the ruling class do when it rules?: State apparatuses and state power under feudalism, capitalism and socialism*. Thetford, Norfolk: Lowe and Brydore.

Therborn, G. (1980). *The ideology of power and the power of ideology*. New York: Schocken Books.

Walker, A., & Maltby, A. (1997). *Ageing Europe*. Buckinghamshire: Open University Press.

Wiegersma, N. (1991). Peasant patriarchy and the subversion of the collective in Vietnam. *Review of Radical Political Economics, 23*(3&4), 174-197.

Williams, F. (1996). Racism and the discipline of social policy: A critique of welfare theory. In D. Taylor (Ed.), *Critical social policy: A reader* (pp. 48-78). Thousand Oaks, CA: Sage Publications.

Women's Edge Coalition. (2003). Retrieved May 16, 2003 at www.womensedge.org/events/conference2000sum.htm

CHAPTER 6

Reciprocal Co-Optation: The Relationship of Critical Theory and Social Gerontology

Dale Dannefer

The relationship between age and critical theory may be characterized as a relation of reciprocal co-optation. By co-optation I mean that an idea or principle is accepted, but is reframed to fit within the assumptions of one or more preexisting paradigms. Therefore, its power is diluted at the same time that it is heralded as a new contribution. When co-optation is reciprocal, it of course poses a double challenge. This chapter suggests that such a condition of reciprocal co-optation has characterized the relation between age and critical theory. The first part of the chapter discusses the co-optation of critical theory by the wider discourse in social gerontology, and the second takes up the co-optation of the problem of aging by critical theory.

THE CO-OPTATION OF CRITICAL THEORY BY GERONTOLOGY

As articulated in social gerontology, critical theory incorporates both structural and hermeneutic perspectives on sociological analysis. The first of these deals with issues of political economy and distributive justice—of material inequality, its consequences, and the processes that sustain it; the second with human whole-ness—with the relationship of consciousness and the symbolic apparatus to the material conditions of life, both at the individual level and at the sociocultural level. I contend that critical scholarship on aging has encountered tendencies toward co-optation in each of these domains, and this chapter supports that contention by presenting an example from each.

THE STRUCTURAL PERSPECTIVE:
AGING AND AGEISM, COHORT PROCESSES,
AND CUMULATIVE ADVANTAGE

Exposing Ageism: A Legacy of the Sociology of Age

In articulating the presence of oppressive social conditions, aging is a field in which critical theory hardly has a monopoly. It is perhaps ironic that some of the most notable pioneers of social gerontology and the sociology of age introduced data, concepts, and analytical perspectives demonstrating that age and the processes of individual aging show considerable variation across history and culture. Thus, they demonstrated that age cannot be reduced to individual-level formulas that assume aging is a universal process; this work always implied, and sometimes made explicit, that such intellectual microfication masked a need for institutional critique (Hagestad & Dannefer, 2001). As prominent examples, Irving Rosow's early critique of retirement and old age suggested that retirement might be more accurately thought of as a "roleless role." Others, such as Bernice Neugarten (1983) and Leonard Cain (1964), offered similar critiques. Vern Bengtson (1973) suggested that aspects of debility in old age could be redefined in terms of labeling theory, and Jaber Gubrium's early work on nursing home life demonstrated powerfully the relevance of a constructivist, interactionist approach to aging (1975, 1976). Most systematic and perhaps most radical of all, Matilda Riley and colleagues argued that age is a property not just of individuals but of social structure and institutions. Like the Riley group, Robert Butler (1975) argued for a need to rethink the shape of social institutions with respect to age. And across disciplines, scholars who documented the importance of the cohort (Baltes & Schaie, 1968; Elder, 1999; Schaie, 1965; Uhlenberg, 1978) in accounting for age-related patterns and outcomes provided some of the most powerful evidence to compel the questioning of traditional notions of aging.

Thus, prior to the development of a distinctly critical approach to aging, the work of these gerontological scholars challenged the assumptions that age is a natural, biologically inevitable, and individual-level phenomenon, and their work also contained a critique, although often largely implicit, of the institutional arrangements and practices that oppressed older people prior to the development of a distinctly critical approach. While such critiques generally focused less on the directly exploitative aspects of existing institutions, they were compelling, and they provided concepts and tools of general use identifying and articulating the role of social forces in aging; though the contributions of such scholarship, both the confounding of history and age (via disentangling the effects of cohorts) and the confounding effects of illness, impoverishment, and prejudicial stereotypes with aging, have been identified as fallacies that have contributed to the stigmatization and oppression of the older people in modern societies and have contributed to what Riley and associates called "structural lag" (Riley & Riley, 1994). In the United States, these voices provided a disciplined analytical framework of empirical social science to add legitimacy to the efforts of effective social movements and lobbies that gave voice to an increasingly large aging population, so that both the economic (Preston, 1984) and cultural (Marquié, Cau-Bareille, & Volkoff, 1998; McNaught, 1994; Thomas, 2004) positions of older people changed markedly over the past half century.

Intracohort Inequality and the Phenomenon of Cumulative Advantage/Disadvantage

Nevertheless, some significant ideas have been inspired by a distinctly critical approach to aging and social structure and have received some attention in the sociology of aging and in social gerontology over the past two decades. Yet these, too, have been challenged by alternative interpretations that co-opt them by a reductionist, individual-level reframing. One such idea is the concept of cumulative advantage/disadvantage.

Cumulative advantage/disadvantage (Crystal, 2003; Dannefer, 1987, 1988, 2003; Hagestad, 1992; O'Rand, 1996) offers a contemporary example of the co-optation of a *structural* concept. This notion invites an analysis of aging as a collective process of intracohort stratification, as social processes allow advantage to cumulate in the life experience of some individuals and disadvantage of others, over the collective life course of a cohort. The end result, *ceteris parabus,* is that greater extremes of affluence and poverty are found within the older population than within other age strata.

As one of the early advocates of this concept of intracohort stratification and cumulation, I can attest to the hope—shared by other early researchers in this area—that this notion would stimulate a more direct acknowledgment of the causative power of social arrangements over the life course of cohorts and of individuals and of the human costs of these arrangements. Speaking personally, I had hoped that if it could be recognized that a systematic process of increasing stratification were an integral part of the life of each cohort, the inadequacies of the microfication and individual-level reductionism would be clear, and the importance of paying systematic attention to the power of social forces in understanding the phenomena of aging would become unavoidably apparent. Indeed, issues of cumulative advantage/disadvantage and other aspects of intracohort diversity in equality have received an increasing amount of attention over the last several years, and the need to get beyond characterization of age strata in modal or average terms are ideas that have been accepted within sociology and neighboring disciplines (Baltes, Staudinger, & Lindenberger, 1999; Bass, Kutza, & Torres-Gil, 1990; Caspi & Moffitt, 1993; Crystal & Shea, 2003; Kelley-Moore & Ferraro, 2003; Maddox & Lawton, 1988; O'Rand, 1996; O'Rand & Henretta, 1999; Pallas, 2002).

However, the associated (and from a critical perspective, crucially important) idea that inequality-generating processes of social reproduction can properly be thought of as a major *causal factor* has not been widely accepted in gerontology. It has been challenged by at least two alternative "explanations" of increasing inequality over the life course, both based on individual-level processes. These may be termed "choice" or "fate."

Choice refers to the presumption that the greater reason for increasing heterogeneity and stratification with age is *not* cumulating advantages or losses, but rather the unique individuality of each person and the efficacy of each individual's agentic force to craft a life plan and lifestyle that cannot be reduced to developmentally determined patterns or social-science generalization. Some scholars have thus speculated that the differentiation of aging cohorts may reflect the flourishing of individuality with the advent of retirement (e.g., Atchley, 1997; Heinz, 2002; Hickey, 1980), which may "open up" new space for individual expression. Advocates of this perspective may proclaim in an almost celebratory affirmation of human uniqueness. For example, Atchley (1999, p. 89) argues that ". . . retirement frees both men and women to take part in activity at a level closer to their ideal." Since social roles no longer impose restrictions upon individuality, diversity flourishes and inequality emerges among the aged. Rather than requiring a concern with a scientific explanation, choice thus celebrates the sanctity of individual free expression.

This emphasis coincides, interestingly, with the targeting of the aged by advertisers as a significant new market. As financial security and affluence have begun to characterize a broader segment of the aged population, they have been embraced, with increasing intensity, by corporate product developers and advertisers, whether for new low-carb frozen dinners, ocean cruises, or pharmaceuticals for a host of age-related maladies (see Binstock, 2003; Ekerdt, 2003; Douthit, this volume; Katz, this volume).

It is true that such commercials may increasingly present a relatively positive and sometimes even vibrant view of older people that in some respects contradicts the negative stereotypes of old age in modernity. In that respect, ironically, the advertising industry may serve as a social force for positive macrolevel change in the cultural imagery of the aged, one that is probably resonant with conventional gerontological images of successful aging. This is true even when one factors in the pharmaceutical and other health-related commercials that emphasize age-related health problems (see Katz and Calasanti & King, this volume.) As discussed by Baars and Walker in this volume, the positive, upbeat assessments that are becoming more familiar as media fare have even been endorsed by thoughtful social analysts (e.g., Gilleard & Higgs, 2001) who have been inspired by the recent work on risk and individualization (e.g., Beck & Camiller, 2000; Beck, Giddens, & Lash, 1995). Yet to take commercials with their images of "successful aging" as evidence that "individual freedom" or "human emancipation" now flourishes in mature adulthood and retirement would be a serious error for at least two reasons.

First, images of elder affluence and even "greedy geezerism" that are nourished by these images eclipse the now well-documented fact that inequality in resources (and perhaps in health as well) is greatest among the aged, and that many older people, especially older women, have limited discretionary income which, especially in the United States perhaps, is increasingly spent on medicine and healthcare (Estes, 1979, this volume). Moreover, the inequality observed within the older age strata underestimates the effects of lifelong economic inequalities in another way: A disproportionate number of those from lower socioeconomic backgrounds have been prematurely removed from the population by mortality (Crystal & Waehrer, 1996; Dannefer, 1988).

Second, such commercial and other media portrayals of successful aging must also be questioned even for those who are economically well off. Historians and sociologists working within a range of traditions, including critical theory, have documented the deliberate and remarkably effective use of advertising to shape consumer demand and taste (e.g., Cohen, 2003; Ewen, 1976, 1999; Wexler, 1977). In view of the pervasiveness of such commercial forces, the "real self" celebrated by symbolic interactionists as a triumph of modernity (Turner, 1976) is actually, in substantial part, a self shaped by instruments of mass information dissemination, which include not only the consumerism promoted in commercial media but also the pronouncements of "professional experts" concerning normal development and aging, mental health, and so on. This brings us to *fate,* the second alternative explanation for increasing diversity and inequality.

Fate refers to a sense of inevitability and predetermination. In the context of discussions of increasing divergence and diversity over the life course, its technical term is "accentuation"—a concept that has been used uncritically by sociologists as well as psychologists. Accentuation refers to a presumption of fixed intraindividual characteristics that become more and more pronounced with the passage of time. This notion, which accounts for increasing inequality primarily on the basis of processes that originate within the organism and are fixed early in the life course, is alive and well. For example, Caspi and Moffitt (1993) proposed an aggressive sociobiological formulation that not only could be used to account for heterogeneity and inequality in terms of prefixed personality differences but also argued that social structure actually serves as a brake on such differentiation. Periods of social change, they argued, which entail institutional breakdown or upheaval, would permit essential and possibly suppressed aspects of personality to flourish and express themselves (Caspi & Moffitt, 1993; see also Light, Grigsby, & Bligh, 1996).

In sum, the notion of increasing heterogeneity and inequality with age itself has found some receptivity: it has contributed to a growing interest in the phenomena of differentiation and stratification among the aged. At the same time, however, its critical force has often been reframed in reductionistic and individualistic terms in which social structure again becomes invisible. Thus, instead of contributing to a rejection of naturalistic accounts of organismically based individual aging or existentially based freedom of choice, a substantial force of gerontological argument has sought to interpret the phenomenon of intracohort stratification as a further substantiation of those accounts. It should be noted that, despite their persistence and robustness, it cannot be said that these impulses to microfication have succeeded. A growing body of work continues to document the primacy of social class and other resource effects on health over the life course, supplying a steady stream of evidence of the power of social forces in shaping individual outcomes (e.g., Crystal & Shea, 2003; Daniels, Kennedy, Kawachi, Cohen, & Rogers, 2000; Farmer, 2001; Marmot, 2004).

The Hermeneutic Perspective: Alienation and Meaning

The hermeneutic dimension pertains to the nature of consciousness and meaning. The issue of *meaning* has been a theme of efforts to apply a critical theory to aging on at least two levels. One level entails a concern with an ideological role specific to behavioral and social-science theories that naturalize and legitimize existing social and economic arrangements (Baars, 1991; Dannefer, 1989, 1999; Estes, 1979; Phillipson, 1982; Stein, 2003; Walker, 1981).

A second level has concerned the need to attend to the actual experience and meaning of aging. This need has been expressed by those concerned to develop a critical approach since the early paper of Marshall and Tindale (1978), who asserted that social gerontology "neglects genuine human concerns" (p. 65) in favor of the study of prestructured attitudes and quantifiable performance characteristics that are easy to measure. Since then, this point has received frequent emphasis by scholars from history, literary criticism, and philosophy, as well as sociology (e.g., Achenbaum, 1991; Andrews, 1991; Cole, Achenbaum, Jakobi, & Kastenbaum, 1992; Cole & Gadow, 1986; Kastenbaum, 1992; Moody, 1996; Weiland, 1992). A common theme of these diverse writings is the contention that a careful look at the experience of aging from the subject's perspective may reveal strengths and abilities that cannot be discerned or accessed through structured measures. For example, Moody (1988) wrote that "Critical gerontology would seek to thematize the subjective and interpretive dimensions of aging" and that, through the careful analysis of these dimensions, it could reveal positive but neglected aspects of aging such as wisdom and creativity (pp. 35-36). More generally, he proposes that "critical theory" as applied to gerontology can encompass perspectives drawn from the humanities and cultural study and the critique of positivism, as well as the political economy tradition (Moody, 1996, p. 244).

The general concern with meaning and subjectivity had become a subtheme of some leading scholars in gerontology for a long time, well before its identification with a critical approach (e.g., Butler, 1975; Clayton & Birren, 1982; Neugarten, 1983; Riley, 1978). Thus, the general point that the firsthand experience of aging needs careful and systematic attention has received a sympathetic reception. Such writings may have contributed to a broad "mainstream" recognition of a problem of "ecological validity" (e.g., Baltes, Staudinger, Maercker, & Smith, 1993).

Over the past two decades, this general concern has manifested in the objectives and designs of several important research enterprises, several of which have even taken up "wisdom"—that most elusive and daunting of concepts that is traditionally associated with age—as a topic for study. These include the work initiated by Birren and associates (Birren & Fisher, 1990; Clayton & Birren, 1982), the MacArthur Project on Successful Midlife Development, and recent efforts to "operationalize" wisdom by researchers in both North America (e.g., Ardelt, 2003) and Europe. Especially important for the sophistication, dedication, and energy brought to bear upon the problem of wisdom are the efforts of the Wisdom Project at the Max Planck Institute in Berlin (e.g., Baltes, 2004; Baltes & Staudinger, 2000; Pasupathi, Staudinger, & Baltes, 2001; Staudinger, 1998, 1999.)

It is encouraging to observe serious efforts by social and behavioral scientists to move beyond a reliance on those characteristics that can be measured through standardized and prestructured instruments and to countenance a broader set of *capacities* and concerns of aging individuals. In assessing such efforts, however, it is important to keep clearly in mind the position of meaning, subjectivity, and conscious experience within the framework of critical theory. In the critical tradition, subjectivity is an essential node of analysis because it is understood that consciousness is the basis of human action at the same time that the regulation of human action is essential to social order. This regulation typically requires a degree of legitimation of the social order, which in all known societies involves a mystification of the connection between the productive labor of individuals and the reproduction of the social order. Inevitably, then, a measure of *false consciousness* is inherent in everyday meaning structures. Thus, a critical analysis cannot proceed without a continuous moment of sociopolitical self-reflexiveness or without a systematic effort to clarify the linkages between consciousness and subjective meaning and the cultural, economic, and political contexts within which social actors are located (Andrews, 1991; Baars, 1991; Dannefer, 1999; Habermas, 1978).

Although the growing concern with meaning and subjectivity in social gerontology may be accompanied by a growing recognition of the importance of the self-reflexive moment as an integral aspect of both wisdom and efforts to theorize about wisdom (Baltes, 2004), it is typically a reflexivity of *microfication* (Hagestad & Dannefer, 2001), in which larger issues of social location as well as political and cultural awareness are not explicitly considered and thus remain invisible. Wisdom-related strengths such as "life insight" (Staudinger, in press) can certainly not be reduced to sociopolitical awareness. From a critical perspective, however, "life insight and wisdom" cannot be achieved while the problem of the relation between individual and collective interest with one's political and social location remain invisible. This becomes even more salient and more urgent as a "critique of wisdom studies" as scholars of wisdom adopt morality and virtue more explicitly as elements of wisdom (Baltes, 2004; Baltes & Staudinger, 2000.) By assuming a universal character of consciousness, meaning, wisdom, etc., it fails to consider the extent to which individualized reflexiveness itself is part of an apparatus of social reproduction—the extent to which ecological destruction or multinational violence is advanced by the everyday practice of wisdom and virtue.

A similar problem of microfication has also applied to discussions of meaning offered from scholars working in the humanities. Here, even those associated with a critical perspective have often not been very distinct from other gerontological writing based on efforts to depict meaning. While valuable for both the analytic frames and the insights they offer, such writings differ from a distinctly critical approach in at least two respects. First, as in the case of the wisdom studies described above, they are characterized by a microfication—a depoliticized and dehistorized reduction that does not analyze the social-structural frames within which meaning is generated, neglecting Marx's classic observation that "men make their own history, but they do not make it just as they please; they do not make it under circumstances chosen by themselves . . ." (1852 [1972], p. 437). Second, they sometimes suggest a universalization of concepts that may be culture specific, e.g., "legitimation of biography" (Marshall, 1980), or "journey of life" (Cole, 1991; Kenyon, 1991). Perhaps the concern to permit the power and authenticity of the actors' voices to be heard—without question a well justified concern—has allowed the need to analyze those voices in terms of their social and cultural circumstances to be obscured. As Bhavnani observes, "empowerment and 'having a voice' are not . . . the same, although the two are often conflated . . ." (1990, pp. 145-146). If the result of a lack of analysis of voice in terms of its linkages to factors of class, ethnicity, cohort specificity, etc. is to permit an implicit (or explicit) universalization of concepts, it risks the same kind of disempowering and legitimating function that has been attributed to traditional organismic theories. Since many of the writings on meaning to which I refer have not been produced by sociologists, but by those working in other fields of the social sciences and humanities (e.g., Cole & Gadow, 1986; Moody, 1988, Weiland, 1989, 1993), it may be that this is a place where the sociological foundations of critical theory are especially needed and can make a particular contribution.

As it stands, such discussions of meaning are detached not only from their structural moorings but also from the extensive literature that provides a critical analysis of the modern self—of a self that is, for example, commodified (Wexler, 1983), narcissistic (Lasch, 1979), saturated (Gergen, 1991), or subjectivized (Berger, Berger, & Kellner, 1973; Dannefer, 1981). These analyses offer themes that might be expected to surface in accounts of the subjective experience of aging individuals in late capitalism. Possible themes include despair, borne of the recognition of the futility of accumulation or of too much time squandered on unfulfilling consumerist pursuits or of memories of blocked opportunities for love and work that leave the actor with a sense of irretrievable loss. Under such circumstances, it is likely to be adaptive for an individual to find a "legitimation of biography," even if it involves a degree of self-deception. But if such themes of critical psychology and cultural analysis are not found in literature, it is reasonable to ask why this is the case. At least three hypotheses suggest themselves.

First, a *cohort* hypothesis would suggest that those cohorts now old did not experience the particular assaults to the self described by the critical theorists of self; rather these aged cohorts—who compose what in the United States has been called "the greatest generation" (Brokaw, 1998) and have endured enormous economic upheaval and war experiences as well as unprecedented technological progress—have, as a whole, a different range of experiences and structures of self than those described by critical analysts who focus on the consequences for the self of institutional forces that hit the young and middle-aged most directly. Although this may be an important factor to consider, the incidence of depression and related psychological maladies indicates the insightful voices published in the literature are not representative of the meaning states of many of those currently aged.

Second, a *sampling* hypothesis would suggest a selection effect: that the often moving and profound character of voices that are heard in many published accounts are chosen for their inspirational value. They represent the strong and wise voices of those who are "aging successfully," at least on the dimensions of insight and reconciliation of oneself. Indeed, the state of the literature (critical literature included) on the subjective meaning of age reminds one of where the sociology of age more generally was about two decades ago. In each case, there is a concern to debunk anti-age myths and to generalize a positive and implicitly homogenous depiction of the aged; in neither case is there a deconstruction of the problems of phenomena in question.

Third, a *measurement* hypothesis concerns how adequately the accounts of meaning provided by respondents reflect their actual sense of self and of their lives, versus some idealized version of it. Many are reluctant to focus on or to express despairing or regretful accounts of precious "water under the bridge." This possibility confronts us head on with a problem of false consciousness that is especially delicate in the study of the aged. The general problem it raises is whether "legitimation of biography" is, under some or all conditions, just such an ideological adjustment—a form of false consciousness. This difficult question poses a deep and central dilemma for a critical analysis of age: If the aged uniformly have come to terms with their past experience in a way that legitimates it, reframing its alienated, painful, and constrictive aspects, is that not a valuable and even admirable adaptation at the individual level? On the other hand, how, were this the case, could one apply a critique of modern consciousness or of oppressive institutions, for that matter, to the aged? For this would imply that we come to the end of life, after all is said and done, with a reservoir of inner strength to draw upon, to bring sense and value to patterns of activity that were for years repressed, hyperhabituated, and constricted.

It is difficult at best to adjudicate among these three hypotheses. However an alternative and perhaps more constructive approach to dealing with this issue is to observe the aging individuals whose lives have been committed to a constructive human cause and who therefore have a radically different sense of meaning than those who live in a relatively uncritical acceptance of modern society. One source of data on such individuals is available from Molly Andrews' unusual study of socialists in Great Britain who were born in the early twentieth century (birthdates 1899-1917). According to Andrews' account, these individuals were unable to speak of the meaning of their own lives without a sense of participation in an ongoing movement and with a deep hope for a future they will not live to see. For example, an 85-year-old woman stated, ". . . I seriously thought and hoped I would live to see a Socialist Society in my lifetime, but it is not to be so all one can do is to put into practice as far as one can in your relationships and never be afraid to speak where there is injustice. We are still working very hard" (Andrews, 1991, p. 205). Another 85-year-old activist said, "I know I'll never turn the world around by myself . . . you don't know where you're dropping a seed . . . the seed will grow, it's not one individual, if you convince one individual and she convinces another, this is the only way that you'll succeed" (1991, p. 199).

These accounts contrast dramatically with those aged individuals in modern society who Kaufman, like others, has found, "did not talk about their lives in relation to social trends or the times in which they lived. They did not place themselves in a broader historical context" (1986, p. 22). Andrews shows not only that the aging activists she studied are focused on the collective future rather than the private past but also that they emphasize certain human strengths, such as patience and staying power, as distinct advantages of age. Interestingly, the sense of historical and social engagement articulated by these aged activists may most closely approximate the late-life stock taking of successful entrepreneurs, who often express gratification in the belief that their work positively changed the world and has provided employment and upgraded living standards for their employees (e.g., Brayer, 1996; Ford, 1926). It is possible to notice several themes in common across these two dramatically divergent classes of biography: a sense of purpose and intention, a sense of control over one's activities, a sense of effort well placed and of meaningful legacy.

Traditional and putatively universal psychological categories, including life review, (Butler, 1963; e.g., Staudinger, 1998) ego integrity, and perhaps even legitimation of biography, seem curiously irrelevant in describing these lives. And it has been shown that such constructs have, for all their popularity, a surprisingly narrow empirical base (Lamme & Baars, 1993). While one might contend that the statements made by these activists are precisely part of a subjective process of legitimating their biographies, the focus of Andrews' respondents on collective and historical concern diverges dramatically from the individual-level and familistic preoccupations that seem to characterize life review. Thus, they suggest, at minimum, the need for a typology of legitimation of biography and probably one with multiple dimensions (e.g., collective vs. individual orientation and future vs. past oriented). Any such typology could then be related to structural experiential characteristics in the background of individuals' lives. The diverse and apparently expanding array of configurations of living arrangements for the aged both in the United States (e.g., Streib, 1993) and in Europe (Baars & Thomése, 1994; Hagestad, 1992) reflect the lengthening life course and provide a set of natural laboratories for exploring the course of subjective experience under diverse social and cultural conditions.

In sum, the mission of a critical approach to aging includes the analysis of both 1) inequality in material resources, and 2) diversity and inequality in symbolic and cognitive resources. These tasks have been deflected by the adoption of insights from critical analyses by mainstream theory, which enhances its legitimation and maintains its dominance. The hegemonic tendencies of mainstream theory thus continue to serve an ideological function, absorbing critiques while blunting criticism of institutions and practices.

THE CO-OPTATION OF THE PROBLEM OF AGE
BY CRITICAL THEORY

As indicated by the above examples, numerous aspects of the sociology of aging and social gerontology are ripe for critical analysis. They lend themselves to a straightforward and compelling critique of much work focused on aging in the social and behavioral sciences. Yet one consequence of a single-minded focus on such critique may be to allow critical scholars to avoid the challenge that the phenomena of aging pose for a critical approach. It obscures the tension between, on one hand, coming to terms with real constraints that, in the physical ontogeny of development and aging, seem to impose on the aging body, and the naming and transcending of oppressive social and cultural conditions that add their own "surplus constraints." It obscures the fact that human lives have a dynamic, organismic material basis that is practically constrained at the biological level by parameters that do impose boundaries upon what is socially possible (Dannefer & Perlmutter, 1990; Foner, 1974).

Those ontogenetic constraints may bear little resemblance to the arbitrary role assumptions that are imposed by current social arrangements (Andrews, 1991; Best, 1980; Riley & Riley, 1994). Nevertheless, once one gets beyond the childhood years, critical theory has offered very little positive acknowledgment of aging as an integral part of living and constructive meaning. While many biological, psychological, and social patterns associated with age are historically and socially conditioned, aging intrinsically involves the universal cumulation of temporal experience and memory; and the concomitant potentials for a seasoning of experience and maturation of perspective. And despite the dangers of naturalizing socially constituted aspects of aging, it must be recognized that biological contingencies of vulnerability, loss, and mortality must ultimately confront every individual who lives to a reasonable age. In short, the organism—one's own body and those of others to whom one is related—embodies sets of material processes to which critical theory, including critical approaches to gerontology, have been conveniently oblivious.

It is undoubtedly easier to point to the mechanisms that generate poverty and inequality among the aged, to illustrate the psychological and social oppression of traditional roles, and to analyze processes of social construction and the ideological functions of theories, than it is to take the task of developing an understanding of the meaning, value, and positive possibilities of a long life constructed in relation to others and in a particular sequence of social and historical locations, one day at a time. Ultimately this must be done; even if there were no oppressive roles, the wisdom and insight that come from a long accumulation of experience would mean that a 70-year-old could not be interchanged with a teenager, to whom the firsthand memories and lessons of a half century are currently unavailable.

Nevertheless, a fine line exists between accepting a configuration of age-graded roles as legitimate when they are actually artifacts of a particular social structure and advocating a vision of complete age-irrelevance as a value, an objective, and a possibility. If one argues that the aged have been oppressed by arbitrary roles and cultural stereotypes, the immediate logical response is to negate those roles and reject those stereotypes and to suspect any assertion that give them a special or qualitatively different character, just as one would reject such assertions made on the basis of cultural differences to avoid engaging in racism.

It may be a useful or necessary heuristic to take such a position at one moment in an analysis. It may offer the most compelling aspect of the analysis. I believe it is also the easiest—the one-dimensional project of "macho Marxists" (Pinar, 1994). And to let it stand without confronting the special meaning of age in articulating a theory that is intrinsically historical is to leave central problems unresolved, and these problems are not merely academic. On what basis, for example, does critical theory oppose the glib superficiality of some versions of "successful aging" or the vision of immortality offered by the "anti-aging industry" (see King & Calasanti, this volume, and also Beckman & Ames, 1998; Binstock, 2003; Kurzweil & Grossman, 2004; Olshansky, Hayflick, & Perls, 2004). While many proponents of the latter can be readily dismissed as crass profiteers, to focus only on its economic opportunism does not resolve the deeper tension between the possibility of social transformation that enhances the life chances of all, with the acceptance of the realities of physical suffering and death as essential elements in the life course (Kleinman, 2004).

Thus, the phenomena of aging pose a challenge to critical theory that is equally fundamental and ultimately more formidable than the challenge to social gerontology posed by critical theory. Ultimately, a critical theory of aging should aspire not only to an exposure of oppressive structures and ideological theories but to the articulation of an understanding of how to balance an assault on the "surplus suffering" produced by human ignorance and injustice with the recognition that physical and other personal suffering and loss are not only ultimately unavoidable but can be a source of human wisdom, strength, growth, and learning.

ACKNOWLEDGMENTS

I wish to thank the editors of this chapter, Elaine Dannefer, my coeditors Jan Baars, Chris Phillipson, and Alan Walker for comments on earlier versions of this chapter, and I also thank Lynn Gannon for editorial assistance.

REFERENCES

Achenbaum, W. A. (1991). "Time is the messenger of the Gods": A gerontologic metaphor. In J. E. Birren & G. Kenyon (Eds.), *Metaphors of aging in the sciences and humanities* (pp. 17-35). New York: Springer Publishing.

Andrews, M. (1991). Lifetimes of commitment: *Aging, politics, psychology.* New York: Cambridge University Press.

Ardelt, M. (2003). Empirical assessment of a three-dimensional wisdom scale. *Research on Aging, 25*(3), 275-324.

Atchley, R. C. (1999). *Continuity and adaptation in aging.* Baltimore: Johns Hopkins.

Atchley, R. C. (1997). Everyday mysticism: Spiritual development in everyday life. *Journal of Adult Development, 4,* 123-134.

Baars, J. (1991). The challenge of critical gerontology: The problem of social constitution. *Journal of Aging Studies, 5,* 219-243.

Baars, J., & Thomése, F. (1994). Communes of elderly people: Between independence and colonization. *Journal of Aging Studies, 8,* 341-356.

Baltes, P. B. (2004). Wisdom as orchestration of mind and virtue. Book in preparation. Berlin: Max Planck. Full text: http://www.mpib-berlin.mpg.de/dok/full/baltes/orchestr/index.htm.

Baltes, P. B., & Schaie, K. W. (1968). Longitudinal and cross sectional sequences in the study of age and generation effects. *Human Development, 11,* 145-171.

Baltes, P. B., & Staudinger, U. M. (2000). Wisdom: A metaheuristic (pragmatic) to orchestrate mind and virtue toward excellence. *American Psychologist, 55*(1), 122-136.

Baltes, P. B., Staudinger, U. M., & Lindenberger, U. (1999). Lifespan psychology: Theory and application to intellectual functioning. *Annual Review of Psychology, 50,* 471-507.

Baltes, P. B., Staudinger, U. M., Maercker, A., & Smith, J. (1993). *People nominated as wise: A comparative study of wisdom related knowledge.* Unpublished manuscript.

Bass, S. A., Kutza, E. A., & Torres-Gil, F. M. (Eds.). (1990). *Diversity in aging: Challenges facing planners and policymakers in the 1990s.* Glenview, IL: Scott, Foresman.

Beck, U., Giddens, A., & Lash, S. (1995). *Reflexive modernization.* Palo Alto, CA: Stanford.

Beck, U., & Camiller, P. (2000). *Brave new world of work.* Malden, MA: Polity/Blackwell.

Beckman, K. B., & Ames, B. N. (1998). The free radical theory of aging matters. *Physiological Reviews, 78,* 547-581.

Bengtson, V. L. (1973). *The social psychology of aging.* Indianapolis: Bobbs-Merrill.

Berger, P. L., Berger, B., & Kellner, H. (1973). *The homeless mind: Modernization and consciousness.* New York: Irvington Publishing.

Best, F. (1980). *Flexible life scheduling: Breaking the education-work-retirement lockstep.* Westport, CT: Praeger.

Bhavnani, K. K. (1990). What's power got to do with it? Empowerment and social research. In I. Parker & L. Shotter (Eds.), *Deconstructing social psychology.* London: Routledge.

Binstock, R. H. (2003). The war on anti-aging medicine. *The Gerontologist, 43,* 4-14.

Birren, J. E., & Fisher, L.E. (1990). The elements of wisdom: Overview and integration. In R. J. Sternberg (Ed.), *Wisdom: Its origins, nature and development* (pp. 317-332). Cambridge: Cambridge University Press.

Brayer, E. (1996). *George Eastman: A biography.* Baltimore: Johns Hopkins University Press.

Brokaw, T. (1998). *The greatest generation.* New York: Random House.

Butler, R. (1975). *Why survive? The tragedy of being old in America.* New York: HarperCollins.

Butler, R. N. (1963). The life review: An interpretation of reminiscence in the aged. *Psychiatry, 26,* 65-70.

Cain, L. D. (1964). Life course and social structure. In R. E. L. Faris (Ed.), *Handbook of modern sociology* (pp. 272-309). Chicago: Rand, McNally.

Caspi, A., & Moffitt, T. (1993). When do individual differences matter? A paradoxical theory of personality coherence. *Psychological Inquiry, 4,* 247-271.

Clayton, V. P., & Birren, J. E. (1982). The development of wisdom across the life span: A reexamination of an ancient topic. In P. B. Baltes & O. G. Brim, Jr. (Eds.), *Life-span development and behavior* (Vol. 3, pp. 103-135). New York: Academic.

Cohen, L. (2003). A *consumer's republic: The politics of mass consumption in postwar America.* New York: Knopf.

Cole, T. R. (1991). *The journey of life. A cultural history of aging in America.* New York: Cambridge.

Cole, T. R., & Gadow, S. (1986). *What does it mean to grow old? Reflections from the humanities.* Durham, NC: Duke University Press.

Cole, T. R., Achenbaum, W. A., Jakobi, P. L., & Kastenbaum, R. (Eds.). (1992). *Voices and visions of aging: Toward a critical gerontology.* New York: Springer Publishing.

Crystal, S. (2003, August). *Out of pocket health care expenditures by older Americans: Cumulative advantage, coverage, choice and equity.* Paper presented at the annual meeting of the American Sociological Association, Atlanta, GA.

Crystal, S., & Shea, D. (Eds.). (2003). *Focus on economic outcomes in later life: Public policy, health, and cumulative advantage.* New York: Springer Publishing.

Crystal, S., & Waehrer, K. (1996). Later-life economic inequality in longitudinal perspective. *Journal of Gerontology, 51,* S307-S318.

Daniels, N., Kennedy, B, Kawachi, I., Cohen, J., & Rogers, J. (2000). *Is inequality bad for our health?* New York: Beacon.

Dannefer, D. (1981). Neither socialization or recruitment: The avocational careers of old car enthusiasts. *Social Forces, 60,* 395-413.

Dannefer, D. (1987). Accentuation, the Matthew effect, and the life course: Aging as intracohort differentiation. *Sociological Forum, 2*, 211-236.

Dannefer, D. (1988). Differential gerontology and the stratified life course: Conceptual and methodological issues. In M. P. Lawton & G. L. Maddox (Eds.), *Annual review of gerontology and geriatrics* (8th ed.). New York: Springer Publishing.

Dannefer, D. (1989). Human action and its place in theories of aging. *Journal of Aging Studies, 3*, 1-20.

Dannefer, D. (1999). Freedom isn't free: Power, alienation and the consequences of action. In J. Brandstädter & R. M Lerner (Eds.), *Action and self development: Theory and research through the life course* (pp. 105-131). Thousand Oaks, CA: Sage.

Dannefer, D. (2003). Cumulative advantage/disadvantage and the life course: Cross fertilizing age and social science theory. *Journal of Gerontology, 58B*(6), S327-S337.

Dannefer, D., & Perlmutter, M. (1990). Human development as a multi-dimensional process: Individual and social constituents. *Human Development, 33*, 108-137.

Ekerdt, D. (2003). *Can't take it with you: Age and consumption.* Section on Aging and the Life Course Invited Symposium, American Sociological Association Annual Meeting, Atlanta.

Elder, G. H. (1999). *Children of the Great Depression.* Boulder, CO: Westview.

Estes, C. (1979). *The aging enterprise.* San Francisco: Jossey-Bass.

Ewen, S. (1976). *Captains of consciousness: Advertising and the social roots of consumer culture.* New York: Basic.

Ewen, S. (1999). *All consuming images: The politics of style in contemporary culture.* New York: Basic.

Farmer, P. (2001). *Infections and inequalities.* Berkeley: University of California Press.

Foner, A. (1974). Age stratification and age conflict in political life. *American Sociological Review, 39*, 187-196.

Ford, H. (1926). *Today and tomorrow.* (In collaboration with Samuel Crowther.) New York: Doubleday.

Ferraro, K. F, & Kelley-Moore, J. A. (2003). Cumulative disadvantage and health: Long-term consequences of obesity? *American Sociological Review, 68*(5), 707-729.

Gergen, K. (1991). *The saturated self.* New York: Basic.

Gilleard, C., & Higgs, P. (2001). *Cultures of aging: Self, citizen and the body.* New York: Prentice-Hall.

Gubrium, J. (1975). *Living and dying at Murray Manor.* New York: St. Martin's Press.

Gubrium, J. (1976). Notes on the social organization of senility. *Urban Life, 7*, 23-44.

Habermas, J. (1978). *Knowledge and human interests* (J. J. Shapiro, Trans.). London: Heinemann Educational.

Hagestad, G. (1992, November). *Aging in international perspective.* Paper presented at thematic session, annual meeting of the Gerontological Society of America, Washington, DC.

Hagestad, G., & Dannefer, D. (2001). Concepts and theories of aging: Beyond microfication in social science approaches. *Handbook of aging and the social sciences* (5th ed., pp. 3-21). San Diego: Academic Press.

Heinz, W. R. (2002). Self-socialization and post-traditional society. In R. A. Settersten & T. J. Owens (Eds.), *New frontiers in socialization* (pp. 41-64). Oxford: Elsevier.

Hickey, T. (1980). *Health and aging*. Monterey, CA: Brooks/Cole.

Kastenbaum, R. (1992). Encrusted elders: Arizona and the political spirit of postmodern aging. In T. R. Cole, W. A. Achenbaum, P. L. Jakobi, & R. Kastenbaum (Eds.), *Voices and visions of aging: Toward a critical gerontology* (pp. 160-183). New York: Springer Publishing.

Kaufman, S. (1986). *The ageless self: Sources of meaning in late life*. Madison: University of Wisconsin Press.

Kenyon, G. (1991). Homo viator: Metaphors of aging, authenticity and meaning. In J. E. Birren & G. Kenyon (Eds.), *Metaphors of aging in the sciences and humanities* (pp. 83-101). New York: Springer Publishing.

Kleinman, A. (2004, March). *Who we are: Illness and other dangers to everyday moral experience*. Lecture delivered at Medical Humanities 2004, Case Western Reserve University.

Kurzweil, R., & Grossman, T. (2004). *Fantastic voyage: Live long enough to live forever*. Emmaus, PA: Rodale Books.

Lamme, S., & Baars, J. (1993). Including social factors in the analysis of reminiscence in elderly individuals. *International Journal of Aging and Human Development, 37*, 297-311.

Lasch, C. (1979). *Culture of narcissism: American life in an age of diminishing expectations*. New York: Norton.

Light, J., Grigsby, J. S., & Bligh, M. C. (1996). Aging and heterogeneity: Genetics, social structure, and personality. *The Gerontologist, 36*, 165-173.

Maddox, G. L., & Lawton, M. P. (Eds.). (1988). *Annual review of gerontology and geriatrics (Vol. 8): Varieties of aging*. New York: Springer Publishing.

Marmot, M. (2004). *The status syndrome: How social standing affects our health and longevity*. New York: Times Books.

Marquié, J. C., Cau-Bareille, D. P., & Volkoff, S. (Eds.). (1998). *Working with age*. Bristol, PA: Taylor & Francis.

Marshall, V. (1980). *Last chapters: A sociology of aging and dying*. Belmont, CA: Wadsworth.

Marshall, V., & Tindale, J. (1978). Notes for a radical gerontology. *International Journal of Aging and Human Development, 9*, 163-175.

Marx, K. [1852] (1972). The eighteenth brumaire of Louis Bonaparte. In R. C. Tucker (Ed.), *The Marx-Engels Reader* (pp. 436-525). New York: W. W. Norton.

McNaught, W. (1994). Realizing the potential: Some examples. In M. W. Riley, R. L. Kahn, & A. Foner (Eds.), *Age and structural lag: Society's failure to provide meaningful opportunities in work, family, and leisure* (pp. 219-236). New York: John Wiley & Sons.

Moody, H. R. (1988). Toward a critical gerontology: The contribution of the humanities to theories of aging. In J. E. Birren & V. L. Bengtson (Eds.), *Emergent theories of aging*. New York: Springer Publishing.

Moody, H. R. (1996). Critical theory and critical gerontology. In G. L. Maddox (Ed.), *The encyclopedia of aging* (2nd ed., pp. 244-245). New York: Springer Publishing.

Neugarten, B. L. (1983). *Interpretive social science and research on aging*. Paper presented at the annual meeting of the American Sociological Association, Detroit.

Olshansky, S. J., Hayflick, L., & Perls, T. T. (2004). Anti-aging medicine: The hype and the reality—Part II. *Journal of Gerontology, 59A*(7), 649-651.

O'Rand, A. (1996). The precious and the precocious: The cumulation of advantage and disadvantage over the life course. *Gerontologist, 36*, 230-238.

O'Rand, A. M., & Henretta, J. C. (1999). *Age and inequality: Diverse pathways through later life.* Boulder, CO: Westview Press.

Pallas, A. M. (2002). Educational participation across the life course: Do the rich get richer? In R. A. Settersten & T. J. Owens New Frontiers in Socialization (pp . 327-354). Oxford: Elsevier.

Pasupathi, M., Staudinger, U. M., & Baltes, P. B. (2001). Seeds of wisdom: Adolescents' knowledge and judgment about difficult life problems. *Developmental Psychology, 37*, 351-361.

Phillipson, C. (1982). *Capitalism and the construction of old age.* New York: Macmillan.

Pinar, W. F. (1994). *Autobiography, politics and sexuality: Essays in curriculum theory 1972-1992.* New York: Peter Lanz.

Preston, S. (1984). Aging and cohort succession: Interpretations and misinterpretations. *Public Opinion Quarterly, 37*, 35-49.

Riley, M. W. (1978). Aging social change and the power of ideas. *Daedaelus, 107*, 39-52.

Riley, M. W., & Riley, J. W. (1994). Age integration and the lives of older people. *The Gerontologist, 34*(1), 110-115.

Rosow, I. (1967). *Social integration of the aged.* New York: Free Press.

Schaie, K. W. (1965). A general model for the study of developmental change. *Psychological Bulletin, 64*, 92-107.

Staudinger, U. M. (in press). Weisheit, lebens- und selbsteinsicht [Wisdom, life insight and self insight]. In H. Weber & T. Rammseyer (Hrsg.), *Handbuch der psychologie.* Göttingen: Hogrefe.

Staudinger, U. M. (1998). What predicts wisdom-related performance? A first look at personality, intelligence, and facilitative experiential contexts. *European Journal of Personality, 12*(1), 1-17.

Staudinger, U. M. (1999). Older and wiser? Integrating results on the relationship between age and wisdom-related performance. *International Journal of Behavioral Development, 23*(3), 641-664.

Stein, P. (2003). *Social life under the evacuation of culture: Lost minds, demented selves and social solidarities.* Unpublished doctoral dissertation, University of Rochester.

Streib, G. F. (1993). The life course of activities and retirement communities. In J. R. Kelley (Ed.), *Activity and aging: Staying involved in later life* (pp. 246-264). Newbury Park, CA: Sage.

Thomas, W. H. (2004). *What are old people for? How elders will save the world.* Acton, MA: Vanderwyk & Burnham.

Turner, R. H. (1976). The real self: From institution to impulse. *The American Journal of Sociology, 81*(5), 989-1016.

Uhlenberg, P. (1978). Changing configurations of the life course. In T. Hareven (Ed.), *Transitions: The family and the life course in historical perspective* (pp. 65-97). New York: Academic.

Walker, A. (1981). Towards a political economy of old age. *Aging and Society, 1*, 73-94.

Weiland, S. (1989). Aging according to biography. *The Gerontologist, 29*, 191-194.
Weiland, S. (1993). Criticism between literature and gerontology. In T. R. Cole, W. A. Achenbaum, P. L. Jakobi, & R. Kastenbaum (Eds.), *Voices and visions of aging: Toward a critical gerontology* (pp. 76-104). New York: Springer Publishing.
Wexler, P. (1977). Comment on Ralph Turner's "The real self: From institution to impulse." *The American Journal of Sociology, 83*(1), 178-186.
Wexler, P. (1983). *Critical social psychology.* London: Routledge.

SECTION 2

Critical Dimensions of Medicalization: Aging and Health as Cultural Products

CHAPTER 7

From Chronology to Functionality: Critical Reflections on the Gerontology of the Body

Stephen Katz

The term "blurred genres," the symposium theme, under which the chapters in this volume were brought together, is a keyword for anthropologist Clifford Geertz. Twenty years ago Geertz observed that the social sciences and humanities were exchanging and transgressing intellectual boundaries, and creating a "refiguration of social thought" (1983), or what others referred to as "the interpretive turn" in social thinking. Interpretive theorists drew upon European critical philosophies (phenomenology, hermeneutics, Frankfurt School Marxism, Bakhtinian semiotics), Kuhnian models of paradigmatic science, and later postmodern, feminist, and global frameworks to undermine the positivist ideals and sterile instrumental reason of professional fields and reintroduce subjective meaning at all levels of analysis.

In a less grand fashion within gerontology, interpretive and critical thinkers have steadily challenged individualist and masculinist life course models, biomedical priorities, and neoconservative political agendas (Moody, 1993; Ray, 1999). In the late 1980s and 1990s, the political economy of aging underscored gender, regional, racial, and ethnic inequalities as widespread structural problems (Minkler & Estes, 1984, 1991, 1999). British sociologists Mike Featherstone, Mike Hepworth, and others looked to the work of Georg Simmel and sociologists of the body to critique consumer capitalist constructions of aging lifestyles (Featherstone & Hepworth, 1991, 1998), while humanities scholars in North America created an exciting Age Studies subfield bringing fictional, performative, poetic, and narrative perspectives to bear on traditional problems of self, memory, biography, and identity (Basting, 1998; Biggs, 1999; Blaikie, 1999; Cole & Ray, 2000; Featherstone & Wernick, 1995; Gilleard & Higgs, 2000; Gullette, 1997; Hepworth, 2000; Woodward, 1999). Since the 1990s, reflexive writers have also rethought gerontology's intellectual progress, placing it within instructive frameworks of "generations," "phases," and "periods" of theorizing (Bengtson, Burgess, & Parrot, 1997; Bengtson, Parrot, & Burgess, 1996; Bond, Biggs, & Coleman, 1990; Hendricks, 1992; Lynott & Lynott, 1996; Marshall, 1999). In short, as Victor Marshall puts it, gerontological theory can be understood as "stories about theories, theorizing and theorists" (1999, p. 435; see also Achenbaum, 1995; Cole, 1992).

However, my question has less to do with the story of gerontological thought than with the reflexive life of gerontological research. In previous writing (Katz, 2003) I engaged in this exercise of reflexivity by borrowing from Pierre Bourdieu his critical analytics of "fields" and theoretical methodology of "fieldwork in philosophy" (Bourdieu, 1990), and from Michel Foucault his critical attitude of "genealogy." Foucault (1977), inspired by Nietzsche's *On the Genealogy of Morals*, sought the momentous events of Western culture "in the most unpromising places, in what we tend to feel is without history"; thus genealogy, says Foucault, "operates on a field of entangled and confused parchments" (p. 139). Hence, in my chronicling of gerontological "handbooks," I examined the "entangled and confused" textual codes, vocabularies, literary designs, and rhetorics by which gerontology represents itself as an authority on aging (Katz, 2000a). In a related study, I traced the currency of the master concept "activity" in gerontology as it circulates as a theoretical model, a cultural ideal, an empirical instrument, a healthcare regime, a political rationality, and a discursive resource (Katz, 2000b). In these writings, I was struck by how ideas overflow their sanctioned boundaries, defy theoretical stasis, wander unpredictably between metaphor and fact, and default on their assigned places in scientific progress. Above all my work on the disciplinary structuring of gerontology seemed to suggest that a genealogical field approach fits well with a critical curiosity about the life of ideas, their social contingencies, and their practical consequences.

My current research involves a critique of how binary concepts of "function" and "dysfunction" have been mobilized in gerontological and sexological research (Katz & Marshall, 2003; Marshall & Katz, 2002). Here too I think we have a case for reflexive, theoretical fieldwork and an opportunity to traipse around the genealogy of ideas. In this chapter I wish to extend these ideas further and ask how and why the idea of "functionality" and its correlates—"functional age" and "functional health"—have become so ubiquitous in gerontology. In addressing this question, the argument below explores the professional transformation of aging in the body from a chronological to a functional process.

THE FUNCTIONAL AGING BODY

Functio (Latin): The action of performing, executing a task, expressing an attribute, administering a policy.

At the outset the idea of functionality as a modern instrument for measuring and standardizing the body is not new. In both nineteenth-century medicine and twentieth-century industrial studies of work and age, the mind and body were portrayed as part of a single somatic system under the sign of functionality. For instance, in *Medical Aspects of Old Age* (1922), Sir Humphrey Rolleston, President of the Royal College of Physicians in London, uses the term "functional" solely in relation to productive "activity" or labor. In the following passage, Rolleston (1922) is concerned with the decline of a worker's functional activity outside of his state of health.

> Although functional activity maintains the tissues in a state of health, it is not an infallible panacea for the prolongation of life; in the first place the danger of overwork and excessive fatigue must be borne in mind. (p. 54)

> Further functional activity while keeping the cells of the body in a healthy state depends on their structural integrity, and this in its turn is the outcome of the modifications due to environment, and possibly of the inborn lease of vitality. So that although an active life may within limits prolong life, there are many instances in which, from extrinsic pathological influences or inherent inadequacy, it fails to do so, and a man becomes unequal to the demands of his position. (p. 55)

Over thirty years later, A. T. Welford's *Ageing and Human Skill* (1958), published as a research survey for The Nuffield Foundation in Britain, also merged functional abilities with labor activities. Indeed, the problem for Welford was how to differentiate between human and mechanical functional breakdowns and determine the causal relationship between the two. There are many other examples of government studies and industrial reports which, in the interests of maximizing productivity, mapped the body's functionally interconnected regions in order to render human capacities knowable and governable (see Von Mayrhauser, 1989).

At the same time, since their emergence in the nineteenth century, geriatrics and gerontology have given the static functions of the body a scientifically observable temporal dimension apart from traditionally spiritual, cultural, and symbolic meanings. Jean-Martin Charcot, one of the most influential medical figures of the nineteenth century and founder of clinical gerontology at the Salpêtrière hospital in Paris, insisted in *Clinical Lectures on the Diseases of Old Age* (Charcot & Loomis, 1881), that his "new physiology . . . absolutely refuses to look upon life as a mysterious and supernatural influence" but rather "purposes to bring all the vital manifestations of a complex organism to workings of certain apparatuses" (p. 20). Part of this scientific initiative for Charcot and those who followed was to plot the aging process along well-defined life events and chronological transitions. Indeed, the establishment of the chronological age of old age and statistical lifespan probabilities distinguished the sciences of aging from premodern medicine and its fanciful ideas about longevity (Katz, 1995). The welfare programs and service economies that arose in the nineteenth and twentieth centuries also used age to create new social and economic groupings apart from earlier kinship and regional traditions (Chudacoff, 1989). Hence, the "ages of" military recruitment, schooling, retirement, etc. became institutionalized within the bureaucracies of a modern life-course regime and the biopolitics of populational rule.

In the later twentieth century, the life sciences began to reconsider chronological age as an obstacle to gerontological research, however, because the concept lacked predictive value, empirical exactitude, methodological validity, and conceptual rigor.[1] Today researchers agree that, despite the ambivalent but rich cultural status accrued to the age of 65 over the last two centuries, 65 as the supposed onset of later life, as with any other age for that matter, is of questionable scientific utility. As leading gerontologist James Birren states, "chronological age is only an index, and unrelated sets of data show correlations with chronological age that have no intrinsic or causal relationship with each other. Thus a goal of theory and research is to replace chronological age with variables that reflect the *causes* of change we initially identify as being closely related to chronological age" (1999, p. 460). Gerontologists, beginning with I. M. Murray (1951) and later Heron and Chown (1967), had already started to work toward Birren's "goal." They claimed that in order to understand the causes of aging, several "ages" were required, along with a new point of articulation emanating from the body—*functional age.*

Murray's paper is credited with first advancing a functionalist, physiological concept of age over a chronological one: "It is well known that chronologic age is not necessarily the same as physiologic age. Physiologic age implies an assessment of the functional capacities of an individual by reference to standards derived from healthy persons of the same chronologic age as the person who is being tested" (1951, p. 120). Here the standardization of functional capacities—visual, auditory, blood pressure, hand grip—are basic, quantifiable, and compounded into the master standard of physiologic age. Murray's research with an all-male group of 21–84 year olds at Dalhousie University demonstrated that physiologic and chronologic ages varied relative to each other, producing in the end a measurable "age" based on "functions" which would be, notes Murray, not only advantageous to researchers but also to life insurance companies. However, Murray's functions are not absolute norms set against deviating pathologies. Rather, they are calculable instances of variation that culminate in the physiological materialization of the aging body. Age is a product of function, and in Murray's research "a man would not be judged physiologically older or younger unless his physiologic age differed by more than +/- 14.7 years from the chronologic age" (p. 123). Murray's methodological work, and that of other biogerontologists, was praised

---

[1] Philosophical and critical gerontologists have also found fault with gerontology's reliance on chronological age, proposing instead more subjective and plural notions of aging in time (see Baars, 1997).

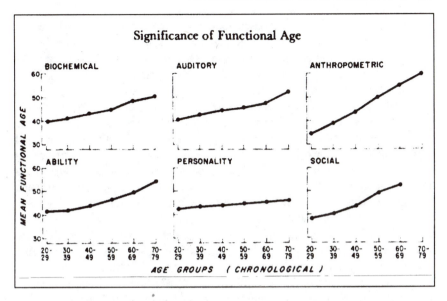

Figure 1. Chronological age profiles of six functional ages:
biochemical, auditory, anthropometric, ability, personality, and social.
Source: Bell (1972, p. 147).

for revealing how individuals of similar chronological ages could have different physiological ages.

Beginning in 1963, these ideas about functional age were elaborated and tested in a major gerontological undertaking called The Normative Aging Study (NAS), conducted at the American Veterans Administration Outpatient Clinic in Boston. Results of the study were gathered into a special issue of the journal *Aging & Human Development* in 1972 (3 [2]); thus, they are worth briefly reviewing in light of their assessment of how health status is configured by functional states. The journal's editorial, "Is Functional Age Functional?" poses functional age as the alternative to chronological age, but also asks: "Are we ready, as a society, to base age-related decisions upon scientific findings rather than tradition and expediency? Are we ready to make individual rather than class decisions?" (p. 143). Benjamin Bell (1972), director of the Boston clinic, responds to this challenge in the affirmative. He states that "we are looking for a unifying concept which would enable the measurement of aging in its various aspects, and the relative rates of age change, both across these areas and over the lifespan. Such a concept might provide a cohesive force in motivating the diverse disciplines to function as a team" (Bell, 1972, p. 145). Bell's unifying concept includes psychological and behavioral as well as biological functions.

Specifically, the NAS study used four indices of functional ages based on biological measurements, sensory and motor abilities, and two more based on "a multifactor description of personality" and "a set of sociological assessments of life style pertaining to family, work, and retirement" (Bell, 1972, p. 146). If the body can be broken down into regions of functionality determined by testable and codifiable biostandards of measurable performance, then the logic of functional health can be extended to a person's whole life and its alignment to the practicalities of professional and commercial interventions. As for Murray, Bell sees the quantitative world of correlations and statistical relationships arising from the NAS research as creating a "practical significance in providing guidelines of the actuarial field, for planning in behalf of aged population in such matters as equipment, housing, health care, and economic assistance, to indicate therapeutic intervention, and to design optimal conditions for working and retirement" (Bell, 1972, p. 147). Such social parameters of functional age are more pronounced in the paper by Rose (1972), a contributing sociologist to the journal who invents "social age" as "a changing composite of social life styles, attributes, and attitudes at various points of the life cycle" (p. 153). Social age is not reducible to chronological age and is "therefore a special case of a larger concept of functional age. . . . Just as an individual may be younger or older in the way he functions socially, so he may also have a psychological or physiological functional age" (Rose, 1972, p. 153). Rose (1972) also implied that the technical batteries and tests used to measure physiological functions are adaptable to social functions, so that, "one is socially old before his time if, relative to the respective age norms, he is more settled in his job, staves off retirement, has a working wife, does not plan to relocate, and sees less of his relatives" (pp. 162-163).

There were several obvious problems with the NAS project. In terms of its empirical research, as Bookstein and Achenbaum (1993) note, the NAS failed to create the sophisticated and durable tools of measurement necessary to fulfill the promise of functional age as a major conceptual breakthrough in gerontology (p. 37). Furthermore, the supposedly objective and population-wide functional standards promoted by the researchers, based on the all-male NAS sample of 2000 mostly healthy veterans aged 28–83, were tainted with the industrialist, masculinist, and familialistic biases of the time. While follow-up research on functional age ensued with more refined, accurate, and culturally nuanced test batteries, (Chappell, Gee, McDonald, & Stones, 2003, pp. 180-181), so did the internal criticisms (Costa & McCrae, 1985; Spiriduso, 1995, pp. 49-52). In particular, the critics stressed four problems. First, it is erroneous to presume that there are uniform rates of aging across different systems, and that such rates correlate to single standards of biological age. Second, gerontology has not really abandoned chronological age, nor could it hope to do so. As Spiriduso (1995) notes, "most critics of multiple regression research on biological age find it ironic that researchers have turned to test batteries of attributes and performances because they are dissatisfied with chronological age as a marker of biological age.

Yet, these researchers base the validity of their biomarkers on the correlation of these markers to chronological age!" (p. 49; see also Fry, 1999, p. 276). Third, rates of aging, even when functionally isolated to specific bodily regions or processes, change over time. Therefore, test results showing a "young heart" and slower-than-average age rate for an individual are far more likely to be due to the interaction between physical and external factors than to physical factors alone. Fourth, different researchers use different combinations of different test-battery criteria. For this reason, according to Spiriduso (1995), "the biological age batteries developed for humans to date have not improved much upon chronological age as a descriptor of the aging process, nor can they successfully predict aging rate. No unitary biomarker has been identified that can predict aging of individuals across several physiological and psychological systems" (p. 52). Given these and other criticisms, the question arises as to whether or not functional age actually exists at all. Indeed, in a Position Statement on Human Aging published in an issue of *Scientific American* that cited fifty-one leading researchers on issues of aging and anti-aging, a sidebar titled "Determining Biological Age": "Despite intensive study, scientists have not been able to discover reliable measures of the processes that contribute to aging. For these reasons, any claim that a person's biological or 'real age' can currently be measured, let alone modified, by any means must be regarded as entertainment, not science" (May 13, 2002).

Despite the internal debate, the concept of functional age seems to have expanded throughout the twentieth and twenty-first centuries. The professional enthusiasm for its potential to measure, standardize, and materialize the aging body, while justifying a new inventory of risks and interventions appropriate to aging individuals, outweighs its conceptual limitations. Functional age also drives the imperative to biologize the aging process apart from chronological aging by coordinating the body's biomarkers. Biomarkers are defined in the recent *Encyclopedia of Aging* (2002) in the following way: "The assumptions that underlie the concept of biomarkers of aging are that organisms age at different rates and thus chronological age is not a good predictor of remaining life expectancy, that different tissues, organs, and organ systems within an organism may age at different rates, that these differences can be measured and predicted, and finally that it may be possible to alter the rate of aging of any or all of the components of organisms" (Sprott, 2002, p. 133). The fact that there is a general division in geriatrics and gerontology today between "disease-oriented" and "function-oriented" approaches also indicates the practical utility of functional age, especially to health promotion programs aimed at healthy aging in areas of mobility, cognition, and social activities. In turn, these activities are measured and tested by a broad set of instruments, such as the popular ADL (Activities of Daily Living) checklists first proposed in 1959, the IADL (Instrumental Activities of Daily Living) in the late 1960s, and the more recent ALSAR (Assessment of Living Skills and Resources), and the Standardized

Test of Fitness developed in Canada. These instruments typically examine the functions of daily life (toileting, dressing, eating, mobility, etc.), highlight their dysfunctional impediments (disease, disability, environmental limitations), and identify possible interventions (physiotherapy, service plans, fitness programs, residential care). There is also a range of cognitive tests, such as clock drawing and the Folstein Mini-Mental test. If one scans the *Abstracts in Social Gerontology* for a snapshot of current research on aging, one would find subheadings under "functional states" that include: disability, environmental stressors, hearing and vision loss, urinary incontinence, environmental adaptability, physical and social mobility, sleep disorders, depression, communication disorders, exercise regimes, risk of death, musculo-skeletal measurements, alcohol consumption, menopause, all forms of cognitive impairment (and psychological dysfunctions), racial and gender groupings, hospitalization, osteoporosis, genetic influences, smoking, sexual health and activity, arthritis and chronic pain, levels of self-esteem, and loneliness. Every kind of common activity however disparate—taking medication, shopping, sitting in a rocking chair, staring into space—are folded into activity studies related to functional health or one of its functional or dysfunctional correlates (see Katz, 2000b). As one abstracted study (Scott, 1995) concludes: "For clinicians working with the geriatric population, one word is becoming the basis of evaluation and rehabilitation: function" *(Abstracts in Social Gerontology,* 1996, p. 167).[2]

Ultimately, the language of functional testing is geared toward independent living and its problematizations. Terms such as "successful," "healthy," and "productive" aging are used interchangeably and premised on empirically driven agendas for avoiding dependency. "Dependency-free life expectancy" is also referred to as "health life expectancy," "active life expectancy," "disability-free life expectancy," and "functional life expectancy" (Chappell et al., 2003, p. 12). However, as noted earlier, the issue of successful living is closely integrated with neoliberal health agendas centered on individualized lifestyle choices, risk management, and self-care skills. The biosocial rationalities of functional age and independent living correspond therefore. Supporting this correspondence are the bioidentities by which people can know themselves as functional selves and participate in a gerontological culture of enablement.

---

[2] Disability research followed a similar route, where, since the 1970s, new definitions and daily-activity testing of functional health were used to evaluate intervention and service needs (Williams & Busby, 2000). A noted difference between disability and gerontological studies is that the former have adapted critical, phenomenological, feminist, and social inequality theories to contest the deficit models and service-based clientelism of disability research practices.

THE FUNCTIONAL AGING SELF

In the 1972 special issue of *Aging & Human Development* on functional age, gerontologist Robert Kastenbaum and coresearchers posit that there is a subjective reality to functional age, determined by correlating the degree of "consensuality" between "personal age" indicators (based on self-reporting status) and "interpersonal age" indicators (based on status viewed by others) (1972, pp. 197-211). By administering an interview schedule called the "ages of me" to a sample of 75 adults aged 20–69, the researchers find that personal age tends to be viewed as younger than chronological age, with the gap increasing further up the chronological scale (p. 206). Their work is important because it introduces subjectivity as a component in the determination of functional age, whereby people acquire the self-skills and professional vocabularies to judge themselves as functional. Released by scientific gerontology from the uncertainties of chronological age, the subjects of the "ages of me" study are free to embrace youth-based self-conceptions and treat functional age as a mediation point between self and body. In their conclusions, the authors ask: "Is it "healthy" or "pathological" to embrace an ever-more-youthful self-conception as one grows older?" (p. 210). In this case, however, standards of healthy, normal, or pathological have little to do with the adjudication of functional or dysfunctional states or their subjective manifestations because functional aging and health are flexible and relative ideals, modifiable through personal actions, attitudes, and lifestyle practices. In gerontology, as in other life sciences where the functional/dysfunctional grid underpins new orders of biosociality,[3] the self and its bio-identities are constitutive elements in gerontological, methodological, networking, informational, professional, and commercial enterprises. In particular, issues of functional identities and aging selves can be illustrated with reference to the research on self-reporting and functional health literacy.

Self-Reporting

A longstanding technique in qualitative gerontological research is self-reporting, whereby participants are asked to self-rate or self-evaluate selected aspects of their everyday activities or life-course careers (He, Colantonio, & Marshall, 2003; Herzog & Markus, 1999; Leinonen, Heikkinen, & Jylhä, 2001; *The Gerontologist*, 2003, pp. 369-411). While discrepancies between the researchers' expectations and their subjects' self-reports can sometimes emerge (e.g., Russell, Hill, & Basser, 1996) along with variations in cross-cultural settings

[3] The term "biosociality" is taken from Paul Rabinow, who uses it to express the contemporary condition in which the fluidity of conventional boundaries between the real and the artificial, the human and the instrumental, and the technoscientific forms of life appear neither natural nor cultural, yet both at the same time. Rabinow argues that in the future, "nature will become known and remade through technique and will finally become artificial, just as culture becomes natural" (1996, p. 99).

(Lee & Shinkai, 2003), self-rated health, depending on how it is coded, is valued as an important predictive indicator of an individual's health status. For instance, in the Nun Study on aging and Alzheimer's Disease carried out in 1991–1993 and 1993–1994, self-rated function meant "the ability to take care of oneself" (Greiner, Snowdon, & Greiner, 1996; see also Snowdon, 2001). The researchers, satisfied with the results, deduced that self-reporting made people in this study more aware of their functional abilities than of their overall health status. However, in other areas the self-reporting of functional health status has created new problems because the self-skills required to differentiate between general health status and functional health status are haphazard. Concepts of functionality first need to be embodied and enacted in everyday contexts in order for subjects then to narrate, reflect upon, evaluate, and assess their status in a vocabulary of expertise (see Gubrium & Holstein, 1998). Thus, several studies repeatedly argue that self-reporting of functional health runs aground because of incongruities between what people say they do and what they actually do (Glass, 1998). Research subjects, particularly in professional research studies, often conspire to make their lives fit the research design by reinterpreting their functional abilities according to its standards. Not surprisingly, many ADL and related self-rated surveys contain measurement errors and inconsistent subjective responses (Rodgers & Miller, 1997).

The theoretical problem of matching self-skills and functional age research is rarely addressed in the literature, nor is the challenge to research subjects to divide their lives into narrow, observable, and standardized zones of functionality. After all, how does one know oneself as functional? How can the activities of everyday life be translated into measurable units leading to interventionist strategies? And even if self-reports question what a person can do, they bypass the question of what a person likes to do or resists doing. In the relevant context of disability, Williams & Busby (2000) remark:

> Measures of health, disability, well-being and quality of life . . . provide a picture of "activities of daily living" devoid of a phenomenological grasp of the individual's own experience, on the one hand and any political analysis of the structures and contexts within which the activity takes place on the other. (p. 171)

Rather, the professionals avoid these and other issues by prioritizing only those self-skills assigned to comprehending subjective functional health status according to authoritative codes of health literacy.

Health Literacy

The skills required to read and understand health-related literature, pharmaceutical products, physicians' instructions, homecare schedules, and therapeutic procedures are typically referred to as health literacy. In contemporary gerontological health promotion campaigns, health literacy and physician-patient communication are seen as key determinants of disease management and prevention (Nutbeam, 2000; Shillinger, 2001), thus various health literacy tests have been devised to support this contention (Baker, Williams, Parker, Gazmararian, & Nurss 1999; Casiano, Paddon-Jones, Ostir, & Sheffield-Moore, 2002). The close connection between being functionally healthy and functionally literate means that individual responsibility has become an expansive resource for establishing neoliberal health networks. For example, Don Nutbeam (2000) argues that for health literacy to be a successful public health goal and "promote greater independence and empowerment among the individuals and communities we work with" (p. 267), functional literacy levels of competence need to be broadened to include "interactional" and "critical" skills. Despite the critical evidence showing that health literacy and associated promotional skills are embedded in class, gender, racial, and regional inequalities and hierarchical forms of cultural capital (Abel, Cockerham, & Niemann, 2000; Blaxter, 2000; Lumme-Standt & Virtanen, 2002), functional health literacy, as with functional status self-reporting, is held aloft as a self-skill that permits the aging individual entry into the privileged and professionally approved realm of quality-of-life autonomy and choice making. Central to this process is the construction of lifestyle as an all-encompassing refuge for the inculcation of risk-management and health promotion ideals. Indeed, a lifestyle is "healthy," "successful," and "active" only when it is capable of linking together functional bodies, literate selves, responsible lives, empowered communities, and public health agendas. Hence, lifestyles have also become classified and measurable through the same codes of functionality applied to individuals and populations (e.g., Chumbler, Foster, Grimm, & Williams, 2000).

CONCLUSIONS

This study has taken a reflexive, genealogical approach to gerontology's shift from chronological to functional notions of age. This shift is significant for what it may signal about the priorities of quantifiable and measurable states of being and their alignment to neoliberal health mandates around activity, enablement, self-care, and independence. Constructed through exhaustive batteries of tests, aggregations of data, scales, indices, and self-reports, such states set the bio-markers of human life and join other life sciences and biosocial rationalities which implicate the individual as an active participant in striving toward new collective ideals of successful aging. Critical gerontology thus faces the important task of questioning the role of functionality as it constitutes dominant ways of knowing about the aging process. Geertz (1983) had cautioned that the refiguration of social thought, "represents a sea change in our notion not so much of what knowledge is but of what it is we want to know" (p. 34). Similarly, my argument has been to suggest that the intellectual opportunities of working in "blurred genres" should inspire us to critique the power of taken-for-granted ideas in

gerontology and glimpse not only "what it is we want to know" but also how
we might know it imaginatively and reflexively.

REFERENCES

Abel, T., Cockerham, W. C., & Niemann, S. (2000). A critical approach to lifestyle and
    health. In. J. Watson & S. Platt (Eds.), *Researching health promotion* (pp. 54-77).
    London & New York: Routledge.
Abstracts in Social Gerontology. (1996). Ankles, functional assessment, knees, physical
    imbalance, rehabilitation, *39*(4), 167.
Achenbaum, W. A. (1995). *Crossing frontiers: Gerontology emerges as a science.* New
    York: Cambridge University Press.
Baars, J. (1997). Concepts of time and narrative temporality in the study of aging. *Journal
    of Aging Studies, 11*(4), 283-295.
Baker, D. W., Williams, M. V., Parker, R. M., Gazmararian, J. A., & Nurss, J. (1999).
    Development of a brief test to measure functional health literacy. *Patient Education
    and Counseling, 38*(1), 33-42.
Basting, A. D. (1998). *The stages of age: Performing age in contemporary American
    culture.* Ann Arbor: University of Michigan Press.
Bell, B. (1972). Significance of functional age for interdisciplinary and longitudinal
    research on aging. *Aging & Human Development, 3*(2), 145-148.
Bengtson, V. L., Parrott, T. M., & Burgess, E. O. (1996). Progress and pitfalls in
    gerontological theorizing. *The Gerontologist, 36*(6), 768-722.
Bengtson, V. L., Burgess, E. O., & Parrott, T. M. (1997). Theory, explanation, and a third
    generation of theoretical development in social gerontology. *Journal of Gerontology,
    52B*(2), S72-S88.
Biggs, S. (1999). *The mature imagination.* Buckingham: Open University Press.
Birren, J. E. (1999). Theories of aging: A personal perspective. In V. L. Bengtson & K. W.
    Schaie (Eds.), *Handbook of theories of aging* (pp. 459-471). New York: Springer
    Publishing.
Blaikie, A. (1999). *Ageing and popular culture.* Cambridge University Press.
Blaxter, M. (2000). Class, time and biography. In S. J. Williams, J. Gabe, & M. Calnan
    (Eds.), *Health, medicine and society: Key theories, future agendas* (pp. 27-50). London
    & New York: Routledge.
Bond, J., Biggs, R., & Coleman, P. (1990). The study of aging. In J. Bond & P. Coleman
    (Eds.), *Aging in society: An introduction to social gerontology* (pp. 17-47). London:
    Sage.
Bookstein, F. L., & Achenbaum, W. A. (1993). Aging as explanation: How scientific
    measurement can advance critical gerontology. In T. R. Cole, W. A. Achenbaum, P. L.
    Jakobi, & R. Kastenbaum (Eds.), *Voices and visions of aging: Toward a critical
    gerontology* (pp. 20-45). New York: Springer Publishing.
Bourdieu, P. (1990). Fieldwork in philosophy (Interview). In P. Bourdieu (Ed.), *In other
    words: Towards a reflexive sociology* (pp. 3-33). Stanford University Press.
Casiano, E. R., Paddon-Jones, D., Ostir, G. V., & Sheffield-Moore, M. (2002). Assessing
    functional status measures in older adults: A guide for healthcare professionals.
    Physical Therapy Reviews, 7(2), 89-101.

Chappell, N., Gee, E., McDonald, L., & Stones, M. (2003). *Aging in contemporary Canada*. Toronto: Prentice-Hall.

Charcot, J-M., & Loomis, A. L. (1881). *Clinical lectures on the diseases of old age*. (L. H. Hunt, Trans.). New York: William Wood.

Chudacoff, H. P. (1989). *How old are you? Age consciousness in American culture*. Princeton: Princeton University Press.

Chumbler, N. R., Foster, A., Grimm, J. W., & Williams, P. (2000). The influence of mid-life Adult status and functional health status on health lifestyles. In J. J. Kronenfeld (Ed.), *Research in The Sociology of Health Care, 18* (pp. 249-267). Elsevier Science Inc.

Cole, T. R. (1992). *The journey of life: A cultural history of aging in America*. Cambridge University Press.

Cole, T. R., & Ray, R. E. (Eds.). (2000). *Handbook of the humanities and aging* (2nd ed.). New York: Springer Publishing.

Costa, P. T., Jr., & McCrae, R. R. (1985). Concepts of functional or biological age: A critical view. In R. Andres, D. L. Bierman, & W. R. Hazzard (Eds.), *Principles of geriatric medicine* (pp. 30-37). New York: McGraw-Hill.

Featherstone, M., & Hepworth, M. (1991). The mask of ageing and the postmodern life course. In M. Featherstone, M. Hepworth, & B. S. Turner (Eds.), *The body: Social process and cultural theory* (pp. 371-389). London: Sage.

Featherstone, M., & Hepworth, M. (1998). Ageing, the lifecourse and the sociology of embodiment. In G. Scambler & P. Higgs (Eds.), *Modernity, medicine and health: Medical sociology towards 2000* (pp. 147-175). New York: Routledge.

Featherstone, M., & Wernick, A. (Eds.). (1995). *Images of aging: Cultural representations of later life*. New York: Routledge.

Foucault, M. (1977). Nietzsche, genealogy, history. In D. L. Bouchard (Ed.), *Language, counter-memory, practice* (pp. 139-164). Ithaca: Cornell University Press.

Fry, C. L. (1999). Anthropological theories of age and aging. In V. L. Bengtson & K. W. Schaie (Eds.), *Handbook of theories of aging* (pp. 271-286). New York: Springer Publishing.

Geertz, C. (1983). Blurred genres: The refiguration of social thought. In *Local knowledge: Further essays on interpretive anthropology* (pp. 19-35). New York: Basic Books.

Gilleard, C., & Higgs, P. (2000). *Cultures of ageing: Self, citizen and the body*. Harlow: Prentice-Hall.

Glass, T. A. (1998). Conjugating the 'tenses' of function: Discordance among hypothetical, experimental, and enacted function in older adults. *The Gerontologist, 38*(1), 101-112.

Greiner, P. A., Snowdon, D. A., & Greiner, L. H. (1996). The relationship of self-rated function and self-rated health to concurrent functional ability, functional decline, and mortality: Findings from the Nun Study. *Journal of Gerontology: Psychological Sciences, 51B*(5), P234-P241.

Gubrium, J. F., & Holstein, J. A. (1998). Narrative practice and the coherence of personal stories. *The Sociological Quarterly, 39*(1), 163-187.

Gullette, M. M. (1997). *Declining to decline: Cultural combat and the politics of midlife*. Charlottesville: University Press of Virginia.

He, Y. H., Colantonio, A., & Marshall, V. W. (2003). Later-life career disruption and self-rated health: An analysis of General Social Survey data. *Canadian Journal on Aging, 22*(1), 45-57.

Hendricks, J. (1992). Generations and the generation of theory in social gerontology. *International Journal of Aging and Human Development, 35*(1), 31-47.

Hepworth, M. (2000). *Stories of ageing.* Buckingham: Open University Press.

Heron, A., & Chown, S. (1967). *Age and function.* Boston: Little, Brown.

Herzog, A. R., & Markus, H. R. (1999). The self-concept in life span and aging research. In V. L. Bengtson & K. W. Schaie (Eds.), *Handbook of theories of aging* (pp. 227-252). New York: Springer Publishing.

Kastenbaum, R., Derbin, V., Sabatini, P., & Artt, S. (1972). "The ages of me": Toward personal and interpersonal definitions of functional aging. *Aging & Human Development, 3*(2), 197-211.

Katz, S. (1995). Imagining the lifespan: From premodern miracles to postmodern fantasies. In M. Featherstone & A. Wernick (Eds.), *Images of aging: Cultural representations of later life* (pp. 61-75). London: Routledge.

Katz, S. (2003). Critical gerontological theory: Intellectual fieldwork and the nomadic life of ideas. In S. Biggs, A. Lowenstein, & J. Hendricks (Eds.), *The need for theory: Social gerontology for the 21st century* (pp. 1-31). Amityville, NY: Baywood.

Katz, S. (2000a). Reflections on the Gerontological Handbook. In T. R. Cole & R. E. Ray (Eds.), *Handbook of the humanities and aging* (2nd ed., pp. 405-418). New York: Springer Publishing.

Katz, S. (2000b). Busy bodies: Activity, aging, and the management of everyday life. *Journal of Aging Studies, 14*(2), 135-152.

Katz, S., & Marshall, B. L. (2003). New sex for old: Lifestyle, consumerism, and the ethics of aging well. *Journal of Aging Studies, 17*(1), 3-16.

Lee, Y., & Shinkai, S. (2003). A comparison of correlates of self-rated health and functional disability of older persons in the Far East: Japan and Korea. *Archives of Gerontology and Geriatrics, 37*(1), 64-76.

Leinonen, R., Heikkinen, E., & Jylhä, M. (2001). Predictors of decline in self-assessments of health among older people—A 5-year longitudinal study. *Social Science & Medicine, 52,* 1329-1341.

Lumme-Standt, K., & Virtanen, P. (2002). Old people in the field of medication. *Sociology of Health & Illness, 24*(3), 285-304.

Lynott, R. J., & Lynott, P. P. (1996). Tracing the course of theoretical development in the sociology of aging. *The Gerontologist, 36*(6), 749-760.

Marshall, B. L., & Katz, S. (2002). Forever functional: Sexual fitness and the ageing male body. *Body & Society, 8*(4), 43-70.

Marshall, V. (1999). Analyzing social theories of aging. In V. L. Bengtson & K. W. Schaie (Eds.), *Handbook of theories of aging* (pp. 434-455). New York: Springer Publishing.

Minkler, M., & Estes, C. L. (Eds.). (1984). *Readings in the political economy of aging.* Amityville, NY: Baywood.

Minkler, M., & Estes, C. L. (Eds.). (1991). *Critical perspectives on aging: The political and moral economy of growing old.* Amityville, NY: Baywood.

Minkler, M., & Estes, C. L. (Eds.). (1999). *Critical gerontology: Perspectives from political and moral economy.* Amityville, NY: Baywood.

Moody, H. R. (1993). Overview: What is critical gerontology and why is it important? In T. R. Cole, W. A. Achenbaum, P. L. Jakobi, & R. Kastenbaum (Eds.), *Voices and visions of aging: Toward a critical gerontology* (pp. xv-xli). New York: Springer Publishing.

Murray, I. M. (1951). Assessment of physiologic age by combination of several criteria—Vision, hearing, blood pressure, and muscle force. *Journal of Gerontology, 6*(1), 120-126.

Nutbeam, D. (2000). Health literacy as a public health goal: A challenge for contemporary health education and communication strategies into the 21st century. *Health Promotion International, 15*(3), 259-267.

Ray, R. E. (1999). Researching to transgress: The need for critical feminism in gerontology. *Journal of Women & Aging, 11*(2/3), 171-184.

Rabinow, P. (1996). Artificiality and enlightenment: From sociobiology to biosociality. In *Essays on the anthropology of reason* (pp. 91-111). Princeton, NJ: Princeton University Press.

Rodgers, W., & Miller, B. (1997). A comparative analysis of ADL questions in surveys of older people. *Journals of Gerontology: Psychological and Social Sciences, 52B*, 21-36.

Rolleston, H. (1922). *Some medical aspects of old age.* London: Macmillan and Company.

Rose, C. L. (1972). The measurement of social age. *Aging & Human Development, 3*(2), 153-168.

Russell, C., Hill, B., & Basser, M. (1996). Identifying needs among 'at risk' older people: Does anyone here speak health promotion? In V. Minichiello, N. Chappell, H. Kendig, & A. Walker (Eds.), *Sociology of aging: International perspectives* (pp. 378-393). Melbourne: Thoth.

Scientific American. Position statement on human aging. Retrieved May 13, 2002 from www.sciam.com/article/e.g.m?articleID=0004F171-FE1E-1CDF-B4A8809EC588EEDF.

Scott, K. F. (1995). Closed kinetic chain assessment rehabilitation for improved function in the older patient. *Topics in Geriatric Rehabilitation, 11*(1), 1-5.

Schillinger, D. (2001). Improving the quality of chronic disease management for populations with low functional health literacy: A call to action. *Disease Management, 4*(3), 103-109.

Snowdon, D. (2001). *Aging with grace. The Nun Study and the science of old age: How we can all live longer, healthier and more vital lives.* London: Fourth Estate.

Spiriduso, W. W. (1995). *Physical dimensions of aging.* Champaign, IL: Human Kinetics.

Sprott, R. L. (2002). Biomarkers of aging. In D. J. Ekerdt (Ed.), *Encyclopedia of aging* (pp. 133-135). New York: Macmillan Reference USA.

The Gerontologist. (2003). Special Section: Self-rated health, gender, and morality, *43*(3), 369-411.

Von Mayrhauser, R. T. (1989). Making intelligence functional: Walter Dill Scott and applied psychological testing in World War I. *Journal of the History of the Behavioral Sciences, 25*(1), 60-72.

Welford, A. T. (1958). *Ageing and human skill.* London: Oxford University Press.

Williams, G., & Busby, H. (2000). The politics of 'disabled' bodies. In S. J. Williams, J. Gabe, & M. Calnan (Eds.), *Health, medicine and society: Key theories, future agendas* (pp. 169-185). London & New York: Routledge.

Woodward, K. (Ed.). (1999). *Figuring age: Women, bodies, generations.* Bloomington and Indianapolis: Indiana University Press.

CHAPTER 8

Empowering the Old:
Critical Gerontology and Anti-Aging
in a Global Context

Neal King and Toni Calasanti

Two competing discourses, those of critical gerontology (CG) and the anti-aging industry (AAI) that it opposes, offer to empower the old. Each responds to twentieth century forms of ageism, including the depictions of the old as passive dependents whose demands upon our economy and time comprise social problems. Where the AAI offers to erase the fact of old age, CG rejects both the notion of the old as an undue social burden and the capitalist ideals of "productivity" that exclude them. Critical gerontologists prefer their emphasis on political economy and collective responsibility to the age-phobic medicine of the anti-aging industry. However, self-reflexivity on the part of critical gerontologists requires that we reckon all that we share with the anti-aging industry, beginning with our common origins in the Global North and then our language of "empowerment." Focusing on U.S. history, we suggest how the combination of massive wealth, dense bureaucracy, and consumer capitalism has shaped both of these discourses, however opposed we might be ideologically. We conclude with what our Global North status might imply about our attempts to enhance the quality of life of old people worldwide.

AGEISM IN A GLOBAL CONTEXT

Particular forms of *ageism*—exclusion of the old—have been shaped by nations' unique interplays of cultures and histories, as well as their positions within the global economy. Western forms of ageism include the depiction of the old as a social burden in an apocalyptic scenario, which provides warnings about the dangers posed by an aging baby-boom generation. The "gray tidal wave" of dependent elders has been linked to forebodings of everything from national bankruptcies to the rise of global terrorism (Peterson, 1999), based on the idea that the aging, rich countries in the Global North will be no match for the masses of angry young men in the Global South whose futures look too dim to bear.

As gerontologists have already demonstrated, dependence in later life— defined here in economic terms as lack of employment and reliance on social support[1]—is not inevitable, but is socially created (e.g., Myles, 1984; Phillipson, 1998; Walker, 2000). Though equations of the old with dependence predate the creation of nationalized retirement schemes (e.g., Haber & Gratton, 1994), they have been linked to these public pensions. The appearance in nations of the Global North of extensive wealth, clashes between industrial labor and management, a burgeoning middle class wishing to free itself of unpredictable family obligations, and a well-developed governmental bureaucracy able to construct a whole category of persons as dependent, are based upon the positions of those nations in the global economy.

At the same time, the creation of the old as dependent in the Global North has not been uniform, even within particular nations. Using the United States as an example, we can see that the monetary basis of capitalism leads us to define only those with obvious ties to paid activities in the public sphere as "productive." The Social Security Act and early amendments to it codified this assessment and thus provided conditions for "dependence" by tying the benefits of retirees to those who were employed, while also designating retirees as nonproductive. The Social Security Act also ensured that wives, already dependent upon husbands, were further tied to their spouses for their own economic well-being, while also stipulating that their work was only half as productive as that of their husbands (Fraser & Gordon, 1994). The Act stratified dependency by leaving some occupations, predominantly those overrepresenting minorities and women, uncovered. These developments stratified and set into legal stone the timing and meaning of "old" as "retired" and differentially dependent upon public monies. Uncovered occupations tend to pay less and leave those workers dependent upon means-tested public assistance in old age. Despite the inclusion of such jobs under Social Security coverage in subsequent decades, the persistence of relatively low pay to women as well as racial and ethnic minorities results in even greater cumulative disadvantages in old age and an increased likelihood of dependence (Dannefer, 200 ; O and, 199 ; Pampel, 1998).

Dependence is also structured by *age relations*—a system of inequality, based on age, which privileges the not-old at the expense of the old (alasanti, 200). n the United States, unions were complicit with management in sacrificing older workers (through mandatory retirement) to obtain shorter workdays and a

---

[1] Other forms of dependence, including physical and mental, are related to this notion of being "nonproductive" and not contributing. That is, much of what is problematic with these forms of dependence upon others—whether the family or the state—is the related "costs" and the assumed lack of reciprocity.

system of seniority (Graebner, 1980). The proposal for Social Security also spoke to the needs of the younger members of a white middle class, struggling to form nuclear, well-to-do units free of the unpredictable burdens of caring for dependent parents (Haber & Gratton 1994). Legislators were thus interested in "ensuring the security of middle-age workers. They felt that people in their prime should not be unduly burdened by caring for dependents at both ends of the life cycle" (Achenbaum, 1999, p. 9).

Age relations structure other aspects of old age as well. For instance, in the Global North, we know that children of, say, ages 0 to 5 will be dependent, more obviously so than people aged 65–70. Yet no major concern was voiced among the wealthy nations when their baby booms created a much higher dependency ratio in the 1960s (Calasanti & Slevin, 2001; Gee, 2000). Ageism targets the old and stigmatizes their dependency as burdensome, just as it maligns their unpaid labor as unproductive.

Divisions by age, and thus definitions of dependence upon public coffers, have proceeded differently in most agrarian and colonized nations in the Global South. Variations in labor-force participation rates across the globe, for instance, affect local constructions of dependence. Only three in ten of the world's workers receive pensions because such plans tend to be quite limited in the Global South, covering mainly the few workers in the civil service, military, and the formal economy. Agricultural workers, often most of the population, go mostly unprotected. Nigeria's program, for instance, covers only 1% of its labor force; Zambia's, only 10%; Morocco's, 21%; and South Korea's, 30% (Kinsella & Velkoff, 2001, p. 117, Figure 11-3). By contrast, access to pensions in the Global North is wider, with more than 9 in 10 workers in most countries now covered by government-based plans (Kinsella & Velkoff, 2001).

For these reasons, in the Global South, older men's and women's labor-force engagement remains substantially above that in the North. They must work longer to survive. In Rwanda, for instance, older men and women display rather high and similar rates of labor force participation; though at every age, the figures for men are slightly above those of women. More than three-fourths of both men and women over the age of 60 (87% and 78%, respectively) are employed, and rates stay elevated, right up to age 75, when they "drop" to 46% for men and 33% for women—figures far above those in countries in the North (Kinsella & Velkoff, 2001, p. 93, Figure 10-1). The impact of globalization in the South appears in data that reveal that, in some countries in the South, such as Argentina, Mexico, Peru, South Korea, and Uruguay, the employment of women over age 65 has actually increased since the 1970s (Kinsella & Velkoff, 2001, p. 102, Figure 10-5c). The fact that both old men and women most likely work in agriculture in rural areas speaks to the element of necessity in much of this continued employment. Retirement remains a privilege of the urban upper class.

From this standpoint, then, it seems clear the economic development of countries in the Global North created the conditions for the construction of the old as "dependent" as well as our solutions to that "social problem." The advancement of capitalism—through its welfare stage into a deindustrialized "disorganization" in which employment rates fall, central-state controls weaken, and public services privatize—enhances an individualism that wears at traditional ties already frayed by the movement of industrial workers away from families of origin (Phillipson, 2003). This position in a global economy, in which corporate might challenges the authority of the welfare state, shapes our solutions by leaning upon ideas of equality, liberty, and service-recipient *empowerment*.[2] While national agendas include a range of solutions to the "burdensome" status of the old, we concentrate on just two empowering strands: critical gerontology and the anti-aging industry. In addition to sharing roots in advanced capitalist and globalizing processes, these opposing discourses share a promise of empowerment through active responses to feelings of stigma.

THE RISE OF GERONTOLOGY AND TWO FORMS OF EMPOWERMENT

The Anti-Aging Industry

The rise of consumer capitalism increased the scope of the medical industry, always in search of new markets. Gerontology, expanded by postwar government investment in science, also played a role. Early theories tended to focus on individual adaptation to aging, wherein "activity" emerged as the key to "healthy adjustment in old age" (Katz, 2000, p. 138). Although such contemporary streams of gerontology as "active aging," "successful aging," and "productive aging" do not necessarily emphasize adjustment, the individual-level focus remains in each perspective. These imply that any individual can govern life satisfaction through lifestyle choices: regimens of activity, diet, exercise, and the like. This individual-based perspective provides expert discourse, policies, and services to the old that direct the flow of some of this medical-industry energy. One result is the formation of an anti-aging industry (AAI). Although we do not claim that social gerontology led to the emergence of this industry, scholars have noted "the kinship between positive activity models of aging in gerontology and consumerist ideologies" (Katz, 2000, p. 138). Further, members of the anti-aging industry often draw upon that gerontology to sell their products

---

[2] The definition of "empowerment" varies with professional context but maintains a focus on agency. From a contemporary social-work text on the strengthening of families, we learn that, "the person who is the help-seeker (learner, client, etc.) must attribute behavior change at least in part to his or her own actions if one is to acquire a sense of control necessary to manage family affairs. This is what we mean when we say a person is *empowered*" (Dunst, Trivette, & Deal, 1994, p. 3). This individualism is built into public-service work, and is typical of the means by which agencies, private and public, provide their services.

and gain scientific legitimacy, while members of the gerontological community advocate many aspects of this industry.

The AAI treats the life course as a set of market segments and consumer profiles (Katz, 2001-2002, p. 29). It includes anti-aging medicine, "a medical specialty founded on the application of advanced scientific and medical technologies for the early detection, prevention, treatment, and reversal of age-related dysfunction, disorders, and diseases" (Klatz, 2001-2002, p. 59; Olshansky, Hayflick, & Carnes, 2002). This "medical specialty," represented by the American Academy of Anti-Aging Medicine (A4M), provides the professional legitimacy for much of the anti-aging industry, whose purveyors liberally avail themselves of A4M's scientific claims that aging can be halted and even reversed. Related anti-aging products include cosmetic surgery, dietary and exercise regimes; and extend to vacations and spas.

Recent investigative reporting valued anti-aging medicine at $30 billion a year (Dateline NBC, March 6, 2001), while the U.S. Senate Special Committee on Aging calculated the figure for the "marketing of dietary and specialty supplements that particularly target . . . elderly and senior citizens" (p. 1) at $27 billion a year. Regardless of the accuracy of these figures, this appears to be a huge and profitable industry (U.S. Senate Special Committee on Aging, 2001). The lucrative aspects of anti-aging, not lost on A4M, represent part of its own assertion of legitimacy as a medical field and its pitch to practitioners who might join. Thus, on the one hand, A4M presents itself as a nonprofit organization.

A4M is a non-commercial, not-for-profit volunteer society of physicians and scientists who approach diseases as being treatable and largely preventable, and *aging as a medical disorder of dysfunctional metabolism* (Wellness Today, 2002). At the same time, they also note that

> Those who choose the privilege of A4M membership recognize that the A4M, as the sole medical society in the world dedicated to the advancement of anti-aging medicine as a clinical science, has been instrumental in the proliferation of this emerging marketplace. By maintaining your membership in the A4M, you rise to the challenge of redirecting our nation's paradigm of health care, whereas the choice to decline A4M membership may, quite simply, leave you in the dust. . . . (American Academy of Anti-Aging Medicine, 2002)

However, as this quote implies, the success of the anti-aging industry doesn't keep A4M from viewing itself as in opposition or rebellion against mainstream medicine. Indeed, A4M's President, Ron Klatz (April, 2001) complains that

> A powerful old-boy network is investing enormous time, personnel, and financial resources on destroying today's most successful, most popular, and fastest-growing medical society. . . . These successes achieved by A4M physicians are perceived as a threat to the medical power elite. . . . We submit that the maturation of anti-aging medicine as a major market segment has

triggered a battle for control of this new leading model for healthcare. (Wellness Today, 2002)

Anti-aging thus poses itself as a critical counterdiscourse, bucking the medical establishment to offer consumers a way out of stigmatized dependency and decline. The industry offers empowerment, inviting the old to embrace and extend youth, to avoid feeling passive and powerless.

Katz (2000, 2001-2002) has documented this emphasis on active lifestyle and its origin in gerontological "activity theory." He has provided a Foucaultian critique of anti-aging as a disciplinary regime, deployed to make old age problematic. In this analysis, these activity regimes, cosmetic procedures, and hundreds of not-so-affordable hormone and drug treatments organize old age into one long retreat from the inevitable. The transition from well-defined modern life stages (youth, productivity, retirement) to a postmodern timelessness conducive to eternal consumption implicitly stigmatizes any of the old among us who might prefer to, say, nap rather than shop, contemplate rather than consume, relax rather than resort, and allow one's skin to wrinkle rather than try to cure the dread disease of aging. Well aware that many people might disapprove of their implicit stigmatization of the old, merchants of anti-aging services promise empowerment and enhancement for the brave consumer. No doubt many of these marketers are sincere in their desire to help the old, anxious to learn what consumers want, ready to take satisfaction in the rescue of the old from stigma and decline. They seek to listen, empower, provide, and serve.

Critical Gerontology

Many, however, prefer to avoid using consumer capitalism as the tool for empowering the old. On another end of this ideological spectrum, we find critical gerontology (CG). It rejects capitalism and individualist approaches and refuses to equate aging with disease. It also provides a mirror image of anti-aging, with its focus on empowering the old to become active on their own behalf.

Mid-century liberation movements (civil rights, student rights, and feminist) defined underemployed peoples as oppressed groups and represented them in public debate, often in opposition to government and private-industry discourses. Social gerontologists learned this analysis as they trained and then brought it to bear on the problems of people as they age. This influenced a strand of gerontology that takes a political-economic approach to the impoverishment of the old (Katz, 2003, pp. 17-18). By the late 1980s, CG coalesced by building upon these neo-Marxist, feminist frameworks and focusing on a variety of forms of inequality and the corporate and government policies that perpetuate it. As a primarily academic field, CG often does not make its pitch directly to the old, but instead fashions position statements geared at policy makers and practitioners.

Critical perspectives in aging pull from a wide array of approaches in the social sciences and humanities, including critical, conflict, and feminist theories as well as cultural studies (Estes, Linkins, & Binney, 2001; Moody, 1988). These traditions contribute to professional activity in political economy, feminist gerontology, and cultural and humanistic gerontology (or what Minkler & Estes, 1991, refer to as moral economy). Critical perspectives question the ways in which old age has been constructed and the conditions of aging at both micro- and macrolevels; "the association of age with disease and inevitable decline is better reframed so that aging is seen as a *social* rather than *biological process*. This alternative view of aging is central to the critical perspective because many experiences related to aging result from socioeconomic conditions and inequalities experienced (and compounded) over the life course" (Estes et al., 2001, p. 31). Thus, they do not urge that we avoid old age. They do not stigmatize those who "grow old," or posit individual responsibility. They are concerned with power in relation to the constructions/conditions of old age and point to the age relations that stigmatize it.

All of this professional activity—AAI and CG—occurs mainly in privileged nations, where freedom from colonial predation allows people to focus on anti-poverty and bourgeois liberation movements rather than other social problems. Activists focus on labor-market status, personal health, and public stigma, rather than famine or civil war. They can join the professional class in large numbers by taking jobs in policy and service institutions. For these reasons, the proliferation of social scientists, medical scientists, doctors, service professionals, and consumer-product marketers who make up gerontology has been a bourgeois phenomenon relatively undeveloped outside of the Global North; so is the rise of the old as a consumer group containing both rich members with money to spend and poor members in need of welfare-state support.

With the following comparison, we paint a picture of two advocacy groups, staffed by many sincere professionals, each of whom want to empower the old to maintain some crucial form of activity. Those forms of empowerment differ in some crucial ways. We begin with the comparison and will turn to the differences between the AAI and CG afterward.

A PROFESSIONAL ETHIC OF EMPOWERMENT

Katz notes that "all dependent non-laboring populations—unemployed, disabled, retired—have become targets of state polices to 'empower' and 'activate' them" (2000, p. 147). Both of these approaches to this task—the anti-aging industry and critical gerontology—define themselves as counterdiscourses in opposition to some mainstream view. Each offers to the old an exciting new way to define themselves and improve their lives. They each invite the old to avoid some other, putatively dominant, discourse; and each invites the old to join in a new quest for full citizenship and better lives. They each involve, in the words of Phillipson and Walker (1987, p. 12) in their discussion of critical gerontology, "a commitment not just to understand the social construction of ageing but to change it." Anti-aging wants to empower old people to prove that they are neither ugly nor passive, that their lives are in their own hands, and that decline need not be inevitable. CG wants to change the view that aging is "bad" and that the old are little more than burdens on the young.

Each offers a way out of stigmatized dependency. The AAI promises a cure to growing old and the utopia of successful aging. Critical gerontologists hope that their exhortations to policy makers help erase the stigma that accrues to old age. They urge policies that would serve old people's needs and offer them access to gainful employment as well as dignified retirement. Each also offers to humanize the old by giving them public voice to articulate their problems and fears, putting human faces on the statistics of scientific reports, and then offering to respond to those voices with either products or policies.

We now compare these discourses of empowerment, to see all that they have in common. We will then turn to their differences and finally to the possible consequences of their Global North origins.

Anti-Aging Claims to Empower Consumers

Bearing in mind their missionary sense of counterprogramming, consider a few claims offered by merchants of anti-aging products, including herbs, drugs, diets, exercises, spas, and knowledge in general.

> Empower-GH is the most advanced all natural Growth Hormone enhancing on the market. If you are looking for a Growth Hormone/Anti-Aging product that works, you will love Empower-GH! As a fitness professional I highly recommend that any one that is over 25 years of age and trying to stay healthy and slow down the aging process should be on this product! (Terry's Total Fitness, 2002)

Note that the quest to deny age by consuming appropriate products is to begin earlier and earlier in life. One should begin denying age in youth.

> Awareness is the greatest gift of all! The steps above will EMPOWER YOU TO TAKE CONTROL of your physical wellness and financial future—so don't delay. You can create the life you've always dreamed of starting today! (Oasis Life Sciences, 2002)

Some take a more religious or reverent tone, one that conveys a morality: if you don't take advantage of the available technology, then you deserve to be old and dependent.

> Our mission can be summed up this way: "We're here to bless your life and to provide value in products that empower people to live younger and healthier lives."
> "We believe in empowering people with a full measure of tools, information, and access." (Anti-Aging Research Laboratories, 2002)

Never mind the gushy punctuation and missionary zeal, consider the salvation offered here. Some work through drugs, but all proffer "alternative" knowledge:

> Knowledge of both traditional Western medicines and alternative therapies of healing the whole person empowers you to make informed choices. (Wellness Today, 2002)

A4M is a professional organization that has successfully proliferated four key elements requisite in a model of wellness-oriented medical care:

- custom compounding of natural (body-friendly) pharmaceutical products
- expanded-label use of medications prescribed by physicians
- patient education and empowerment
- patient and physician advocacy for application of innovative medical therapies (Wellness Today, 2002).

Others recognize diversity and seek to empower marginalized groups by addressing their specific needs.

> Enhanceme.com® is a company for women, by women, that strives to provide accurate, reliable, and educational information to women interested in enhancing and empowering their lives spiritually and physically. (Enhance Me, 2002)

Tides of Life goes even further in terms of "diversity"—puts the consumer in charge of her experience while implying that the product will benefit everyone.

> Our goal is to empower YOU to make informed, intelligent healthcare decisions because every woman is different and unique. Learn more about health! (2002)

Here, empowerment means learning from sympathetic professionals, who seek the greater good of a people often lied to by such major industries as conventional medicine. Aligning with alternative, "Eastern" medicine, advocates for women, and others resistant to the dominant industry, one may find health and happiness. Empowerment awaits those who join the friendly resistance to the tyranny of old age.

Ads include testimonials by those who have been able to "stop aging" through the use of these products. Such stories remind us that these products DO in fact make users feel like they are empowered and have taken control of their lives and futures.

> "The Oasis products are amazing! I'm on the Level 2 products, Bone and Joint, Female Formula, and Inthinity. I'm noticing wonderful differences in my skin tone. My face looks so much smoother and more vibrant, and those little wrinkles seem to be disappearing. I also have unbelievable energy. It's incredible!" – Diane, CO.

"I have more energy than I ever thought possible. I rode my bike for 45 miles the other day and 35 miles the very next day. When I first took the ACI test I was aging at the rate of a 72-year-old. I took the test again the other day and it reported that I'm aging at the rate of a 32-year-old." – Leon, FL.

"I've been on other products from other companies and they just don't compare to Oasis. I feel so energetic now and my muscular activity is much easier. I'm able to keep up with my 20-year-old gardener and I'm about 4 times his age! No one wants to grow old. Oasis is simply the solution for health and wealth!" -C.G, CA.

"I am so blown away with the big picture of what Oasis is all about. This is the only company that is making products that are tested and have a huge amount of science that are behind them. Oasis delivers true anti-aging at 4 levels— the physical being, the organism, the organs, the cells, and the DNA. And we have proof that all 4 of those areas are positively affected by taking those products." – Bea, CO (Oasis Life Sciences, 2002)

Drawing on a language often seen as "alternative," empowerment through consumption can also be communal, with individuals working together to help one another realize their potential. Thus, from a plastic surgeon we receive "mentor testimony" that "provides . . . clients with personal mentors, or women who can offer invaluable 'girlfriend' advice":

Lynne, Upper Eyelids, Mini Face-Lift, Laser Skin Resurfacing, Botox

I'm in my forties and have known I would have cosmetic surgery for a very long time. My mother had a face-lift and many of my friends have had various procedures performed as well. I travel a great deal and have interviewed several surgeons. A friend suggested I interview an enhanceme.com® Doctor. I went to the consultation and the surgeon spent over 2 hours answering my questions and addressing my concerns. By the end of my appointment, I knew I had found the right doctor for me. My doctor told me that botox would be able to take care of the large crows feet near my eyes. It hurt a little, but my crow's feet were gone 72 hours later! No surgery, no recovery, no wrinkles. You have to love that . . .

I will be glad to share my thoughts, hopes and fears from both before and after surgery if you contact me. lynne@enhanceme.com or 1-877-7enhance (1-877-736-4262).

Kathy, 3 Breast Augmentations, Liposuction, Eye Lift, Botox

Hello, I am 40ish. That's close enough. I have been a flight attendant and facilitator for a major airline for the past 10 years. I am also single and have no children. I had my first breast augmentation done about 15 years ago. . . . I just had my first botox injection about a week ago (yes, it hurt and yes, I love the results) and scheduled an eyelift for early January.

If I can offer any advice, answer any questions or you just want to talk, contact me kathy@enhanceme.com or call me at 1-877-7enhance (1-877-736-4262).

Finally, on the "mentor/it happened for me" page from the same site we find:

Cynthia,

> I just wanted to thank you so much for making it possible for my dream to come true. You and your staff were so very helpful and made everything so easy! I'm lying in bed recovering right now and I feel great about myself! And thank you for the beautiful flowers! That was very thoughtful of you and made a big difference to me—you really are a different kind of financing company. Your help has been invaluable to me.
>
> Again, Thank You So Much,
> Jenny Lynn Baldwin
> (Enhance Me, 2002)

Through consumer research and the testimonials, the old are empowered to speak and claim what they want (in this case, escape from unattractiveness and decline). The approach is humanistic: it puts faces to cold figures and illustrates its claims with personal stories. Anti-aging advertising is generous with its pictures of smiling consumers. It offers new rituals to facilitate transitions through later life. Based upon either consumer research or grassroots organizing, professionals then suggest products.

In his analysis of health discourse and consumer empowerment, Thompson argues that the decentralized natural health marketplace "encodes values of pluralism, diversity, and the ideal of informed consumer choice" (2003, p. 103) and cautions that those of us skeptical of such medical empowerment not be too quick to distinguish it from "experiences of authentic self-discovery." Postmodern empowerment works through such professional interventions—the raising of consciousness and proliferation of options for the citizen-consumer through education. So, indeed, proceeds much of the empowerment offered by critical gerontology.

CRITICAL-GERONTOLOGICAL CLAIMS TO EMPOWER THE OPPRESSED

A similar language of empowerment appears across the spectrum of social gerontology, language used by service providers as well as those who theorize the power relations that govern their research and service provision. One may read of "user empowerment" in the healthcare strategies of old people (Andrews, 2002), or their use of the Internet to gather information for themselves (McMellon & Schiffman, 2002). The Center for Aging at the University of Alabama-Birmingham reports empowering old people with crossword puzzles and television news shows to exercise their minds ("Empowering the Elderly," 2003). Representing state agencies as well as private research centers, critical gerontologists use this language in ways that at least superficially resemble those of the anti-aging merchants, no doubt in part because the two discourses are aware of each other (Katz, 2001-2002, p. 30).

Critical gerontology teaches that professionals who serve clients or customers do well to listen to the old and spur them to life-improving action. Retirees in search of yet another counterdiscourse to the mainstream wisdom on aging could put down their anti-aging ads and instead read about "revolution," "empowerment," "knowledge," and "emancipation" in the promises that critical gerontologists make in their academic literature. Moody (1988, p. 27) urges models of development that foster "self-criticism, self-interpretation, and critical consciousness," as vital features of emancipation. "Without that 'utopian' ideal of development, old age risks becoming a self-fulfilling prophecy of decline, a public burden or a private despair" (p. 28). He defines CG not only in terms of self-reflexivity of its theories (indeed, the purpose of this very essay) but also in terms of the "positive ideal of human development . . . toward freedom beyond domination" that it can offer (p. 33).

Minkler (1996) also posits "empowerment" as the uniting thread that runs through CG in its humanist, political-economic, and feminist forms. This empowerment is "the process by which individuals and communities are enabled to take such power and act effectively to transform their lives and their communities" (p. 472). More communal than AAI tends to be, this empowerment works either "through societal transformations in the redistribution of wealth and income or through the creation of new rituals and other means to facilitate transitions to and through later life" (p. 471).

As Cusack (1999) puts it, "The major task is one of liberating people of all ages from a view of old age as an expensive, expansive wasteland and older people as useless burdens on society" (p. 22). In these ways, critical gerontologists have joined their anti-aging counterparts in the war on damaging stereotypes, wishing to paint the old in more flattering colors, though by different means. When not battling stereotypes, critical gerontology provides information with which people can understand the world and make the best choices for their lives. Empowerment can operate through self-inspection, a search for "empowering ways to re-interpret and re-articulate midlife and beyond" (Ray, 1999, p. 181). For instance, the combination of personal experience and feminist discourses can produce "a counter-narrative which challenges middle-ageist assumptions that life is all 'down hill' after 40" (Ray, 1999, p. 181) Only here the information takes a more political form. This work becomes "potentially empowering and emancipating 'by [providing people] the resources to understand the intrinsic relationship between culture and the various forms of power, and thus to develop strategies for survival' (Sardar & Van Loon, 1997, p. 43, quoted in Estes et al., 2001, p. 39). With such knowledge among the people, the potentially revolutionary human subject may act."

Active engagement with old people is also crucial. While calling old people to self-redefinition, critical gerontologists hope to include the old in conversations about what they want and how various agencies might provide it. In Minkler's (1996, p. 474) words, empowerment demands "elders themselves must be afforded a much greater role in deciding both the project agenda and the steps for achieving it." Such gerontologists wish the old to speak, shape research, and then direct service offerings.

Many critical gerontologists maintain sharp awareness of the class politics of such provider/receiver relationships. For instance, Minkler (1996, p. 476) observes that, "Behind the euphemisms of community participation and empowerment lay the realities of power, control, and ownership"; while Walker (1998, p. 31) cautions that we not seek to empower "only to benefit the professional group or service providers." Professionals govern conversation by providing terms that bolster unstated values and agendas. However sensitive the provider, the unequal relationship remains, and "empowerment" can too easily turn into learning the rules that the service provider sets and disciplining oneself accordingly.[3] Nevertheless, critical gerontologists join our anti-aging colleagues in calling upon the old to speak their minds, stake their claims, and guide us in the invention of policies and services that will empower them.

In sum, AAI and CG discourses amount to competing forms of discipline. Each claims to represent the old and offer the best hope for enhancing their lives. Each responds to the fact of ageism with a solution available to any old people willing to define themselves within the terms of the respective discourse: as diseased people unfairly cast aside when a cure is at hand, or as oppressed people stigmatized as unproductive and diseased.

DIFFERENT IDEOLOGIES AND CONSEQUENCES

When they turn to empowerment, these (counter) discourses can sound alike, and audiences can become confused. Listening to our critiques of the anti-aging industry, coupled with our concerns for the well-being and life satisfaction of the old, some audience members approach us and ask why we wouldn't want old people to exercise and be healthy. In such cases, critical gerontologists have failed to make plain how these two discourses differ, given that both promise empowerment.

The anti-aging industry promises individual control and demands individual responsibility of each consumer. The challenge it poses to ageism does not revolve

---

[3] While there are notable exceptions (predominantly feminist gerontologists such as Calasanti & Slevin, 2001; Estes & Associates, 2001; Holstein, 1999; Minkler, 1996; and Ray, 1999), critical gerontologists sometimes present "the old" and aging as homogenous by ignoring the diversity among groups of old and aging experiences. Even among those who mention gender, race, and ethnicity (sexual preference rarely comes up), these tend to be subsumed under class. Finally, discussions of theory assume but rarely examine age relations explicitly (Katz's work provides one exception). Such omissions limit the ability of critical gerontology to achieve its goals.

around questioning the logic of the stereotypes or asking why they should lead to devaluation. Instead, it promises to help individuals avoid the stigma through disciplined shopping. It embraces the inequality between age groups in order to motivate consumption by the old. It recognizes some diversity, especially that of gender, but otherwise defines health in terms of images of white, leisure-class athleticism. Critical gerontology pays far more attention to class relations in its critique of the consumer capitalism that anti-aging celebrates. Walker (1998, p. 32), for instance, notes "the importance of emphasizing the *collective* basis of welfare so as to avoid conflict between different groups of service users (e.g., across generations)."

Critical gerontologists vary in the degree of their attention to inequality. Some theorize the age relations underlying these discourses of empowerment—relations that intersect with those of class, gender, race, religion, and nation in a global consumer capitalism. Where the anti-aging industry celebrates its free-market individualism and scientific progress, critical gerontology values diversity not as a marketing tool but as a way to discover the many facets of exploitation and neglect in a world torn by inequality. Similarities in our missionary languages of empowerment, though they indicate our shared Global North origins, finally give way to the crucial distinction between marketing on the one hand (which can veer into organized white-collar crime, as merchants peddle expensive "snake oil" in the name of beauty and health, according to the 2001 Senate Special Committee on Aging), and attempts to help those most in need, on the other.

Each solution to the problem of ageism comes at its price: the AAI requires discretionary spending on the props of successful aging, available only to the most privileged. CG requires, to realize its own goals, massive reorganization of such large institutions as the labor market, its pensions and social security entitlements, the medical industry, the housing market, international trade, and so on, as well as reflection on the ageism within our cultures and within ourselves. Though the old can share common cause with the disabled rights movement, feminism, antiracism, and other new social movements, they cannot achieve the goals of critical gerontology without decades of hard-fought battles and a massive redistribution of wealth and esteem. And the benefits of the anti-aging industry are available only to the wealthy, its most lavish promises liable to come true only in science fiction. Neither discourse offers easy ways out, though both promise empowerment to those who can train themselves to think (and consume) appropriately, to become active on their own behalf, to listen to the professionals who beckon.

CG reaches out to the activists who would challenge a "free-market" capitalism to care for a group who have been long used as reserve labor and a consumer market; the AAI reaches out to those with money and a belief in store-bought solutions. In either case, many resources, freedom to act, and a strong focus on "the old" as a group worth serving are required. These phenomena occur largely in the Global North.

CONCLUSION: LIMITS OF THE GLOBAL NORTH

This shared language of empowerment results from a Global North location, one structured by the advances of capitalism and movements of liberation that modernity brings. AAI may or may not concern itself with the ways in which people outside the Global North interpret its marketing. But unless critical gerontologists plan to speak only amongst ourselves, we must attend to how others hear us. As activists, we distance ourselves from individualist approaches such as that of the anti-aging industry, which embraces the corporate, nondemocratic ethics of modern capitalism. We organize around age relations; and though our rhetoric of empowerment sounds at times like that of anti-aging, we ground it differently. We fight stereotypes of aging, but by valuing all aspects rather than denying the reality of this time of life or striving to remain ageless. The work of critical gerontologists often ignores diversity or subsumes such power relations as age, gender, and race under class. In becoming more attuned to inequality in our quest for empowerment, we must consider global relations as well, which include complexities of nationality, religion, and economic development, which involve more than linear progressions toward democracy and capitalism.

Malcolm Johnson (1995) has written, "We have the global capacity to support all the world's people, but to do so will require a revolution in economic and political action which re-establishes human solidarity and reciprocity as central features of our social order" (p. 262). Assumptions about a bygone "human solidarity" aside, we might consider the global derivation of some of our most cherished values. The critical gerontologist calls for anticapitalist activism; global redistributions of wealth, and equal valuation of people seem perfectly sound but have their roots in Global North political economies. This sense of responsibility for stewardship of wealth leads to a patron mentality, a paternalism for which the United States (chief among patron nations) has been rightly criticized.

These last several years, we citizens of absurdly wealthy nations have been told by people around the world that our well-intentioned spread of modernity's blessings—mass education; individual freedom; democratic government; and the partial dismantling of slavery, patriarchy, and caste—may have angered some of our neighbors, who value those ideals less than those of traditional rank, orthodox authority, and communal sacrifice. CG avoids individualism in its assessment of social processes, but most of us cherish the modern notions of empowerment and freedom that enlightenment ideals and loosening of patriarchal ties have brought. Many of us, witness to the rise of postmodern consumer-capitalist behemoths that trample nation-states in their path, wish for more robust democratic governance. And all of us who take part in new social movements revere equality. Still, these values may, to an important extent, result from our Global North history and not always export as well as we might like. People from some of the many orthodox cultures that we seek to serve reject the individualist moral vacuity at the heart of modern and postmodern liberty and our professional-class culture (Barber, 1995; Gole, 1997; Larrain, 2000). For instance, Barber (1995) chronicles the rise of nationalist movements that reject the pluralism, rational-ization, and individualism that capitalist development brings. And Gole (1997) recounts the responses of different groups of women in Turkey, some of whom crave more individual freedom, but others who veil themselves in communal solidarity with their nationalist brothers. In all cases, responses to the ideological currents of modernity are complicated by concerns that they will fragment the traditional communities that sustain so many people. Gerontology in many forms seeks to empower the stigmatized with knowledge, representation, service, and a critical eye. Tired of exploitation and in search of stability, no one turns down economic security when offered it. But debt relief and developmental funds come with ideological strings attached; and many peoples of the world tell us that some of these values—corrosive of tradition and community—may as well stay in the capitalist Global North from which they came.

Certainly the worst of this corrosion proceeds under the banner of the corporate ethics that drive the anti-aging industry: the embrace of a new hierarchy based upon possession of capital even as one rejects patriarchy, and the focus on individual agency at the expense of communal ties. Here, the attention to diversity that marks the best of critical gerontology can help it avoid the pitfalls of modernity inherent in our models of empowerment. Keeping in mind the differences in outlook as well as wealth and status coupled with race, gender, religion, national, and other inequalities, we must maintain a self-critical focus on the force of our own needs as professionals, and the way in which those forces shape solutions to the problems of the old. We shall not turn our backs on our responsibilities to shepherd the wealth exploited from other lands and to try to lend esteem to old people in all circumstances that oppress them. But our gerontology must remain critical of the global relations as well as the age relations that shape our best intentions to empower the old.

REFERENCES

Achenbaum, W. A. (1999). In the U.S., we've (usually) expected our elders to remain productive. *The Public Policy and Aging Report, National Academy on an Aging Society, 10*(2), 7-10, 13.

American Academy of Anti-Aging Medicine. (2002). Retrieved November 1, 2002 from http://www.wellnesstoday.com/april2001/anti_aging_under_attack!.htm.

Andrews, G. J. (2002). Private complementary medicine and older people: Service use and user empowerment. *Aging & Society, 22*, 343-368.

Anti-Aging Research Laboratories. (2002) Retrieved November 1, 2002 from http://www.antiagingresearch.com/aboutus.e.g.m.

Barber, B. (1995). *Jihad vs. McWorld: How globalism and tribalism are reshaping the world.* New York: Ballantine Books.

Calasanti, T. M. (2003). Theorizing age relations. In S. Biggs, A. Lowenstein, & J. Hendricks (Eds.), *The need for theory: Critical approaches to social gerontology for the 21st century* (pp. 199-218). Amityville, NY: Baywood.

Calasanti, T. M., & Slevin, K.F. (2001). *Gender, social inequalities, and aging.* Walnut Creek, CA: Alta Mira Press.

Calavita, K. (1996). The new politics of immigration: Balanced-budget conservativism and the symbolism of Proposition 187. *Social Problems, 43*(3), 284-306.

Cusack, S. (1999). Critical educational gerontology and the imperative to empower. *Education and Ageing, 14*(1), 21-37.

Dannefer, D. (2003). Cumulative advantage/disadvantage and the life course: Cross fertilizing age and social science theory. *Journal of Gerontology, 58B*(6), S327-S337.

Dunst, C. J., Trivette, C. M., & Deal, A. G. (1994). *Supporting and strengthening families: Methods, strategies and practices.* Cambridge, MA: Brookline Books.

Empowering the Elderly: Calisthenics for the brain. (2003). *Insight on Aging, 10*(1), 1. University of Alabama at Birmingham, Center for Aging, Geriatric Education Center.

Enhance Me (2002). Retrieved November 1, 2002 from http://www.enhanceme.com/about/index.html

Estes, C. L., Linkins, K. W., & Binney, E. A. (2001). Critical perspectives on aging. In C. A. Estes & Associates (Eds.), *Social policy & aging: A critical perspective* (pp. 23-44). Thousand Oaks, CA: Sage.

Estes, C. L., & Associates. (2001). *Social policy & aging: A critical perspective.* Thousand Oaks, CA: Sage.

Fraser, N., & Gordon, L. (1994). A geneology of 'dependency': Tracing a keyword of the U.S. welfare state. *Signs, 19*(2), 309-336.

Gee, E. M. (2000). Population politics: Voodoo demography, population aging, and social policy. In E. M. Gee & G. M. Gutman (Eds.), *The overselling of population aging* (pp. 5-25). New York: Oxford University Press.

Gole, N. (1997). *The forbidden modern: Civilization and veiling.* Ann Arbor, MI: University of Michigan Press.

Graebner, W. (1980). *A history of retirement: The meaning and function of an American institution.* New Haven, CT: Yale University Press.

Haber, C., & Gratton, B. (1994). *Old age and the search for security.* Bloomington, IN: Indiana University Press.

Holstein, M. (1999). Women and productive aging: Troubling implications. In M. Minkler & C. L. Estes (Eds.), *Critical gerontology: Perspectives from political and moral economy* (pp. 359-373). Amityville, NY: Baywood.

Johnson, M. (1995). Interdependency and the generational compact. *Ageing and Society, 15*(2), 243-265.

Katz, S. (2000). Busy bodies: Activity, aging, and the management of everyday life. *Journal of Aging Studies, 14*(2), 135-152.

Katz, S. (2001-2002). Growing older without aging? Positive aging, anti-ageism, and anti-aging. *Generations, 25*(4), 27-32.

Katz, S. (2003). Critical gerontological theory: Intellectual fieldwork and the nomadic life of ideas. In S. Biggs, A. Lowenstein, & J. Hendricks (Eds.), *The need for theory: Critical approaches to social gerontology* (pp. 15-31). Amityville, NY: Baywood.

Kinsella, K., & Velkoff, V. A. (2001). *An aging world: 2001*. U.S. Census Bureau (Series P95/01-1), Washington, DC: U.S. Government Printing Office.

Klatz, R. (2001-2002). Anti-aging medicine: Resounding, independent support for expansion of an innovative medical specialty. *Generations, 25*(4), 59-62.

Larrain, J. (2000). *Ideology and cultural identity: Modernity and the third world presence.* Cambridge: Polity Press.

McMellon, C. A., & Schiffman, L. G. (2002). Cybersenior empowerment: How some older individuals are taking control of their lives. *Journal of Applied Gerontology, 21*(2), 157-175.

Minkler, M., & Estes, C. L. (1991). *Critical perspectives on aging: The political and moral economy of growing old.* Amityville, NY: Baywood.

Minkler, M. (1996). Critical perspectives on ageing: New challenges for gerontology. *Ageing and Society, 16*, 467-487.

Moody, H. R. (1988). Toward a critical gerontology: The contribution of the humanities to theories of aging. In J. E. Birren & V. L. Bengtson (Eds.), *Emergent theories of aging* (pp. 19-40). New York: Springer Publishing.

Myles, J. (1984). *Old age in the welfare state: The political economy of public pensions.* Boston: Little, Brown.

Oasis Life Sciences. (2002). Retrieved November 1, 2002 from http://www.longevitysystems.com/html/recommerce.html.

Olshansky, S. J., Hayflick, L. & Carnes, B. A. (2002). No truth to the fountain of youth. *Scientific American, 286*(6), 92-95.

O'Rand, A. M. (1996). The precious and the precocious: Understanding cumulative disadvantage and advantage over the life course. *The Gerontologist, 36*(3), 230-238.

Pampel, F. C. (1998). *Aging, social inequality, and public policy.* Thousand Oaks, CA: Sage.

Phillipson, C., & Walker, A. (1987). The case for a critical gerontology. In *Social gerontology: New directions* (pp. 1-15). London: Croom Helm.

Phillipson, C. (1998). *Reconstructing old age: New agenda in social theory and practice.* London: Sage.

Phillipson, C. (2003). Globalization and the reconstruction of old age: New challenges for critical gerontology. In S. Biggs, A. Lowenstein, & J. Hendricks (Eds.), *The need for theory: Critical approaches to social gerontology* (pp. 163-179). Amityville, NY: Baywood.

Peterson, P. G. (1999, Jan/Feb.). Gray dawn: The global aging crisis. *Foreign Affairs, 78*, 43-56.

Ray, R. (1999). Researching to transgress: The need for critical feminism in gerontology. *Women and Aging, 11*(2/3), 171-184.

Terry's Total Fitness (2002). Retrieved November, 2002 from http://www.ttfit.com/empower-gh.htm.

Thompson, C. J. (2003). Natural health discourses and the therapeutic production of consumer resistance. *The Sociological Quarterly, 44*(1), 81-108.

Tides of Life. (2002). Retrieved November, 2002 from http://www.tidesoflife.com/.

U.S. Senate, Special Committee on Aging. (2001). Swindlers, hucksters and snake oil salesman: Hype and hope marketing anti-aging products to seniors (Serial No. 107-14). Washington, DC: U.S. Government Printing Office.

Walker, A. (1998). Speaking for themselves: The new politics of old age in Europe. *Education and Ageing, 13*(1), 13-36.

Walker, A. (2000). Public policy and the construction of old age in Europe. *The Gerontologist, 40*(3), 304-308.

Wellness Today. (2002). Retrieved November, 2002 from http://www.wellnesstoday.com/april2001/anti_aging_under_attack!.htm.

Wilson, G. (2000). *Understanding old age: Critical and global perspectives.* London: Sage.

CHAPTER 9

Dementia in the Iron Cage: The Biopsychiatric Construction of Alzheimer's Dementia

Kathryn Douthit

Over the past quarter century, Western psychiatry has undergone significant transformation from a profession predicated largely on psychoanalytic thought to one that draws heavily on the success and apparent scientific authority of modern medicine (Ingleby, 1980). As a result of its new stature as a legitimate medical discipline, Western psychiatry has bolstered its eminence among the many professionals engaged in the treatment of psychological distress. The power of the biomedical model has elevated the influence of psychiatry in the Western world, and that influence reverberates around the globe, challenging indigenous non-Western understandings of mind and healing (Maser, Kaelber, & Weise, 1991).

In its quest for scientific grounding, however, psychiatric care has itself become increasingly constrained by the late-modernist privileging of rationalism, positivism, technical efficiency, componentiality, and scientific method (Berger, Berger, & Kellner, 1974). In a marked divergence from the constructivism and subjectivism characterizing postmodern thought (Ingleby, 1980), psychological distress is understood in terms of a delimited nosology (classification system) consisting of objectified, atomized categories of mental disorder. Psychological disturbances are decontextualized and divorced from inter- and intrasubjective meaning. Thus, both the social sources of psychiatric distress and its existential human significance are eclipsed from diagnosis and treatment. Most disturbingly, the new biomedical model of psychiatry shares a reciprocal relationship of legitimation and support with the market-driven policies and practices of the healthcare and pharmaceutical industries.

In its approach to the diagnostic process, Western psychiatric nosology thus fails to consider the multidimensional configuration of forces—sociocultural as well as biopsychosocial—that constitute the human psyche. Instead, categories delineating particular configurations of behavioral and affective descriptors are introduced based on a presumption that for each of the identified disorders, medical science will elucidate the underlying neuropathology. This late-modern brand of psychiatry, privileging in vitro molecular understanding and medical intervention, is known as biopsychiatry and is sharply distinguished from what is largely considered by the profession to be its archaic and ill-informed predecessor, Freudian or psychoanalytic psychiatry (Kirk & Kutchins, 1992).

While the late-modern themes of biopsychiatry play a major role in defining early twenty-first century understanding of psychological distress, market forces guiding the policies and practices of managed care impose a distinct character on the structure of contemporary mental health by bolstering the use of interventions that can readily be assessed for their ability to render expeditious cost-effective outcomes (Dana, Conner, & Allen, 1996; Lerner, 1995; Miller, 1996a, 1996b). Pharmacological, behavioral, and strictly time-limited psychotherapeutic interventions have provided a centrally important response to the political and economic priorities exerted by biopsychiatry and managed care, respectively. Alternative forms of mental health delivery have become marginalized and more medicalized, efficiency-based clinical practice has been reflexively reinforced (Breggin, 1991a, 1991b).

The biopsychiatric approach can point to some notable successes, including the life-saving pharmacological treatments in severe cases of schizophrenia, bipolar disorder, and major depressive disorder. Such examples notwithstanding, biopsychiatry seldom suffices as the sole approach to treatment, and in some instances its uncritical application can be seen as counterproductive. When clinicians focus all of their attention on the biological treatment of disorders such as attention deficit/hyperactivity disorder, generalized anxiety disorder, and major depressive disorder, just to name a few, they become complicitous in the exoneration of sociostructural configurations that limit human possibility (Douthit, in press) and fail to provide genuine caring, empathic, emotionally sustaining, and humane relationships (Breggin, 1997).

Recent advances in the science of dementia of the Alzheimer's type (DAT) show that biologizing trends in dementia care follow a similar pattern of exonerating the social and denying the humanity of the victim. Scientists working to understand the ways that social life contributes to the DAT disease process have suggested that a number of social conditions are detrimental to brain health generally, and to DAT resistance more specifically (Snowdon, 2001). Professionals who work closely with people with Alzheimer's disease claim that there are lessons about the essence of human social life to be learned from the seemingly convoluted and halcyon expressions of dementia, and that amidst the diminishing grasp of a historical self remains a yearning for a self-in-relation (Stein, 2002). Yet these compelling understandings and the possibilities they represent remain eclipsed from mainstream trends in dementia care by the hegemony of the medical model. In the place of the continued need for human contact and responsiveness, the one-dimensional "expert knowledge" of biopsychiatric medicine is often used to confine persons with dementia to a Weberian "iron cage" (Weber, 1958) of scientifically sanctified and bureaucratically administered knowledge.

This chapter will analyze the hegemonic forces and processes that eclipse the possibilities for dementia-preventive and palliative care. It will show how trends in biopsychiatry, favoring pharmacological and time-limited instrumental therapies, have ignored the multidimensional aspects of DAT treatment in favor of interventions that focus on genetic and neurophysiological aspects of mental disorder. These therapies are tacitly imposed on the global mental health community through the American Psychiatric Association's (APA) widely disseminated *Diagnostic and Statistical Manual of Mental Disorders* (*DSM*). For almost a half century, the *DSM* has been the sole source of diagnostic authority for psychiatric problems and illnesses, despite the fact that the text itself has undergone several "updatings" that have involved revision of disorder descriptions. In this chapter, proposed associations between the increasing influence of the biopsychiatric paradigm, through imposition of the *DSM*, and ill-informed practices surrounding current management of DAT are elaborated.

The chapter is organized in four main sections as follows: It first offers an overview of DAT, including symptoms, epidemiology, and treatment. Second, it reviews the history of *DSM* over the past quarter century relative to movements in academic psychiatry that espoused, during this time period, a shift to a more biomedically informed mental health practice. Originating in the United States, this impact has long been felt throughout the modern world and is increasingly global in scope. Third, the *DSM* depiction of DAT is closely examined. Fourth, two particular outcomes of the *DSM* depiction of DAT are then considered that together comprise significant missed opportunity for palliative and preventive care; namely, 1) the reliance on time-efficient behavioral therapies and depersonalized psychopharmacological treatment strategies, and 2) the lack of attention to preventive and sociostructural interventions harboring significant promise for circumvention of suffering for both the elderly and their caregivers.

DEMENTIA OF THE ALZHEIMER'S TYPE: A BRIEF OVERVIEW

Alzheimer's disease, as described by the Alzheimer's Association (2004), is a neurological disorder that destroys brain cells leading to the symptoms of DAT, including progressive memory loss, disorientation, decline in the ability to perform routine tasks, deterioration of language skills, impairment of judgment, and changes in personality that are distressing for caregivers and family members. Brain cell loss associated with Alzheimer's disease eventually compromises the function of general body systems and is fatal. The rate of disease progression varies widely with the time from symptom onset to death, ranging between 3 and

20 years. Upon autopsy, the brains of Alzheimer's victims display the amyloid plaques and neurofibrillary tangles that are the hallmarks of the disease.

Drawing upon epidemiological data, the Alzheimer's Association (2005) estimates that approximately 10% of people age 65 and above are stricken with Alzheimer's and that half of persons age 85 and older are similarly afflicted. Family history is a risk factor for the disease as well. To date, one gene has been shown to increase the risk of disease after age 65 (Alzheimer's Association, 2004).

The pharmacological and behavioral interventions that dominate Alzheimer's care may confer some relief, albeit temporary and incomplete, from the cognitive deficits that plague the lives of Alzheimer's patients and their caregivers. The first line of treatment in a battle to retain as much cognitive capacity as possible is to administer one of several recent incarnations of acetylcholinesterase inhibitors. Known by their brand names Aricept, Exelon, and Reminyl, these pharmaceuticals appear to delay the decline of cognitive and mental function in many Alzheimer's disease patients (Bullock, 2001). Although the disease process is not permanently thwarted, these drugs in some cases can temporarily, and thankfully improve cognitive function. Likewise, the 20% to 40% of DAT patients who suffer from the clinically significant depression that is a part of the Alzheimer's disease process can be treated with the spectrum of available antidepressant medications (Kennedy & Scalmati, 2001; Small et al., 1997).

Many behavioral therapies should also be acknowledged for their success in addressing the routine difficulties encountered by caregivers tending to the needs of the DAT patient. Simplifying tasks, utilizing safety locks for doors and gates, establishing predictable routines, using labels to serve as reminders or to jog memory, and simplifying the environment for easier negotiation all contribute to a more manageable caregiving experience both at home and in institutional settings (Slone & Gleason, 1999; Stewart, 1995).

THE *DSM* AND GLOBALIZATION OF BIOPSYCHIATRY

The current focus on interventions that address expressions of the neurological deficits of Alzheimer's disease clearly reflect a more general trend in biopsychiatry that privileges time-efficient, instrumental therapies whose outcomes can be assessed using objective measures. On a fundamental level, this scientized trend toward efficiency and instrumentality has been foisted upon the breadth of the mental health community through contemporary editions of the *DSM*. Veiled theoretical assumptions in the manual supporting the biopsychiatric model are imposed on mental health practitioners through coercive practices that tie the use of the *DSM* to professional legitimation and remuneration. What follows is an accounting of the political forces that catapulted the transformation of *DSM* from its mid-twentieth century psychoanalytic roots to its present-day bio-organic orientation.

The medical/biological leanings of psychiatry, which gained considerable momentum in the 1970s, are deeply embedded in the current version of the *DSM,* the *DSM-IV-TR* (fourth edition, textual revision) (American Psychiatric Association, 2000). This publication represents the latest instantiation of a largely unarticulated but persistent trend in biopsychiatry over the last several decades. As described earlier, the *DSM* provides a classification system for the diagnosis of mental disorders. To date, nearly 400 disorders are included within its classification system. Like its predecessors, *DSM-III* (third edition) (American Psychiatric Association, 1980), *DSM-IIIR* (third edition revised) (American Psychiatric Association, 1987) and *DSM-IV* (fourth edition) (APA, 1994), the *DSM-IV-TR* (APA, 2000), dictates the language and conceptualization of mental disorder not only for psychiatrists, but for the range of nonpsychiatric mental health professionals working in hospitals, mental health clinics, community agencies, long-term care facilities, schools, and private offices. Third-party reimbursements, services in special education, governmental research funding awards, and legal questions of mental competency versus incompetency are uniformly contingent upon the codifications of the *DSM-IV-TR* (Kutchins & Kirk, 1997).

While the *DSM* clearly dominates mental health administration in the United States, it is also published in 22 languages (American Psychiatric Association, 2005) and along with its closely related counterpart, the World Health Organization's *International Classification of Disease (ICD)* (World Health Organization, 2005), enjoys increasing global expansion (Maser, Kaelber, & Weise, 1991). Considerable attention is devoted to ensuring that *DSM* and *ICD* codifications are compatible so that uniform standards of disorder identification exist across geographic boundaries. This global effort to standardize psychiatric diagnosis is accompanied by an inevitable export of some of the injurious practices arising from *DSM*.

It is to be acknowledged that the new biopsychiatry, disseminated through the *DSM* and *ICD,* can claim a number of clear successes. For example, clients suffering from severe battles with bipolar disorder or schizophrenia often find the psychopharmacological interventions offered by biopsychiatry to be effective, sometimes in ways that have life-saving value for patients. This knowledge, however, is not predicated upon a unidirectional organic model of causation. While molecular geneticists have supplied credible evidence of inherited, biological vulnerability to some disorders (for a review, see Faraone, Tsuang, & Tsuang, 1999), they have simultaneously implicated powerful environmental influences on genetic expression and have bolstered the notion that inherited vulnerability does not constitute an unequivocal endorsement of biomedical intervention (Douthit, in press; Rose, 1998; Sapolsky, 1998). Because of these powerful environmental effects whose operation directly on genetic expression is now understood, contextually informed prevention and intervention can interrupt destructive cycles of psychological distress even in the case of serious mental disorders that have a known genetic basis. Intervention that disregards this powerful link to environmental exigency is inevitably bankrupt in its ability to holistically intervene in episodes of psychological distress.

More broadly, indiscriminate applications of the biopsychiatric paradigm not only limit the scope of clinical practice to one that is injuriously bounded by biomedical epistemology, it also directs myopic research agendas limited to search for organic attributions of mental disorder, and more generally constrains both the professional and lay understanding of etiology, treatment, and prevention of psychological distress This paper will explore how this general problem is manifested in the specific case of DAT, as it is characterized by the current *DSM*. Before proceeding to that specific task, however, it will be useful to review some of the historical and political context within which the *DSM* was itself initially developed, and how it has changed.

Psychiatry's Paradigm Shift

Over the past three decades, the field of psychiatry has witnessed sweeping changes in the fundamental epistemological assumptions that govern both research and practice in the profession. Although some of these changes have occurred in response to compelling empirical evidence, many have been the outcome of political shifts within the psychiatric community. Like many political struggles, the conflicts among factions of the APA during the 1970s were premeditated, clearly articulated, and resulted in irreconcilable divisions in the organization's philosophical underpinnings (Caplan, 1996; Kirk & Kutchins, 1992; Kutchins & Kirk, 1997).

Discord in the APA was precipitated by a small, but powerful contingent of academic research psychiatrists who aggressively challenged the dominant role of psychoanalytic theory in the psychiatric conceptualization of mental disorder. Starting in the 1950s, it was becoming clear that the psychoanalytic paradigm informing much of American psychiatry was suitable for wealthy neurotics, but was failing miserably in addressing the needs of the poor, the disenfranchised, and institutionalized psychotics. As psychiatry was already considered a low-status subspecialty in medicine, the growing public and professional awareness of its failures only exacerbated the generally denigrating view of the discipline (Kirk & Kutchins, 1992).

Clearly, due to the paucity of scientific evidence supporting its established practices, the field of psychiatry in the mid-twentieth century was suffering from a crisis of legitimation (Habermas, 1976). Nothing else served to publicly high-light the pseudoscientific sand upon which the profession of psychiatry stood like the famous debate over whether or not homosexuality should be classified as a mental disorder. Beginning in 1970, gay activists, infuriated by the fact that homosexuality was being officially classified as a mental disorder, began staging a series of disruptive protests at national meetings of the APA. On one side of the homosexuality controversy was the contingent of vocal and persuasive gay activists (including a number of gay psychiatrists) and on the other was the large body of psychiatrists outraged at the notion of changing a diagnosis based exclusively on political exhortation (Caplan, 1996; Kirk & Kutchins, 1992; Kutchins & Kirk, 1997).

The outcome of the controversy was a compromise proposal that eliminated the classification of homosexuality as a mental disorder and instead focused on those unable to adjust to what was now being characterized as a type of variation in sexual development (Spitzer, 1981 in Kirk & Kutchins, 1992). Although this compromise addressed the dispute among factions within the APA, it did little to bolster the organization's image. General doubt about the scientific legitimacy of psychiatry was exacerbated by this apparently arbitrary decision to classify, and then declassify, homosexuality as a mental disorder. To preserve its prestigious position within the mental health arena and to shore up its eroding status relative to the remainder of the medical profession, psychiatry needed to address skepticism concerning its fundamental legitimacy. It urgently needed an epistemology that would afford the profession the objectivity in diagnosis and treatment enjoyed by their nonpsychiatric medical counterparts (Caplan, 1996; Ingleby, 1981; Kirk & Kutchins, 1992).

The emergent biomedical model of "mental disorder," a term that intentionally comports the notion of individual mental pathology, clearly reflected a victory for both the academics and the accountants. Research methods in psychiatry are increasingly predicated on positivist rather than interpretivist epistemology; costly, labor-intensive psychoanalytic practice has been rejected in favor of time-limited therapies and psychopharmacological intervention, and a dramatic shift has occurred from a complex psychodynamic view of deviant behavior to one which reflects organic attribution and "cost-effective," pharmacologically driven individual-level solutions.

The Birth of DSM-III

A core assumption accompanying the new biomedical paradigm was that scientific legitimation for psychiatrists would ultimately come from biopsychiatric research elucidating the physiological, biochemical, and anatomical causes of mental illness. Ultimately, biopsychiatry would assume a dominant role within the scope of psychiatric practice. One major problem remained, however, in psychiatry's biopsychiatric transformation: It is impossible to elucidate biological causation of mental disorders when members of the profession cannot agree on how to define categories of illness. Clinicians were generally unable to agree on diagnostic criteria for discrete "illnesses" making it quite difficult to categorize individuals for research purposes. Unlike their medical counterparts, practicing Freudian psychoanalysts had little use for diagnostic handbooks. Contrastingly for the psychoanalyst, the push to develop diagnostic criteria was antithetical to a long history of interpretive subjectified practice strategy (Ingleby, 1981; Kirk & Kutchins, 1992).

The *DSM-III* (American Psychiatric Association, 1980), developed through the 1970s and published in 1980, was crafted in a manner that gave primary focus to interclinician reliability. Categories of disorder and the criteria describing them were the product of extensive conferencing among clinicians and a massive field study (Kirk & Kutchins, 1992). Further refinement and expansion of the disorder categories are reflected in subsequent editions of *DSM* including the *DSM-III-TR* (American Psychiatric Association, 1987), *DSM-IV* (American Psychiatric Association, 1994), and *DSM-IV-TR* (American Psychiatric Association, 2000). In its current incarnation, the *DSM-IV-TR*, the manual contains classification schemes and textual descriptions for over 400 categories of mental disorder, all predicated on the importance of interclinician reliability.

Although *DSM-III* addressed, to a limited degree, the interclinician reliability problem, several other problems were not addressed. Most notably, no attention was given to the nosology's construct validity (Kirk & Kutchins, 1992). This absence of construct validity is troubling, particularly in light of the fact that the Manual erroneously claims that all of the disorder characterizations contained within its pages are atheoretical with regard to etiology and that each of the entries is exclusively confined to a descriptive profile: "*DSM-III* introduced a number of important methodological innovations, including explicit diagnostic criteria, a multiaxial system, and *a descriptive approach that attempted to be neutral in relation to theories of etiology* (italics added)" (American Psychiatric Association, 2000, p. xxvi). Many of the criteria sets are, in fact, not actually atheoretical and few were generated using scientific evidence. *Deconstructive theoretical analysis of a number of the sets of descriptive criteria, as well other supporting text in the manual, clearly reveals the underlying assumption of an organic disease model* (see, e.g., Douthit, 2001). Not surprisingly, such bias privileges intra-individual psychiatric interventions that are both cost-effective and scientifically legitimated.

Although the categories and their descriptors were generated primarily through clinician consensus rather than through scientific evidence, they have, since their introduction in 1980, gone through a process of reification that has afforded them an air of objective truth. The apparent truth value of the nosology has been reinforced by the wide array of venues where *DSM* terminology and conceptualization serve as the intellectual currency through which mental health issues are negotiated. Not only do *DSM* categorizations influence clinical intervention strategies, they scaffold academic and pharmaceutical research agendas and are the basis for third-party reimbursement policies, social security support, legal decisions of mental competency versus incompetency, and decisions regarding school-based support services (Kutchins & Kirk, 1997). The *DSM* has, in essence, been instrumental in disseminating its compartmentalized organicist model of mental disorder, whose primary support comes in the form of clinician consensus and whose wide proliferation comes through reciprocal multisystemic reinforcement to all reaches of mental health enterprise.

DSM-IV-TR and Its Depiction of DAT

Although *DSM-IV-TR* heralded a new standard in scope with unprecedented claims of the strength of its neuroscientific evidentiary base (American Psychiatric Association, 2000), many concerns prevail regarding its organic psychopathological view of psychiatric diagnosis, the credibility of its claims to "theory neutrality," and its exclusion of socially constituted and phenomenological perspectives. Such concerns have previously been raised in relation to selected entries in *DSM* such as attention-deficit/hyperactivity disorder (Douthit, 2001), and depression (Kleinman & Cohen, 1997), and it is an extension of these concerns that brings us to the central task of this chapter; namely, to analyze the *DSM* depiction of DAT and its implications for later life mental health services.

A clear example of the manual's theoretical adherence to an organic disease model can be found in the *DSM-IV-TR* (American Psychiatric Association, 2000) entry for DAT. Essentially, three diagnostic criteria, "A," "B," and "C" are included in the criterion set describing DAT. Criterion A is the most elaborate of the three and includes a host of cognitive deficits:

A. The development of multiple cognitive deficits manifested by both:
 (1) memory impairment (impaired ability to learn new information or to recall previously learned information)
 (2) one or more of the following cognitive disturbances:
   (a) aphasia (language disturbance)
   (b) apraxia (impaired ability to carry out motor activities despite intact motor function)
   (c) agnosia (failure to recognize or identify objects despite intact sensory function)
   (d) disturbance in executive functioning (i.e., planning, organizing, sequencing, abstracting) (American Psychiatric Association, 2000, p. 157)

Criterion B specifies the degree to which A1 and A2 affect daily life: "The cognitive deficits in Criteria A1 and A2 each cause significant impairment in social or occupational functioning and represent a significant decline from a previous level of functioning" (American Psychiatric Association, 2000, p. 157). Rather than suggesting additional forms of disability, criterion B gives definition to how the cognitive disabilities in criterion A shapes day-to-day living.

Criterion C gives temporal definition to the cognitive disabilities in criteria A1 and A2: "The course is characterized by gradual onset and continuing cognitive decline" (American Psychiatric Association, 2000, p. 157), while criteria D, E, and F caution against confusing DAT with other types of disorders that can potentially manifest with symptoms similar to DAT. Disorders likely to produce cognitive disabilities that mimic DAT include central nervous system conditions such as brain tumors, cardiovascular disease, and Parkinson's disease; systemic conditions such as hypothyroidism, HIV infection, folic acid deficiency, and hypercalcemia; delirium, and other mental disorders such as schizophrenia and major depressive disorder. Finally, various types of DAT are specified, including early or late onset, and associated delirium, delusions, and/or depressed mood.

The gestalt that emerges from consideration of criteria A through E is one that clearly underscores a host of cognitive disabilities and their impact on occupational and social functioning. The *sine qua non* of the disorder, reflected in criteria A-F, is situated exclusively in the cognitive domain. While an explicit reference to disorder etiology is not cited in the criteria for DAT, implicitly, it can be said whatever the etiology, the most salient and clinically significant outcome of that etiology is one that affects a wide array of cognitive operations, including executive function, memory, speech, motoric facility, and sensory interpretation.

Although no explicit reference is made to disorder etiology in the set of criteria, explicit etiological reference is made in the text that accompanies the criteria. References in the text clearly frame the disorder as a "central nervous system condition" (American Psychiatric Association, 2000, p. 154) for which there is a genetic predisposition (American Psychiatric Association, 2000). Additional descriptors guide the reader to distinguish between early and late onset; thereby, conveying the notion of a regularized, predictable biologically age-driven disorder genesis.

Logical analysis of the criteria and text for DAT reveals the following theoretical points in regard to etiology:

1. The symptoms related to DAT reflect a central nervous system disruption resulting in dysfunction in one or more primary cognitive functions.
2. The disruption in cognitive function is likely correlated with the presence of specific genes.
3. The manifestations of the responsible gene(s) is/are dependent upon a predictable degree of biological maturation.

Additional information about the presumed etiology of DAT can be gleaned from the *DSM-IV-TR* entry for "mood disorder due to a general medical condition" (MDDGMC), which includes Alzheimer's Disease in a list of "neurological conditions" leading to depressive disturbance (American Psychiatric Association, 2000, p. 403). This particular piece of MDDGMC text echoes the theoretical assumptions found in the DAT entry; namely, that Alzheimer's disease is a neurological condition.

While the etiological theory that emerges from the DAT diagnostic criteria presents few ambiguities, references in the DAT text to "depressed mood" introduce a theoretical uncertainty that is central to this critique of later-life mental health practice. For the clinician diagnosing DAT, a classification option, "with depressed mood," can be adopted to account for symptoms of dysphoria associated with the disorder presentation. The *DSM*'s attention to DAT symptoms of depression gives the appearance that the manual is considering the patient's affective response to their devastating condition. This apparent attention to affect is an important theoretical/etiological consideration that seems to acknowledge the importance of lived experience in the disease process. It would concede that the phenomenology of the disease process, or the notion of the disease itself, has subjective meaning to the patient-in-relation and that this subjective meaning is an integral component of the disease experience. However, upon closer analysis, the DAT entry in the *DSM-IV-TR* reveals that the references to depressed mood are, in substance, unrelated to the phenomenological experience of the disorder.

Returning to the MDDGMC section of the manual, several points, taken together, help to elucidate the theoretical roots of the depressive features of DAT. As a category, MDDGMC is designed specifically to account for depressive symptoms generated by medical conditions. The manual specifically states that "(t)he essential feature of MDDGMC is a prominent and persistent disturbance in mood that is judged to be due to the direct physiological effects of a general medical condition" (American Psychiatric Association, 2000, p. 401). Unlike other *DSM* categories of depressive disorder for which the symptoms of depression are not specifically tied to an organic disease entity, i.e., major depressive disorder and dysthymia, for the diseases subsumed under the MDDGMC classification, depression is a predictable outcome of disease process. The fact that Alzheimer's disease is referenced, along with other diseases with direct nervous system involvement, in a detailing of the prevalence of MDDGMC across organic diseases implies that DAT is indeed among those disorders that the *DSM* portrays as being associated with disease generated depression. It should be noted that unlike the other diseases with noted nervous system involvement (e.g., Parkinson's disease, Huntington's disease, cerebrovascular disease) (American Psychiatric Association, 2000), however, depression associated with DAT has its own distinct classification code (i.e., a code distinct from the generic MDDGMC code), but its status in the *DSM* as an example of a mood disorder generated by organic disease process is still quite clear. The logical conclusion that can be drawn concerning the "with depressed mood" specifier is that depression, as an affective response to the exigencies of life as a DAT patient, is not the focus of the specifier. Rather, the "with depressed mood" designation is intended to denote the depressive symptoms that are often the outcome of Alzheimer's neuropathology.

Drawing on the preceding analysis of *DSM* text, the following summary statement concerning the *DSM* profile of DAT emerges: *DAT is a neurodegenerative mental disorder, likely related to specific genes, that results in disruption in one or more primary cognitive functions. Manifestation of DAT symptoms generally depends on biological maturation, and the affect generated by the experience of being a victim of the disorder is not considered to be a germane identifying feature of DAT.* Further, predicated on the knowledge that *DSM-IV-TR* categories of disorder were originally composed with the primary objective of creating interclinican reliability (Kirk & Kutchins, 1992), it can be said that the clinicians and researchers who authored *DSM-IV-TR* and participated in all of the relevant field trials generally agree that this DAT profile provides an apt description of the Alzheimer's dementia patient. These clinicians and academicians are content to limit the defining features of DAT to those associated with the range of cognitive deficits and depressive symptoms linked to disease pathology.

Thus, the *DSM-IV-TR* profile of DAT is deceptively myopic. Although the theory underlying the *DSM-IV-TR* depiction of DAT reflects contemporary understanding of the biological mechanisms that generate the disease, further consideration of the DAT entry reveals a specious profile that is theoretically reductionistic, ignoring nonbiomedical sources and failing to capture many of the poignant and profound clinical exigencies endured by the disorder victim. By focusing exclusively on the cognitive and behavioral outcomes stemming from the neurodegenerative/genetic roots of the disorder, the *DSM-IV-TR* depiction of DAT contributes to both a naturalized understanding of the disease and the support of established economic interests. Thus, attention is focused on expanded pharmacological usage and simultaneously deflected from difficult social-structural conditions that could play a role in prevention.

THE IMPACT OF DAT BIOMEDICALIZATION

Eclipsing the Affective Domain: The Increasing Reliance on Behavioral and Pharmacological Interventions

A particularly disturbing consequence of the cognitive and neurodegenerative focus of DAT in the *DSM-IV-TR* is that it fails to capture the profound sense of anxiety, grief, sadness, loss of self-esteem, and need for relatedness experienced by Alzheimer's disease victims (Bahro, Silber, & Sunderland, 1995). The image of dementia that emerges from the *DSM* entry is one that is estranged from affect and assumes that the most significant aspects of the victim's transcendence from competency to incompetency, from self to selfless, is marked exclusively by cognitive and behavioral phenomena. Any affect generated by the phenomenological realities of living with the disorder is parceled into alternative diagnoses such as generalized anxiety disorder or adjustment disorder.

As explained above, the *DSM-IV-TR* entry for DAT includes, as coding options, early or late onset DAT "with depressed mood" (American Psychiatric Association, 2000, p. 155) and this apparent inclusion of affect in the disorder profile is used to account for the depressive features generated by the neuropathology of the disease process. Empirical evidence, in actuality, points to a predictable major depressive syndrome of Alzheimer's disease, i.e., a major depression related to the neurobiological changes of Alzheimer's disease. In a collaborative study reported by Zubenko et al., (2003), major depressive episodes are observed in nearly 50% of their most severely demented subjects; a number that is considerably higher than what is observed in age-matched controls. Zubenko et al. (2003) state that

> (t)he high rate of major depressive episodes that occur after the onset of cognitive impairment among patients with Alzheimer's disease (the majority of whom had no premorbid history of major depression), common emergence in the early stages of dementia when symptoms of cognitive impairment are least likely to contribute to the syndromal diagnosis of major depression, and differences in the clinical presentations of major depressive episodes of Alzheimer's disease patients and nondemented elderly comparison subjects, all support the validity of the major depressive syndrome of Alzheimer's disease. Our findings suggest the major depressive syndrome of Alzheimer's disease may be among the most common mood disorders of older adults. (p. 857)

Evidence from pharmacological and neurobiological studies also supports the existence of a form of depression related to the degenerative neuropathology of Alzheimer's disease. Specifically, research on plasma levels of the tricyclic antidepressant nortriptyline indicates that the clinical responses of patients with Alzheimer's disease with depression differ from those of late-life patients who have depression in the absence of Alzheimer's disease, and that these differences are not attributable to alterations in drug metabolism or decreased tolerance of side effects (Streim et al., 2000 in Weintraub, Furlan, & Katz, 2003). Zubenko et al. (2003) report the findings of a number of studies (see Curcio & Kemper, 1984; Iversen et al., 1983; Tomlinson, Irving, & Blessed, 1981; Yamamoto & Hirano, 1985; Zubenko & Moossy, 1988) that implicate the Alzheimer's disease related degeneration of brain stem nuclei involved in mood and thought. "Projections from the dorsal and median raphe nuclei provide extensive serotonergic innervation of the forebrain. The noradrenergic cells of the locus ceruleus project axons widely to both the neocortex and the hippocampus. Alzheimer's disease is associated with the loss of neuronal cells from both of these nuclei, and a substantial fraction of those that remain develop neurofibrillary tangles" (pp. 859-860).

Still, in spite of the compelling evidence implicating the direct involvement of Alzheimer's disease pathology in the etiology of a depressive syndrome, it is erroneous to assume that the depression suffered by Alzheimer's disease patients, particularly those who have not yet experienced a high degree of cognitive decline, is uniformly an outcome of the neurological degeneration associated with the disease. A consensus statement of the American Association of Geriatric Psychiatry, the Alzheimer's Association, and the American Geriatrics Society contends that the impact of Alzheimer's disease extends beyond the cognitive and behavioral manifestations of the disorder to impart an "emotional toll on patients and their families (that) is profound" (Small et al., 1997, p. 1366).

Supporting the notion that focus is disproportionately aimed at the behavioral and biological challenges of Alzheimer's disease, Bahro et al. (1995) conclude that "the psychodynamics of Alzheimer's disease have been largely overlooked by a research community that is, perhaps, more familiar with mechanisms for observing objective, measurable ratings of behavioral or biological criteria. There are fewer studies on the phenomenology of Alzheimer's disease patients' subjective experiences, their individual beliefs or self-perceptions" (p. 41). Bahro et al. (1995) acknowledge the complexity of the phenomenological experience of their DAT patients and conclude that "A comprehensive perspective of . . . (DAT) . . . patients must include recognition of the meaning of their experience from the vantage point of their 'inner world'. The clinical manifestations of their illness result from a complex interaction of neurological deficits, the meaning of these impairments to the patient, and the defense mechanisms used by the patient in coping with her illness" (p. 45). Some of the impairments suffered by the DAT patients include: "loss of self-esteem as well as the loss of a sense of mastery and control" (p. 45).

Clearly, the predictable and comprehensible emotional responses of Alzheimer's disease victims to their ongoing, progressive loss of self-in-relation is not a direct outcome of the genetic expression of the Alzheimer's disease genes associated with the plaques and tangles of brain tissue from Alzheimer's disease patients. But from a theoretical standpoint, it is particularly relevant that the affective, phenomenological sequelae of DAT are not factored into the diagnostic criteria. Experience is excluded. Instead, the criteria are aimed, with great precision, at the neurological foundations of the disorder and are divorced, for the victim, from its psychosocial and cultural meaning. In spite of the fact that intense feelings are associated with the disorder, they are not considered by the authors of *DSM-IV-TR* to be relevant to a description of the disease process. *Thus, the DSM-IV-TR characterization of DAT, with its emphasis on degenerative neurological mechanisms, encourages neglect of the phenomenological experience by the research community as well as medical practitioners, and eclipses its import in the clinical intervention regimen.*

Without the phenomenological perspective that goes beyond neurologically generated symptomatology, the main focus of intervention thus continues to be aimed at that which is economically expedient and rooted in the objectivity of Western medicine. A dehumanized clinical picture of the DAT client/patient emerges that ironically mirrors the difficulty commonly experienced by friends and relatives scrambling to find a vehicle that will connect them to the humanity of the DAT victim and reinforces the victim's own sense of their impending loss of self. The disproportionate focus of drug and behavioral therapies on the cognitive misguidedly equates cognition with the totality of human essence. The loss of cognition, and its attendant loss of a historical self-identity, are mistakenly equated with the loss of a relational self. Afflicted elderly, suffering unspeakable losses, are thus objectified as an infantilized and disabled "other."

Cognition and humanity—knowing and being—remain inextricably intertwined in the late-modern understanding of the essence of humankind. For older persons needing to name their subjective experience and to find comfort in human relationship, a meager solace is salvaged from a hard-edged practice of mental health that embraces efficient, instrumental biologically informed solutions and behavioral manipulations.

Denial of Sociogenic Contributions to Disease

The second fallacy predicated on the *DSM*'s bioorganic presentation of DAT is the manual's instantiation of a false dichotomy between the internal biological self and external systemic sociocultural structures. DAT is depicted as a disorder arising as a consequence of intrinsic biological failure, while the various compelling contextual factors that have been shown to influence manifestation of the disorder are diminished. This failure to consider the "individual-in-relation" places serious constraints on clinical and investigative practices. What is at issue here is not the accuracy of the *DSM*'s depiction of DAT symptoms; rather, it is that its focus on existing organic disease process eclipses key psychosocial risk factors for DAT, many of which are correlates of inequitable social and economic resource allocation. *DSM*'s compartmentalization of DAT into the bounds of a circumscribed neurogenetic disorder draws attention from important relationships between DAT and the physical and emotional sequelae of social, economic, cultural, political, and historical challenges. *Emerging research suggests that DAT symptoms, at least in part, are the tangible embodiment of an individual's life-course history, and that the correlates of DAT extend far beyond the boundaries of simple later-life inherited neurological disease.*

Numerous examples exist of DAT risk factors that bear a relationship to socioeconomic status. Moceri et al. (2001), in a retrospective study of Alzheimer's disease patients, show that the children of unskilled manual laborers harbor a greater risk of being diagnosed with Alzheimer's disease than randomly chosen subjects. The same group of researchers showed that the children of fathers employed in manual labor are at a greater risk for Alzheimer's disease both in groups that carried the apolipoprotein epsilon-4 allele (APOE-4), a strong genetic risk factor for Alzheimer's disease, and in groups that did not carry the APOE-4 allele. Another retrospective study of Alzheimer's patients (Letenneur et al., 1999) shows that for both men and women, the risk of being diagnosed with Alzheimer's disease is associated with lower educational attainment.

Data drawn from the well-known "Nun Study," launched by David Snowdon, raise compelling questions concerning the relationship between early childhood literacy practices and acquisition of Alzheimer's disease in later life (Snowdon et al., 1996). In this exceptional analysis, information on the nuns' linguistic ability and performance in early adulthood (measured by idea density in the autobiographical writing) was available and was combined with data on later life

Alzheimer's disease and cognitive function and then with autopsy reports. The studies showed that poor cognitive function and Alzheimer's disease in late life is related to low linguistic ability in early life. In a population of women ages 75 to 95 years, early age linguistic ability was assessed through autobiographical writing completed when the women were a mean age of 22 years. The findings indicate that linguistic ability is positively associated with the presence, upon gross examination, of the neuropathological markers of Alzheimer's disease and with low cognitive functioning. The correlation between early linguistic ability and the presence of late-life plaques and tangles strongly suggests that the higher cognitive ability scores in the more linguistically adept nuns are not merely a reflection of genetically determined intelligence. Snowdon (2001) suggests that these data may shed light on the importance of early-childhood literacy practices in maintaining cognitive health in later life. If the quality and quantity of childhood interaction with text, both written and spoken, translates into a more complex handling of text in young adulthood, Snowdon's speculation concerning the importance of early-childhood literacy practices may indeed have important implications for DAT prevention.

The potential preventive value of life-course cognitive development also receives support from Snowdon (1997). In a case study of a particularly vital 101-year-old woman he calls "Sister Mary," Snowdon shows that even in the presence of abundant senile plaques and neurofibrillary tangles, i.e., the neuro-pathological lesions indicative of Alzheimer's disease, the cognitive and behavioral manifestations of the disease can be averted. Sister Mary, who displayed exemplary physical and cognitive facility, had surprising findings when autopsied. In spite of the fact that she had consistently demonstrated high levels of cognitive functioning and no signs of dementia, her brain tissue presented with numerous lesions diagnostic for Alzheimer's disease. Although there are no conclusive findings from this case study, it suggests a hypothesis that may ultimately prove to be quite germane to Alzheimer's prevention efforts: That the quantity and quality of synaptic connections developed in early life may compensate for destruction of neurological pathways in old age.

Early development, outside the bounds of cognition, holds additional clues to Alzheimer's prevention. A preponderance of evidence implicates poor cardio-vascular health in the cognitive and behavioral manifestations of Alzheimer's disease (Bowler, 2004; Breteler, 2000; Iadecola, 2003; Tzourio, 2003). Athero-sclerosis of arteries in the circle of Willis, an arterial configuration that is a part of the central blood supply to the brain, is associated with brain infarct, i.e., stroke. Brain infarcts, both large and small, are in turn linked to marked exacerbation of Alzheimer's pathology. A study by Snowdon et al. (1997) shows that poorer cognitive function and higher prevalence of dementia result from the simultaneous presence of stroke and Alzheimer's neuropathology than either the stroke or Alzheimer's neuropathology condition alone. Understanding the connection between DAT and cardiovascular health provides several key avenues for prevention, many of which are linked to social-systemic intervention strategies dealing with exposure to stress (Sapolsky, 1996; Turner, 2003), poor nutrition (Minehira & Tappy, 2002), tobacco (Kilburn, 2003; Niaura & Abrams, 2002), and other correlates of vascular disease (Torpy, Cassio, & Glass, 2003).

Retrospective studies linking poor prenatal nutrition with later-life obesity suggest that prevention of DAT expression ideally begins before birth (Kuzawa, 2004). Increasing evidence points to the impact of early-life dietary practices on later-life cardiovascular health (see, for example, McGill & McMahan, 2003) that in turn favors protection from DAT expression. Efforts directed at prenatal nutritional education and access to high quality whole food sources rich in vitamins, phytochemicals, and fiber and low in saturated fat could provide the foundation DAT resistance in aging populations (Adair & Prentice, 2004; Martin, 2003; Shatenstein, Payette, Nadon, & Gray-Donald, 2003). Contemporary global trends propagating inexpensive, processed, low nutrient, high fat foods (Martorell, Stein, & Schroeder, 2001; Sawaya, Martins, Hoffman, & Roberts, 2003) impose a powerful countercurrent to healthy nutritional practices and may increase the risk of DAT expression.

Early-life commitment to an exercise regimen may also prove to be helpful in prevention of DAT symptoms. Studies suggest that exercise, and its accompanying brain perfusion, promotes brain development that is resistant to the later-life manifestations of DAT (Dik, Deeg, Visser, & Jonker, 2003). Regular participation of youth in an exercise program requires that minimally, children and adolescents must have safe, accessible community facilities that have needed equipment, adequate supervision, and informed staff. Parents, caregivers, and children need to understand the long-term benefits of regular exercise and devise strategies for counteracting the deleterious health effects of technologically and socio-structurally mediated physical stagnation.

While the DAT correlates explored in this chapter do not represent an exhaustive list of associated factors related directly or indirectly to contextual challenge, they collectively exemplify several notions of central importance to the critique of biopsychiatry. The medical model, in its quest for biological solutions, overlooks more costly humane disruptions of existing social arrangements and consequently abandons the vision for universal health across the life course. By focusing its resources on biological pathology that reflects a life-long accumulation of structurally constrained practices, biopsychiatry fails to implement its knowledge in ways that could alleviate a considerable amount of needless suffering.

CONCLUSION: CAN THE IRON CAGE BE UNLOCKED?

Biomedical trends in mental health reflect a robust tension with the postmodern vision of privileged subjectivity and blurred genres. While psychiatry's adoption of an objectivist/positivist paradigm has been fueled by a long-standing identity struggle and legitimation process within the profession, it is also intimately tied to market-driven, corporatizing trends in mental health administration. These forces together form a powerful hegemony that serves to protect and strengthen the expertise and knowledge monopoly of the medical profession, the cost containment pressures of the corporate interests of HMOs and insurance companies, and the relentless pressures for market expansion faced by the pharmaceutical industries. Thus, mental health care related to genuine quality of life concerns in older adults is eclipsed by priorities of cost-effective patient management achieved through scientized intervention strategies that are justified by the powerful combination of expert knowledge, market expansion, and low-cost treatment aimed at patient management. This unfortunate set of circumstances disregards potentially transformative strategies for both prevention and humanizing palliative care.

In accordance with medicalizing trends in psychiatry, a highly disproportionate allocation of resources is directed toward research committed to increasingly refined understandings of genetic and other molecular mechanisms. Potentially life-altering data about the regulation of genetic expression by the various sources of environmental influence—from cells to societies—is eclipsed by increasingly detailed studies of decontextualized, in vitro, biological processes. Gene regulation, when viewed as a process guided by both macro- and microenvironmental factors, becomes a matter of compelling political, economic, and ethical importance.

In the light of such discoveries, it is becoming recognized to an increasing extent that the key to unlocking the iron cage is not merely a matter of psychiatric theory or knowledge of genetic markers and biochemical reactions. The truths in these domains are known to many practitioners whose work is increasingly governed by the constraints of the market and who regret that they cannot spend extra minutes of quality time that might enable a greater understanding of the existential dimensions of mental disorder or are unable to contribute to prevention practices that could ease human suffering.

To avert the profound human suffering imposed by the devastation of Alzheimer's disease will require changes in the other domains, such as politics, economics, and ethics. If such domains seem far removed from the worlds of psychiatric theory, it is only because of a failure to recognize the degree to which mental health diagnosis and treatment are constrained by biomedicalization and the relentless pressure to economize the cost of care. This circumstance leads to the unavoidable conclusion that progressive change in the knowledge base, research vision, and treatment and diagnosis of DAT will ultimately require bolstering several forms of will. It will require the political will to oppose the short-term professional self-interests that accrue from narrowly defined, overspecialized, reductionist understandings of psychiatric illness; the economic will to invest in medical care that countenances and values universal quality of life rather than cost minimization; and the ethical will to denaturalize human suffering in later life, challenging the presumption that all aspects and forms of suffering encountered late in life represent inevitable manifestations of the decline of aging.

REFERENCES

Adair, L. S. & Prentice, A. M. (2004). A critical evaluation of the fetal origins hypothesis and its implications for developing countries. *The Journal of Nutrition, 134*(1), 191-193.

Alzheimer's Association. (2003). Fact: About understanding Alzheimer's disease. Retrieved February 21, 2004 from basie.g.acts.asp.

Alzheimer's Association. (2004). Fact sheet: About Alzheimer's disease. Retrieved September 21, 2005 from http://www.alz.org/Resources/FactSheets/FSADFacts.pdf.

Alzheimer's Association. (2005). Fact sheet: About Alzheimer's disease statistics. Retrieved September 21, 2005 from http://www.alz.org/Resources/FactSheets/FSAlzheimersStats.pdf.

American Psychiatric Association. (1980). *Diagnostic and statistical manual of mental disorders* (3rd ed.). Washington, DC: Author.

American Psychiatric Association. (1987). *Diagnostic and statistical manual of mental disorders* (3rd ed., text rev.). Washington, DC: Author.

American Psychiatric Association. (1994). *Diagnostic and statistical manual of mental disorders* (4th ed.). Washington, DC: Author.

American Psychiatric Association. (2000). *Diagnostic and statistical manual of mental disorders* (4th ed., text rev.). Washington, DC: Author.

Bahro, M., Silber, E., & Sunderland, T. (1995). How do patients with Alzheimer's disease cope with their illness?—A clinical experience report. *Journal of the American Geriatric Society, 34,* 41-46.

Berger, P., Berger, B., & Kellner, H. (1974). *The homeless mind: Modernization and consciousness.* New York: Vintage.

Bowler, J. V. (2004, February). Vascular cognitive impairment. *Stroke, 35*(2), 386-388.

Breggin, P. R. (1991a). *Toxic psychiatry: Why therapy, empathy and love must replace the drugs, electroshock and biochemical theories of the 'new psychiatry.'* New York: St. Martin's Press.

Breggin, P. R. (1991b). Psychotherapy in the shadow of the psycho-pharmaceutical complex. *Voices, 27,* 15-21.

Breggin, P. R. (1997). *The heart of being helpful: Empathy and the creation of a healing presence.* New York: Springer Publishing.

Breteler, M. M. B. (2000). Vascular risk factors for Alzheimer's disease: An epidemiologic perspective. *Neurobiological Aging, 21,* 153-160.

Bullock, R. (2001). Drug treatment in dementia. *Current Opinion in Psychiatry, 14*(4), 349-353.

Caplan, P. (1996). *They say you're crazy: How the world's most powerful psychiatrists decide who's normal.* Cambridge, MA: Perseus.

Curcio, C. A., & Kemper, T. (1984). Nucleus raphe dorsalis in dementia of the Alzheimer's type: Neurofibrillary changes and neuronal packing density. *Journal of Neuropathology and Experimental Neurology, 43,* 359-368.

Dana, R., Conner, M., & Allen, J. (1996). Quality of care and cost-containment in managed mental health: Policy, education, research and advocacy. *Psychological Reports, 79,* 1395-1422.

Dik, M. G., Deeg, D. J. H., Visser, M., & Jonker, C. (2003). Early life physical activity and cognition in old age. *Journal of Clinical and Experimental Neuropsychology, 25*(5), 643-653.

Douthit, K. Z. (2001). The psychiatric construction of ADHD: A critical evaluation of the theoretical precepts. (Doctoral dissertation, University of Rochester, 2001). *Dissertation Abstracts International, 62,* 774.

Douthit, K. Z. (in press). The convergence of counseling and psychiatric genetics: An essential role for counselors. *Journal of Counseling and Development.*

Faraone, S. V., Tsuang, M. T., & Tsuang, D. W. (1999). *Genetics of mental disorders: A guide for students, clinicians, and researchers.* New York: Guilford.

Habermas, J. (1976). *Legitimation crisis* (T. McCarthy, Trans.). London: Heinemann.

Iadecola, C. (2003). Atherosclerosis and neurodegeneration: Unexpected conspirators in Alzheimer's dementia. *Arteriosclerosis, Thrombosis & Vascular Biology, 23*(11), 1951-1953.

Ingleby, D. (1980). *Critical psychiatry: The politics of mental health.* New York: Penguin.

Iversen, L. L., Rossor, M. N., Reynolds, G. P., Hills, R., Mountjoy, C. Q., Foote, S. L., Morrison, J. H., & Bloom, F. E. (1983). Loss of pigmented dopamine-[beta]-hydroxylase positive cells from the locus coeruleus in senile dementia of the Alzheimer's type. *Neuroscience Letters, 39,* 95-100.

Kennedy, G. J., & Scalmati, A. (2001, July). The interface of depression and dementia. *Current Opinion in Psychiatry, 14*(4), 367-369.

Kilburn, K. H. (2003). Stop inhaling smoke: Prevent coronary heart disease. *Archives of Environmental Health, 58*(2), 68-73.

Kirk, H., & Kutchins, S. A. (1992). *The selling of DSM: The rhetoric of science in psychiatry.* New York: Aldine de Gruyter.

Kleinman, A., & Cohen, A. (1997, March). Psychiatry's global challenge. *Scientific American,* 86-89.

Kutchins, H., & Kirk, S. A. (1997). *Making us crazy: DSM: The psychiatric bible and the creation of mental disorders.* New York: Free Press.

Kuzawa, C. W. (2004, January). Modeling fetal adaptation to nutrient restriction: Testing the fetal origins hypothesis with a supply-demand model. *The Journal of Nutrition, 134*(1), 194.

Lerner, M. (1995, September-October). The assault on psychotherapy. *Family Therapy Networker,* 44-52.

Letenneur, L., Gilleron, V., Commenges, D., Helmer, C., Orgogozo, J. M., & Dartigues, J. F. (1999). Are sex and educational level independent predictors of dementia and Alzheimer's disease? Incidence data from the PAQUID project. *Journal of Neurology, Neurosurgery, and Psychiatry, 66*(2), 177-183.

Martin, A. (2003, February). Antioxidant vitamins E and C and risk of Alzheimer's disease. *Nutrition Reviews, 61*(2), 69-73.

Martorell, R., Stein, A. D., & Schroeder, D. G. (2001). Symposium: Obesity in developing countries: Biological and ecological factors—Early nutrition and later adiposity. *The Journal of Nutrition, 131*(3), S874-S880.

Maser, J. D., Kaelber, C., & Weise, R. E. (1991). International use and attitudes toward *DSM-III* and *DSM-III-R:* Growing consensus in psychiatric classification. *Journal of Abnormal Psychology, 100*(3), 271-279.

McGill, H. C., & McMahan, C. A. (2003). Starting earlier to prevent heart disease. *Journal of the American Medical Association, 290*(17), 2320-2322.

Miller, I. (1996a). Managed care is harmful to outpatient mental health: A call for account-ability. *Professional Psychology: Research and Practice, 27*(4), 349-363.

Miller, I. (1996b). Time-limited brief therapy has gone too far: The result is invisible rationing. *Professional Psychology: Research and Practice, 27*(6), 567-576.

Minehira, K., & Tappy, L. (2002). Dietary and lifestyle interventions in the management of the metabolic syndrome: Present status and future perspective. *European Journal of Clinical Nutrition, 56*(12), 1264-1269.

Moceri, V. M., Kukull, W. A., Emanual, I., van Belle, G., Starr, J. R., Schellenberg, G. D., McCormick, W. C., Bowen, J. D., Teri, L., & Larson, E. B. (2001). Using census data and birth certificates to reconstruct the early-life socioeconomic environment and the relation to the development of Alzheimer's disease. *Epidemiology, 12*(4), 383-389.

Niaura, R., & Abrams, D. B. (2002). Smoking cessation: Progress, priorities, and pros-pectus. *Journal of Consulting & Clinical Psychology, 70*(3), 494-509.

Rose, S. (1998). *Lifelines: Biology beyond determinism.* New York: Oxford University Press.

Sapolsky, R. M. (1996). Why stress is bad for your brain. *Science, 273,* 749-750.

Sapolsky, R. (1998, March/April). Is biology destiny?: Genetic predisposition is not the same as genetic inevitability. *Family Therapy Networker,* (Suppl.), 9-11.

Sawaya, A. L., Martins, P., Hoffman, P., & Roberts, S. B. (2003). The link between childhood undernutrition and risk of chronic diseases in adulthood: A case study of Brazil. *Nutrition Reviews, 61*(5), 168-175.

Shatenstein, B., Payette, H., Nadon, S., & Gray-Donald, K. (2003). An approach for evaluating lifelong intakes of functional foods in elderly people. *The Journal of Nutrition, 133*(7), 2384-2391.

Slone, D. G., & Gleason, C. E. (1999). Behavior management planning for problem behaviors in dementia: A practical model. *Professional Psychology: Research and Practice, 30*(1), 27-36.

Small, G. W., Rabins, P. V., Barry, P. P., Buckholtz, N. S., DeKosky, S. T., Ferris, S. H., Finkel, S. I., Gwyther, L. P., Khachaturian, Z. S., Lebowitz, B. D., McRae, T. D., Morris, J. C., Oakley, F., Schneider, L. S., Streim, J. E., Sunderland, T., Teri, L. A., & Tune, L. E. (1997). Diagnosis and treatment of Alzheimer disease and related disorders: Consensus statement of the American Association for Geriatric Psychiatry, the Alzheimer's Association, and the American Geriatrics Society. *Journal of American Medical Association, 278*(16), 1363-1371.

Snowdon, D. A. (1997). Aging and Alzheimer's disease: Lessons from the Nun Study. *The Gerontologist, 37*(2), 150-156.

Snowdon, D. (2001). *Aging with grace: What the Nun Study teaches us about leading longer, healthier and more meaningful lives.* New York: Bantam.

Snowdon, D. A., Greiner, L. H., Mortimer, J. A., Riley, K. P., Greiner, P. A., & Markesbery, W. R. (1997). Brain infarction and the clinical expression of Alzheimer's disease: The Nun Study. *Journal of the American Medical Association, 277*(10), 813-817.

Snowdon, D. A., Kemper, S. J., Mortimer, J. A., Grenier, L. H., Wekstein, D. R., & Markesbery, W. R. (1996). Linguistic ability in early life and cognitive function and Alzheimer's disease in late life: Findings from the Nun Study. *Journal of the American Medical Association, 275*(5), 528-532.

Stein, P. (2002, November). Paper presented at the meeting of the American Gerontological Association, Boston, MA.

Stewart, J. (1995). Management of behavior problems in the demented patient. *American Family Physician, 52*(8), 2311-2322.

Streim, J. E., Oslin, D. W., Katz, I. R., Smith, B. D., DiFilippo, S., Cooper, T., & Ten Have, T. (2000). Drug treatment of depression in frail elderly nursing home residents. *American Journal of Geriatric Psychiatry, 8*, 150-159.

Tomlinson, B. E., Irving, D., & Blessed, G. (1981). Cell loss in the locus coeruleus in senile dementia of the Alzheimer's type. *Journal of Neurological Science, 49*, 419-428.

Torpy, J. M., Cassio, L., & Glass, R. (2003). Risk factors for heart disease. *Journal of the American Medical Association, 290*(7), 980.

Turner, R. J. (2003). The pursuit of socially modifiable contingencies in mental health. *Journal of Health and Social Behavior, 44*(1), 1- 17.

Tzourio, C. (2003). Vascular factors and cognition: Toward a prevention of dementia? *Journal of Hypertension, 21s*(Suppl. 2), S15-S19.

Weber, M. (1958). *The Protestant ethic and the spirit of capitalism.* (T. Parsons, Trans.). New York: Scribner.

World Health Organization. (2005). *International classification of diseases and related health problems* (10th rev.). Retrieved September 23, 2005 from http:/www.who.int/classifications/icd/en/.

Yamamoto, T., & Hirano, A. (1985). Nucleus raphe dorsalis in Alzheimer's disease: Neurofibrillary tangles and loss of larger neurons. *Annals of Neurology, 17*, 573-577.

Zubenko, G. S., & Moossy, J. (1988). Major depression in primary dementia: Clinical and neuropathologic correlates. *Archives of Neurology, 45*, 1182-1186.

Zubenko, G. S., Zubenko, W. N., McPherson, S., Spoor, E., Marin, D. B., & Farlow, M. R., Smith, G. E., Geda, Y. E., Cummings, J. L., Petersen, R. C., & Sunderland, T. (2003). A collaborative study of the emergence and clinical features of the major depressive syndrome of Alzheimer's disease. *American Journal of Psychiatry, 160*(5), 857-866.

SECTION 3

Age and Inequality: Local, National, and Global Dynamics

CHAPTER 10

The Emerging Postmodern Culture of Aging and Retirement Security

Larry Polivka and
Charles F. Longino, Jr.

The aging experience in the twenty-first century is likely to be substantially different in many respects from what it has been over the last several decades or since the creation of publicly supported retirement systems in most developed countries after World War II. Some of these differences are cultural in nature. Members of the baby-boom generation, who constitute the next generation of retirees, have been deeply influenced by post–World War II cultural changes, many of which are associated with the protest movements of the 1960s and 1970s. These movements for social justice were largely focused on recognizing and protecting the rights and freedoms of individuals regardless of race, ethnic, or gender identities. These movements were also organized to change, and often diminish, the role(s) of traditional institutions and to limit their capacity to shape and control the lives of individuals for the benefit of small institutional elites. The fundamental, common objective of these movements, their organizing principle, was the valorization of individual autonomy, which affected virtually every institution in Western societies.

The effects of these cultural changes can be seen today in the values and aspirations of individuals across socioeconomic, religious, ethnic, and age divisions. According to Allen Wolfe (2001):

> Moral freedom has become so ubiquitous in America that we sometimes forget how pathbreaking it is. . . . What so many philosophers and theologians for so long considered an impossible idea has become the everyday reality in which modern Americans live. (p. 184)

This focus on the value of moral autonomy is likely to have a great influence on how members of the baby-boomer generation experience aging and manage retirement. Many of them will be committed to organizing their lives around the exercise of freedom, choice, and control, even, or especially, under conditions of impairment. These changes in cultural values and the way baby boomers intend to live in retirement may be referred to as the emerging postmodern or posttraditional culture of aging. We attempt to describe some of the major features of this culture within the context of larger societal trends toward postmodern values and cognitive styles. We also address the implications of the ideological differences between what we call the neoliberal and progressive postmodern perspectives on the aging experience in the years ahead. These differences are especially salient for the social and economic well-being of future retirees, most of whom will be as dependent on publicly supported income and healthcare benefits as current retirees. Our argument is that the dismantling of programs providing the benefits would undermine any opportunity for most retirees to experience the kind of freedom, creativity, and self-development that are potentially a part of the postmodern aging experience. Postmodern cultural trends create greater space for individual agency and public welfare programs, including income support and healthcare programs for retirees, and should be designed to nurture individual choice and control. This does not require, however, the dismantlement of programs, which would leave most retirees without the resources required to exercise choice and control in any effective manner. Neoliberal proposals to dismantle the welfare state would resurrect the hazards of old age characteristic of the premodern past, including poverty, poor healthcare, and powerlessness.

The chapter is organized into four sections. It begins with an overview of some of the cultural and social changes and trends associated with the emergence of posttraditional, postmodern society, with particular reference to its valorization of individual freedom and agency. Those changes will be examined that, we think, have the greatest salience for the future of aging. This brief overview of some of the major tenets of postmodern social theory, or theories of posttraditional societies, is not intended to be comprehensive. Rather, our intention is to use these theoretical tools to identify a few of the more salient trends and changes in Western societies as a prelude to discussing their implications for social policy in general and policies for the frail elderly in particular.

The second section examines neoliberal postmodernism and the public policies that emerge from its perspective. This section is critical of the neoliberal approach to policy, which may make sense for affluent, elite "third agers," but ignores physical vulnerability, impoverishment, and other barriers to the exercise of agency.

In the third section, we review a range of economic data on current and future retirees. In our judgment, these data clearly demonstrate that most retirees over the next several decades will be dependent on maintaining and even enhancing current income support and healthcare programs.

The fourth section proposes a progressive, postmodernist approach to public policies related to the elderly. This approach emphasizes autonomy and self-determination, hallmarks of postmodernism, but weds this emphasis with maintaining and improving publicly supported retirement security. We describe the kind of public policies we think would be most compatible with the kinds of lives older persons are likely to experience in the future. These policies differ from the neoliberal privatization policies that are often associated with a strand of postmodern thought that celebrates the role of the market and self-expression through consumption. We refer to our recommended approach to new policies for the elderly as the "new synthesis." It gives equal weight to ensuring the economic security of the elderly and creating more flexible self-empowerment-oriented policies that reflect the opportunities for freedom and individual autonomy created by the emergence of posttraditional, postmodern societies.

THE POSTMODERN WORLD AND THE
NEW INDIVIDUALISM

The postmodern world, or late modernity, which is still largely a Western phenomenon, is increasingly shaped by conscious, intentional change that tends to radicalize life by eroding traditions and exposing society and the individual to growing contingency and risk. These trends also produce more opportunities for freedom and creativity for individuals and society. The influence of traditions, and the institutions that embody them, has faded over the last several decades, and social organizations and individuals increasingly have had to write their own scripts and make decisions about a wide range of issues that were once largely made for them by adherence to strong traditional values and ways of life. For Beck and Beck-Gernsheim (2002) this means that

> All metaphysics and transcendence, all necessity and certainty are being replaced by artistry. In the most public and the most private ways we are helplessly becoming high-wire dancers in the circus tent. And many of us fall. Not only in the West, but also in the countries that have abruptly opened their doors to Western ways of life. People in the former GDR, in Poland, Russia or China, are caught up in a dramatic "plunge into modernity." (p. 2)

One of the features of modernity is the shifting balance between tradition and expert knowledge, favoring the latter. The fading of traditions is liberating in the sense that choices are no longer so strongly prescribed. As this shift occurs, people face the task of building their own identities and mastering the tools of self-creation—of making their own decisions about values and behaviors.

This self-creation does not mean that people make decisions and live their lives completely independent of others. We often look to others for guidance and support, but they are just as much on their own as we are, and the collective expression of values is more likely to take the ephemeral form of fads and fashions rather than traditions. Where tradition once stood, producing the expected goals and routines of life, we have in its place an increasing degree of self-reflexivity that requires us to make decisions on our own in terms of self-generated criteria and rationales.

The growing importance of autonomously constructed narratives of the self creates the conditions for the proliferation and diversification of cultural perspectives, lifestyle options, belief systems, and the eclectic blending of values and behaviors. This trend toward multiple cultural perspectives and openness has major implications for older persons and the retirement experience.

> . . . in relation to retirement as a whole, the scope for decision-making has been drastically widened. Increasingly, people are being called upon to build retirement around their own individual planning, both in relation to finances and the timing and manner in which they leave the workplace. These questions indicate that older age has simultaneously become a major source of "risk" but also a potential source of "liberation." Old age does threaten disaster—poverty, severe illness, and the loss of a loved one. But it also can bring the opposite: freedom from restrictive work and domestic roles; new relationships; and a greater feeling of security. People do truly ride a "juggernaut" in older age, and this is making the period more rather than less central as an issue of concern for social policy. (Phillipson, 1998, p. 125)

In posttraditional society, reasons have to be given for attitudes and behaviors in the growing absence of tacit assumptions based on widespread acceptance of traditional culture and belief systems. These reasons are increasingly drawn from self-constructed life narratives that open up space for discursive personal relationships and expanded cognitive activity. In the postmodern world, individuals bear greater responsibility for articulating their own attitudes, values, and behaviors.

Ronald Inglehart (1997) and his colleagues have been tracking changes in values since the early 1970s in over 25 countries with the use of survey data. In the vast majority of these countries, the data indicate movement from materialist to postmaterialist and postmodern values. The shift involves a movement away from values associated with the search for economic security to a growing emphasis on individual autonomy, self-expression, tolerance, human rights, ecological awareness, and rejection of institutional and hierarchical authority in all domains. All of these trends are accompanied by a deepening quest for personal meaning and morality; for spiritual development; close, affectionate ties with family members and friends; and existential significance in work.

In summarizing the overall impact of these changes in values, Ingelhart (1997) writes that

> . . . the publics of advanced industrial societies are moving toward Post-modern values and placing increasing emphasis on the quality of life. Empirical evidence from around the world shows that cultural patterns are closely linked with the economic and political characteristics of given

societies. The Modernization syndrome is linked with a shift from traditional to rational-legal values; but the emergence of advanced industrial society gives rise to a shift from survival values to postmodern values, in which a variety of changes, from equal rights for women to the emergence of democratic political institutions, become increasingly likely. (p. 339)

The decline in traditions has brought with it a decline in the robustness of human values rooted in authoritative external systems, and a corresponding shift toward individualized values, worked out to fit the individual's needs and goals. This shift in the locus of values has strong implications for organizational commitments and behavior, favoring the democratization of social arrangements. The institutional response to the pursuit of individual autonomy and reflexivity is eroding hierarchical command and control systems throughout society and creating greater opportunities and requirements for the exercise of autonomy and choice.

Individual autonomy and reflexivity are expanding the scope of ethics in everyday life and making philosophers of us all. Beck and Beck-Gernsheim (2002) notes that it is in the

. . . everyday experiments in living that we will find out about a new ethics that combines personal freedom with engagement with others and even engagement on a transnational basis . . . we are living in a highly moral world despite what the cultural pessimists try to tell us. But it is not a world of fixed obligations and values. Rather, it is one that is trying to find out how to combine individualization with obligations to other, even on a global scale. (p. 212)

These trends toward a posttraditional society, characterized by revisable, contestable expert knowledge, provisional authority, and self-reflexivity, are creating the conditions for the democratization of social institutions, which must increasingly accommodate individual autonomy as the organizing principle of posttraditional, late modern society. Democratizing processes now operate at every level of society, including personal relationships characterized by mutual understanding, intense communication, sensitivity, and equality. This democracy of the emotions offers many rewards, but also puts relationships under considerable strain. This pressure is less likely to be experienced in more traditional societies where the form and substance of relationships are more likely to be inherited than made. The relational pressure in traditional societies tends to arise, on the contrary, from oppressive power relationships.

There is no guarantee that the trends and changes described here, under the broad conceptual framework of posttraditional or postmodern society, will eventually culminate in institutions and cultures that are fundamentally characterized by institutional and individual reflexivity, discursivity, flexibility, and openness. Nor is it a certainty that fluctuating networks of power, leveled hierarchies, and a politics and ethics based on extensive equality and individual autonomy will prevail. These broad trends are arrayed against powerful forces, including atavistic nationalisms, religious and ethnic fundamentalisms of many kinds, and the drive of transnational corporations to control the global economy and create a global culture through relentless marketing, deregulation, and privatization.

Neoliberal Postmodern Theory and Public Policy

There are multiple strands of postmodern thought, including a neoliberal version that emphasizes the privatization of social, economic support and healthcare services that must be examined before we propose a progressive, postmodern approach that emphasizes both security and freedom, or what we call the new synthesis of public policy. The neoliberal variant is

> . . . a celebrationist, Saatchi-style postmodernism, commodified to the gills—regardless of whether the shopping is done in the mall or cyberspace. It sidesteps disparities in wealth just as a group of advertising executives might circumnavigate a homeless beggar on their lunchtime return to the office. In this way it ignores the differential ability of groups to become active consumers and bestows full human status only on those able to choose. Its designation of gender and ethnicity and the like as merely lifestyle choices misses the point that these are also social divisions and still significant sites of inequality. This then is a complacent and selfish postmodernism, which, with its hyper-commodification of the cultural realm, serves to exclude the poor just as efficiently as any caste system in history. (Carter, 1998, p. 21)

This kind of "celebrationist" postmodernism reduces social, political, and public life generally to participation in the market and the citizen to just another consumer whose rights are determined by their power in the market—by their wealth or lack of it. This is a kind of postmodernism that is consistent with neoliberal economics and its agenda for privatization of public sector programs and for moving control of tax-funded programs from the public to the private sector where they can be used to generate profits in the name of increased choice and efficiency.

Neoliberal postmodernism is expressly designed to divide the elderly into those who can fully provide for themselves and those who cannot and to dramatically reduce public support for the latter. According to Gilleard and Higgs (2000):

> The relative affluence of occupational and private pension holders separates them out from those older people as primarily welfare benefit recipients. It is the latter group who now constitute the "problem" of "old age." The same dichotomy is played out in relation to health care. Here people are presented with two images: one the physically frail and dependent "fourth-ager" lacking the necessary "self-care" skills to sustain a third-age identity, the other the active and healthy individual producing and consuming his or her "third age." (pp. 103-104)

Neoliberal postmodernism uses many of the same concepts and categories (individualization, reflexivity, autonomy of the self, detraditionalization) we and others use to describe the emerging trends of the posttraditional/postmodern societies of Europe and the United States. Neoliberal postmodernism, however, does not support public policies we think are necessary if the opportunities (freedom, creativity) of postmodern aging are to be extended to more than just affluent elite. According to neoliberal postmodernists, the full potential of post-modern aging cannot be achieved without the dismantling of the age-based entitlements of the welfare state, which has trapped retirees in a labyrinth of structural dependency, stigmatizes elderly people, and is inconsistent with their increasing affluence and capacity to construct their own identities through patterns of creative consumption. The fundamentally antistatist, promarket "eclipse of the social" tendencies of this perspective are clearly evident in the following passages from Gilleard and Higgs' exegesis of the aging experience under conditions of what they refer to as "advanced liberalism." The expectation that

> . . . individuals themselves should take responsibility for achieving and maintaining health, wealth and well being throughout their adult life. Such a perspective represents later life as the culmination, or final reckoning, of how well such responsibilities have been exercised. Too much government is seen as constraining the space where individual liberty can be expressed. . . . While interpretations of this political shift may vary, the outcome is every-where evident in the growing emphasis upon reducing public expenditure, privileging the role of "market forces," criticizing state paternalism, resisting the collectivization of social identity and expressing skepticism toward all "grand narratives," and their attempts to claim the ideological high ground." (Gilleard & Higgs, 2000, p. 63)

According to this scenario for the future of aging

> . . . third-age identities are likely to be elaborated through increasing material consumption, a sense of "packing life in" to a period of adulthood of uncertain length and a wary and ambivalent position in relation to providing for "old age." Third-agers, while acknowledging old age, are likely to prefer to live at a considerable physical and psychological distance from it. (Gilleard & Higgs, 2000, p. 45)

For those with the resources, participation in the market can be a means of escaping assignment to the ghetto of old age. They have the ". . . cultural capital to avoid getting locked into a generational ghetto increasingly distanced from the global 'youth' culture of the late twentieth century" (Gilleard & Higgs, 2000, p. 64).

According to the neoliberal narrative, economic hardship and poor health in old age indicates that the individual has failed to ward off disease through preventive measures and a failure to keep up with the times in terms of lifestyles and attitudes. This view of old age and its vicissitudes as wholly the responsibility of the individual is fundamentally a construction of neoliberal ideology and the corporate agenda that focuses on reducing the public sector through tax cuts and privatization of programs like Social Security and Medicare and on the marketing of a growing array of anti-aging products to aging baby boomers.

Anthony Giddens (1994), a representative of the so called "third-way," has adopted much of the neoliberal position on aging public policy by advocating a reduction of public pensions in order to make individual agency the organizing principle of old age.

> . . . governments should concern themselves with the creation and promotion
> of the "autotelic self" who not only has self-respect and ontological security
> but also challenges risk as a way of achieving self-actualization. The abolition
> of the state retirement pension may be a fundamentally radical idea as far as
> contemporary politics is concerned, however, it is not so far from the practice
> of recent British governments who have insured that state pensions have
> become less and less valuable in real terms. (p. 98)

One may ask at this point how older persons, who have not earned enough during their work careers to support families, make investments, and build savings all at the same time, can be expected to experience ontological security and self-actualization in the absence of basic economic and healthcare security. Gilleard and Higgs (2000) claim that the growing affluence and disenchantment with the state are dissolving the link between the citizen and the state and diminishing the need for and desirability of state welfare systems to meet the needs/demands of older persons.

As states increasingly require individuals to take responsibility for their later life, they target economic and healthcare assistance to only the poorest and most impaired (from universal to means-tested benefits). According to Gilleard and Higgs (2000):

> It seems doubtful that their [the poor and impaired elderly's] lot has worsened
> in consequence and relatively speaking their numbers have diminished;
> nevertheless they remain as an iconic warning against "improvidence"—both
> during and after working life. (p. 120)

There is an extraordinarily chilling tone to this plainly written description of what would become of the frail elderly in the neoliberal version of postmodern society where they would have value, primarily "as an iconic warning against improvidence"—a breathtakingly aggressive form of blaming the victim. One can only imagine what the cost to the frail elderly will be if this neoliberal vision of society and public policy becomes dominant. And what would be the costs to everyone else if this heartless view of the frail elderly were to become characteristic of Western societies?

Furthermore, it should be noted that according to Gilleard and Higgs (2000), citizenship is not only an illusion for the frail elderly requiring long-term care, but increasingly for the affluent (successful) elderly and everyone else as well in a postmodern society where the consumer is replacing the citizen, and one's value is largely a function of a purchased lifestyle. There is, of course, one other implied source of value for the frail elderly who have become hopelessly damaged consumers—they have value as commodities within the long-term care industry where profits are made by minimizing the number of caregiving staff hired, paying them poorly, and providing no benefits. In the neoliberal postmodern society, the frail elderly may be the canaries in the coal mine, providing an "iconic warning" to many other less-than-optimal consumers for whom citizenship is becoming illusory.

> If government policies continue to treat "the elderly" simply as another category of need, alongside the disabled, the mentally ill and other "marginalized communities," few retired people are likely to find such a "politics of age" either of personal interest or of collective concern. Instead they may turn away from the idea of citizenship altogether, preferring their own constructed self-identities. (p. 123)

The authors' reference to the disabled in this context is curious—the disabled have, at least in the United States, effectively extended the scope of citizenship in recent years by achieving, through protest, legislation, and other forms of political activity, an extensive array of social rights. The disabled community is, in fact, a model of effective action for aging advocates committed to making healthcare and long-term care more humane and responsive to the needs and preferences of the elderly and their families—to the creation of a new synthesis in public policy of security and freedom.

We have many misgivings about the kind of neoliberal, postmodern society described by Gilleard and Higgs (2000), which largely center on their reduction of value and meaning to the workings of the market and the acquisition of consumer goods, which eviscerates the necessary conditions for any morally and politically effective sense of social solidarity. We think they are right, however, in their analysis of what neoliberal, postmodernism intends for the future of the welfare state and the status of the many elderly and members of other groups who cannot pretend to be completely self-sufficient. Indeed, most retirees depend on Social Security for half or more of their income and could not afford private insurance in the absence of Medicare. Precise predictions are impossible, but these realities are not likely to be any different for most members of the next generation of retirees who will carry more debt and fewer defined benefits pensions into retirement than their parents.

CURRENT AND FUTURE RETIREE
FINANCIAL STATUS

The neoliberal version of postmodern aging is fundamentally at odds with the economic realities of current and future retirees in Western societies. The neoliberal notion that most retirees are now affluent and that an even greater majority will be independently well off in the future is not supported by the facts of economic life among current and future middle-class retirees.

In the United States, the median household income of those aged 65+ is $24,000 for whites and a little over $16,000 for African Americans and Hispanics; and Social Security constitutes 41% of the income of all retirees on average, which is 6% greater than 40 years ago. Over two-thirds of all retirees depend on Social Security for 50% of their income; this percentage is 75% for female retirees and 77% for minority retirees (Wu, 2001). In terms of financial wealth, the median net worth (minus value of home) of the bottom three income quintiles of those aged 70+ (75% of total population 70+) is $68,500, $15,000, and $1,000 respectively. Only the top quintile has sizable financial assets with a median net worth of $285,000. The median net worth of minority elderly aged 70+ is less than one-third that of whites (Reynolds-Scanlon, Reynolds, Peek, Polivka, & Peek, 1999).

What about the income and financial status of the next generation of retirees, those now between ages 47 to 64? Will they have enough income and wealth to make them qualitatively less dependent on entitlement programs than current retirees and more capable of experiencing the pleasures of neoliberal, postmodern aging as envisioned by Gilleard and Higgs (2000)? A greater percentage of future retirees are likely to have high incomes and substantial wealth than among current retirees due to higher incomes and asset accumulation during their working years and continuing employment after age 65. An analysis, however, of projected retirement wealth among those aged 47–64 indicates that most retirees over the next 30 years will not be substantially better off than their parents (Wolff, 2002).

Mean retirement wealth, which is defined as projected income from defined benefits and fixed contribution pension plans and Social Security, increased by 10% from 1983 to 1998 for those aged 47+ and total wealth (net work and retirement wealth) increased by 2%. In terms of median values, however, retirement wealth fell by 7% during this period and total wealth by 9%. Mean retirement wealth declined from 1983 to 1998 for all households age 47+ with less than $500,000 in net wealth, stagnated for those with $500,000–$999,000 in net wealth, and grew by 44% for those with $1 million plus in net worth. The retirement wealth of African Americans and Hispanics fell by 14.6% for the age 47+ group and by 20% for those aged 47–64. These trends reflect the growing income and wealth inequality in the United States over the last 25 years (Wolff, 2002). The increasing dominance of defined-contribution pension plans and declining or stagnant wages among most workers is likely to increase inequality in retirement wealth over the next several decades.

A recent study by the Employee Benefits and Retirement Institute (EBRI) found that retirees will have $45–$50 billion less in income in 2030 than they will need to cover basic needs (food, housing, transportation, out-of-pocket acute-care costs, etc.) and any costs arising from an episode of care in a nursing home or from a home health provider (VanDerhei & Copeland, 2003). The cumulative shortfall by 2030 will be over $400 billion. Increased savings could be used to cover or reduce this projected shortfall. For most, however, the increase would have to be very substantial (5% to 25% of earnings more than they are saving now). Current average savings in the United States have fallen to about 1% from 11% in 1983, with higher income groups saving up to 10%–20% and lower income groups accumulating more debts than savings. For example, older, lower income women would have to save 25% of earnings to close the gap. In fact, all women in the lowest quintile (bottom 25%) income group, regardless of age (64 or 38) would have to save 25%+, which is simply impossible given their low incomes (VanDerhei & Copeland, 2003).

It should be noted that the EBRI model projections are based on very conservative assumptions, such as everyone works until age 65 (most workers now retire well before age 65); and individual retirement account balances are annuitized over a period of time that expands life expectancy by five years, even though annuitization rarely occurs now; and no changes in Social Security. In short, the retirement income prospects of the preboomers and boomers are decidedly mixed and are likely to be most challenging for the 1936–1945 cohort and lower income single women across all cohorts (VanDerhei & Copeland, 2003). Also, recall that Wolff's projections indicate that the age 47–55 boomers have lower retirement income than age 56–64 boomers. Furthermore, is it realistic to think that workers aged 47–64 will be able to increase their savings by 5% to 10% of income in order to have a 75% to 90% chance of achieving retirement income sufficient to cover basic expenses?

Basic expenses for future retirees may actually be higher than those projected by the EBRI model, especially for healthcare. According to an analysis by Johnson and Penner (2004), out-of-pocket healthcare costs for the retiree population, given current policies and projected cost increases, will increase from 12.7% to 27.3% for married couples between 2000 and 2030 and from 11.6% to 21.8% for unmarried adults. As a result, married couples in the lowest income quintile will see their net income shrink from $13,326 on average to $11,981 and those in the second quintile will see an increase of only $1,680, from $23,184 to $24,764. The same trends hold for unmarried persons as well, but at substantially lower income levels—$7,000 and $12,000 for the two lowest quintiles.

Any notion that families will be able to save and invest enough to cover projected shortfalls in retirement income over the next several decades is largely eviscerated by the current financial condition of most families that are caught in the vise of rising costs and declining or stagnant incomes and are unable to generate adequate retirement wealth. The decline in discretionary family income cannot be explained by excessive consumption. The average family in the United States spends 21% less on clothing than in the 70s ($750 less than in 1973), 22% less on food, and 44% less on major appliances. They spend 23% more on home entertainment/computers, but this amounts to only $170.00 annually. There is little evidence for more frivolous spending today than 25 years ago (Warren

& Tyagi, 2003). Overspending can't explain a 255% increase in foreclosures, 430% increase in bankruptcies, and 530% increase in credit card debt since the 70s. These trends are largely the result of big increases in family expenses. These increases in fixed costs (home mortgage, child care, education, and health insurance) have reduced discretionary income for dual income families below the amount available to single earner families in 1975.

Families now spend a lot more on houses, 60% of which are 25 years or older and most are no bigger than in 1975. Housing prices increased by 79% from 1983 to 1998 for families (from $98,000 to $175,000 on average—a lot more even with lower interest rates). Mortgage debt increased by 39% for the highest 10% of earners between 1989 and 2001, 94% for the middle 20%, 124% for the next lowest 20%, and 191% for the lowest 20% of earners. Owners' equity as a percentage of their real estate value fell from 70% in 1983 to 55% in 2003. This increase is driven by the pursuit of safety and better educational opportunities (schools) for their children—a 5% increase in fourth grade math and reading tests in a school adds $4,000 to nearby houses. With more flexible lending strategies (5%–10% down payments) and increased housing prices, mortgage costs have increased 69% (inflation adjusted) since the 70s (Warren & Tyagi, 2003).

Education costs have also risen rapidly. Over 60% of three- and four-year-olds now attend preschool, compared to only 4% attendance 30 years ago. In Chicago it costs $6,500 a year for prekindergarten, and few receive public support. College education has become an economic necessity. The gap between available slots and the number seeking admission is growing, costs are increasing faster than inflation, and available aid is not keeping up with the growing need for help. Tuition fees at public universities have doubled in 25 years (inflation adjusted). Tuition, room, and board now cost $8,600 annually on average or 17% of the average family's pretax income, and private universities are two to five times more expensive (Warren & Tyagi, 2003).

Health insurance premiums have risen severalfold since the 1970s, and individuals are 49% more likely to be uninsured than 25 years ago. The number declaring bankruptcy in the wake of a serious illness has increased by 3000% since 1975. As housing costs, mortgage debt, healthcare, and education costs soared and job security declined, lending industries (mortgages and credit cards) were substantially deregulated after a 1978 Supreme Court Ruling allowing banks to export interest rates from state to state, essentially eliminating usury laws which capped interest rates at 10% to 14%. Credit, even with defaults, is now a highly profitable consumer product (Warren & Tyagi, 2003).

These 25-year trends toward increasing reliance on mortgage and credit card debt are substantially driven by declining or stagnant family incomes. Real wages declined from a high of $15.14 an hour for nonsupervisory workers in the 1964–1967 period to $13.91 in 1981–1992 and $13.60 in 1993–2000. Wages have lagged far behind productivity growth since 1973. Wages tracked productivity only from 1997 to 2001, but the gap remains huge (10 times greater than in 1973 when the gap was 25%). In percentages, wages fell by 15% between 1973 and 2000, and the poverty levels increased even as the per capita GDP was 70% higher in 2000 than in 1974; productivity was 61% higher and the stock market was up 603% (Pollin, 2003). Stocks were driven up by unprecedented increases in price earning ratios (44.2 times in 1998 vs. 14.5 times from 1880–1989). This occurred in response to the new economy myth, reduced regulation, reduced corporate and capital gains taxes, and the emergence of stock options (CEO compensation). The integration of the United States into the global economy, which increased employer access to low wage workers in other countries, and declining union membership/power are major sources of wage stagnation/decline.

These trends appear likely to persist far into the foreseeable future, given current domestic economic and trade policies. The latest recession may have ended in 2002, but unemployment remains high, new job growth remains slow, wages are stagnant, and productive capacity utilization remains below 80%. The currently modest recovery is based on historically low interest rates, modest inflation, and strong consumer spending that is debt driven, including second and third mortgages. Bond and mortgage rates are still well above interest rates, but housing costs continue to increase rapidly (10%–15% annually) and now consume almost 40% of income compared to 28%–32% in 1990. Real interest rates (interest rates minus inflation) are 6% compared to 4.8% between 1972 and 2001. Average household debt reached 107% of disposable income in 2002—in the past, debt ratios have always fallen during recessions (Warren & Tyagi, 2003).

One reason for this increasing level of debt is that wages fell for most U.S. workers from 2001 to 2004 after rising modestly (1% to 2%) from 1995 to 2001. This decline was largely a function of increased unemployment and the generally lower wages or meager benefits of new jobs compared to those lost as faster growing industries pay less than shrinking industries (Economic Policy Institute, 2004). Rising employment is likely to improve wage levels in the future, but the probability of a big surge in the number of higher quality, higher income jobs is relatively low. As noted in a report (Gould, Mishel, Bernstein, & Price, 2004) from the Economic Policy Institute, Bureau of Labor Statistics, employment projections show that

> . . . there will not be any surge in the need for college-educated workers over the next decade that will offset losses from offshoring [outsourcing] (a factor not incorporated in the current BLS projections). Moreover, there is unlikely to be any skills mismatch between the jobs available and the skills of the workforce.

> . . . employment will be shifting to occupations with higher median annual wages, but the effect will be to raise annual wages by only 1% over 10 years (or 0.1% per year). This is not a large change compared to the real wage growth that occurs each year or to the effects of occupational shifts identified in earlier years.

In short, the economic status of most future retirees is likely to be about the same as current retirees. Most future retirees will have no more in private retirement wealth than the current 65+ population and are likely to be as dependent on publicly provided retirement benefits (Social Security and Medicare) for their economic well-being, which makes the preservation of these benefits a critical political challenge. It should be understood, however, that the economics of this challenge are less a function of rising payroll taxes and population aging per neoliberal doctrine than the rising cost of private healthcare and increasing income and wealth inequality. Dean Baker (1998) writes:

> The public attention given to the problems the nation will face as the baby boomers retire has been largely misplaced. By itself, the retirement of the baby boom generation will not prevent workers in the future from enjoying substantially higher living standards than do workers today. But tomorrow's workers still face another, more serious problem: rising health care costs and growing wage inequality threaten to greatly diminish the future living standards of most workers. In order to protect the well being of future generations, it will be necessary to bring health care costs under control and to stop, if not reverse, the trend toward greater wage inequality.

Baker's (1998) analysis, which is based on projections from the Social Security Trustees and the Health Care Financing Administration (now Centers for Medicare and Medicaid Services), shows that if there were no increase in wage inequality, after-tax wages and family income would be 30% higher in 2030 for an average family than in 1998, and after-tax, after-healthcare income would be 41% higher. The retirement costs of the baby boomers in 2030 would reduce after-tax wages and family income by only 6%. If, however, healthcare costs rose at the rate projected by the Health Care Financing Administration in 1998, then after-tax, after-healthcare income would be 27% higher in 2030 for the average family. After declining from 1998 to 2001, annual healthcare cost increases returned to the levels projected in 1998. Rising income inequality, which has continued largely unabated since 1998, will reduce after-tax income for families in the middle of the income distribution by 22% between 1998 and 2030.

> The combined effects of rising health care costs and increased wage inequality lead to an actual decline in after-tax, after-health-care income for most of the population through the next century. The projected loss in the year 2030 for a family in the middle of the income distribution, compared to the baseline, is 37%, or more than six times as large as the impact of changing demographics. (p. 7)

Clearly, the future costs of Social Security and Medicare are not a threat to the economic well-being of families over the next 30 years. In fact, these programs are essential to their well-being in that they ensure the financial status of older relatives. The true threat to the economic well-being of families arises from neoliberal policies of tax cuts for the wealthy, reductions in spending for education, childcare, and other social programs, privatization and deregulation, anti-union measures, and other policy initiatives that fuel rising inequality and healthcare costs.

TOWARD A PROGRESSIVE POSTMODERN PUBLIC POLICY FOR THE ELDERLY

As public policy debates acknowledge the decline in traditional sources of truth and the rise of individualism, is there a different route to a viable postmodern old-age policy other than the neoliberal alternative discussed above? In this section, we will attempt to show that current policies are largely not consistent with our emerging posttraditional society, and that this gap will become increasingly evident and difficult to justify as the huge baby-boom generation ages over the next 30 years. This generation is the first to feel the full weight of the change and trends we described in the first section, and this influence is likely to effect their expectations of social policy in the future.

The trends and changes caused by the emergence of posttraditional society and its associated values and behaviors represent a growing challenge to current social policy. Any effective response to this challenge will require the creation of new conceptual and explanatory frameworks in the development and execution of policies and programs. Frameworks that reflect posttraditional values (autonomy, reflexivity, self-determination, equality) will gain support. The outlines of neoliberal social-policy alternatives are already evident, but they are not the only ones possible. The postmodern world is full of alternatives that are more responsive to the needs and desires of individuals whose identities are drawn from a sense of the self as

> . . . a multiple personality, with plural, distinct and often conflicting facets and needs, finding expression in ever-changing and highly personalized, eclectic lifestyles, now more usually held together by particular patterns of personalized preferences and values than by the imposition of the dull routine of everyday life or of social-structural and functional necessities. Giddens, Connolly, Taylor and we ourselves have hypothesized that accompanying the "disembedding" of the self from its traditional social location is a process of the "reinvention" of the self (Connolly, 1991; Giddens, 1991a; Taylor, 1989). We hypothesize the emergence of new structures of feeling and new patterns of values and preferences amongst western citizens that have an impact on behaviour, practices and institutions, including areas considered in social policy (Gibbins & Reimer, 1995). (Gibbins, 1998, p. 41)

Abandoning positivistic notions of an essential, innate human nature and tradition-based metanarratives that support the normalizing tendencies of conventional social theories and practices creates space for exploring the diversity, difference, and indeterminacy that are inherent in all discourse and behavior. In the absence of metanarratives or grand theories about human behavior designed to generate a consensus around comprehensive controlling social practices, we can begin to recognize the realities of pluralism, fragmentation, diversity of culture, and subjective realities, the contingency and ambivalence of postmodern life. Gibbins (1998) has noted that

> . . . if social policy has to deal with new selves and groups who are more self-authored, autonomous and assertive, it will need to change its assumptions, aims and practices. . . . How to reconcile the results of the processes of disembedding, pluralisation and empowerment is the problem inherited by postmodern social policy, with which every police force, prison, school, hospital and community must grapple. Changing needs, desires, problems, uncertainties and risks, emerging from the new situations and relationships, also pose immediate challenges. (pp. 43-44)

These challenges are also present in the provision of health- and long-term care services for older persons.

In responding to these challenges, a new theoretical framework and criteria are needed for the development of social policy.

> The outlines of this can be found in various recent texts, which advocate for the future (rather than celebrate the arrival of) the empowerment of citizens: the encouragement of autonomy, self-actualisation and expressivism at the individual level; the development of new politics, and new political structures and organizations, such as new social movements, at the group level; the recognition, legitimation, and support of new types of family, network and lifestyle; the search to craft particular packages of services for particular cases; the prioritizing of particularism (not selectivism) over universalism . . . the pluralizing of services; the recognition that a new set of welfare values and principles is needed to deal with a more cosmopolitan and differentiated society. . . . (Gibbins, 1998, p. 44)

These are the kind of empowerment-oriented values and realities that should guide the development of postmodern public policies designed to support a new syntheses of security and freedom for older people; they are expansive policies that are flexible enough to be responsive to individual needs and desires.

What we are proposing here is a synthesis of elements from the emerging postmodern culture and the welfare systems that have emerged and evolved since World War II in the United States. This synthesis would emphasize individual choice, agency and autonomy, but would wed these values to a strong awareness of needs of the vulnerable and of society's responsibility for seeing that their basic needs are met (security).

Chris Phillipson (1998) describes this new synthesis perspective well when he writes that he is not arguing

> . . . for a narrow "postmodern" view of ageing which focuses simply on choice and reflexivity, ignoring the profound inequalities of class, gender and ethnicity which continue to shape the lives of older people. In fact, I wish to

draw a middle position between these two: arguing, first for a framework which provides the necessary financial support for older people; but, second, for greater flexibility as regards the way in which older age is allowed to develop within society. (p. 127)

In terms of economic security, this approach makes the case for a broader, more expansive Social Security system that provides more equal benefits, especially for minorities and women; and that responds to the increasing level of risk experienced by employees in rapidly changing economies across the developed world, including declining private pensions and the growth of pensions based on defined contributions. This means that public pensions should be redesigned to reflect the value of productive activities, such as caregiving, that occur outside the formal marketplace, and that are responsive to the realities of contemporary work, such as multiple entries and exits from formal employment. Flexibility within the occupational system should not come at the price of exclusion from provisions for financial security in old age.

Neoliberal proposals to privatize public pensions, including the U.S. Social Security system, would make them as risky as private pensions have become with the spread of defined contribution (DC) plans (401 & IRA plans) over the last 25 years. As noted earlier, only half of all employees in the United States now have private pensions and most of these are defined contribution plans. The level of benefits generated by these plans is contingent upon employee and employer contributions and the performance of the equity and bond markets in the years prior to retirement. The growth of these plans over the last 25 years has not enhanced the retirement security of most employees who cannot afford to maximize their contributions and are often forced to cash out their accumulations prior to retirement to cover family expenses and reduce debt. Accumulation levels have been greatly restrained by stagnant/declining wages and rising costs over the last 30 years. The average 55-year-old employee now has less than $55,000 in her defined contribution account, which would generate less than $2,000 annually if converted to an annuity at retirement. Seventy percent of employees cash out their accounts at retirement rather than purchase annuities (Munnell, Sundén, & Lidstone, 2002).

Privatizing Social Security would only increase the economic insecurity of future retirees with defined-contribution private pension plans or no private pension at all. Social Security in its current form may be a more essential source of income for future retirees, especially women, minorities, and lower income workers generally, than it is for current retirees. Privatization of Social Security, along with the growth of DC private plans, would put retirement income at greater risk *without* solving the Social Security Trust Fund shortfall problem and creating a huge, $1 to $2 trillion transition cost problem for which no one has offered a feasible solution. Preserving Social Security as a publicly funded program would require relatively minor adjustments over the next 40 to 50 years. These adjustments should include improvements in benefits for minority retirees, women, and other lower income employees.

Privatization would undermine retirement security for low- and middle-income retirees and increase their dependence on family resources, which are already barely sufficient to keep most families afloat. Twenty-five years of stagnant wages, low savings, rising housing, health and education costs have squeezed families to the point of relying on debt to cover necessities. In short, privatization of the publicly supported retirement system represents a profound threat to the financial and emotional capacities of the intergenerational family. These capacities will come under additional stress in the years ahead as the number of elderly requiring caregiving assistance grows by 50% to 100%.

A recent analysis of the impact of the two privatization proposals developed by the President's Commission on Social Security found that a sizable majority of future retirees would have lower retirement incomes under both proposals than under the current programs. Those who had the misfortune of retiring during a turndown in the stock market would be especially disadvantaged. During the most recent market decline (2001–2003), defined contribution accounts lost 20%–40% of their value and are still far short of their 2001 predecline levels (Diamond & Orszag, 2003).

The new synthesis of retirement security will require major enhancements in health- and long-term care policies in order to expand opportunities for freedom in old age. Out-of-pocket medical expenses under Medicare have grown dramatically over the last 15 years (from 10% to 20%+ of discretionary income) and have put routine medical care beyond the reach of many less affluent older people, especially women. Adding a prescription drug benefit to Medicare will help reduce out-of-pocket costs for some retirees, but many older people will not have adequate access to healthcare until Medicare copayments and deductibles are substantially reduced and long-term care is made an affordable Medicare benefit.

The recently passed Medicare Prescription Drug Improvement and Modernization Act of 2003 (MMA), which includes a relatively meager, bizarrely designed drug benefit, is fundamentally a neoliberal proposal that includes several provisions designed to privatize Medicare, including private sector administration of the drug benefit, health savings accounts, a lot more money for HMOs, and six demonstration projects designed to test the relative cost-effectiveness of managed care versus fee-for-service Medicare beginning in 2010. What MMA does not include is any plausible prospect of cost containment. All major components of the healthcare industry do well in the bill with pharmaceutical companies and HMOs set to make many billions of dollars over the next five to ten years and physicians and many hospitals receiving rate increases. It is difficult to see how Medicare costs will be contained by reimbursing HMOs at rates 5% to 20% above payment levels in the fee-for-service system.

If Medicare costs are contained following implementation of the MMA, it is likely to occur as a result of increased beneficiary out-of-pocket spending, which is already three times the percentage spent by those under age 65. Without effective regulation, Medicare costs and beneficiary spending are both likely to increase. The MMA essentially leaves the struggle over the privatization of Medicare unresolved and guarantees that it will intensify in the future as health-care costs continue to increase and the population aged 65 and older grows.

Publicly provided, long-term care is now only available to poor Medicaid-eligible elders, the vast majority of whom are in nursing homes. A new synthesis long-term care policy would make long-term care universally available under Medicare and far more flexible than the current Medicaid program. A long-term care policy designed to support the autonomy of impaired elderly persons (new synthesis: freedom) would give them much greater control over the provision of care by allowing them to decide how resources are used.

The flexible, reflexive, self-creating lives of many middle-age members of the baby-boom generation will change the aging experience over the next 30 years. However, there must be a parallel effort to retain and enhance the security provisions (Social Security and Medicare) of the new synthesis for older persons, especially minorities and women. Social Security and Medicare have greatly increased economic security among older people. These two programs have created the necessary conditions for a new synthesis of public welfare and cultural resources. This synthesis includes the freedom of a postmodern culture that offers personal meaning as well as more opportunities for multiple, diverse, and creative narratives of the self. Public policies should be redesigned to provide more support for this kind of postmodern aging through greater flexibility and responsiveness to individual needs and desires. This approach, however, is antithetical to neoliberal policies of cutting and privatizing welfare programs and reducing choice in what individuals can afford to consume through the private market.

In response to neoliberal claims that the welfare state is antiquated, Alan Walker (2002) points out that

> . . . there is little or no evidence for the contention that the welfare state has outlived its usefulness or is unable to cope with new risks. Although there are new risks, many of the old ones continue, and the welfare state has proved itself to be a flexible institution well able to accommodate new risks. More-over, if we consider the nature of the emergent risks, it is very clear that some form of collective welfare is required to pool their costs and to take preventative action. There are four main ones (see Boscoe & Chassard, 1999):
>
> - a reduction in the financial risk associated with old age but with a new risk of becoming unemployable after 50;
> - the emergence of a new risk associated with longevity—long-term care;
> - a change in the nature of the labor market and unemployment so that, for the unemployed, it is not just a matter of geographical mobility to find work but also skills mobility to remain employable;
> - new forms of insecure work with no or very low workers' rights to social protection.

CONCLUSION

The struggle between progressive and neoliberal postmodernism over the future of public policy for the elderly is likely to play a major role in shaping the direction of politics in the West for the next several decades and the aging experience of the baby-boom generation. The future of Social Security and Medicare in the United States has already been placed in great jeopardy by the emergence of huge, long-term deficits in the federal budget and the possibility of large, continuing increases in military spending necessary to sustain a long, open-ended war against terrorism and to create a system of international security that could become the foundation for an empire.

These developments could greatly damage the potential for a progressive form of postmodernism, undermine the potential for new synthesis of freedom and security in old age, and create the economic, cultural and political conditions for the neoliberal dismantling of health and economic security programs for the elderly as well as others. This would leave baby boomers and later generations with their market-dependent private pensions and privately purchased health insurance. This is not a prescription for freedom, creativity, and personal fulfillment in old age for most people.

Neoliberalism, of course, is not limited to an agenda of privatization of public pensions and healthcare for the elderly. The neoliberal agenda includes the privatization of public programs for all age groups and across all policy domains from education and childcare to housing, healthcare, employment, and income support programs. These proposals are as risky and counterproductive for society as a whole as the neoliberal agenda for Social Security and Medicare is for retirees. Maintaining the income and healthcare pillars of the publicly supported retirement system is essential for the economic security of future retirees. The neoliberal agenda, however, must also be opposed in all of the other policy domains through the renewal of the social democratic vision of a just, generous, and productive society. In the globalizing, postindustrial societies of the developed world, privatization policies will not only undermine retirement security, they will also restrict economic growth and erode living standards.

A more social democratic policy agenda based on public welfare as an essential form of social investment is more likely to achieve growth and a high quality of life for the vast majority through a comprehensive family support program, a high priority on gender and ethnic equality, and public provision for old age security. A family support program designed to prevent poverty and featuring extensive investments in early childhood cognitive development can qualitatively reduce levels of educational failure and increase employability and overall productivity. Gender equality has several dimensions; but from a growth and development perspective, programs that help to harmonize child rearing with employment can prevent child poverty and reduce the severe labor force and birth shortages confronting many developed countries over the next several decades. These growth-oriented social investments can better position countries to meet the increasing costs of ensuring retirement security and enhance the labor force participation of women through publicly supported caregiving programs for the growing population of frail elderly persons in all developed countries.

Neoliberal proposals to privatize education, health, and caregiving activities would greatly increase the economic and psychological burdens on families already short of resources, generate greater inequality, diminish the employability potential of many people, especially minorities and women, restrict longer term productivity growth, and undermine the capacity of nations to meet the income and healthcare needs of retirees. The damaging consequences of neoliberal policies for education, healthcare, and public welfare can already be seen in countries across the developing world where privatization, deregulation, and cuts in public spending have occurred in tandem with stagnant or negative growth and declining living standards (Polivka & Borrayo, 2004).

REFERENCES

Baker, D. (1998). *Defusing the baby boomer time bomb: Projections of income in the 21st century.* Washington, DC: Economic Policy Institute.

Beck, U., & Beck-Gernsheim, E. (2002). *Individualization.* Thousand Oaks: Sage.

Carter, J. (1998). Studying social policy after modernity. In J. Carter (Eds.), *Postmodernity and the fragmentation of welfare.* New York: Routledge.

Diamond, P., & Orszag, P. (2003). *Reforming social security: A balanced plan.* Policy Brief #126, Washington, DC: The Brookings Institution.

Economic Policy Institute (2004). *Snapshot for July 21, 2004.* Economic snapshots. http://www.epinet.org.

Gibbins, J. (1998). Postmodernism, poststructuralism and social policy. In J. Carter (Ed.), *Postmodernity and the fragmentation of welfare.* New York: Routledge.

Giddens, A. (1994). Living in a post-traditional society. In U. Beck, A. Giddens, & S. Lash (Eds.), *Reflexive modernization: Politics, tradition and aesthetics in the modern social order.* Stanford, CA: Stanford University Press.

Gilleard, C., & Higgs, P. (2000). *Cultures of aging: Self, citizen and the body.* New York: Prentice Hall.

Gould, E., Mishel, L., Bernstein, J., & Price, L. (2004). *Assessing job quality.* EPI Issue Brief #200, http://epinet.org/content/e.g.m/issuebriefs_ib200.

Inglehart, R. (1997). *Modernization and postmodernization: Cultural, economic, and political change in 43 societies.* Princeton: Princeton University Press.

Johnson, R., & Penner, R. (2004). *The long-run financial burden of health care on aged households.* Prepared for the Sixth Annual Conference of Retirement Research Consortium, The Future of Social Security: Washington, DC.

Munnell, A., Sundén, A., & Lidstone, E. (2002). *How important are private pensions?* Issue Brief Number 8. Chestnut Hill, MA: Center for Retirement Research at Boston College.

Phillipson, C. (1998). *Reconstructing old age: New agendas in social theory and practice.* Thousand Oaks: Sage.

Polivka, L., & Borrayo, E. (2004). Globalization, population aging and ethics: Reflections on global disorder and justice. *The International Journal of Health Services* (accepted).

Pollin, R. (2003). *Contours of descent: U.S. economic fractures and the landscape of global austerity*. New York: Verso.

Reynolds-Scanlon, S., Reynolds, S., Peek, M., Polivka, L., & Peek C. (1999). *Profile of older Floridians*. Prepared for State of Florida Department of Elder Affairs, Contract #XM823.

VanDerhei, J., & Copeland, C. (2003). *Can America afford tomorrow's retirees: Results from the EBRIERF retirement security projection model*. EBRI Issue Brief Number 263: Washington, DC.

Warren, E., & Tyagi, A. (2003). *The two-income trap: Why middle-class mothers and fathers are going broke*. New York: Basic Books.

Walker, A. (2002). *Cultures of ageing: A critique*. Cultures of Aging Symposium, British Society of Gerontology Annual Conference: Birmingham, UK.

Wolfe, A. (2001). *Moral freedom: The impossible idea that defines the way we live now*. New York: W. W. Norton & Co.

Wolff, E. (2002). *Retirement insecurity: The income shortfalls awaiting the soon-to-retire*. Washington, DC: Economic Policy Institute.

Wu, K. (2001). *Income and poverty of older Americans in 2001: A chartbook*. AARP Public Policy Institute: Washington, DC.

CHAPTER 11

Dynamics of Late-Life Inequality: Modeling the Interplay of Health Disparities, Economic Resources, and Public Policies

Stephen Crystal

Over the life course, health status and economic resources interact in a complex and dynamic fashion to shape late-life outcomes. Understanding of this process and its implications for health and retirement income policy has been hampered by several factors that include inadequate data to disentangle these complicated relationships; insufficient analysis of distributional consequences of policies; and lack of clear conceptualization of interactions across domains usually studied separately.

Empirically, economic resources; health status and health-related quality of life; and access to and use of health services have typically been studied in separate "silos." Surveys and panel datasets developed to focus on one of these domains often contain inadequate measures in the other domains. For example, health-oriented surveys have often failed to incorporate income and asset measures of sufficient quality and have inadequately addressed measurement problems in these domains, such as high nonresponse rates. Surveys with an economic orientation, for their part, have often failed to incorporate adequate measures of health, health services use, and functioning.

On a theoretical level, quite separate and distinct conceptual frameworks have been dominant in understanding health outcomes and economic outcomes. Theoretical models applied to studies focusing on one domain have seldom incorporated well-developed conceptualizations in the other domain and of inter-actions between the two.

This chapter presents a theoretical framework for understanding and analyz-ing this process. This framework integrates cumulative advantage theory with perspectives from disablement theory that characterize the process by which biological changes in individuals, such as particular chronic diseases, ultimately do or do not lead to role-performance differences affecting economic status, and ultimately to late-life outcomes. It provides a structure for modeling the reciprocal relationships over the lifecourse of economic resources and health; and the process by which disparities cumulate in later life. While this approach is in the tradition of lifecourse studies, it also explicitly incorporates the role of structural factors, such as healthcare systems, in shaping the distribution of outcomes. Public policy choices interact with lifecourse processes to shape these distributional outcomes, including patterns of health and economic disparities at each stage of the lifecourse. By explicitly examining these relationships, we can understand more clearly what is at stake in public policy choices concerning the design of retirement income systems and healthcare financing systems.

POLICY CHOICES AND LATE-LIFE INEQUALITY

Among the most important life events that shape late-life outcomes are occupational and labor-force participation histories; health changes; and marriage, divorce, and widowhood, as well as many other individual lifecourse changes. These events interact with the institutional setting formed by societal public policy choices, such as the structure of retirement income and healthcare coverage systems, to produce the distribution of economic outcomes experienced by the older population. There has been considerable debate over the net effect of these factors on late-life inequality, stemming both from differences in underlying assumptions and in measurement. Some have argued that the pattern of outcomes reflects a "leveling" process, as preretirement sources of income, largely from the employment market, are replaced by sources that are more dominated by income from social insurance programs such as Social Security pensions (Fuchs, 1984). Others have argued that preretirement relative economic status is replicated in postretirement income in a process of "status maintenance" (Henretta & Campbell, 1976).

However, particularly when methodological issues such as underreporting of unearned income in survey data are adequately addressed, it appears to be fairly clear that the level of economic inequality, at least in the United States, increases after retirement age, both in cross-sectional studies and in longitudinal studies of multiple cohorts followed over time (Crystal, 1982, 1995; Crystal & Shea, 1990; Crystal & Waehrer, 1996). There is also evidence that the influence of initial advantages, such as the level of formal education received early in the lifecourse, is at least as determinative of economic outcomes after age 65 as it is earlier in the lifespan, despite the many, individually unpredictable life events that take place in the interim (Crystal, Shea, & Krishnaswami, 1992).

Based on these findings, the cumulative advantage model proposed by Crystal and Shea (1990) has suggested that the influences of many socioeconomic characteristics that act through a variety of pathways to influence economic well-being often cumulate over the lifecourse. For example, knowledge-based careers that entail high early investments in human capital may bring their greatest rewards in midlife and beyond. The economic return to experience in such careers may be greater; the potential for injury may be lower; ability to perform the work may be less reliant on age-related physical strength and endurance; and pension and healthcare coverage may be better. These four pathways reflect, respectively, differences in the market value of work, the health impact of work, the dependency of work productivity on health, and the impact of societal choices about retirement income and healthcare financing systems.

The probability of adverse events such as disablement varies across socio-economic subgroups; however, the impact of these events depends on structural or policy factors such as occupationally or governmentally based benefit systems. High levels of late-life inequality, therefore, are not a "law of nature" but depend in large part on societal choices. For example, economic inequality among the elderly is much higher in the United States, where private pensions account for a high proportion of retirement income, which tends to outweigh the redistributional effects of the Social Security system, than in countries that rely more heavily on public retirement income systems that have flat-rate or high-minimum benefits, or a substantial role for means-tested benefits (Whitehouse & Disney, 2003). Thus, in countries with lower late-life inequality, such as the Scandinavian nations, Australia, and the Netherlands, pensioners at the ninetieth percentile of pensioner income enjoy retirement incomes that are in the range of 2 to 2.5 times as high as those of pensioners at the tenth percentile. In the United States, by contrast, the ratio exceeds 5 to 1. Countries with comprehensive earnings-related public pensions paying larger benefits to higher earners produce intermediate levels of inequality (Whitehouse & Disney, 2003).

HOW MIDLIFE SETS THE STAGE FOR LATE-LIFE INEQUALITY

While early advantages and disadvantages, such as parental status and formal education, have long-persisting influences, it is the resources and events of midlife that are the immediate precursors to late-life economic and health status. By midlife, as well, the relationship between the economic and health domains becomes more apparent. The cumulative consequences of differences in socio-economic status on health are often long-term in nature; they become more marked in midlife after decades of exposure to differential stresses and risks. Disparities are generated through multiple pathways, including socioeconomic differences in risky health behavior; differences in access to healthcare (particularly in the U.S. system which, uniquely among the world's wealthy countries, lacks universal health coverage); and differences in occupational stress and occupationally based coping resources (Marmot & Fuhrer, 2004).

Conversely, health differences begin to have a sharper impact on economic outcomes at midlife, as the baseline risk of chronic illness and functional impairment increases. Differential age of onset of work disability is an important pathway by which these effects operate. This can be illustrated, for example, by Figure 1, which presents rates of disablement by age and years of education (less than high school graduate, high school graduate, college graduate). Decennial census data were used from the 5% sample of the 1990 census; this extremely large dataset made it possible to graph disability rates (respondent reported that "health conditions prevent working at a job") by exact years of age, so that the pattern of increasing disablement rates with age for each subgroup could be shown.

These figures provide, literally, a graphic illustration of the increasing divergence between disability rates for individuals who entered the workforce with different levels of formal education, as they approach and move through midlife. Between the ages of 40 and 60, the rates for non-high school graduates increase more sharply year-to-year than for the other groups, as illustrated in the steeper slope of the line representing that group. By the time individuals reach their late fifties, more than one in five of this group reports being disabled, as compared with about 4% of the college educated group.

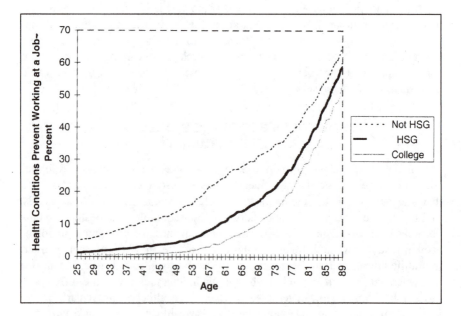

Figure 1. Percentage with work disability, by education and age, 1990 Census 5% sample.

Factors Shaping Midlife Disparities

Understanding the factors that lead to such dramatic divergences is one key to clarifying the dynamics of late-life inequality. Scholars such as Marmot have emphasized the adverse effects on health of job characteristics, which include decision authority and use of skills, and the stress of occupying subordinate positions in the occupational social hierarchy. Those who share this school of thought have viewed differential access to and use of healthcare services as a relatively minor contributor to such disparities, concluding that the causes of the social gradient in health lie outside the medical sector. However, this factor may be more important in the United States, with its absence of a universal health coverage program, than in some other settings; it is also plausible that it is increasing in importance as tools improve for medical management of chronic illnesses such as diabetes; moderating the risks created by hypercholesterolemia, hypertension, and similar conditions; and the prevention of disabling events such as myocardial infarctions and stroke.

Differential health behavior by socioeconomic status is also a key factor in shaping disparate late-life health outcomes. Many risky health behaviors, such as tobacco smoking, have become increasingly concentrated among persons of lower socioeconomic status in the wake of health education campaigns and publicity about the risks that were responded to more readily by more-advantaged individuals. In this way, health education efforts aimed at the general population, while having a positive impact on overall population health, can, ironically, actually contribute to disparities. This does not, of course, justify a defeatist position in terms of the role and responsibilities of public policies in relation to personal health behaviors, as the discussion below will clarify.

Finally, it is important to appreciate the socioeconomic as well as the "medical" dimensions of disability. A particular medical condition may have a very different impact on the ability to function in occupational or other roles, depending on the individual's ability to overcome the impact of the problem—for example, through restorative health treatment or technological assistance—and, clearly, on the demands of the position. An orthopedic problem that may be disabling for a heavy equipment operator may not be disabling for a teacher.

HEALTH, HEALTHCARE, AND ECONOMIC OUTCOMES IN MID AND LATE LIFE: A CONCEPTUAL MODEL

As discussed above, while health-related life events are important determinants of late-life economic outcomes, their effects can be moderated by a number of factors, many of which are the result of policy choices. These moderating factors can be illustrated by the following conceptual framework, which combines the cumulative advantage/cumulative disadvantage perspective with perspectives from disablement theory that characterize the process by which biological changes in individuals, such as particular chronic diseases, ultimately lead (or do not lead) to role performance differences, such as discontinuation of employment (Johnson & Wolinsky, 1993; Verbrugge & Jette, 1994). Research informed by the cumulative advantage perspective has typically focused on issues of financial well-being, while research in the disablement tradition has typically focused on health-status differences. Since health status and financial well-being are so intimately interrelated, however, there is considerable potential for integrating aspects of the two perspectives. An important compatibility between the two perspectives is that both treat individual-level outcomes as the result of interactions between life-course events on the one hand and socioeconomic settings, constraints, and institutions on the other (Crystal & Waehrer, 1996; O'Rand, 2003; Verbrugge & Jette, 1994).

Cumulative-advantage theorists, for example, would note that intermittent labor-force participation patterns by women juggling family and career may or may not cause financial privation in late life, depending on the structure of vesting rules in private pension systems. Disablement theorists would note that an accident leading to the need to use a wheelchair may or may not lead to work disability, depending on whether the individual's occupation is manual or professional and the extent to which the employer is willing to make accommodations. We therefore conceptualize the impact of individual-level life-course events on changes in bodily functioning and the impact of this in turn on role performance, health perceptions, and other more distal outcomes, as being moderated by resources and demands of the social and institutional environment. Drawing from the disablement tradition, this model conceptualizes health difficulties and their impact in terms of a process that proceeds from physiological dysfunction to performance limitation to disability. We extend this conceptualization by integrating into the model the impact of health problems at these various levels on financial well-being (which is, of course, also shaped by the social and demographic characteristics in the leftmost block of the model and by other variables). We identify moderating variables that can buffer the effects of disease on impairment, impairment on disability, and disability on financial disadvantage (see Figure 2).

Many of the moderating factors are related either to the continuing effects of early advantage; to systems of occupational stratification and differential privileges and accommodations; and/or to social policy choices. Effects of education, for example, are pervasive. Those with less formal education are at higher risk of specific chronic diseases. They may be less able to reduce the impact of these conditions or slow their progression by seeking out and accessing appropriate healthcare or by self-care/behavioral change strategies, thus experiencing increased impact of their conditions on functional impairment (e.g., the ability to perform specific tasks such as lifting, climbing stairs, or walking specified distances). These impairments in their turn increase the risk of disability with respect to employment (difficulty or inability to work at a job) or with respect to performance

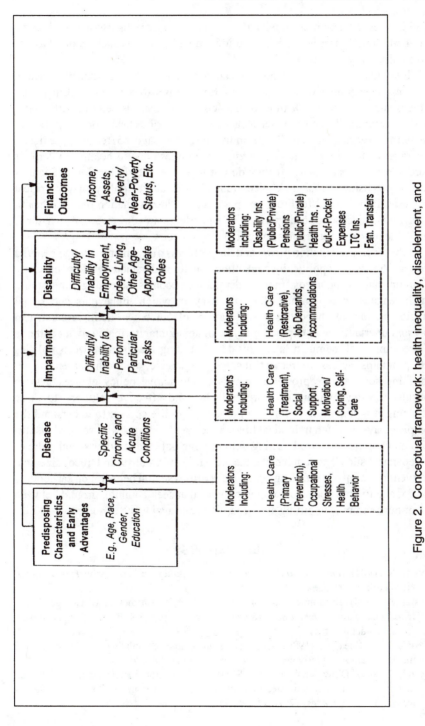

Figure 2. Conceptual framework: health inequality, disablement, and cumulative advantage over the life course.

of other roles and activities. Finally, the financial impact of disablement on income may be buffered for a better-educated individual by actions such as purchase of private disability insurance.

While such individual advantages can reduce the adverse impact of health problems on economic outcomes, this relationship is also shaped by public policy choices and institutions. Healthcare financing and access is central, particularly for those individuals who experience disability and serious health problems before the normal retirement age. While individuals over age 65 receive Medicare, coverage for those who become "premature retirees" due to health problems is more uncertain, particularly if they do not meet the criteria for Social Security disability pensions. Societal choices related to disability policy play a critical role, especially in midlife. From this perspective, the association between health disparities and economic disparities in late life is not the result of a natural, inevitable process, but reflects specific policy choices.

As the elderly population grows and the problems of financing old-age benefits become increasingly politically contentious, better understanding of the diversity of circumstances and needs among older people becomes increasingly important. Much remains to be learned about the way in which life events and social policies interact to shape this varied pattern of outcomes. Such research can play an important role in exploding myths of aging; monitoring evolving patterns of economic well-being in later life; demonstrating the links between policies and programs across retirement income, healthcare, and other arenas; and clarifying some of the probable impacts of alternative policy choices. As we consider the development of more equitable and effective solutions to these problems, it is important to think of the long-term life course; to understand the complex ways in which individual life-course events interact with societal institutions and policies; to avoid dealing with old-age policy and other social policies in separate "silos"; to appreciate the key role of midlife and recognize that interventions aimed at reducing late-life disparities should begin much earlier than age 65; and to craft social-protection policies that seek common ground between generations rather than pitting age-group interests against one another.

REFERENCES

Crystal, S. (1982). *America's old age crisis: Public policy and the two worlds of aging.* New York: Basic Books.

Crystal, S. (1995). Economic status of the elderly. In R. Binstock & L. George (Eds.), *Handbook of aging and the social sciences* (4th ed., pp. 388-409). San Diego and New York: Academic Press.

Crystal, S., & Shea, D. (1990). Cumulative advantage, cumulative disadvantage, and inequality among elderly people. *The Gerontologist, 30*(4), 437-443.

Crystal, S., Shea, D., & Krishnaswami, S. (1992). Educational attainment, occupational history, and stratification: Determinants of later-life resources. *Journal of Gerontology: Social Sciences, 47*(5), S213-S221.

Crystal, S., & Waehrer, K. (1996) Later-life economic inequality in longitudinal perspective. *Journal of Gerontology: Social Sciences, 51B*(6), S307-S318.

Fuchs, V. R. (1984). Though much is taken: Reflections on aging, health, and medical care. *Milbank Memorial Fund Quarterly: Health and Society, 62,* 143-166.

Henretta, J., & Campbell, R. (1976). Status attainment and status maintenance: A study of stratification in old age. *American Sociological Review, 41,* 981-992.

Johnson R. J., & Wolinsky, F. (1993). The structure of health status among older adults: Disease, disability, functional limitation, and perceived health. *Journal of Health and Social Behavior, 34*(2), 105-121.

Marmot, M. G., & Fuhrer, R. (2004). Socioeconomic position and health across midlife. In O. G. Brim, C. D. Ryff, & R. C. Kessler (Eds.), *How healthy are we? A national study of well-being at midlife* (pp. 64-89).Chicago: University of Chicago Press.

O'Rand, A. (2003). Cumulative advantage and gerontological theory. In S. Crystal & D. Shea (Eds.), *Economic outcomes in later life: Public policy, health, and cumulative advantage* (2002 volume of the Annual Review of Gerontology and Geriatrics, pp. 14-30). New York: Springer Publishing.

Verbrugge, L. M., & Jette, A. M. (1994). The disablement process. *Social Science and Medicine, 38*(1), 1-14.

Whitehouse, E., & Disney, R. (2003). Cross-national comparisons of retirement income. In S. Crystal & D. Shea (Eds.), *Economic outcomes in later life: Public policy, health, and cumulative advantage* (2002 volume of the Annual Review of Gerontology and Geriatrics, pp. 60-94). New York: Springer Publishing.

CHAPTER 12

Health, Aging, and America's Poor: Ethnographic Insights on Family Co-morbidity and Cumulative Disadvantage

Linda M. Burton and Keith E. Whitfield

Low-income populations are more likely to suffer from serious physical and mental health problems that are often exacerbated by limited access to quality healthcare (Heymann, 2000; Whitfield, Weidner, Clark, & Anderson, 2002; Williams & Collins, 1995). In the current scholarly and political discourse on this issue, notable attention is given to the prevalence of certain diseases among the poor with an eye toward reducing socioeconomic and ethnic/racial inequalities in health or what is popularly termed "health disparities" (National Research Council, 2001). However, in seeking to reduce health disparities, social scientists, health professionals, and policy makers alike have devoted little attention to exploring health experiences "inside" low-income families—that is, 1) the degree to which family household members are co-morbid (e.g., evidencing both physical and mental health problems); 2) the social, as well as biological etiology of family co-morbidity; and, 3) the factors that exacerbate the incidence of chronic and acute physical and mental illnesses individuals experience in the context of families as they move from childhood to old age.

In ways similar to the family co-morbidity approach, social scientists have yet to maximize the potential of cumulative disadvantage theory as a guiding framework in research on poverty, health, and aging (Crystal & Waehrer, 1996; Dannefer, 1988, 2003). Cumulative disadvantage theory is concerned with the ways in which social inequality creates the successive accumulation of debilitating risks for society's "have-nots" as compared to the "haves" (Merton, 1968). Dannefer (p. 105 this volume) contends that, with the exception of a few notable studies (Crystal, Shea, & Schaie, 2003; Ferraro & Kelley-Moore, 2003), relatively few gerontologists have acknowledged the impact of cumulative disadvantage on health and aging among America's poor and that popular images of successful aging and elder affluence "eclipse the now well-documented fact that inequality in resources (and perhaps in health as well) is greatest among the aged . . . and that inequality observed within the older age strata underestimates the effects of lifelong economic inequalities in another way: A disproportionate number of those from lower socioeconomic backgrounds have been prematurely removed from the population by mortality." Geronimus' (1996, p. 590) conceptual and empirical work on the "weathering" hypothesis comparably suggests that the effects of social inequality on health in certain populations may compound with age, leading to growing gaps in health status for individuals across and within families. Moreover, a high incidence of individual and family co-morbidity experienced early in the life course may have long-term and enduring consequences for chronic morbidity later in life (Blackwell, Hayward, & Crimmins, 2001).

In this chapter, we use family co-morbidity and cumulative disadvantage perspectives as guiding principles to examine ethnographic data on health and aging in poor families. This chapter is an empirical extension of Dannefer's and Crystal's (this volume) discourse on cumulative disadvantage and aging and highlights the profound ways in which lifetime poverty experiences in families snowball across economic, social, interpersonal, and psychological domains to exacerbate compromised health among family members throughout the life course. We contend that a contextually grounded, more insightful under-standing of poverty, health, and aging is achieved when family co-morbidity and cumulative disadvantage perspectives guide the generation of knowledge on this topic.

We explore patterns in cumulative disadvantage and family co-morbidity in a sample of 256 economically disadvantaged families who participated in the longitudinal ethnographic component of *Welfare, Children, and Families: A Three-City Study* (Winston et al., 1999). The families are multigenerational and headed by young adult and midlife women with young children. These young families give us a unique window into cumulative disadvantage, family co-morbidity, and aging in ways that punctuate the social processes and mechanisms that influence health disparities among America's poor across the life course. We address two questions: 1) In what ways do "cumulative disad-vantages" that poor families experience on a daily basis create the context for their health experiences? 2) How are these disadvantages evidenced in family co-morbidity?

THE *THREE-CITY STUDY* ETHNOGRAPHY

The data on cumulative disadvantage and family health featured in this chapter derive from the ethnographic component of a larger research project, *Welfare, Children, and Families: A Three-City Study*. The study was carried out over a period of four years in Boston, Chicago, and San Antonio to monitor the consequences of welfare reform for the well-being of children and families. The study comprises three interrelated components: 1) a longitudinal in-person survey of approximately 2,400 families with children aged 0–4 and 10–14 in low-income neighborhoods, about 40% of whom were receiving cash welfare payments when they were first interviewed in 1999; 2) an embedded developmental study of a subsample of about 630 children aged 2–4 in 1999 and their caregivers; and 3) an ethnographic study of 256 families residing in the same neighborhoods as the survey families, recruited according to the same family income criteria, and who were followed intensively until the project ended in August 2003. African American, Hispanic, and non-Hispanic white families are represented in all three components and in all three cities. A detailed description of the *Three-City Study* and a series of reports are available at www.jhu.edu/~welfare.

All families who participated in the ethnography had household incomes at or below 200% of the Federal Poverty Line. The majority of ethnography participants (42%) were of Latino or Hispanic ethnicity (e.g., includes Puerto Ricans, Mexican Americans, and Central Americans). Of the remaining participants, 38% were African American and 20% were non-Hispanic white. Over half of the mothers were aged 29 or younger, and a majority of the respondents had a high school diploma or a GED (General Education Diploma), or attended trade school or college. Forty-nine percent of the families were receiving welfare when they entered the study; one-third of these, in compliance with welfare regulations, were also working. Fifty-one percent of the sample was not receiving welfare benefits, and the primary earner in the household was either working a low-wage labor job or unemployed. The 256 mothers identified a total of 685 children in their households. Fifty-three percent of the children were aged 4 or younger; 47% of the children were elementary school age or adolescents. Twenty-five percent of the mothers were responsible for one child, and 28%, 25%, and 23% for two, three, and four or more children, respectively. Fifty-six percent of mothers were not married and did not have a partner (e.g., boyfriend) living with them; another 17% were not married, but were cohabiting with a partner; 17% were married and living with their spouse; and 10% were married or separated, and their spouses were not living in the home.

Families were recruited into the ethnography at formal childcare settings, such as Head Start, WIC offices, neighborhood community centers, local welfare offices, churches, and other public assistance agencies, as well as in less formal neighborhood settings, between June 1999 and December 2000. Of the 256 families participating in the ethnography, 44 were recruited specifically because they had a child, aged birth to 8 years, with a moderate or severe disability. We recruited families of children whose disability might make a difference in their mother's ability to work. We purposely included a broad range of disabilities to represent children who have different needs and thus present different issues for families (e.g., autism—high impact behavioral issues; Down syndrome—

significant cognitive delays and possible health problems; spina bifida—high impact medical problems; and cerebral palsy—physical and perhaps cognitive delays). Medical diagnoses of these children include cerebral palsy, Down syndrome, seizure disorder, severe ADHD, significant developmental delays, visual and hearing impairments, spina bifida, Pervasive Developmental Disorder, autism, chondrodysplasia punetata, various syndromes (e.g., Kartagener syndrome, Angelman syndrome, and Cri-du-chat syndrome), severe asthma, and other involved medical conditions (e.g., congenital heart problems; brain damage, lung disease) that have resulted in developmental delay and disability (Skinner, Lachiotte, Cherlin, & Burton, 2002). We include this purposive subsample of families with a child with a disability in the analysis reported here because they are similar on cumulative disadvantage issues and health to the sample of 212 families that were recruited for the overall ethnography, but not on the basis of having a child with a disability. This circumstance indicates how prevalent health problems were in the families we studied even when they were not purposively recruited for health conditions.

To gather ethnographic data on families, we employed a method of "structured discovery" in which in-depth interviews and observations focused on specific topics, but allowed flexibility to capture unexpected findings and relationships among topics (Burton et al., 2001; Winston et. al., 1999). The interviews addressed: health and health access; experiences with welfare and other public assistance programs; education, work experiences and future plans; family economics; child development, parenting, and intimate relationships; support networks; family routines; and home and neighborhood environments. Ethnographers also engaged in participant observation with the family, accompanying the mother and her children to the welfare office, doctor, hospital, clinic, or workplace, and taking note of the interactions and overall contexts.

Ethnographers met with each family once or twice each month, on average, for 12 to 18 months, with two follow-up interviews at six months and one year after the 18-month intensive period. Interview transcripts, field notes, and other documents were coded for entry into a qualitative data management (QDM) software application and summarized into a case profile for each family. The QDM program and case profiles enabled counts across the entire sample of ethnographic families as well as detailed analysis of individual cases.

A team of Qualitative Data Analysts (QDAs)—using profiles developed on each family and the QDM software—assessed each family's health status and level of cumulative disadvantage. Tables with health and employment information were constructed for each of the 256 families in our sample. Data on each family were cross-checked through an iterative process: information drawn from family profiles was compared to information available from the data-collection team, information from the data-processing team (the QDAs), and information that had been coded into our QDM software.

CUMULATIVE DISADVANTAGE:
THE CONTEXT OF AGING AND FAMILY HEALTH

In the context of often severe cumulative disadvantage, the circumstances in which poor families live and negotiate health are highly variable. The personal circumstances of at least 61% of the families participating in the ethnography can best be characterized as highly challenging, with the remaining 39%, relatively speaking, experiencing moderate and fewer personal challenges. We define the most challenged families as those who are consistently confronted with harsh situations that compromise their abilities to meet their most basic of needs (Earle & Heyman, 2002; Olson & Pavetti, 1997). These families couldn't, as one participant indicates, "ever get a break." Their ability to negotiate complex issues was commonly usurped by unpredictable monthly incomes and expenses, inadequate housing, physical threats to personal and family safety, tragic family deaths including the deaths of very young children, difficult work schedules, and inconvenient and unreliable transportation that resulted in mothers "spending most of their time on the bus [getting to work, the doctor, and home]."

Highly Challenging Family Lives

Several families provide a glimpse of highly challenging lives. These families persistently face myriad adverse circumstances with limited financial resources and inadequate social support. For example, Marla is a 35-year-old mother of three who began adulthood in one of the three cities as a 16-year-old runaway from the South, unprepared for the partner violence and substance abuse that lay ahead. With physician-confirmed HIV and cancer diagnoses, she is susceptible to bouts of major depression that incapacitate her and prompt her to voluntarily surrender her children to protective services or send them to relatives when she is going through "a bad spell." Life is very unpredictable for Marla and her children. Marla cannot plan long-term for the future, let alone the next day.

Barbara is a 37-year-old grandmother dedicated to providing a home for the grandchildren she now raises as a result of their mother's drug addiction and imprisonment. In addition to making a home for her three grandchildren aged 2, 6, and 10, Barbara is still recovering from the nervous breakdown she had last year after her husband left her. His leaving was too much to bear given all of her chronic mental and physical health conditions, including bipolar disorder, depression, anxiety, migraines, back injury, diabetes, high cholesterol, eczema, three hernias, back injury, kidney problems, and a slide into morbid obesity. She is doing the best that she can, but admits to being challenged by just making it through the day.

Colleen has been trying to make good the expectation that one must work or go to school to make a better life. She was cut off welfare when she started working a job that paid slightly more than minimum wage—$6.00/hour. Despite her persistence in trying to "get it together," she and her two young children found themselves homeless yet again. Since the last homeless shelter she and her children lived in enforced very rigid rules about young children and feeding schedules, Colleen decided not to take the homeless shelter route this time. So, she found herself and her children sharing a relative's public housing unit with *twenty-two* other people. The housing unit has two bedrooms and one bathroom. Colleen continues her multiyear wait on the public housing list. There's not much else she can do right now except wait. She lost her welfare and Medicaid twice in the last year. She says, "no home, no mailbox, no check, no medical card."

The experiences of the Jones family are particularly illustrative of the cumulative impact of extremely challenging lives. Evette Jones and her children once lived in the suburbs and believed they were finally setting a new family path out of poverty. Evette held on tightly to her dream until one day, reeling from the sequential and unexpected deaths of her parents and brother, and overwhelmed by financial difficulties, she made a decision to "just stop working." Evette and her children then left the suburbs and moved back into the same housing project she grew up in even though she feared for her children's safety. This seemingly "irrational" move had a very specific rationale from Evette's perspective. She was hedging her bets because she knew that moving back into the projects greatly increased her chances for getting government assisted housing in a better neighborhood. Nonetheless, her fears were realized when she and her family were victimized and the windows in her apartment were continuously broken by people attempting to break in. Evette's young daughter, Candice, was in the room during one such incident.

> When they busted the windows, my baby was in the kitchen, and it was something that just knocked me off my feet. I was over overwhelmed cause I was like, my precious baby, she's just a doll, she would hurt no one. Why would you want to hurt a baby, you know? And just think that if you know the baby's in there, to hurt them and they helpless, they just babies, they don't deserve this. How you gonna just end their life or hurt them and they just, you know, babies? They gotta grow like you did to grow to bust that window. That's why I was just real overprotective, and now that I am living in fear because I feel like now, you gonna bust my windows, you throw a cocktail in here, you gonna burn me up.

Evette was markedly affected by the break-ins because of her special attachment to Candice. However, Evette continued to live in her apartment because she hoped she would soon be relocated to one of the new townhomes being built for residents of her complex. To protect herself and her family, Evette had her windows boarded up, leaving only one small area exposed. In the meantime, afraid for her children's safety, she was hesitant to let them play outside. This was particularly difficult for one of her six sons who has hypertension. He, along with three of her other children, also has asthma.

[My son] feels like he is caved in, he never goes outside and he don't go outside playing and running around. [My] number one priority in life is having safety. And I don't have that right now.

Issues of financial insecurity and safety played a major role in Evette's fate. After living in the housing project a little less than a year, Evette was arrested for participating in illegal drug activities. She was sent to jail; relatives assumed responsibility for her children's care.

Although the boarded-up windows may have helped prevent people from breaking into Evette's apartment, they appeared to be a major factor in endangering the lives of her children. While in the care of family members, a fire broke out in Evette's apartment and Candice was killed. Since she was incarcerated, Evette was not able to attend her daughter's funeral.

Moderately Challenging Family Lives

Relatively speaking, approximately 39% of the families experienced moderate to low-level challenges in their lives, in large part because their experiences, while also difficult, were not of sustained duration. Several of these families plummeted into poverty via unanticipated job loss or divorce, while others are "just getting by" and still others "getting ahead." These families commonly receive support from extended kin or friends or through links established with community agencies.

Anna's family is an example of one family for whom life became complicated as a function of an unexpected decline in its economic resources. Anna, her husband Alan, and their two children recently became homeless after Alan lost his job. Anna and Alan were expecting a child at the time and decided, because of their current status, to give the child up for adoption. Some time after their child was adopted, Alan went back to work. With the assistance of programs available through the homeless shelter, the family was able to acquire stable housing and health insurance. For now, Anna and Alan believe that their lives are back on track. They have, in a sense, "caught a break." However, as with all families in the ethnography, we continue to monitor Anna and Alan's family closely, knowing that perhaps the impact of having to give their child up for adoption has not be fully realized just yet because their current attention is so firmly directed on stabilizing life for their family "right now."

Sandy and her family are just getting by. Sandy, her two daughters, and her mother and step-father live in a rented trailer. Sandy took her parents in after her stepfather lost his job. While living quarters are tight and finances dip sometimes, this family pools its resources to stay afloat. Sandy's mother has multiple disabilities, but watches the children while Sandy works long hours. Sandy's stepfather, despite his failing health, continues to look for employment. Sandy earns $7.00/hour at her current job and receives Medicaid for her children. She goes without health insurance because she can't afford to pay for it with her limited wages. Sandy describes her health as "pretty good right now, so I'm not going to worry about not having insurance for myself until I need it."

A few families are getting ahead. In most of these families, children and their mothers and fathers co-reside, and both parents typically work low-wage jobs. These families do not receive welfare and juggle work schedules, childcare, and doctor's visits, often within the context of lengthy journeys on public transportation. Rita and Raul, both of whom work low-wage jobs "in the city," recently purchased a home with the assistance of a HUD-type program after their former landlord encouraged them to become homeowners. They take long sojourns by bus to work and to get medical care for their children. However, Rita, unlike Evette, can say that the extra effort it takes to get to work and the doctor are worth it because, "When I go to sleep at home, a train could pass by, and I wouldn't wake up because I feel so safe."

MEASURING HEALTH

In the context of cumulative disadvantage and challenging lives, we asked mothers to tell us about those illnesses affecting them and their children that have been diagnosed by a physician or mental health professional. In some cases, mothers and children were receiving medical care, but physicians or mental health professionals had not yet rendered a definitive diagnosis about their health problems. In these instances, we asked the mother to simply tell us what the doctor was treating them for, acknowledging that it was a "temporary diagnosis until the real one came in."

The precision with which health problems within families were articulated by the primary caregivers was somewhat variable. Most were quite precise in delineating their health problems because they were applying for SSI for themselves or a child. Such applications require a physician's report and precise descriptions of disabling ailments. Some mothers were less exact in reporting health problems because they: 1) had other things to worry about, and as one young primary caregiver who had "some form of cancer" indicated, " I don't want to deal with it yet;" 2) were not acknowledging their children's disabilities or overt behavioral problems because they didn't want their children to be thought of as "slow, crazy, dumb, wild, sickly, or uncontrollable" in social settings such as family reunions, school, or church; 3) didn't understand the diagnoses physicians or mental health professionals had given them because it "wasn't explained in a way that I could understand;" or 4) used cultural terms to describe their mental and physical ailments, such as "nervosa" which encompasses anxiety, panic attacks, and depression; "getting in a mood," which in some families is a synonymous term for mild schizophrenia, paranoia, and anxiety disorders; "sugar," which implies diabetes; and "water," which in one neighborhood setting meant hypertension characterized by notable water retention and extremely swollen hands, wrists, ankles, and feet.

Gathering precise health data on the families involved considerable effort on our part and was only achieved after months of in-depth discussions with, observations of, and verification of illnesses by the primary caregivers. While our families experienced numerous episodes of short-term illnesses, our analysis focused specifically on the *major* health problems our families experienced as defined by the National Center for Chronic Disease Prevention and Health Promotion (Center for Disease Control, 2002), the Surgeon General's Call to Action to Prevent and Decrease Overweight and Obesity, and recent National Institutes of Health reports that outline principal population health concerns, including diseases of the nervous, endocrine, metabolic, circulatory, and respiratory systems (National Research Council, 2001). The most common physical ailments mothers reported were severe obesity, hepatitis, hypertension, cancer, arthritic conditions, cardiovascular disease, and diabetes; and for their children, diabetes, severe asthma, seizures, and lead poisoning. Chronic dental problems, such as "brown teeth" and advanced gum disease were also common for adults and children, particularly in San Antonio.

In terms of mental health, 76% of the mothers ($N = 223$) reported mental health problems based on a diagnoses provided by their mental health professional (e.g., psychiatrist). Recent reports on mental health issues in low-income populations also guided our analysis (Beardslee, Versage, & Gladstone, 1998; Danzinger et al., 2000; Jayakody, Danzinger, & Pollack, 2000; Kessler & Zhoa, 1999; Lennon, Blome, & English, 2002), as well the *DSM IV* listing of conditions (American Psychiatric Association, 1994). The most frequently reported mental health conditions experienced by mothers were depression, anxiety, post-traumatic stress disorder, and chronic stress; and for their children, attention deficit hyperactivity disorder, autism, anxiety, and depression.

FAMILY HEALTH

Our analysis of health problems focuses on the family as the principal unit of analysis. Families are defined as the primary caregiver(s) and the children she/he is responsible for. The decision to examine health as a family issue rather than just the mother or the children was based on emergent findings in the ethnographic data. The data suggest that the health problems of mothers and fathers and their children were integrally linked and could not be discussed as separate issues. The chronic health conditions of children, as well as other family members their mothers were responsible for, proved equally as problematic in families' day-to-day efforts to economically sustain themselves.

The presence of multiple health problems in families was common. Family health profiles fell into four categories ($N = 256$ families): 1) *Concurrent Family Health Problems (63%)*—where two or more members had chronic physical and mental health conditions; 2) *Primary Caregiver Health Problems Only (15%)*—where only the primary caregiver had one or more chronic physical and mental health conditions; 3) *Child Health Problems Only (9%)*—where a child was the only member of family with one or more chronic physical and mental health conditions; and 4) *No Reported Family Health Problems (13%)*—where no one in the family reported chronic physical and mental health conditions.

Families experiencing concurrent illnesses usually included a mother who had multiple health conditions. Seventy-eight percent of the mothers in the sample reported multiple physical illnesses or a combination of physical and mental illnesses. Although the combinations of physical illnesses experienced by the mothers varied, they were quite frequently accompanied by depression, as in the case of Earlene. Earlene, a 45-year-old primary caregiver of two grandchildren, has hepatitis C, high blood pressure, and vision problems, and she suffers from constant pain in her stomach and arthritis in her knees. She also suffers depression and anxiety and didn't leave her house during the preceding year. During the first few months of her involvement in the ethnography, Earlene checked herself into a mental hospital because she "was so depressed that she felt like the walls in her house were closing in on her." One of her daughters took care of her grandchildren while she was in the hospital. Currently, Earlene takes numerous daily medications for her mental and physical health conditions.

The mothers in the sample were relatively young, with approximately 83% aged 39 or younger. The young ages of the primary caregivers coupled with the high incidence of multiple chronic physical and mental illnesses made them justifiably fearful for their middle and later years. Females with severe chronic physical and mental health problems early in life are likely to have exacerbated health problems as they approach midlife and old age (Blackwell et al., 2001; Geronimus, 1996; National Research Council, 2001). Lupe, a 21-year-old mother of two, was aware of the problems associated with having poor health at a young age. She notes

> Me and my mom talk about how many problems I've had. I'm only 21, and
> I've had all these problems (asthma, gynecological tumors, and depression),
> and I worry about in coming years what's going to happen. There are women
> out there in their thirties having hysterectomies. Is that going to be me?

Many of the mothers became melancholy about their health when reflecting on the lives of their own mothers. Most of these respondents' mothers were disabled or had died of cardiovascular disease, strokes, or cancer before the age of 55. Like their daughters and their grandchildren, these women had lengthy histories of infectious and chronic illnesses dating back to their childhoods.

Mothers' Health and Meeting Family Needs

Mothers in the study tended to neglect their own physical and mental health needs to meet the economic and healthcare needs of their children and extended family members. While over 56% of the mothers received some support from their spouses, partners, or the fathers of their children, nearly all the women in the study, even those who reported no current health problems, often put symptoms of their illnesses "out of their minds" and postponed regular check-ups and treatment of diagnosed illnesses because "being sick" interfered with their abilities to take care of their children and older family members and their ability to keep going on the job. For example, some mothers refused to take medication prescribed for severe hypertension because they feared it would keep them from being "alert enough" to care for their young children. Rena, whose story follows, was too busy and too worried about the impact of medications to follow medical advice.

Rena is a 25-year-old working, single mother of three children, aged 1, 5, and 10. She works the third shift at her job, so she survives on less than five hours of sleep daily. Rena does not have a car, so every day she rides the bus at least five hours to and from work as well as delivering and picking up her children from school and childcare at her mother's house. In fact, Rena travels everywhere by bus or cab.

Rena told us that she has been diagnosed with clinical depression but has, in her own opinion, "little time to be depressed." Her 10-year-old child is autistic and takes up quite a bit of her time. And all too often, Rena spends her time defending herself during episodes of physical violence with her current live-in partner. Rena refuses to take her depression medication, even though there are some days she is so depressed that it is hard for her to get out of bed.

Rena puts off her healthcare needs as much as possible because of the cost and limited childcare options for her children. With an autistic child and a toddler and preschooler, both of whom have asthma, in addition to her job and dealing with domestic violence, Rena feels a bit overwhelmed with life—a fact reflected in her attitude toward health. Rena says she goes to the doctor when her chest gets tight, she can't breathe, or she is in intense pain. Unless it is one of these situations, she usually does not go to a doctor because she "could spend $5.00 looking on the wall at Walgreen's [buying over-the-counter remedies to self-medicate] as opposed to a $20 co-pay for a visit to the doctor . . . with working, the kids, and cleaning you don't have time to stop and listen to your body, even when there are warnings sign of a problem . . . you just 'do' until you can just sit in a chair and nod off."

Francine, a 30-year-old mother of three children, aged 4, 6, and 8, also had too many other responsibilities to take care of her own health problems. Francine explained that, as a baby and toddler, she was often in the hospital with pneumonia; she was not expected to live into the elementary school years. She made it, but she was hospitalized every year with pneumonia until her freshman year of high school.

When Francine joined the ethnographic study, she had just received a "temporary diagnosis of stomach cancer," but Francine did not return to the doctor. She only returned when the pain was unbearable and she "didn't have other folks to take care of." Her six-year-old asthmatic son required constant attention. Francine's mother suffered a recent stroke and heart attack. Francine, like many of the mothers in the study, was her own mother's primary caregiver. With no alternatives for caring for her mother or children, Francine could not accept treatment for her own medical conditions.

Some mothers, like Camille, actually discounted the serious nature of their illnesses. Camille does not attend to her health according to her doctor's recommendations. In fact, she is fairly nonchalant about the chronic conditions that affect her life and the lives of her children. Her youngest son has severe asthma that often requires late night emergency room visits and short-term hospital stays. Camille's own upper respiratory difficulties have required at least one hospital stay per year from birth to age 17, and she currently suffers from asthma. When she is under a great deal of stress, she has to use her inhalers more frequently and visit the doctor every two weeks for breathing treatments.

Six years ago, Camille was diagnosed with a form of cervical cancer. She has been treated with chemotherapy and medication, but the cancer does not stay in remission for long. Camille notes that, "My doctor says it is eating up my stomach, but not spreading yet. Some days I am fine with it, but other times it hurts so bad I just lay down and cry." Still, flare-ups of her asthma or the return of her cancer don't seem to cause her any extraordinary alarm. She says that, "someone has to make me go to the doctor" because past interactions with her healthcare providers (primary and emergency room) has led to immediate mandates that she present herself for hospitalization, even against her wishes.

Camille believes that her healthcare providers can do nothing for her, but she doesn't seem to think she is terminally ill either. Recently she reported that she might be pregnant, she is planning her wedding, and she has no plans to return to her doctor soon. Camille believes that in spite of what her doctor says, she will always be able to take care of her children and the needs of others.

Not only did family health problems force mothers to put their own health on the backburner, but the health of their dependents, including their children and elderly relatives, could interfere with their ability to keep their jobs and provide for their family's needs. For example, mothers who reported losing or resigning from their full time jobs ($N = 50$) frequently cited family health-related responsibilities as a barrier to work. Mothers with physically and mentally ill children and older relatives who required care reported that they resigned from or lost their jobs because they missed work to take their "children and parents to the doctor by bus." Mothers responsible for children with mental illnesses such as depression, ADHD, and suicide-ideation were also more likely to leave work early to manage a medical crisis with their children or to take extended periods of time off work when their children were hospitalized or when they could not find "sick-child care." Denise, the single mother of eight boys, lost at least three jobs during the course of the study because she missed several weeks of work caring for one of her children who has "rheumatic fever and heart problems that require frequent hospitalization." Eventually, 68% of these full-time working mothers "lost their jobs trying to keep their children well," also forgoing healthcare for themselves. For example, Gina says,

> I worry a lot about how I'm going to cover myself when my kids get sick, and I'm going to have to miss work. It's happened before where just one of us would get sick, and it just affects our whole life. Our whole life can fall apart like that. I just pray that my children don't get too sick. If I have to make a choice whether I'm going to stay home and take care of my sick kids or go to work, I'm going to stay home.

This problem applied not just to mothers, but to other caretakers of young children, including the grandmothers who were often called on to take over when mothers were not there. For example, Beatrice, the grandmother and custodial guardian of her three grandsons, was unable to maintain a job because she was too busy attending to the needs of Malcolm, who was nine years old and had sickle-cell anemia. In fact, Beatrice owned her own beauty salon, and she often had to shut it down in order to attend to Malcolm's needs. Having to put her family's health needs ahead of family financial needs and concerns and her own health needs was not new for Beatrice. She had also found it difficult to keep a job when raising her own children, because her son had kidney disease. When she had difficulty making ends meet, she sold her kitchen appliances, such as the microwave, to the pawnshop. "Healthcare for myself is like, I refuse. I try and use my mind in a positive way. My mind tells me that no matter what sickness I have, it's not going to last more than seven days. So deal with it! Even if I am sick, I get up, I walk around with it, because if I get into bed, it's going to last me longer. . . . I just refuse it!"

Lourdes, a 34-year-old mother of three children (one with severe Attention Deficit Hyperactivity Disorder), continues to work despite her and her family's illnesses. She describes herself as "just getting a little sicker everyday, but still having to work." Her physician tells her that she is "very, very overweight." In addition, Lourdes has been diabetic for at least ten years, and her psychiatrist says she "is also suffering from depression." Lately, Lourdes has been experiencing a lot due to her diabetes and working. She has glaucoma and is having problems with her vision, sometimes "seeing black circles." She says that her diabetes has already begun to damage her kidneys and that she has difficulty walking because of dizziness and numbness in her legs. She would like to get a medical exemption from work, although to complete the process she will need a note from her doctor. Her current doctor won't give her the note because he said that she could still work. Now she is trying to see another doctor at a "diabetes place" to see if she is going to be paralyzed. Lourdes feels that she handles her illnesses and doctor's appointments and those of her children the best she can even though she knows that she can't predict how her family's health will be from one day to the next. However, there is one thing she does know for sure: no matter how sick she is, she still must work.

SUMMARY AND CONCLUSION

This chapter was an empirical extension of Dannefer's and Crystal's (this volume) discourse on cumulative disadvantage and aging and highlights the profound ways in which life-time poverty experiences in families snowball across economic, social, interpersonal, and psychological domains to exacerbate compromised health among family members throughout the life course. We also discussed health from the perspective of family co-morbidity to highlight the complex ways in which multiple illnesses across generations in families contribute to the further accumulation of disadvantage in poor families.

We explored pattern of cumulative disadvantage and family co-morbidity in a sample of 256 economically disadvantaged families who participated in the longitudinal ethnographic component of *Welfare, Children, and Families: A Three-City Study*. Our intent in focusing on families headed by young-adult and midlife women with young children was to illustrate how early and sustained experiences with cumulative disadvantage affect the health experiences of individuals in later life.

The preliminary findings from this ethnography point to several implications for future research. First, the majority of families in the ethnography "accumulated disadvantage" on a daily basis, leading to challenging lives. While it is true that families often "weathered the storms of life," the results of social inequality towards the poor, including consistent unemployment and the lack of quality housing, healthcare and quality education, took a serious toll on family health. Thus, it is important that scientists examining issues of health and aging consider the multiplicative effects of cumulative social disadvantage not just in late life but across an individual's life course.

Second, most of the families in the study are co-morbid, meaning that at least one person and in most cases several family members have both physical and mental health problems. These data suggest that researchers must widen their lenses in designing studies of health, aging, and the poor to include simultaneous attention to physical and mental health for children, their caregivers, and older family members.

Third, the high incidence of chronic physical and mental health problems mothers and their children experience at very young ages is, in itself, cause for serious concern. There may be serious lifetime cumulative effects of the early onset and persistence of certain disease states (e.g., rheumatic fever, hypertension, diabetes, cardiovascular disease, and depression) that result in chronic morbidity in mid- and latelife (Blackwell et al., 2001). For many families, multiple health problems make it more difficult for adults to work and sustain economic security. In addition, these diseases compromise other important aspects of their lives, including accelerated entries to "disability status" and "premature" mortality. In developing future studies on aging and health among America's poor, researchers must consider the implications of poverty on health across the entire life course, devoting special attention to cumulative debilitating effects of compromised health in childhood on health in later life.

ACKNOWLEDGMENTS

We gratefully acknowledge the funders of the ethnographic component of *Welfare, Children, and Families: A Three-City Study* including: The National Institute of Child Health and Human Development; Assistant Secretary for Planning and Evaluation, United States Department of Health and Human Services; Social Security Administration; The Henry J. Kaiser Family Foundation; The Robert Wood Johnson Foundation; The W.K. Kellogg Foundation; The John D. and Catherine T. MacArthur Foundation; The Hogg Foundation for Mental Health; and The Kronkosky Charitable Foundation. We extend special thanks to our 215-member ethnographic team (see project website www.jhu.edu/~welfare) and particularly the Penn State team who provided the infrastructure, organization, and data management for the multisite ethnography. Most importantly, we thank the families who have graciously participated in the project and have given us access to their lives. Where specific examples are used in this chapter, families have been assigned pseudonyms.

REFERENCES

American Psychiatric Association. (1994). *Diagnostic and statistical manual of mental disorders (DSM-IV)* (4th ed., Rev.). Washington, DC: American Psychiatric Association.

Beardslee, W., Versage, C., & Gladstone, A. (1998). Children of affectively ill parents: A review of the past 10 years. *Journal of the American Academy of Child & Adolescent Psychiatry, 37*(11), 1134-1141.

Blackwell, D. L., Hayward, M. D., & Crimmins, E. M. (2001). Does childhood health affect chronic morbidity in later life? *Social Science and Medicine, 52,* 1269-1284.

Burton, L. M., Jarrett, R., Lein, L., Matthews, S., Quane, J., Skinner, D., Williams, C., Wilson, W. J., & Hurt, T. (2001). *"Structured discovery": Ethnography, welfare reform, and the assessment of neighborhoods, families, and children.* Paper presented at the biennial meeting of the Society for Research in Child Development, Minneapolis, MN.

Center for Disease Control. (2002). *Chronic disease prevention.* http//www.cdc.gov/nccdphp/about.htm.

Crystal, S., Shea, D., & Schaie, K. W. (Eds.). (2003). *Focus on economic outcomes in later life: Public policy, health, and cumulative advantage.* New York: Springer Publishing.

Crystal, S., & Waehrer, K. (1996). Later-life economic inequality in longitudinal perspective. *Journal of Gerontology, 51,* S307-S318.

Dannefer, D. (1988). Differential gerontology and the stratified life course. In G. L. Maddox & M. P. Lawton (Eds.), *Annual review of gerontology and geriatrics 8: Varieties of aging* (pp. 3-36). New York: Springer Publishing.

Dannefer, D. (2003). Cumulative advantage/disadvantage and the life course: Cross-fertilizing age and social science theory. *Journal of Gerontology: Social Sciences, S8B*(6), S327-S337.

Danzinger, S., Corcoran, M. Danzinger, S., Heflin, C., Kalil, A., Levine, J., Rosen, D., Seefeldt, K., Siefert, K., & Tolman, R. (2000). *Barriers to employment of welfare recipients*. Retrieved from: www.ssw.umich.edu/poverty/pubs.htlm.

Earle, A., & Heymann, J. (2002). What causes job loss among former welfare recipients: The role of family health problems. *Journal of American Medical Women's Association, 57*, 5-10.

Ferraro, K. F., & Kelley-Moore, J. A. (2003). Cumulative disadvantage and health: Long-term consequences of obesity? *American Sociological Review, 68*, 707-729.

Geronimus, A. T. (1996). Black/white differences in the relationship of maternal age to birthweight: A population-based test of the weathering hypothesis. *Social Science and Medicine, 42*(4), 589-587.

Heymann, J. (2000). *The widening gap: Why America's working families are in jeopardy and what can be done about it.* New York: Basic Books.

Jayakody, R., Danzinger, S., & Pollack, H. (2000). Welfare reform, substance use, and mental health. *Journal of Health, Politics, Policy, and Law, 25*, 623-652

Kessler, R. C., & Zhoa S. (1999). Overview of descriptive epidemiology of mental disorders. In C. Aneshensel & J. Phelan (Eds.), *Handbook of the sociology of mental health.* New York: Kluwer/Academic Plenum Publishers.

Lennon, M. C., Blome, J., & English, K. (2002). Depression among women on welfare: A review of the literature. *Journal of American Medical Women's Association, 57*(1), 27-32.

Merton, R. K. (1968). The Matthew Effect in science. *Science, 159*, 56-63.

National Research Council. (2001). New horizons in health: An integrative approach. In B. H. Singer & C. D. Ryff (Eds.), *Committee on future directions for behavioral and social sciences research at the National Institutes of Health.* Washington, DC: National Academy Press.

Olson, K., & Pavetti, L. (1997). *Personal and family challenges to the successful transition from welfare to work.* Washington, DC: The Urban Institute.

Skinner, D., Lachicotte, W., Cherlin, A., & Burton, L. M., (2002). *Disability, health coverage, and welfare reform.* The Kaiser Commission on Medicaid and the Uninsured.

Whitfield, K. E., Weidner, G. Clark, R., & Anderson, N. B. (2002). Sociodemographic diversity and behavioral medicine. *Journal of Consulting and Clinical Psychology, 70*(3), 463-481.

Williams, D. R., & Collins, C. (1995). US socioeconomic and racial differences in health: Patterns and explanations. *Annual Review of Sociology, 21*, 349-386.

Winston, P., Angel, R. J., Burton, L. M., Chase-Lansdale, P. L., Cherlin, A. J., Moffitt, R. A., & Wilson, W. J. (1999). *Welfare, children, and families: Overview and design.* Baltimore, MD: Johns Hopkins University.

CHAPTER 13

Culture, Migration, Inequality, and "Periphery" in a Globalized World: Challenges for Ethno- and Anthropogerontology

Sandra Torres

This chapter focuses on the implications of a globalized world for the study of the impact of ethnicity and culture on the experience of aging. The discussion that follows takes for granted that globalization is bringing about the growth of interactions between a range of social, economic, and cultural networks across the world. Archer (1990) summarizes the implications of these changes by stating that each "major aspect of social reality . . . is simultaneously undergoing globalization" (p. 1).

Among the transformations that have been identified as constitutive features of globalization processes are: the geographical expansion and increased density of international trade; the development of a worldwide capitalist economy and of multinational corporations; the emergence of what Beck (2000) calls "polycentric world politics" (p. 11); the dispersion of mass media across the world; and the variety of innovations that have taken place in information and telecommunications technology. The transnational actors, communities, social spaces and structures that these transformations imply, have brought about a variety of worldwide exchanges that have made the transcendence of traditional national boundaries possible. It is because of this that Smart (1993) suggests that

> . . . an adequate understanding of social life, social relations, identity and experience can no longer be derived from an analysis limited in scope to "society," particularly when the latter is conceptualized as equivalent to the geopolitical order of the modern nation-state. (p. 135)

Globalization is, in other words, assumed to make a tangible impact not only on the world as we know it but on the way through which we acquire knowledge about that world. That is why it seems appropriate to consider some of the challenges that a globalized world could pose to the study of those who age as a minority. In this context the term "minority" will henceforth be used to refer both to those elders that are in the minority as a result of their disadvantageous ethnicity- (and social class-) related positions within specific societies (as is the case of migrants in relation to the majority population) and those whose cultural backgrounds are relatively peripheral to theory building within mainstream social gerontology (i.e., those whose cultures of origin could be classified as non-Western). In short, the discussion that follows will address the impact that globalization is expected to have on key areas within ethno- and anthropogerontology, namely, those relating to culture, migration, inequality and periphery.

STUDYING THE IMPLICATIONS OF CULTURE IN GLOBALIZED TIMES

The implications of ethnic, social, economic, and religious backgrounds for identity formation and maintenance have traditionally been located via "national versions" of society and community. In this version of reality, culture is conceived to be a point of reference that is essentially territorial—one that "belongs" to a particular society. Cultural values are consequently assumed to be taught through the submersion into the specific localities that socialization entails. By contrast, the emergence of transnational communities is likely to challenge the manner in which we think about culture. As Tomlinson (1999) has stated, "Globalization disturbs the way we conceptualize 'culture' for culture has long had connotations tying it to the idea of a fixed locality" (p. 27). Thus, in a globalized world, culture must be thought of as "general human software" that is not necessarily locally learned and that is most definitely not confined to a specific territory (Swindler, 1986).

To this effect, Hannerz (1992) has argued that "the autonomy and boundness of cultures must nowadays be understood as a matter of degree" (p. 261). All of this could most likely contest the way in which we think in terms of culture's impact on the experience of growing old, because if the fixed locality of culture is no longer tangible, neither are, for example, assumptions regarding cultural differences about the way in which old age is conceived and experienced. The state of affairs that globalization may bring about suggests, in other words, that intracultural differences might become more important in the future and that investigating intercultural differences might pose difficulties for social research. Gille and Riain (2002) suggest here that our "ability to straightforwardly access the social by going to the local becomes problematic under conditions of globalization" (p. 273)—an issue in regard to which anthropogerontologists need to develop an effective response.

The loss of correspondence between cultures and geographical territories has been defined as "deterritorialization" (Tomlinson, 1999). With respect to the displacement of culture that deterritorialization alludes to, King (1991) suggests that the study of culture becomes much more complex since "it's not just that, increasingly, many people have no roots; it's also that they have no soil" (p. 6). With regard to the displacement of culture, Tomlinson (1999) and Hannerz (1992) have suggested that globalization is prompting the replacement of real localities with "non-places" (like airports, lounges, motorways, cyberspace, etc.) and that these, in turn, are contributing to a globalized culture that is increasingly deterritorialized. Tomlinson (1999) argues that such trends have, however, led to premature claims that the emergence of "a world culture" (i.e., a single, unified system of meaning shared globally) will eventually emerge. In this respect, Hannerz (1990) has stated:

> There is now a world culture, but we had better make sure we understand what this means. . . . No total homogenization of systems of meaning and expression has occurred, nor does it appear likely that there will be one for some time soon. (p. 237)

King (1991) and Tomlinson (1999) have also argued that because we are "embodied and physically located," deterritorialization can never completely bring about "the end of locality." Tomlinson (1999) suggests further that the emergence of such a monolithic culture is not necessarily going to bring the destruction of "real" localities, since the importance of localized experience to identity formation is not easily compromised. Moreover, "global culture" will itself continue to be divided with respect to dimensions such as age, race, gender, and social class (Robertson 1992, 1995). Experiencing the world as a single place is becoming possible, but this does not in and by itself suffice to undermine the importance that differing positions have for the acquisition of cultural, social, and economic capital and/or, as Mittleman (2000) would suggest, for the importance that the hierarchization of cultures has for our understanding of the world. Within the context of gerontology specifically, it has been suggested that this hierarchization is responsible for the fact that the Western template is often used when sense is being made of cultural differences (Thomas & Chambers, 1989). This leads, in turn, to the treatment of Western understandings of old age and aging as the norm and non-Western understandings as aberrations from the ideal (Torres 2001a, 2004).

It is, in other words, important not to confuse being able to overcome physical distance (i.e., being close) with being capable of overcoming cultural distance (i.e., being the same). In this regard, Beck (2000) stresses that it is within the context of the "local" that the effects of globalization are experienced. Thus, although globalization is bringing about a sense of a unified world, our respective localities will most likely continue to be our primary points of reference. Having said this, it must also be stressed that, regardless of whether or not globalization has the potential to create a global culture, it is nowadays assumed that global-ization challenges the manner in which we conceive not only the geographical location of culture but its "impact." Moreover, culture homogenization notwith-standing, most social scientists engaged in the globalization debate now take for granted the profound effects of deterritorialization and global interconnectivity. Giddens (1994) summarizes this by claiming that globalization alters ". . . the context of meaning construction: how it affects people's sense of identity, the experience of place and self in relation to self, how it impacts on the shared understandings, values, desires, myths, hopes and fears that have developed around locally situated life" (p. 95).

The study of culture's impact on the experience of aging and/or on the way in which understandings of aging are constructed is, of course, not exempted from the transitions identified above. The question at this point in time is not whether globalization is going to affect the way in which we study the relationship between culture and aging but *how* it is going to affect the way in which ethno- and anthropogerontogical research questions are posed and the manner in which research in these areas is conducted.

GLOBALIZATION AND THE STUDY OF INTERNATIONAL MIGRATION AND MIGRANTS

Warnes, Friedrich, Kellaher, and Torres (2004) make the point that one of the implications of globalization is that "the number of older people who have been international migrants and have cultural differences from the host population will undoubtedly increase during the coming decades" (p. 309). According to Castles and Miller (1998) and Castles (2000), globalization is one of the trends that are likely to play an important role in how social scientists approach the study of migration and those who migrate in the future. The transnational exchanges identified earlier are also among the trends expected to change the way in which studies of international migration and migrants are conducted (Faist, 2000a). Glick-Schiller, Basch, and Szanton-Blanc (1992, 1995) assert, for example, that the politics of "belonging" have started to become transnational in the case of some migrants. Thus, when talking about the implications of globalization for the study of international migration, consideration must be made of the transnational communities formed by some migrants around the world. These are believed to represent one of the pillars upon which the phenomenon of transnationalism rests. The concept of transnationalism encompasses a variety of phenomena— from communities and social networks to financial corporations and political organizations. In this chapter, the focus is upon the microlevel, or trans-nationalism, as viewed "from below" (Faist, 2000b). The type of transnationalism in question refers to the variety of multistranded social ties established and sustained by migrants across national borders and the linkages between countries of origin and host countries that these bring about.

Transnationalism is expected to have unprecedented implications for all aspects of migration studies: from the way in which we study migration movements and their implications for national and international policies (Castles & Davidson, 2000), to the manner in which we approach the study of migrants and policies relevant to their needs (Kivisto, 2001). In regard to the study of migration, Richmond (2002) argues that globalization weakens the distinction between "sending" and "receiving" countries, as well as the stereotypical assumptions about immigrants and refugees that are often made. This will also, as a consequence, challenge the way in which gerontological studies about migrant aging are conducted. Such studies often rest on knowledge gathered through migration-related research and will therefore need to become accustomed to the way in which globalization is changing the premises upon which such research is based and also the assumptions that are often made about the needs of elderly migrants. With regards to the latter, it can, for example, be argued that transnational interactions have intensified the diversity of older migrants and are posing numerous challenges when it comes to the design of programs and services meant to cater to their needs (Warnes, Friedrich, Kellaher, & Torres, 2004).

It should, however, be mentioned that the transnational ties in question are different from those that are often sporadically upheld by "conventional" migrants. Portes, Guarnizo, and Landolt (1999) make the point that not all contemporary immigrants belong to the transnational category, since only those who have access to the transportation and technological prerequisites of transnationalism can sustain such ties over time. Thus, when speaking of transnationals, they are referring to people that "live dual lives: speaking two languages, having homes in two countries, and making a living through continuous regular contact across national borders" (Portes, Guarnizo, & Landolt, 1999, p. 217). This excludes, in other words, the "occasional and fleeting contacts between migrants and relatively immobile people in the countries of immigration and the countries of emigration" (Faist, 2000b, p. 190). With regard to transnationalism and the study of aging and/or elders, research on international retirement migration has been an important area of investigation (Gustafson, 2001; King, Warnes, & Williams, 2000) and is likely to become an important focus within gerontology as transnational migrants and lifestyles become more common.

The fact that transnational ties are bound to challenge the way in which the study of immigrants' culture of origin and host culture is conducted is also particularly relevant. After all, culture's relationship to "locality" is shaken by transnationalism just as much as it is challenged by globalization. Transnational migrants are people that stay "connected" with (and are simultaneously influenced by) more than one culture at a time. It is because of this that migration scholars have referred to transnationalism's influence on culture in "translocal" terms (Smith & Guarnizo, 1998). Thus, transnationalism brings about what has been referred to as the "hybridization" of cultures (Nederveen, 1994), with important implications as a result for the study of culture, ethnicity, and aging. Research on the notions of "aging well" that are upheld by Iranian immigrants in Sweden shows, for example, that being-in-between cultures can challenge the way in which growing old is understood (Torres, 2001a, 2001b). Such a state of affairs can, in some cases, lead to great variety with regard to how ideas of what constitutes a good old age are constructed, since a synthesis of ideas could occur which does not, in the end, resemble what is considered to be typical of one's culture of origin or what is assumed to be characteristic of the host culture that has become one's own. The fact that transnational migrants are, by virtue of their lifestyle, simultaneously exposed to two (often different) cultures suggests therefore that their experiences and understandings of aging are an unexplored but most likely fruitful source of information regarding the study of old age and aging.

The changes in question have also made the formulation of immigrant policies and the "business" of coping with cultural diversity much more complex (Faist, 2000b; Kivisto, 2001). The weakening of the sovereignty of national boundaries that globalization entails means that established models for the "handling" of cultural diversity are also being destabilized. This is a further challenge since "the global character of international migration results in the intermingling and cohabitation of people from increasingly different physical and cultural settings" (Castles & Miller, 1998, pp. 286-287). When it comes to the impact of transnationalism on culture, Portes, Guranizo, and Landolt (1999) argue for the distinctiveness of current forms of immigrant adaptation, making the point that

> . . . the immigration literature has generally assumed that, once newcomers arrive, they settle into the host society and undergo a gradual but inevitable process of assimilation. . . . For immigrants involved in transnational activities and their home country counterparts, success does not so much depend on abandoning their culture and language to embrace those of another society as on preserving their original cultural endowment, while adapting instrumentally to a second. (pp. 228-229)

The being-in-between culture that is characteristic of the first stages of immigrants' adaptation is a permanent state of affairs for transnational migrants. This is why it can become difficult to speak of territorially bounded cultural values in their case. With regard to the study of aging minorities, if transnationalism poses a challenge to the design of policies that cater to migrant populations, then we must also foresee that it can have an impact on, for example, the design of culturally appropriate elderly care programs and services, an issue of particular interest to research on service provision for ethnic minorities. Warnes, Friedrich, Kellaher, and Torres (2004) summarize the issues here as follows:

> The diverse studies of older migrants that are becoming available across Europe also show that policy gaps and service deficiencies are widespread in creating income deprivation, social exclusion and unmet social support and health care needs. . . . There is a widespread need and indeed obligation to develop culturally sensitive and responsive services, but the spread of

such services is slow. Common problems are inadequate guidance on the prevalent problems and unmet needs, and too little sharing of experience especially in approaches to the development of feasible and effective services. Many studies report not only the absence of interpreter services in health and welfare agencies and facilities, but also the unsympathetic reactions of "front-line" staff, a consequence of the lack of training and of consciousness-raising by employers. . . . Researchers and academics could do more to assist managers and clinicians gain an understanding of how new services are successfully developed. (p. 318)

Inequality affecting migrant groups will require major initiatives within receiving countries, especially in relation to the organization of social security and related services. However, crucial issues must also be considered in relation to problems affecting resource issues between poorer and richer nations. It is to a consideration of the implications of this area for researchers in ethno- and anthropogerontology that we now turn.

GLOBALIZATION'S IMPACT ON THE STUDY OF INEQUALITY, MINORITIES, AND "THE PERIPHERY"

Most globalization theorists agree that the processes discussed in this chapter are likely to intensify resource gaps that already exist between rich and poor nations, the First and Third World, the so called "center and the periphery" and between the West and the rest (Bauman, 1998; Beck, 2000; Giddens, 1994; Mittleman, 2000; Richmond, 2002). Although globalization has the potential to challenge such distinctions, various "winners" and "losers" among social groups and nations will continue to develop. Beck (2000) argues, for example, that the study of social justice (to which inequality studies belong) is bound to be challenged by globalization since the transformations in question will eventually demand that the ". . . very losers of globalization will in the future have to pay for everything—from the welfare state to a functioning democracy" (p. 6). In a similar manner, Richmond (2002) claims that: "in a global economy based on unregulated free market principles, the rich are bound to get richer and the poor relatively poorer" (p. 715). The "power geometry" implied in this assumption is also addressed by Castles (2000) as well as by Massey (1994), the latter giving particular emphasis to the link between globalization on the one side and inequality on the other. Bauman (1998) presents the relationship between globalization and localization as reflecting the polarization of the world into the "globalized rich and the localized poor." The former have the world as their point of departure while the latter are confined to the locality in which they "belong." In this regard, Bauman (1998) argues that

For the first world, the world of the globally mobile, the space has lost its constraining quality and is easily traversed in both its "real" and "virtual" renditions. For the second world, the world of the "locally tied," of those barred from moving and thus bound to bear passively whatever change may be visited on the locality they are tied to, the real space is fast closing up. This is a kind of deprivation which is made yet more painful by the obtrusive media display of the space conquest and of the "'virtual accessibility' of distances that stay stubbornly unreachable in non-virtual reality." (p. 88)

Speaking of the poor in local terms does not, however, mean that they are excluded by globalization or that affluence is a prerequisite for the impact of globalizing forces to be felt. Tomlinson (1999) argues, for example, that globalization has a basic "applicability" to most people and countries. In other words, no one is really exempt from globalization, even though we are bound to experience its effects differently. With regard to the main pillars of social differentiation (i.e., race, class, gender, and age), Tomlinson (1999) argues that

> . . . it is clear that some are going to live deterritorialized culture more intensively, actively and (on balance) enjoyably than others. The distance between "yuppie" couple and [poor] pensioner is illustrative of this. But it would be a mistake to see the experience of deterritorialization as something which only arrives at a certain threshold of socio-economic advantage, above which is a switch to the "hyper space" of a "cosmopolitan" lifestyle and below which there is a simple exclusion from the whole process of globalization and a different *order* of experience. (p. 132)

Thus, when speaking of inequality and globalization at the macrolevel, it is imperative that we do not mistakenly assume that lack of resources and power means exemption from the process. Most globalization theorists assume, for example, that the transformations in question will have, to varying degrees, an impact on us all, regardless of whether or not we live in the First or Third World. In fact, as Tomlinson (1999) argues, the poor and marginalized might actually be more affected by globalization since lack of power does not necessarily impede the global nexus from intruding into their localities as well as their daily lives.

Gerontologists might draw parallels between this discussion and earlier arguments in the discipline concerning the impact of modernization on the lives of older people. Cowgill (1974) as well as Cowgill and Holmes (1972) argued that social processes associated with modernization were likely to result in a lowering of the status of older people. The key features producing this effect were held to be: 1) the introduction of new technology, 2) the impact of urbanization, and 3) the importance attached to education. These factors, according to Cowgill (1974), set up a chain reaction that undermined the status of older people, as compared with their position in preindustrial societies. The empirical works of Palmore and Manton (1974) and Bengtson (1975), however, questioned the inevitability of the scenario presented by modernization theorists. The question is, therefore, whether the same will happen with globalization, i.e., whether the "worst scenario" anticipated by globalization theorists in regard to the anticipated growth in resource gaps between countries and the inequalities these presuppose will, in fact, turn out to be the case. If so, we must also question whether this will in turn have the damaging effects on elders that are invariably assumed (Beck 2000; Massey 1994). Ackers & Dwyer (2002) and Dwyer & Papadimitriou (2003) have shown, for example, that transnational senior citizenship can bring about the widening of inequalities in old age. If resource inequalities continue, premonitions regarding the negative impact of globalization may turn out to be correct. However, we must also keep in mind the extent to which globalization is challenging the way in which we think about ethnic minorities within Western societies. As Warnes, Friedrich, Kellaher, and Torres (2004) have argued, global-ization is increasing the diversity that exists with regard to migrants' back-grounds and social positions. Thus, although globalization could bring about disadvantages for some minority elders (i.e., those in the so called "periphery"), there is also the possibility that others (i.e., some of the more wealthy migrants in the West) will be beneficiaries of globalization.

With regard to the intrusion of the global, it might further be argued that globalization challenges the study of inequality, not only because it brings about the growth of inequalities between the center and the periphery, but also because the experience of marginalization within the periphery will also be challenged. This is the case because telecommunication-related advances seem to be changing the way in which marginalization is experienced. In this regard, Appadurai (1990) asserts that advances in telecommunications and access to the global mass media mean that an increasing number of marginalized people are con-fronted with the spectrum of possible (and most importantly, prosperous) lives on a daily basis. This means therefore that "imagined worlds" are now virtually accessible to most people. Thus, globalization affects the study of inequality, not only because of transformations at a macrolevel (i.e., and the accentuation of existing inequalities, hierarchies, and modes of exclusions that these presuppose), but also at the microlevel of everyday life given the more intense way in which inequality may be experienced.

CONCLUSION: THE CHALLENGE OF GLOBALIZATION FOR THE STUDY OF MINORITY AGING

This chapter has argued that globalization will almost certainly challenge the manner in which studies of culture, migration, and aging are conceived and conducted. Four aspects to this will be reviewed in this concluding section: first, the relationship between cultural values and national contexts; second, the issue of "intersectionality"; third, the "visibility" of peripheral societies; fourth, globalization and processes of informal care.

The first issue points to the way in which constructions of old age are challenged by the unsettling of the relationship between cultural values and the national locality to which these relate. Assumptions regarding cultural homogeneity within nationally bounded spaces are undermined by globalization, this leading to an extension of social and cultural differences within aging populations. Phillipson (2002) makes the point here that: ". . . diverse populations will . . . have greater variability in respect to images and definitions of aging. The notion of what it means to grow old, when old age begins, and normative behaviors for old age, will all show much wider variation in one society than has historically been the case" (p. 6). As Kearney (1995) has suggested with regard to anthropology, cross-cultural studies take for granted a variety of classifications that have made the comparative study of cultures possible. However, in a globalized world, it has become difficult to conceive of individuals as members of bounded and/or of "either or" groups and to study culture while assuming bounded and fixed territoriality. In this respect it has been implicitly suggested that further research on transnational lifestyles in old age is needed, as transnational migrants become a significant group within the population. The hybridization of cultural values implicit in such lifestyles is still relatively unexplored within gerontology. One of the challenges of globalization for the study of aging and old age, therefore, concerns the way in which elderly transnational migrants "negotiate" the meanings they attach to the experience of aging when growing into old age takes place while being both Here-and-There and when both Either-Or applies. At the core of social gerontological knowledge lies a variety of assumptions regarding, among others, continuity across the life course. Transnational migrants, in contrast, have precisely the opposite experience. With continuities in identity becoming increasingly less common, future gerontological research will need to focus on the impact of "biographical discontinuity" on adjustment in old age.

A second issue concerns discussions regarding "intersectionality" in research on ethnicity and migration. This refers to the way in which the social position that is allocated through minority ethnic and cultural background interacts with other sociocultural power differentials such as gender, sexuality, and class, thus influencing the construction of subjectivity as well as access to social resources (Anthias, 2001). Although age is not always addressed in such discussions, it is clear that age is also a social differential around which power is accorded and through which we make sense of ourselves as subjects. Thus, when speaking of the challenges that globalization poses to the study of aging, developing awareness of intersectionality as a concept and issue will be important to consider.

A third issue identified in this chapter concerns the way globalization provides greater visibility to peripheral or poorer societies (Austin-Broos, 2003). Polivka (2000) brings to our attention the fact that the elderly populations of "peripheral" societies are growing even faster than their counterparts in developed countries— a matter that he claims has gone unrecognized by social gerontologists. In this respect, it seems necessary to reiterate his argument, namely that "the elderly in developing countries will not only outnumber those in developed countries— they are and will be incomparably poorer and less healthy than those in the West" (Polivka, 2001, p. 156). As far as globalization is concerned, it must be further emphasized that the aging of non-Western elders cannot be relegated to the periphery of the "gerontological imagination" (Estes, Binney, & Culbertson, 1992). This is the case since globalization is bound to augment existing inequalities and can therefore challenge the study of disadvantaged "others" as well as the formulation of elderly policies in peripheral and poor societies. The fact that such elders run the risk of being relegated to the "second world" that Bauman (1998) identifies is yet another issue to take into consideration when an agenda for a globalized gerontology is being set.

Finally, associated with the relevance of globalizing processes to the study of ethnic minority elders is also the fact that globalization (but most specifically transnationalism) is changing the political economy of informal care. This is the case since "globalization is producing a new kind of aging in which the dynamics of family and social life may be stretched across different continents and across different types of societies" (Phillipson, 2002, p. 3). As Wilson (2002) suggests: "globalization has been accompanied by changes in the patterns and numbers of people migrating . . . [and this has] implications for support in later life, as families are fragmented and entire communities lose their mid-life members" (p. 657). This means that the pressures to secure care and support in old age might be intensified in a globalized world, which is why it might become necessary to develop social policies that can handle the transnational interactions mentioned earlier and the various effects that these could have in unsettling, for example, filial obligation norms. Moreover, it is Phillipson's (2002) contention that the transnational communities discussed earlier, may have a significant impact on the well-being of older migrants. In this regard, Wilson (2002) argues that "one benefit of globalization . . . is that it allows migrant groups to maintain their own culture and opens new cultural roles for older migrants if they and their children have been able to benefit from migration" (pp. 658-659). However, inasmuch as fixed locality is a prerequisite for the kind of stability deemed to be necessary for "successful aging," we must also keep in mind that globalization might pose certain risks to what Phillipson and Biggs (1998) refer to as "a viable identity for living in old age" (p. 21). So the effects of transnational lifestyles on the experience of aging seem to be an interesting new angle of investigation for the fields with which this chapter is concerned.

Having suggested some areas of inquiry within ethno- and anthropogerontology that could be potentially challenged by globalization, we conclude by restating the point that globalizing processes challenge the ways in which research agendas concerned with the study of minority aging are set and question both the problems with which we are concerned and the ones that we insist on disregarding. Globalization and the hybridization of cultures that such a state of affairs presupposes challenge mainstream conceptualizations of what aging means and how old age is experienced. The question is whether the peripheral elders that have been the main concern of ethno- and anthropogerontology can share the protagonist role that mainstream gerontologists have so far exclusively accorded to "majority" and "native" elders. In a globalized and deterritorialized world, it is these minority and peripheral elders who are particularly interesting, not only for the expansion of our "gerontological imagination," but for the advancement of theory development within social gerontology.

REFERENCES

Ackers, H. L., & Dwyer, P. (2002). *Senior citizenship: Retirement migration and welfare in the European Union*. Bristol: Policy Press.

Anthias, F. (2001). The material and the symbolic in theorizing social stratification: Issues of gender, ethnicity and class. *British Journal of Sociology, 52*(3), 367-390.

Appadurai, A. (1990). Disjuncture and difference in the global cultural economy. In M. Featherstone (Ed.), *Global culture: Nationalism, globalization and modernity*. London: Sage.

Archer, M. (1990). Foreword. In M. Albrow & E. King (Eds.), *Globalization, knowledge and society*. London: Sage.

Austin-Broos, D. (2003). Globalization and the genesis of values. *The Australian Journal of Anthropology, 14*(1), 1-18.

Bauman, Z. (1998). *Globalization: The human consequences*. New York: Columbia University Press.

Beck, U. (2000). *What is globalization?* Cambridge: Polity Press.

Bengtson, V. (1975). Modernization, modernity and the perception of aging: A comparative study. *Journal of Gerontology, 30*(6), 688-695.

Castles, S. (2000). *Ethnicity and globalization: From migrant worker to transnational citizen*. London: Sage.

Castles, S., & Miller, M. J. (1998). *The age of migration: International population movements in the modern world*. London: Macmillan Press Ltd.

Castles, S., & Davidson, A. (2000). *Citizenship and migration: Globalization and the politics of belonging*. London: Macmillan Press Ltd.

Cowgill, D. O., & Holmes, L. D. (1972). *Aging and modernization*. New York: Appleton Century Crofts.

Cowgill, D. O. (1974). The aging of population and societies. *Annals of the American Academy of Political and Social Science, 415*, 1-18.

Dwyer, P., & Papadimitriou, D. (2003, October 23-26). *The social security rights of older international migrants in the European Union*. Paper presented to the European Science Foundation Scientific Network on International Migration in Europe: Welfare Policy and Practice Implications for Older People, York, UK.

Estes, C. L., Binney, E. A., & Culbertson, R. A. (1992). The gerontological imagination: Social influences on the development of gerontology, 1945-present. *International Journal of Aging and Human Development, 35*(1), 49-65.

Faist, T. (2000a). *The volume and dynamics of international migration and transnational social spaces*. Oxford: Oxford University Press.

Faist, T. (2000b). Transnationalization in international migration: Implications for the study of citizenship and culture. *Ethnic and Racial Studies, 23*(2), 189-222.

Giddens, A. (1994). Living in a post-traditional society. In U. Beck, A. Giddens, & S. Lash (Eds.), *Reflexive modernization*. Cambridge: Polity Press.

Gille, Z., & Riain, S. O. (2002). Global ethnography. *Annual Review of Sociology, 28*, 271-295.

Glick-Schiller, N., Basch, L., & Szanton-Blanc, C. (Eds.). (1992). *Towards a transnational perspective on migration: Race, class, ethnicity, and nationalism reconsidered.* New York: New York Academy of Science.
Glick-Schiller, N., Basch, L., & Szanton-Blanc, C. (1995). From immigrant to transmigrant: Theorizing transnational migration. *Anthropological Quarterly, 68*(1), 48-63.
Gustafson, P. (2001). Retirement migration and transnational lifestyles. *Ageing and Society, 21*(4), 371-394.
Hannerz, U. (1990). Cosmopolitans and locals in world culture. *Theory, Culture and Society, 7*(2-3), 237-251.
Hannerz, U. (1992). *Cultural complexity: Studies in the social organization of meaning.* New York: Columbia University Press.
Kearney, M. (1995). The local and the global: The anthropology of globalization and transnationalism. *Annual Review of Anthropology, 24,* 547-565.
King, A. D. (Ed.). (1991). *Culture, globalization and the world-system: Contemporary conditions for the representation of identity.* Binghamton: SUNY Press.
King, R., Warnes, A. M., & Williams, A. M. (2000). *Sunset lives: British retirement to the Mediterranean.* Oxford: Berg.
Kivisto, P. (2001). Theorizing transnational immigration: A critical review of current efforts. *Ethnic and Racial Studies, 24*(4), 549-577.
Massey, D. (1994). *Space, place and gender.* Cambridge: Polity Press.
Mittleman, J. H. (2000). Globalization: Captors and captive. *Third World Quarterly, 21*(6), 917-929.
Nederveen, P. J. (1994). Globalization as hybridization. *International Sociology, 9*(2), 161-184.
Palmore, E., & Manton, K. (1974). Modernization and the status of the aged: International correlations. *Journal of Gerontology, 29,* 205-210.
Phillipson, C., & Biggs, S. (1998). Modernity and identity: Themes and perspectives in the study of older adults. *Journal of Aging and Identity, 3*(1), 11-23.
Phillipson, C. (2002, August 29-32). *Transnational communities, migration and changing identities in later life.* Paper presented at the 34th European Behavioral and Social Science Research Section's (EBSSRS) Symposium on Aging and Diversity, Bergen, Norway.
Polivka, L. (2000). Postmodern aging and the loss of meaning. *Journal of Aging and Identity, 5*(4), 225-235.
Polivka, L. (2001). Globalization, population, aging and ethics. *Journal of Aging and Identity, 6*(3), 147-163.
Portes, A., Guarnizo, L. E., & Landolt, P. (1999). The study of transnationalism: Pitfalls and promise of an emergent research field. *Ethnic and Racial Studies, 22*(2), 217-237.
Richmond, A. H. (2002). Globalization: Implications for immigrants and refugees. *Ethnic and Racial Studies, 25*(5), 707-727.
Robertson, R. (1992). *Globalization: Social theory and global culture.* London: Sage.
Robertson, R. (1995). Globalization: Time-space and homogeneity-heterogeneity. In M. Featherstone, S. Lash, & R. Robertson (Eds.), *Global modernities.* London: Sage.
Smart, B. (1993). *Postmodernity.* London and New York: Routledge.
Smith, M. P., & Guarnizo, L. E. (Eds.). (1998). *Transnationalism from below.* New Jersey: Transaction Publishers.

Swidler, A. (1986). Culture in action: Symbols and strategies. *American Sociological Review, 51,* 273-288.

Thomas, L. E., & Chambers, K. O. (1989). Successful aging among elderly men in England and India: A phenomenological comparison. In L. E. Thomas (Ed.), *Research on adulthood and ageing: The human science approach.* New York: SUNY Press.

Tomlinson, J. (1999). *Globalization and culture.* Chicago: The University of Chicago Press.

Torres, S. (2001a). *Understanding successful aging: Cultural and migratory perspectives.* Sweden: Uppsala University.

Torres, S. (2001b). Understandings of successful aging in the context of migration: The case of Iranian immigrants in Sweden. *Aging and Society, 21*(3), 333-355.

Torres, S. (2004). Making sense of the construct of successful aging: The migrant experience. In S-O. Daatland & S. Biggs (Eds.), *Aging and diversity: Multiple pathways and cultural migrations.* Bristol: Policy Press.

Warnes, A. M., Friedrich, K., Kellaher, L., & Torres, S. (2004). The diversity and welfare of older migrants in Europe. *Ageing and Society, 24*(3), 307-326.

Wilson, G. (2002). Globalization and older people: Effects of markets and migration. *Ageing and Society, 22*(5), 647-663.

CHAPTER 14

Globalization and Critical Theory: Political Economy of World Population Issues

John A. Vincent

Population change is the product of human action. Demography tends to produce mathematically-based descriptive models. Critical theory is a major tool with which to understand why population is changing and the power relationships that lie behind these changes. Demography may describe and analyze the components of population change, but critical theory seeks to understand them. Demography, because it is such a powerful descriptive tool, is in constant use by economic and governmental institutions with specific aims and briefs. However, analysis of global population in a macrosocietal and historical perspective is not frequently attempted. Demography does not usually seek to theorize this broad-brush perspective on world population, which is more often debated within economic history and anthropology (Caldwell, 1982; Greenhalgh, 1996; Wilkinson, 1973).

A proper analysis of globalization must include thinking about and understanding the world as a single economic, social, and demographic system and understanding it in new ways that are not immediately apparent from within the social horizons of everyday life. The critical perspective requires us to consider the ideological significance of the way the problems of globalization and demography are constructed and understood. This chapter attempts to look at modern global demographic change and understand how these changes relate to the growth in the global power and influence of pension funds in the United States and Britain. The relationship between demography and pension-fund capitalism will be explored by an examination of the institutions that underpin the redistributive processes of the modern global economy and the ideological construction of gerontological issues within this framework. This involves critical examination of the interests, attitudes, and behaviors of key social groups who contend for control of the power embedded in the accumulated savings of Western pensioners and would-be pensioners.

POLITICAL ECONOMY THEORIES
OF POPULATION

Political-economy theories of population concentrated their perspective on the reproduction of labor power (Cancian, 1976). They were particularly effective in two areas. One was the analysis of precapitalist societies of all kinds studied by anthropologists. In different tribal and peasant societies, control of labor and reproductive power could be compared using the categories and general approach of political economy. Particularly influential were writers in the tradition of French Marxist anthropology (Bloch, 1973; Meillassoux, 1975; Terray, 1972) and those American anthropologists writing in the tradition of Leslie White (Polgar, 1975; Sahlins, 1974; White, 1959). The same methods play an important role in some feminist critiques used to understand the relationship between female domestic labor and macrothemes of reproduction and population change, particularly where these drew on third-world and developmental themes (Anker, Buvinic, & Youssef, 1981; Kuhn & Wolpe, 1978; Lowe & Hubbard, 1983; Moore, 1988; Raphael, 1975; Rogers, 1980; Rosaldo & Lamphere, 1974; Smith, Wallerstein, & Evers, 1984). The limitations of the method, which played a major part in its fall from fashion, were twofold. Firstly, although there was attention to culture and cultural variation, the macroscale of the approach tended to underemphasize human agency, and so it could be seen as simplistic determinism (Barrett, 1980; Goody, 1976; Hammel & Howell, 1987; Johnson & Earle, 1987). Secondly, while the ideas worked well in dealing with domestic, agricultural, and largely unmechanized labor, which were organized predominantly by nonmarket mechanisms and could also be used to understand how capitalist institutions linked to noncapitalist ones, they were not well-adapted to looking at rapid technological change. Development and population issues changed—East Asia industrialized, the Soviet Union collapsed, and neoliberal economics dominated national policies and global agendas. There was a parallel shift in emphasis within the critical perspective, from trying to understand the barriers to development to understanding the consequences of globalization. The priority was to expose the human and environmental costs of marketization and new technologies, and there was less need to counter Malthusian views that the crucial issue was curbing population growth (Roseberry, 1988; Sklair, 1994; Toye, 1987). Nevertheless, critical perspectives have key insights to make about contemporary population issues.

> Human populations, then, respond to environmental factors such as scarce or bountiful resources but never in an "objective" mechanical way. We much think in terms of a *politics of populations* which will take into account the structure of power influencing fertility, morbidity, mortality, migration,

expressing differential access to local resources and the control of space.
(Narotzky, 1997, p. 11, emphasis in original)

A necessary first step is to outline the basic approach taken in a political economy of population. It is work—the time, skill and effort spent—that transforms natural objects into something useful. The "division of labor" is the social coordination of useful work. People play different parts in the overall labor of society that collectively creates value/economic output; hence, the contrast between "use value" and "commodity value." Commodity value is the price that something can command in a market when it is bought or sold. Use value is the contribution, without any necessary cash price, that summarizes the labor that went into its creation and the benefits to society of that work. Children, a healthy environment, or a religious ritual have a "use value," but most people hold it morally repugnant when they have a commodity value.

Exploitation is the acquisition of the value of other people's labor without return. Capital, that is, the resources to invest in future production, is only accumulated labor power. It is the tangible result of work, but alienated from those who expended the effort and under the control of others. How does that accumulation of capital occur? The classic answer to the question "how, if people only exchange things that are of equal value, can capitalist entrepreneurs make a profit?" lies in the difference between use value and commodity value. The capitalist is paying a commodity price for labor that is lower than the use value, thus allowing the employer to accumulate "surplus" value and make a profit. In practice, the division of labor has become so complex and economic relationships so lacking in transparency in contemporary global economy that it is not always immediately obvious who is exploiting whom (e.g., Emmanuel, 1972; Roxborough, 1979; Spybey, 1992). Are modern pensioners, receivers of income from pension funds, a new capitalist class living from other people's work? Or would it be better to try and understand the class position of older people in terms of "entitlements." What are the key social relationships through which older members of society have a claim on part of the cornucopia produced by the modern global economy? The use of the term here is as a sociological concept rather than as a specific concept in U.S. law (Quadagno, 1996, pp. 391-392). An example of the successful use of a theory of entitlements is that of Amartya Sen's (1982) analysis of the Bengal famine of 1943. He demonstrated that there was enough food in Bengal to feed the population; those who died were people whose entitlement to subsistence failed. The government ensured that the urban markets had rice, but specific categories of rural poor who could not claim part of the grain harvest were unable through their traditional occupations to afford to buy food (Devereux, 1993; Sen, 1982). By analogy, world production is today sufficient to give all older people a decent material standard of living. Only some of them get it. What is the nature of the entitlement failure that excludes so many from a decent old age?

DEMOGRAPHIC ISSUES IN THE REPRODUCTION
OF CAPITAL

Under capitalist social relationships, labor is a commodity. It can be bought and sold, and its price varies depending on supply and demand. When there is extra labor supply, wages go down. However, wages cannot go down indefinitely. People need to eat; they need to survive in order to work. Hence there is a subsistence minimum necessary for the reproduction of labor power. By analogy to the daily and weekly need to reproduce labor through having food and shelter and a minimum of good health, the investment of labor in the cycle of generations is also required. Women have to be supported while they give birth and suckle their babies; parents need the time and resources to bring up the next generation; society needs to provide the knowledge, skills, and human resources to create the next generation of the labor force. Unless the economy is to regress, the new labor force needs the investment of social capital at least equivalent to the previous generation. Thus, the value of labor is the value of the work it took to create it. That is to say, it is the activities of women and families (largely unpaid) that produces the next generation of workers (e.g., Narotzky, 1997, pp. 158-177).

The current world demographic trend to lower fertility is tightly associated with labor market opportunities for women (McDonald, 2000; Sen, 1998, p. 735; Singh, 1994). In highly specialized societies in which a great deal of labor and education is needed to bring a skilled person into the productive process, the costs of reproduction are high. In these societies, women have choices: whether to raise children or take the material rewards of participation in the labor market. Conversely, the places in the world with the highest fertility are where women's labor is cheap and unpaid; where women's opportunities are restricted by a combination of poverty and discrimination that forces them into subordinate positions in families and in work hierarchies. This analytical framework makes sense of why it appears that, in global terms, the poor have more children than the rich; why towns and newly developing areas are full of young people who did not grow up there; and why rural backwaters are left with old populations struggling to look after themselves. This analysis has been linked with the idea of exploitation as Marxist feminists sought to theorize the relationships of female oppression. The owners of capital had an interest in maintaining unpaid female household labor to sustain male workers who could thus be more effectively exploited (Barrett, 1980; Smith, Wallerstein, & Evers, 1984). This household-economy perspective was also taken up by World System theorists, who used it to demonstrate how people (largely women reproducing an army of cheap labor) who were used to produce cheap primary products for the manu-facturers of the developed world, were the bottom end of a chain of exploitation (Wallerstein, 1979). Capitalism produces population growth in the cheapest areas to produce labor just as it organizes the production of motor cars or videos in the cheapest location where production costs are low and profits can be maximized. It is also caught in a dilemma whereby the increasing incorporation of women in the labor market produces declines in fertility such that the most advanced capitalist countries have rapidly aging populations and fertility rates below that of natural replacement.

The final step in this introduction to a critical approach to demography is to note that systems of exploitation are always associated with methods of justifying those relationships. Ideologies are intellectual and symbolic tools for constructing legitimations for unequal social relationships; they "explain," among other things, the social relationships through which reproduction is organized. Older men in tribal societies can justify their control of women's horticultural production by reference to kinship ideologies and to their use of ritual knowledge to ensure fertility (Meillassoux, 1975; Sahlins, 1968). Similarly, the elites running modern nation-states identify it as in their interests to control demographic trends; they use dominant ideologies such as "nationalism" or "modernization" to justify their actions and turn to science and social engineering for the tools with which to achieve their goals (Yuval-Davis, 1997, pp. 27-38). I suggest that much of the writing on the aging of populations forms just such an ideological function (Gee & Gutman, 2000; Mullan, 2000; Parsons, 1977; Vincent, 1996). The following examples, from a deluge of reportage on the topic, illustrate the ideological use of demography to specify the economic interests of national elites and indicate how economic interests are articulated through the rhetoric of demographic expertise. Experts define the problem:

> In addition to population size and growth, the age structure of a population can significantly affect national economic performance. Those countries with a high proportion of people at the extremes of the age structure—large percentages of young and old—tend to devote a relatively high proportion of resources to these groups, often resulting in limits of economic growth. By contrast, countries where the largest portion of population is at prime working age may experience economic growth because more people are earning and accumulating capital, and spending less on dependents. This phenomenon is called the "demographic dividend." (Population Resource Center, 2003)

Experts identify its origins.

> Robert Stowe England, analyzing demographic factors, believes that the next 50 years will be economically grim ones. . . . England's . . . results from the Center for Strategic and International Studies' Global Aging Initiative, . . . central thesis is that the aging of populations in most major developed countries in the 2000–2050 period will produce a much slower rate of economic growth, from two factors: the fiscal strain of funding excessive pension payments and the savings deficit produced by a society dominated by old people running down their savings. (Hutchinson, 2002)

Hence, elites identify certain demographic changes as a threat, and their ideologies can identify not only the cause but also the moral responsibility for these threats. These ideologies, having defined the problem, imply courses of action. Powerful elites select tools to exert control to tackle the perceived crises. If population is thought to be too high, they initiate carefully orchestrated family planning programs; they may even consider sterilization campaigns, population expulsion, or gas chambers. Or, if the population is too low, family allowances, nursery schools, and medals for the mothers of the nation might ensure the necessary competitive demographic advantage. Historically there have been strong links between demography, eugenics, and social engineering (Solway, 1995).

Key Factors in World Demographic Aging

Thus, demographic processes are specific to particular forms of political economy. Each have their institutionalized relationships which (a) systematize the division of labor (whose work creates the next generation?), (b) organize the distribution of the product of that labor (who benefits from the work of the new generation?), and (c) articulate the ideological justifications for those distributions (explaining the good reasons why the rich should get richer and the poor get poorer). What have been the consequences for the world's population of the growth of global capitalism? From the fifteenth century onwards, the growth of world-wide (but European dominated) maritime empires is credited with an intensification of the global division of labor. The growth of the world's population accelerated dramatically from about the seventeenth century onward (McEvedy & Jones, 1978). Over the last three decades, these exceptional growth rates have fallen back. In most countries of the world, fertility rates are declining and population growth is slowing or even declining. In most places in the world, there is increased life expectancy. This is predominantly as a result of declines in infant mortality. There are significant regional and class variations within this overall global picture. Africa, for example, continues to have very high fertility rates, and in many areas AIDS has shortened life expectancy (U.N., 2001). It is also the continent that arguably has suffered most from colonial exploitation (being on the wrong end of the transatlantic slave trade) and benefitted least from increased global productivity.

Overall, compared to fifty years ago, the world's mothers are having fewer babies and fewer people are dying before they reach old age. This will produce a significant aging of the world's population in the next thirty years (Day, 1992). Among the consequences suggested are economic slow-down, a difficulty sustaining pensions in the developed world, and a shift in military power to the limited numbers of countries with expanding numbers of young men of military age (CIA, 2001). It is possible to question whether these demographic threats are of the nature that they are sometimes made out to be: to what extent are they ideological? However, these crises are certainly real in that the belief that they exist moves people and powerful institutions to act in certain ways.

What is the relationship between these demographic processes and the contemporary changes within capitalism? What can we retrieve from critical approaches to population theory in order to understand the conflicts embedded in population change?

THE HISTORY OF PENSION FUND CAPITALISM

In the last two decades of the twentieth century, a combination of 1) innovations in pension provision that established funded pension schemes for significant sections of British, American, and other populations; 2) aggressive neoliberal policies to expand global markets; and 3) a stock-market boom (partly in response to the optimism of a technological revolution) has produced profound change in modern capitalism. On rising stock-markets—funded pension schemes seemed incontrovertibly the best option and have dominated policy making at national and international levels. U.S. and British funds looking for investment opportunities are themselves a factor in stock-market growth. These pension funds have expanded to such an extent that they have changed key characteristics of capitalism. They have changed the size, global reach, and institutional structure of capital. These enormous amounts of capital are linked to investment opportunities across the world by a host of new financial institutions that have greater reach and higher levels of specialization than ever before. The new global capital markets are only possible because of the nature of the pension funds that supply a continuing stream of cash to invest derived from the incomes of a mass of investors. This new capital has a character that makes it unlike the accumulated capital in the ownership of an elite. Specific characteristics, in terms of the institutional structures that distribute the risks and set the pattern of interests and incentives, together with the cultures of the elites that have risen by the power of these accumulated funds, give this kind of capitalism a distinctive form (Blackburn, 2003; Clark, 2000; Minns, 2001). The development of these institutions will be as significant to the development of capitalism in the twenty-first century as the joint-stock merchant-adventure companies were in the seventeenth and eighteenth centuries.

Capital markets, through which a worldwide trade in money and assets is conducted, bring together a set of institutions with enormous transactional power. More traditional relationships between finance capital and business, commerce and the state have been severely undermined. The bank-financed heavy industrial complexes that have defined late industrializing countries such as Germany and Japan over the past 50 years appear too inflexible under the pressure of global-market forces. The globalization of investment and technology exposed these structures to direct competition for the first time. Fashionable financial doctrines emphasize that in a rapidly changing world, efficiency dictates agile, swift-moving capital for start-ups, restructuring, mergers, and acquisitions. From this perspective, in the 1990s the absence of highly developed stock and bond markets in Asia exposed the region to unsustainable levels of short-term bank debt (Carter, 2000). The solution to the Asian financial crisis was seen as the development of larger capital markets because securities markets were credited with a superior ability to allocate assets efficiently. These new financial relationships could integrate Asian productive capacity with global sources of capital. Some commentators make the case that these capital markets arose not only for the needs of entrepreneurs of investment capital but also, more fundamentally, for pension funds to find rewarding investment opportunities (Blackburn, 1999). Those mainly continental European countries with pay-as-you-go pension schemes are seen not only as under pressure from changing dependency ratios but missing out on the dynamic potential of capital accumulation in pension funds.

Minns (2001) gives as an idea of the scale of these institutions.

> People's private savings for retirement, represent[ing] over $12,000 billion in worldwide assets—more than the combined value of all the companies quoted on the world's three largest stock markets. (p. xi)

Funded pensions in America grew from only $20 billion in assets in 1950 to over $7 trillion in 2000—70% of the United States GDP. In the last twenty years of the twentieth century, U.K. individual pension and retirement assets increased about twelvefold to around $1.5 trillion. Managing these assets is extremely lucrative. The U.K. investment consulting market is estimated to be worth around £80 million a year for actuarial services of roughly £250 million and an estimated £4.9 billion for institutional fund management (Myners, 2001).

> We examined the roles of institutional investors, boards of directors, and technological opportunity in relation to international diversification. . . . In data on 197 large U.S. firms, we found significant relationships between institutional ownership and international diversification. International diversification was favored by (1) professional investment funds along with outside board members and (2) pension funds along with inside board members. Also, pension funds' long-term orientation facilitated internationalization in industries with high technological opportunities. The results suggest that different institutional owners have different stakes in firms' international strategies. (Tihanyi, Johnson, Hoskisson, & Hitt, 2003, p. 195)

The scale of these institutions gives them enormous power. This power ensures their continuity and success compared to competitive institutions. Other power brokers, such as those running state institutions, can be relied upon to maintain those interests. These vast resources also enable them to, both directly and indirectly, frame the context for intellectual work from economists, demographers, journalists, and many other fields of cultural activity. The importance of these institutions in the global economy give those in control of them power across and within nations.

Different elites contended for control of the accumulated capital located in pension funds. With the long-term stock-market boom through the 1980s and 90s, the assets of the pension funds grew at such a rate that they were worth more than was required to pay the pension liabilities of the fund. In a significant number of firms offering their employees funded pensions, the pension funds came to be worth more than the company itself. Astute members of the financial elite could plunder these funds. Pension holidays were periods when the employers made no contributions to the pension fund because it could be actuarially shown that such contributions were not needed to meet the funds liabilities. In hindsight, now that many of these funds look like they will find it difficult to meet their liabilities, these windfall profits with their effective reduction in the value of the fund look rather like expropriation. Further, financial elites were able to prosper at the expense of the less-successful industrial employers by buying up and "rationalizing" firms, "downsizing" the labor force, and acquiring the residual (but frequently substantial) assets of the pension fund.

Large institutions can, to some extent, dominate markets and actively seek to do so; in this way they seek to gain more predictability for themselves (Fligstein, 1996). However, it is not possible for even the largest institutions to remain immune from the global swings in the world capitalist economy, although they may be in the best position to pass on the consequences of downturns to others. At the very end of the twentieth century and the start of the twenty-first, the "dot com" bubble burst, and there was a downturn in global stock markets. Pension funds making up such a high proportion of the finance markets suffered considerable loss of value, in some cases to such an extent that they could not meet their liabilities. In most problem cases involving default, this was the result of fraud, dishonesty, or imprudent promises to customers, and overreliance on volatile stocks that caused failure to meet pension obligations. The public justification for employer pension holidays of the 1980s and 1990s was on the grounds that employers would be responsible for making up any future deficits by additional contributions. *De facto*, in an economic downturn, it proved difficult to prevent employers from avoiding these increased liabilities. Many firms closed their defined-benefit schemes and changed to defined-contribution schemes; a move that passes the risks of saving for the future from employer to employee.

The stock-market downturn has not altered the fundamental structure of global pension-fund capitalism; pension funds still dominate the market in capital. However, the change reveals more clearly the class relationships integral to this form of political economy. Issues of the location of power, processes of exploitation, and the structure of economic interests are opened to critical examination. The powerlessness of the apparent "owners" of pension rights can be contrasted with the sustained high salaries and multimillion dollar pay-offs to the directors of firms with declining rates of profit. The financial elites are able collectively to protect their group interests as money managers. One illustration of this process is the unwillingness of pension funds to take an active role as shareholders and challenge management practices, or to involve themselves in replacing failing management teams (Blackburn, 2003). Davis and Thompson

(1994) present a somewhat different picture in which they convincingly demonstrate the growth in the United States of a social movement of stock holders, in which the executives of pension funds play a distinctive role. However, my point is a broader one. Although clearly there are conflicts within the financial elite, members of which are in competition with each other, on the global scale they have a powerful set of common interests. Davis and Thompson (1994) contrast the regional-(state) level politics of specific firms and their local interests with the frame-setting agenda of national (federal) politics. In parallel, I suggest there is a further, even broader, level of global-class interests, which sets the framework for national politics. These interests focus on the stability of a global financial system of currency markets, the value of the dollar, and the institutional mechanisms that underwrite the international trade in money.

Pension-fund capitalism is a political economy. It requires politics as well as market relationships to succeed.

> Pension funds are backed by tax laws. That puts them into their strong position as the "backbone of Wall Street": pension funds are growing through permanently streaming flows of money from savers of pension schemes, which collect claims from these funds for their old age. Without the tax redemptions, they would maybe give their money to other securities. (Blomert, 2001, p. 13)

It requires politics to provide social stability, coordination of markets, and regulation and policing of the system; hence, for many the globalization of finance is tightly associated with United States political hegemony. The military dominance of the United States and its domination of world economic institutions are inseparable from the ability of pension funds to make transnational investment strategies work. World political leadership enables the United States to shape globalization to its advantage. Shinn and Gourevitch (2002) advocate that the United States actively engages in negotiating international agreements on corporate governance that follow a U.S. model and spell out the benefits that will follow for its own financial interests. They suggest some caveats about how far the American model can be pushed and the degree of financial security it can provide, but overall argue that

> International capital flows are creating incentives for countries to adopt greater shareholder protections, or "corporate governance reforms." When adopted, these protections reorient the priorities of both industrial firms and banks in ways that can defuse many trade disputes and reduce the likelihood of destabilizing financial meltdowns. Corporate governance reforms abroad can also buffer the U.S. domestic securities regulatory model from some contagion risks caused by tighter integration with foreign capital markets. (Shinn & Gourevitch, 2002, p. 1)

In other words, the safety of pension-fund investments across the world depend on an effective policing of the financial markets. In such an integrated world, there is a severe danger that loss of confidence in investments in one part of the world will rapidly come to affect all major financial institutions across the world. It is the power of the United States, its economic, political, and military dominance, that underpins the necessary legal framework and climate of investor confidence in order for the financial elites of pension-fund capitalism to prosper.

The Consequences of Pension-Fund Capitalism

It is necessary to emphasize that capital is a social relationship, not a bookkeeping entry. We are analyzing the fundamental social relationships that structure society, not conducting an economic market analysis of money flows. Thus the questions that need to be asked about pension-fund capitalism include: who benefits, who carries the risks, whose work is sustaining which members of society? These are essentially questions about exploitation. We need to ask questions about how the institutional arrangements of pension-fund capital are seen as legitimate, right, and proper ways to look after older people. These are essentially questions about ideology and how the hegemony of particular views are established. We further need to examine the potential for political stability and change embedded in those relationships. In particular, we can ask how these new relationships of pension-fund capitalism mediate the social ties between generations and influence the ability of global society to reproduce itself demographically and economically.

One of the characteristics of pension-fund capitalism is its extreme fragmentation of the role of capital. There is no simple relationship of capital to labor. Those saving for a pension, who might be thought of as the owners of capital, often have very restricted legal rights of ownership either collectively or individually. They clearly have interests in not losing the value of their savings and getting a good return on their investment; but most pension savers have no say in and are completely ignorant of the investment activities of their funds. The interests of the savers are usually represented by the specialist role of trustee. However, even these representatives of the investors have very restricted options. They are constrained by legal frameworks, such as that of "fiduciary duty," to maximize return on investment regardless of social consequences and by legal frameworks that prescribe proportions of government bonds, or overseas investments the fund may or may not make. The trustees themselves seldom have the knowledge to run such funds; they therefore employ a range of specialists. There are institutions whose staff administer the funds and make the daily financial transactions that are required. There are institutions that provide independent advice on the performance of the funds and their management. There is a close link between demography and the actuarial profession that provides the expertise to estimate the future liabilities of the pension funds. There are even specialist custodians whose function is merely to securely hold and account for the large volumes of cash and other assets.

Thus, there is a multiplicity of layers of financial institutional relationship that lie between the accumulated savings of would-be pensioners and the entrepreneurs and managerial elites who actively use that money to employ people and engage in industrial, commercial, extractive, or other productive activity. This highly complex division of financial labor creates a variety of interests. The interests of the agents do not always coincide with those for whom they are acting. Thus, on the one hand, there is competition between firms and sets of specialist interests. On the other hand, the financial-services industry represents a common set of interests in the continuing stability and · profitability of managing the global capital market and develops a common culture, including accounting standards, economic theories, and common symbols of value, power, and prestige. Sometimes the common culture and the social networks embedded in the financial elite compromise the institutional checks and balances that are meant to regulate the boundary between fraud and corruption and innovative entrepreneurship. There are numerous incidents from Robert Maxwell in the United Kingdom and Enron in the United States where pensions have been lost through the actions of high-profile but compromised corporate executives.

INTERGENERATIONAL RELATIONSHIPS

Pension-fund capitalism as a form of political economy has profound problems with dealing with the relationships between generations. These problems can be summarized on at least two levels. On an ideological level, as a system of entitlements, it has a struggle to explain and justify why one generation should support another. On a demographic level, the dynamic of pension-fund capitalism generates its own imbalances in the size, composition, and opportunities of successive generations. I will elaborate each of these in turn.

On an ideological level, the values of neoliberalism emphasize individuality and choice. The image of human beings as rational, self-interested "economic man" is at the core of this view of the world. As an institution, the pension fund tries to balance the contradictions of the capitalist hero: the hard-working, prudent saver versus the risk-taking entrepreneur. While older people might like a good return on their investments, security of income is the prime objective of those preparing for their old age. However, a "no risk" investment is a "no return" investment: pension-fund capitalism would fail if it followed a "sock-under-the-bed" savings regime.

The neoliberal ideology stresses that the rational, self-interested individual would invest an optimum contribution during a lifetime in a pension fund (or family or other institution) to take care of his/her financial needs in old age. But the concept of the rational, self-interested individual logically precludes strategies that produce returns beyond the lifespan of the individual. Economic individualism reduces the relationships between generations to a rational calculation of self-interest (e.g., Anand & Sen, 2000; Laslett & Fishkin, 1992). Such an ideological view leaves the intergenerational contract—the passing down to each generation the obligation to care for the one before and the one after—vulnerable to dissolution if individuals do not find it to their benefit when they calculate their financial self-interest. It is only when people orient themselves to some greater collectivity (family, nation, the brotherhood of believers, etc.) that multi-generational solidarity can result. Further, those mutual obligations that stem from collective orientations include the rule of law. Such transcendent rules are required to provide reassurance and some predictability before it can be rational to expect current prudence—savings made today to result in benefits in the future. Known risks can be calculated and discounted, which is precisely what the actuaries calculating the life tables for life insurance and pension funds do. Calculating risks requires a prior social order. It is difficult to be rational in the face of unknown risks. There is thus a manifest contradiction between the ideology of rational individualism and the substantive need for intergenerational solidarity to provide security in old age.

Capitalism's core ideological concept is that of private property. Paradoxically, pension-fund capitalism fragments and undermines that concept. Under pension-fund capitalism, the dominant route to an entitlement to a reasonable standard of living in old age is through pension rights accumulated through work history and the individual's, employer's, and government's (through tax concessions) contribution record. A system based on individual property rights is compromised by the complex division of functions of ownership within pension-fund capitalism. People don't own their pensions in the classic sense of untrammeled possession and right to buy and sell in a market (a very limited proportion of pensions are merely private transactions; the basis of the expansion in the last twenty years has been on the basis of employer contributions and tax concessions). An individual subscriber to a pension fund effectively has very little knowledge and no control of how that fund is used. In many cases, they cannot pass their pension rights on to others, and the right to inherit a pension, for example by a partner, is frequently limited in value and constrained by eligibility rules. The entitlement to pension is not merely a matter of private property.

The reproduction of successive generations is affected by pension-fund capitalism, which, like any other political economy, has its own distinctive demography. Insofar as pension funds and new international finance markets do allocate global capital "efficiently," they will also make the pressure to expand markets more effective. There are at least two problems that this will create for pension-fund capitalism itself, both of which involve increases to the cost of fertility—the work burden to families raising children. They are the expansion of labor markets and the commodification of new areas of social life.

Labor markets expand; entrepreneurs seek profitability by drawing new sources of labor where it is scarce and finding cheaper sources of labor to substitute for existing producers. For example, in Britain and Europe, the use of women's labor has grown significantly since the 1950s. The major noncapitalist institution that demands women's labor is the family. Domestic labor is necessary to look after dependants—children, frail older people. However, the more the system is successful in attracting the labor of reproducers into market relationships, the greater the costs to the family of having children and producing the next generation. In much of the twentieth century it was thought that mechanization and automation would eliminate labor shortages, that the future would be a life of leisure. In practice, while across the world many productive techniques have been labor displacing and many industries have shed labor, the total demand for labor has increased. Increases in service and tertiary occupations have more than made up for labor displacement in manufacturing. Women's work is in even greater demand in jobs from nursing to hotel maids and sewing shoes. Thus, it is in the interests of those managing increasing amounts of pension-fund investments to back entrepreneurs who draw ever-increasing numbers of people (particularly women) away from domestic work and into the labor market. However, women's employment and women's education are the best predictors of reduction in national fertility rates (e.g., Caldwell, 1982; McDonald, 2000; Sen, 1998). The success of pension-fund capitalism is thus linked to further declines in fertility worldwide and an increase in the average age of the world's population.

Larger and more efficient financial institutions with access to larger and larger amounts of pension savings has led the drive to find more and more consumers who purchase more and more commodities. One method is to extend the lines of credit to more and more consumers, the ubiquitous credit card being one concrete example, expansion in mortgage lending is another. Expansion of the labor market into new areas also increases the number of consumers. Global companies compete for control of consumption through the use of brands and other methods. The continued success of capitalism has required that each consumer consumes more commodities. In the developed world, consumption behavior has come to dominate culture. Even children become consumers, and parents are targeted with greater and greater demands—education fees, fashionable clothes, healthcare, books and toys—making it more and more expensive to bring up children. In other words, the commodification of childhood produces a further twist in the downward spiral of fertility.

It is the decline in fertility rates that has caused the aging of the world's population and, in many countries, means that each successive generation becomes smaller. Many commentators have seen this demographic regime as producing an inequity between generations and the potentiality for "age wars." I have argued elsewhere that these views are both erroneous and are ideological at root (Vincent, 1995, 1999). The irony of pension-fund capitalism, as the cause rather than the solution to such issues, should not blind us to the need to find alternative and secure ways to create social solidarity and ensure secure entitlements to a decent standard of living in old age.

THE IDEOLOGICAL FRAMEWORK OF PENSION-FUND CAPITALISM AND THE FUNCTION OF POPULATION AS A SOCIAL PROBLEM

Superficially it would seem that an aging population would be in the interests of pension-fund capitalism. It would appear to be a situation that would create more business. Much effort has been put into convincing people that personal, private savings (using the institutions of pension-fund capitalism) is the better solution to fund old age than state-organized pay-as-you-go pension schemes. However, pension-fund capitalism is just as vulnerable to the changing workers-to-pensioners ratio as state welfare systems are. The fundamental problem for both is how to redistribute current production from a smaller number of active workers to those receiving pensions. State welfare systems have to extract cash for pensions from taxpayers and national insurance contributors. Private pension funds extract resources to pay pensions from the (a) enterprises (and thus the workers) in which they invest and (b) governments (and thus taxpayers) via investments in gilt-edged securities. The different redistributive mechanisms do not create more wealth, they merely rearrange who is entitled to it. To make the case that increased private savings will provide the solution to the problem of retirement incomes for an aging population thus requires an enormous amount of ideological work. To sustain the illusion that entitlements to a secure old age are safer in private than public hands and to bolster confidence in pension funds as reliable, fair, and just ways to obtain a secure old age, demographic change has to be portrayed as a crisis and older people portrayed as unproductive, burdensome, and unworthy of collective responsibility. Therefore it is essential for pension-fund capitalism to successfully define the demographic position as one in which the aging population constitutes a crisis.

Fears about population have shifted from overpopulation to underpopulation—too many babies to too many old folks. One way to examine this issue is to look at the way demographic issues enter the agenda. The critical gerontological questions are "in what circumstances do population changes become social issues, who is defining those problems, and to what purpose?" There were concerns in the first part of the twentieth century about declines in fertility, loss of population in war, and the possibility of falling populations. In the thirty years following the Second World War—the development decades—that saw unprecedented economic growth and the ending of direct imperial rule, the major concern was population growth. Population time bombs, it was argued, were waiting to blow up economic progress and environmental stability. In more recent years, the time bomb has become that of an aging population. There has been an almost cyclical process whereby different and contrasting demographic concerns come to dominate international political and economic agendas. I would suggest that this changing demographic agenda is best understood as reflecting the ideological concerns—economic, military, and political—of dominant elites. National and global economic elites want labor for their enterprises and customers for their products. In general terms, if demographic expansion promotes economic expansion all well and good, but if rapid growth leads to instability, then concerns emerge. Military elites are concerned about military manpower for themselves and their enemies (e.g., CIA, 2001, p. 5). Political elites need to sustain state control and manipulation of populations. On a global level the concerns of these elites are expressed in multinational forums. There are three key international organizations that have set the global agenda on population aging. They are the UN, the World Bank, and OECD.

The United Nations conferences can be used to mark the timing of the inclusion of population aging onto the international agenda. The UN is the principal forum in which all sovereign nation-states can debate and attempt to resolve issues. The UN Vienna conference in 1982 created the International Plan of Action on Ageing that was endorsed by the United Nations General Assembly in its resolution 37/51 of 3 December 1982. Aging issues were identified as developmental ones.

> The developmental issues relate to the socio-economic implications of the ageing of the population, defined as an increase in the proportion of the ageing in the total population. Under this heading are considered, inter alia, the effects of the ageing of the population on production, consumption, savings, investment and in turn general social and economic conditions and policies, especially at times when the dependency rate of the ageing is on the increase. (UN, 1982)

Twenty years later, a Second World Assembly on Ageing was held in Madrid, Spain in April 2002. The Assembly adopted a "Political Declaration" and the "Madrid International Plan of Action, 2002," which commit governments to act to meet the challenge of aging (Sidorenko & Walker, 2004). What is revealing about the documentation and reports from that conference is the tacit definitions of what that challenge is (e.g., NGO Committee on Ageing, 2003). Embedded in the conclusions is evidence of the influence of a particular form of political economy that defines the rights, powers, and entitlements of older people in relationship to the rest of society. In their specification of what constitutes the issues and problems about an aging population, they say:

> Where social security systems based on accrued retirement benefits exist, the growth in the number and longevity of retired persons is now emerging as a major aspect of the husbandry of national economic resources, and is sometimes presented in terms of a gradual freezing of a large share of national wealth for so-called non-productive purposes. On the other hand, it will probably be recognized that the accumulation of retirement funds could constitute a stabilizing factor in the national economy, in the sense of providing for long-term and conservatively utilized sources of funding on a substantial scale, whose impact on otherwise fluctuating economic systems can be beneficial. In such systems, the purchasing power of the pensions paid should as far as possible be maintained. (UN, 2002, p. 19)

These are concerns of the financial and economic elites of the developed countries. They are the concerns of older people in those countries insofar as they guide the actions of those in economic power to change the value of their postretirement incomes. A different set of problems is prioritized for developing countries.

> Where formal retirement benefit systems do not yet exist, the economic implications of the ageing of societies are for the time being largely negative, and will probably continue to be so, unless serious and far-reaching efforts are made to turn this liability into a potential benefit for the whole of society. Governmental initiatives to promote material development and social well-being, and international action to sustain such initiatives, could be taken jointly in an effort to prepare for the future of those approaching old age in areas where traditional structures of protection are about to dissolve. (UN, 2002, p. 19)

If these are the problems, the document specifies issues and objectives by way of a solution. Issue 7 in the document is about "Income security, social protection/social security and poverty prevention" and the authors recognize the international dimension to material security in old age and its relationship to issues of social cohesion. They say:

> Globalization, structural adjustment programmes, fiscal constraints and a growing older population are often perceived as exerting pressure on formal social protection/social security systems. Sustainability in the provision of adequate income security is of great importance. In developing countries with limited coverage formal systems of social protection/social security, populations are vulnerable to market shocks and individual misfortunes that strain informal family support. In countries with economies in transition, economic transformations have impoverished whole segments of the population, in particular older persons and many families with children. Where it has occurred, hyperinflation has rendered pensions, disability insurance, health benefits and savings almost worthless. (UN, 2002)

As a consequence, the conference sets the very honorable objective of the promotion of programs to enable all workers to acquire basic social entitlements including, where applicable, pensions, etc. The actions required to achieve this objective include

> (f) Strive to ensure the integrity, sustainability, solvency and transparency of pension schemes, and, where appropriate, disability insurance;
> (g) Establish a regulatory framework for private and supplementary pension and, where appropriate, disability insurance;
> (h) Provide advice and counselling services for older persons regarding all areas of social protection/social security. (UN, 2002)

It is particularly noteworthy that paragraph (g) sets up a framework for private markets for global capital. The relationship between the Action Plan and the interests of international financial institutions and pension-fund capitalism is most explicit in Action (e)

> Invite international organizations, in particular the international financial institutions, according to their mandates, to assist developing countries and all countries in need in their efforts to achieve basic social protection, in particular for older persons. (UN, 2002)

Insofar as globalization is about cross-national coordination of standards and actions, so is the plan. This coordination of standards needs to read in conjunction with the developed world's trade priorities as expressed by the "Singapore Agenda"—the World Trade Organization's attempts to open up developing-world finance markets to Western investment institutions. The Singapore Agenda is shorthand for global financial liberalization involving four key points. These are: open investment rules, competition policy, transparency in government procurement, and trade facilitation. The global finance and investment elites have pushed hard for a "level playing field" whereby new markets would be opened up and freed from local control or "interference."

The World Bank published its report *Averting the Old Age Crisis* in 1994 and its central recommendations have become a form of financial orthodoxy. They advocate a "three-pillar" approach to overcome what they see as the limitations of "government-managed" pension entitlements. The first, or public, pillar would have the limited objective of alleviating old-age poverty and be based on the government's power of taxation; it would be a residual limited floor below which the poorest would not be allowed to fall. The second pillar would be a mandatory, fully funded, privately managed pension scheme designed to provide an income-smoothing device that defers income until later life. The third pillar is a voluntary additional private savings scheme for old age for those with the resources to enhance their pension. The World Bank has been extremely active in pushing for particular kinds of policies and ensuring that governments in need of international credit move toward their three-tier model. Latin America and the former Soviet Bloc countries have moved most rapidly in this direction (Bonoli, 2003). The effectiveness of these policies, in terms of providing financial security for older people has been much debated. However, what is clear is that the policy has created opportunities for expansion for the global financial elites who provide the management for pension funds.

The Organisation for Economic Co-operation and Development also reflects the dominant international agenda on aging populations. The OECD (1998) Policy Brief *Maintaining Prosperity in an Ageing Society* states that population aging could threaten future economic growth and prosperity and suggests that yet greater "reform" of countries' welfare and financial structures are needed. By way of identifying the critical issues, they ask the following questions:

> Will it continue to be possible to share societies' resources between the working generation and its dependent non-working members in ways that do not give rise to unacceptable societal and inter-generational conflicts?

How can the contribution of older people to society and economic prosperity be enhanced?

How should pension, health and long-term care best be reformed?

Which changes in the financial infrastructure are needed to support the development of funded pension systems?

To what extent will ageing OECD countries be able to improve their well-being through growing trade in goods and services and assets, in particular with younger, faster-growing non-OECD countries? (OECD, 1998, p. 1)

But these questions, from the point of view of the dominant agenda, are rhetorical. The ideology of pension-fund capitalism dictates that the answers are obviously that older people should expect less, everyone will have to contribute more towards pensions, people will have to work longer for their pensions, the private sector should be left to manage the funds, and we better rely on the United States to make sure the younger states do not step out of line.

CURRENT AMERICAN CONCERNS ABOUT WORLD POPULATION: THE CIA AGENDA

The United States is the largest source of pension funds and the prime location of the institutions of pension-fund capitalism. It is possible to read the primary strategic concerns of the elites in the United States through CIA reports on the global challenges that currently face the United States. A report produced by the CIA in July 2001 entitled *Long-Term Global Demographic Trends: Reshaping the Geopolitical Landscape* is both prescient and a good example of the agenda of political interests that are felt by the U.S. economic and military establishment. The report debates migration issues, urbanization and poverty, health (particularly AIDS) and environmental issues, but the prime focus of the report is the strategic consequences of changing world demography. The expert advice they assemble for easy digestion sees global demographic trends as having far-reaching consequences for U.S. national power—economic, military, and political. They argue that the U.S. role as dominant superpower and world policeman means the United States will probably be expected to assume a larger share of the burden for increased financial and humanitarian aid and military interventions "needed" around the world. They see some U.S. allies being weakened by demographic change. Both Europe and Japan, they suggest, stand to lose global power and influence. Key allies in the developing world could be destabilized.

The images, which form the background to the report's headings, reflect their anxieties—an older Arab man and a crowd of African and Asian children. They express concern that more immigrants will seek to enter the United States.

The world will be older and far less Caucasian, and it will be far more concentrated in urban areas; these population shifts will demand concessions of political influence at the expense of the young and middle aged and at the expense of traditional rural constituencies, as well as from traditional US allies and toward states currently outside our orbit of influence. (CIA, 2001, p. 5)

The report concentrates specifically on concerns about aging populations in the developed world and the youth bulge in parts of Africa and the Middle East. For the developed world, they predict economic downturn and political pressures. They worry that there will be economic consequences in terms of slower economic growth in the developed world, which could threaten U.S. exports, U.S. interests in global capital markets, and U.S. investments, while U.S. equities at home and abroad would be at risk from increased violence and widespread infectious disease. They argue that population aging means fewer workers to support retirees and that these issues will be especially problematic for Europeans, who they say "harbor cultural biases against working later in life." Their economic problems resulting from population aging include smaller work forces that could depress economic output, create inflation, and hold back investment. These in turn could lead to overcapacity and diminishing returns on investment in a version of the classic overproduction crises of capitalist economies identified since the time of Marx. Their neoliberal analysis suggests that, while the United States is in a better position to cope with the aging issue than the rest of the developed world, they still see a challenge to develop retirement systems that do not undermine private savings and investment through crippling levels of taxation on the young. They voice political fears that there is already polarization among age groups and a rise in intergenerational conflict.

This population agenda mirrors U.S. strategic concerns with the Middle East and with fears of terrorism. The youth bulge is concentrated in areas of poverty and political instability. They mention, among other locations, Afghanistan, Pakistan, Colombia, Iraq, occupied Palestinian territories, and Yemen. The strategic consequences they identify include: large numbers of Afghan and Pakistani youth willing to engage in terrorist activities, increased numbers of Palestinians compared to Israelis, and an increased volume of cannon fodder available to U.S. enemies.

THE INTERNATIONAL FINANCIAL CLASS AND THE IDEOLOGICAL FUNCTIONS OF DEMOGRAPHY

Population issues are frequently described in terms of "time-bombs," and this has been labeled apocalyptic demography (Robertson, 1997). Although population projection is an enterprise fraught with difficulty and is frequently of dubious reliability, its quantitative base gives it the facility to calculate alarming exponential trends into the future. These "time bombs" have frequently been used uncritically to promote the agendas of particular interest groups. We can identify from the above material at least two ways in which the demography of aging of the world's population has been constructed and used to promote pension-fund capitalism. The first is market expansion and the second is standardization and regulation. The potential for market expansion is enhanced through demographic analysis that suggests that welfare-state provision and pay-as-you-go pension schemes are unsustainable. It inhibits aspiring developing countries from following this model and directs them to the World Bank three-tier model with its built-in advantages for the private pensions industry. Population scares provide the ideological justification for governments to let the pensions industry enlarge its role in national pensions provision. For pension funds to benefit from transnational investment, there must be a system of standardization, comparability, and regulation that enables them to judge the return of investment and the level of risk they will incur. International agreements, made within UN and international trade regulation frameworks, are made in the face of overwhelming U.S. political, military, and economic power and ensure that international finance remains highly profitable.

Do the global elite of finance managers represent a distinct class? They represent the distinctive social group of pension-fund capitalism whose position within the international division of labor grants them access to such power and wealth. Sklair (2001) discusses the people as well as their attitudes who he regards as a transnational elite. They come from various national, religious, and ethnic backgrounds, but they much more uniformly come from elite educational institutions and have top quality business qualifications. They are an integrated elite who recruit from within their own ranks and do not co-opt outsiders, i.e., they are a technical elite. These people don't own capital, they manage it. However, they are, in there own right, extremely rich. Although they have organizational ability and entrepreneurial ability, their central technical function is the management of capital. Their pivotal role in the global political economy lies in the fact that they are at the allocative center of the distribution of surplus value.

> Pension funds are steering the fate of the same firms where their clients may work, and they are steering the steps of rationalisations for the sake of more profits. Pension funds work for the pensioners, who can gain a better living by raising share values while the payers may lose their jobs. So the power of pension funds might be called the rule of gerontocracy. The gerontocratic interest in raising the shareholder value helped bring into existence a huge mass of lawyers and judges fighting for the distribution of profits to the pensioners, and gaining themselves high provisions. (Blomert, 2001, p. 13)

These people are a social group with common perspectives and values closely associated with neoclassical economics (e.g., Davis & Thompson, 1994). They do not allocate the resources they control for reproduction, not for demographic reproduction and very little to social reproduction. Studies such as Clark (2000) indicate why the aspiration for socially responsible pension funds investing in civic or urban renewal has not materialized. Paradoxically, pension-fund capitalism's high degree of specialization makes it socially irresponsible; there is no room for the paternalism of the family firm. The ultra specialization within financial management creates greater alienation, in that there is less transparency about where the labor value is going, and a greater necessity for a blind faith in the market as the allocative solution to all problems.

Those women who depend on their children rather than having any entitlement to a pension have a direct interest in their own successful fertility. Other situations are more complex. Individual and collective logic differ. The rational reproducer would aim for fewer babies for themselves, but enough babies from other mothers for society to continue. Free-riding on other women's child-rearing labor has been characteristic of many economies and is positively advocated by some who see immigration as a solution to the "problem" of dependency ratios. The effective costs of raising the next generation through women's labor constitutes a problem for families in terms of their allocation of time. "Can I ask granny to look after the kids again while I go to work?" is the kind of dilemma that increases as "efficient" markets expand still further. Communities and nations have to find increasing resources for education for longer and longer periods or have to pass more of the increased investment in an educated and trained workforce on to families.

CONCLUSION

To conclude, we can return to the ideas of entitlements set out in the introduction. An entitlement is in essence a social relationship. Entitlements to a materially secure old age under pension-fund capitalism are largely mediated through employment-based relationships. As a result, these entitlements are skewed by gender because of gender bias in the workplace—the fact that women tend to hold lower-paid, less-secure jobs and more often fall outside employment (including pension) rights. Migrants also have these characteristics. However, those from poor areas who return home with pension rights fare well compared to their compatriots who stayed at home. Those social groups, where political and economic security and poverty preclude access to pension rights, have to rely on diminishing possibilities of entitlement through family support.

The extreme form of segregation of capital management and ownership functions, which characterizes pension-fund capitalism, has particular consequences. For example, highly mobile capital requiring standardized and predictable returns tends to rely on sophisticated quantitative models to manage risk rather than personal knowledge. Paradoxically, it has been suggested that computerized trading and other manifestations of this financial culture actually creates volatility in markets.

We would expect, however, that over time institutional investors will increase
the liquidity, volatility and price informativeness of the financial markets
in which [they] participate. (Gillan & Starks, 2002, p. 2)

A further consequence is the export of risk to the weakest nations, enterprises,
and social groups at the periphery of the global economy. Therefore, it is the
rural poor, particularly the old and the women, whose entitlement is the most
insecure. Older people in the developed world also have a struggle to defend their
position, although they have greater resources at their disposal than the rural
poor. Pensioners have had great difficulty defending their entitlement to a pension
when it is challenged by controlling elites. British state pensioners have seen the
value of their national insurance contributions eroded, some women actually
received less from National Insurance than they put in. Very high proportions of
those taking out private pensions in Britain fail to sustain their contributions
and, as a result, incur financial losses. In the final analysis, the pension entitlement
is underpinned by the state, which tends to act where possible to ensure confidence
in the financial system. Where state support is withdrawn, as in Argentina, it can
be catastrophic for pensioners. In situations where lack of confidence threatens
the whole system, states and multinational power brokers step in to keep, as far as
possible, the turbulence localized. Some commentators from a critical perspective
have seen the growing accumulation of pension funds as a step forward with
the potential for socially directed control of capital and investment (Blackburn,
1999; Drucker, 1976). The perspective developed here takes a much less positive approach seeing increased alienation as people have less control and understanding of their own economic activity. Like all political economies, pension-
fund capitalism relies on an ideological framework to obtain consent from those
that it exploits.

Capitalism developed with the division of labor between owners and managers.
Managers run enterprises profitably and are experts in organizational skills;
however, investor-owners are experts at risk. Pension fund capitalism sees the
hyper-division of labor within the ownership function. The risk function is
dissected and separated from the nominal beneficial owners. The experts in risk
flourish in globalized capital markets. However, those skills enable them to
efficiently pass the risks of the pension business to others: down the line to
enterprises and their employees and in particular those shut out of the potential for
investment; and up the line by excluding those whose incomes are too small and
insecure to buy into a pension entitlement or to the pension recipients and others
whose entitlements become eroded.

The shift to culture in social studies, while having many benefits, has lost
sight of several key ideas. Cultural analyses dissect cultures in their own terms,
not in relation to power or the causes and consequence of institutional practices.
Cultural studies can show how cultures instill meaning and give people fulfillment, for example by having babies. Children can be a joy as well as work to

their parents. The critical approach enables us to compare social, economic, and demographic systems and ask why some societies have more children than others and why some see too many babies as a threat, while others see too few babies as a problem. Cultural analysis of a category proceeds by use of other cultural categories, how they fit together, how they came into being; at best it will illustrate the contested nature of the category. It does not seek to explain the outcome of such contests. It omits the collective power of some people to have their definition of the meaning of a category stabilized into institutional practice. Thus, for example, the category of "elder" or "pensioner" can be contrasted with other life-cycle stages, for example, by reference to changing constructions of "youth" or "worker." The meanings of this set of terms can be dissected by reference to cultural history and to alternative usages of the categories in different times and places. A political economy, in contrast, asks "in whose interests is it that some people are regarded as 'elders' and others as 'workers'?" Processes of social stratification mark some people out by age criteria and institutionalize a set of social positions within which they are required to live out their lives. Cultural analysis can tell us what this feels like, but a critical analysis is required if we want to find out how such processes happen and how they might be changed.

There are two insights that can be retrieved from the political-economy perspective to inform a discussion of demography and pension-fund capitalism. The first of these is that bringing up the next generation of those contributing to the economy requires large amounts of domestic, unpaid labor, usually that of women. Modern global capitalism is no different in this respect than any other political economy and is caught in a contradiction between the commercial demand for women's labor time and unpaid, domestic labor required for the reproduction of the labor force. A shift in the concerns of global elites from too many babies to too few, from overpopulation to underpopulation in a period of less than fifty years can be seen to reflect that problem. Problematic and contended policing of the international labor market is another aspect of the same process. The second of these insights relates to the circulation of capital and the key role in which transnational investment mediated through pension funds has come into play in control and redistribution of the world's productive assets. A globalized financial system works because of a hegemonic global political system that underpins standardized and predictable international financial transactions. But those groups striving to achieve a financially secure old age in less-favored parts of the global economy find themselves beset by new risks and uncertainties as a result. Mothers and families argue about the problems of childcare against work opportunities; national elites clash over immigration and population policies; and pension-fund managers strive to outcompete their rivals in a fluctuating stock market. Critical theory has a key role in understanding how those conflicts are interlinked and in turn they form the context in which people struggle to obtain an entitlement to a decent lifestyle in old age.

REFERENCES

Anand, S., & Sen, A. (2000). Human development and economic sustainability. *World Development, 28*(12), 2029-2049.

Anker, R., Buvinic, M., & Youssef, N. H. (Eds.). (1981). *Women's roles and population trends in the Third World.* London: Croom Helm.

Barrett, M. (1980). *Women's oppression today: Problems in Marxist feminist analysis.* London: Verso Editions and NLB.

Blackburn, R. (1999). The new collectivism: Pension reform, grey capitalism and complex socialism. *New Left Review, 233,* 3-66.

Blackburn, R. (2003). *Banking on death or, investing in life: The history and future of pensions.* London: Verso.

Bloch, M. (Ed.). (1973). *Marxist analyses and social anthropology.* London: Malaby Press.

Blomert, R. (2001, January). Sociology of finance—Old and new perspectives. *Economic Sociology, 2*(2), 9-15. Retrieved February 16, 2004, from http://econsoc.mpifg.de/archive/esjan01.pdf..

Bonoli, G. (2003). Two worlds of pension reform in Western Europe. *Comparative Politics, 35*(4), 399-416.

Caldwell, J. C. (1982). *Theory of fertility decline.* London: Academic Press.

Cancian, F. (1976). Social stratification. *Annual Review of Anthropology, 5,* 227-248.

Carter, M. N. (2000). Capital markets and occupational pensions: Opportunities for the United States and Japan. Retrieved Aug 24, 2001, from http://www.us-japan.org/boston/carter.htm.

Central Intelligence Agency. (2001). *Long-term global demographic trends: Reshaping the geo-political landscape.* Retrieved June 13, 2003, from http://www.odci.gov/cia/reports/index.html

Clark, G. L. (2000). *Pension fund capitalism.* Oxford: Oxford University Press.

Davis, G. F., & Thompson, T. A. (1994). A social movement perspective on corporate control. *Administrative Science Quarterly, 39*(1), 141-173.

Day, L. H. (1992). *The future of low-birthrate populations.* London: Routledge.

Devereux, S. (1993). *Theories of famine.* Hemel Hempstead: Harvester Wheatsheaf.

Drucker, P. F. (1976). *The unseen revolution: How pension fund socialism came to America.* London: Heinemann.

Emmanuel, A. (1972). *Unequal exchange.* New York: Monthly Review Press.

Fligstein, N. (1996). Markets as politics: A political-cultural approach to market institutions. *American Sociological Review, 61,* 656-673.

Gee, E. M., & Gutman, G. M. (2000). *The overselling of population aging.* Oxford: Oxford University Press.

Gillan, S. L., & Starks, L. T. (2002). *Institutional investors, corporate ownership and corporate governance global perspectives* (Discussion Paper No. 2002/9). World Institute for Development Economics Research/United Nations University. Retrieved 20 June 2003 available from www.tiaa-crefinstitute.org/Publications/wkpapers/wp_pdfs/wp03-29-02.pdf.

Goody, J. (1976). *Production and reproduction: A comparative study of the domestic domain.* Cambridge: Cambridge University Press.

Greenhalgh, S. (1996). The social construction of population science: An intellectual, institutional, and political history of twentieth-century demography. *Comparative Studies in Society and History, 38*(1), 26-66.

Hammel, E. A., & Howell, N. (1987). Research in population and culture: An evolutionary framework. *Current Anthropology, 28*(2), 141-160.

Hutchinson, M. (2002). Analysis: Will aging make us poor? By Martin Hutchinson UPI Business and Economics Editor From the United Press International Business & Economics Desk Published 11/21/2002 9:27 PM. Retrieved August 4, 2003 from http://www.upi.com/view.e.g.m?StoryID=20021121-045815-8085r

Johnson, A. W., & Earle, T. (1987). *The evolution of human societies from foraging group to agrarian state.* Stanford: Stanford University Press.

Kuhn, A., & Wolpe, A. (Eds.). (1978). *Feminism and materialism: Women and modes of production.* London: Routledge and Kegan Paul.

Laslett, P., & Fishkin, J. S. (Eds.). (1992). *Justice between age groups and generations.* New Haven: Yale University Press.

Lowe, M., & Hubbard, R. (Eds.). (1983). *Women's nature.* New York: Pergamon Press.

McDonald, P. (2000). Gender equity in theories of fertility transition. *Population and Development Review, 26*(3), 427-439.

McEvedy, C., & Jones, R. (1978). *Atlas of world population history.* Harmondsworth: Penguin.

Meillassoux, C. (1975). *Femmes, greniers et capitaux* [Maidens, meal and money]. Paris: F. Maspero.

Minns, R. (2001). *The Cold War in welfare: Stock markets versus pensions.* London: Verso.

Moore, H. L. (1988). *Feminism and anthropology.* Cambridge: Polity Press.

Mullan, P. (2000). *The imaginary time bomb: Why an ageing population is not a social problem.* London: I.D.Taurus.

Myners, P. (2001). The Myners Review of Institutional Investment in the UK: Report March 2001 Retrieved January 17, 2005, from http://www.hmtreasury.gov.uk./documents/financial_services/securities_and_investments/fin_sec_mynfinal.e.g.m

Narotzky, S. (1997). *New directions in economic anthropology.* London: Pluto Press.

NGO Committee on Ageing. (2003, September). *Human rights and older persons: Panel report Geneva:* Geneva International Network on Ageing.

OECD. (1998). Policy Brief "Maintaining prosperity in an ageing society" June 1998. Retrieved June 20, 2003, from www1.oecd.org/publications/Pol_brief/1999/9907eng.pdf.

Parsons, J. (1977). *Population fallacies.* London: Elek Books.

Polgar, S. (Ed.). (1975). *Population, ecology, and social evolution.* The Hague: Mouton.

Population Resource Center. (2003, April 30). Banking the "demographic dividend": How population dynamics can affect economic growth, Retrieved June 20, 2003, from http://www.prcdc.org/programs/davanzony/davanzony.html.

Quadagno, J. (1996). Social Security and the myth of the entitlement "crisis." *The Gerontologist, 36*(3), 391-399.

Raphael, D. (Ed.). (1975). *Being female: Reproduction, power and change.* The Hague: Mouton.

Robertson, A. (1997). Beyond apocalyptic demography: Towards a moral economy of interdependence. *Ageing and Society, 17*(4), 425-446

Rogers, B. (1980). *The domestication of women.* London: Tavistock.

Rosaldo, M. Z., & Lamphere, L. (Eds.). (1974). *Woman, culture and society.* Stanford: Stanford University Press.

Roseberry, W. (1988). Political economy. *Annual Review of Anthropology, 17*, 161-185.

Roxborough, I. (1979). *Theories of underdevelopment.* London: Macmillan.

Sahlins, M. D. (1968). *Tribesmen.* Englewood Cliffs, NJ: Prentice-Hall.

Sahlins, M. D. (1974). *Stone Age economics.* London: Tavistock Publications.

Sen, A. (1982). *Poverty and famines: An essay on entitlement and deprivation.* Oxford: Clarendon Press.

Sen, A. (1998). Human development and financial conservatism. *World Development, 26*(4), 733-742.

Shinn, J., & Gourevitch, P. (2002). *How shareholder reforms can pay foreign policy dividends.* Council on Foreign Relations: New York. Retrieved June 20, 2003, from Gov_paper.pdf.

Sidorenko, A., & Walker, A. (2004). The Madrid International Plan of Action on Aging: From conception to implementation. *Aging and Society, 24*(2), 147-166.

Singh, R. D. (1994). Fertility-mortality variations across LDCS—Women's education, labor-force participation, and contraceptive use. *Kyklos, 47*(2), 209-229.

Sklair, L. (Ed.). (1994). *Capitalism and development.* London: Routledge.

Sklair, L. (2001). *The transnational capitalist class.* Oxford: Blackwell.

Smith, J., Wallerstein, I., & Evers, H-D. (Eds.). (1984). *Households and the world economy.* Beverly Hills: Sage Publications.

Solway, R. A. (1995). *Demography and degeneration: Eugenics and the declining birthrate in twentieth-century Britain.* London: University of Chapel Hill Press.

Spybey, T. (1992). *Social change, development and dependency.* Cambridge: Polity Press.

Terray, E. (1972). *Marxism and "primitive" societies* (Mary Klopper, Trans.). New York: Monthly Review Press.

Tihanyi, L., Johnson, R. A., Hoskisson, R. E., & Hitt, M. A. (2003). Institutional ownership differences and international diversification: The effects of boards of directors and technological opportunity. *Academy of Management Journal, 46*(2), 195-211.

Toye, J. (1987). *Dilemmas of development reflections on the counter-revolution in development theory and policy.* Oxford: Basil Blackwell.

United Nations. (1982). *Vienna International Plan of Action on Ageing.* Retrieved August 4, 2003, from http://www.un.org/esa/socdev/ageing/ageipaa.htm.

United Nations. (2001). *World population prospects: The 2000 revision.* New York: Population Division, Department of Economic and Social Affairs, United Nations.

United Nations. (2002, April). *Report of the Second World Assembly on Ageing.* Retrieved August 4, 2003, from http://www.unece.org/ead/pau/age/conf2002frame.htm.

Vincent, J. A. (1995). *Inequality and old age.* London: University College Press.

Vincent, J. A. (1996). Who's afraid of an ageing population? *Critical Social Policy, 47*, 3-26.

Vincent, J. A. (1999). *Politics, power and old age.* Buckingham: Open University Press.

Wallerstein, I. (1979). *The capitalist world-economy: Essays by Immanuel Wallerstein.* Cambridge: Cambridge University Press.

White, L. (1959). *The evolution of culture.* New York: McGraw-Hill.

Wilkinson, R. G. (1973). *Poverty and progress.* London: Methuen.

World Bank. (1994). *Averting the old age crisis.* Oxford: Oxford University Press.

Yural-Davis, N. (1997). *Gender and nation.* London: Sage.

Contributors

JAN BAARS, Ph.D., studied Sociology and Philosophy in Amsterdam and is Professor of Interpretive Gerontology at the University for Humanistics in Utrecht, Netherlands and Professor of Philosophy of the Social Sciences and the Humanities at Tilburg University, Netherlands. He has published and (co-)edited a dozen books and published many articles about philosophical and geronto-logical subjects in English, German, French, Finnish, and Dutch. His main interests are theoretical and practical presuppositions in approaches to aging, especially concepts of time and temporality. He has lectured at many universities in Europe and the United States and chaired gerontological symposia in Australia, the United States, and Japan.

LINDA BURTON is Director of the Center for Human Development and Family Research in Diverse Contexts and Professor of Human Development and Sociology at Penn State University. She was a Spencer Foundation Fellow, Brookdale National Fellow, William T. Grant Faculty Scholar, Fellow at the Center for Advanced Study in the Behavioral Sciences at Stanford University and is the former Director of the National Institute of Mental Health-sponsored Research Consortium and on Diversity, Family Processes, and Child Adolescent Mental Health and the Consortium's Multisite Postdoctoral Training Program. Her research explores the relationship between community contexts, poverty, intergenerational family structure and processes, and development and outcomes across the life course in ethical/racial minority populations. She is currently principal investigator of the ethnographic components of two longitudinal studies of families and poverty in urban and rural settings, Welfare, Children, and Families: A Three-City Study and The Family Life Project.

TONI CALASANTI, Professor of Sociology and Faculty Affiliate of the Center for Gerontology at Virginia Tech, is the author (with Kathleen Slevin) of *Gender, Social Inequalities, and Aging* (2001, Alta Mira Press). Previous research centered on gender, race, and class inequality and aging, particularly as these relate to retirement, and paid and unpaid labor. More recent work includes a more explicit focus on the intersection of age relations with other inequalities, especially in terms of aging bodies and anti-aging industry. She and Kathleen Slevin are co-editing *Age Matters* (Routledge), a volume that explores the significance of age relations for feminist theory, research, and practice.

STEPHEN CRYSTAL (Ph.D., Harvard, 1981) has been a pioneer in the development of the cumulative advantage perspective in aging and the "two worlds of aging" that result from cumulative advantage processes. In an influential line of work that began with his book *America's Old Age Crisis: Public Policy and The Two Worlds of Aging* (Basic Books, 1981) and has continued to the present, he has explored in numerous publications the impacts of lifecourse events and public policies on later-life economic outcomes, and the role of cumulative advantage processes in shaping the distribution of resources in old age. Dr. Crystal is Chair, Division on Aging, and Director of the Center for Health Services Research Development, Institute for Health, Rutgers University.

DALE DANNEFER is a Professor of Sociology at Case Western Reserve University. His scholarly work has been concerned with the links between cultural representations and the characterization of age and aging in science, and with the interrelation of social structure and life course processes. A pioneer in developing cumulative advantage theory as a life-course framework, his research interests also include age segregation and the restructuring of social institutions, and the implications of globalization and life course theory.

KATHRYN DOUTHIT, Ph.D., is an Assistant Professor of Counseling and Human Development at the Margaret Warner Graduate School of Education and Human Development of the University of Rochester. Her interdisciplinary research interests reflect her diverse background in biomedical sciences, human development, and counseling. Dr. Douthit's research, situated broadly within the field of critical biopsychiatry, looks specifically at life course stress-diathesis models of Alzheimer's dementia, geriatric depression, and attention-deficit/hyperactivity disorder. With an eye toward psychopathology prevention, her research attempts to integrate her understanding of human physiology, social determinants of cumulative advantage, and the etiology of mental disorder.

CARROLL L. ESTES, Ph.D., is a Professor of Sociology at the University of California, San Francisco (UCSF). She is the founding and former director of the Institute for Health and Aging (1979-1998) and the former chair of the Department of Social and Behavioral Sciences, School of Nursing, UCSF. Dr. Estes is a member of the Institute of Medicine and the National Academy of Sciences, and past president of the Gerontological Society of America (GSA), the American Society on Aging (ASA), the Association for Gerontology in Higher Education (AGHE). She has served as a consultant to the U.S. Commissioner on Social Security and the U.S. Senate and House committees on aging for more than two decades.

STEPHEN KATZ, Professor of Sociology at Trent University in Peterborough, Canada, is author of *Disciplining Old Age* (1996), *Cultural Aging* (2005), and several journal articles and book chapters on theoretical gerontology, cultures of expertise, and the sociology of the body. His contributions to Canadian and international scholarship address the changing social patterns, political programs, and popular imagery associated with aging populations.

NEAL KING is Associate Professor of Interdisciplinary Studies at Virginia Tech. He is author of *Heroes in Hard Times,* co-editor of *Reel Knockouts,* and has published articles on inequality and culture in such journals as *Gender & Society* and *Men and Masculinities.* Research interests include controversies over media violence, men's justifications for sexual assault, changes in the racial attitudes of whites in the United States, and the intersections of forms of social inequality.

CHUCK LONGINO is the Washington M. Wingate Professor of Sociology and Director of the Reynolda Gerontology Program at Wake Forest University. He was editor of the *Journal of Gerontology: Social Sciences* from 2002 to 2006, and President of the Gerontological Society of America, 2006. He earned his Ph.D. from UNC-Chapel Hill and held a post-doctoral fellowship in the Midwest Council for Social Research in Aging. In addition, he taught at the University of Virginia, University of Kansas, and the University of Miami earlier in his career.

CHRIS PHILLIPSON has held the post of Professor of Applied Social Studies and Social Gerontology, at the University of Keele since 1988. He is Pro-Vice Chancellor (Learning and Academic Development) for the University. He has published extensively in the field of critical gerontology and related areas. He is currently undertaking research on issues relating to social exclusion in old age and the impact of urbanization on the lives of older people. His books include: *Reconstructing Old Age, The Family and Community Life of Older People* (co-authored), *Women in Transition: A Study of the Experiences of Bangladeshi Women Living in Tower Hamlets* (co-authored).

LARRY POLIVKA has served as Director of the Florida Policy Exchange Center on Aging, which is part of the School of Aging Studies at the University of South Florida, since September of 1992. Since August 2003, he has served as Associate Director of the USF School of Aging Studies. Dr. Polivka worked at the State of Florida's Health and Rehabilitative Services as Assistant Secretary for Aging and Adult Services from August 1989 through September 1992 and as Policy Coordinator for Health and Human Services, Office of Planning and Budgeting, Executive Office of the Governor from 1986 through August 1989. Dr. Polivka's primary research interests are in long-term care, housing, ethics and politics of care, globalization/population aging, cultures of aging, and the arts/humanities and aging.

SANDRA TORRES is an Associate Professor in Sociology at Mälardalen University and at the National Institute for the Study of Ageing and Later Life at Linköping University. She is also one of the researchers affiliated with the Social Gerontology Research Group of Uppsala University. Her research interests lie at the crossroads between the sociology of aging and the sociology of migration and ethnic relations. Her publications have dealt with, among others, the lack of culture relevance in gerontology; the relationship between cultural values and understandings of successful aging; issues related to late in life migration and the effects that cross-cultural encounters have in the planning and provision of elderly care.

JOHN VINCENT is a Senior Lecturer in the Department of Sociology at Exeter University. He is an anthropologist by original training and has written on the sociology of old age, the politics of old age, and cultural gerontology. He is interested in integrating issues of old age more effectively into the wider sociological agenda of identity and inequality. Amongst other work he has published *Inequality and Old Age* (University College Press, 1995); *Politics, Power and Old Age* (Open University Press, 1999); *Politics and Old Age: Older Citizens and Political Processes in Britain* (with Guy Patterson and Karen Wale, Ashgate, 2001); and most recently *Old Age* (Routledge, 2003).

DR. ALAN WALKER is Professor of Social Policy at the University of Sheffield, United Kingdom. He is Director of The European Research Area in Ageing. Previously he was Director of the Economic and Social Research Council's Growing Older Programme and the European Forum on Population Ageing Research. He is co-founder and Chair of the European Foundation on Social Quality. He was a member of the Technical Committee responsible for drafting the 2002 UN Plan of Action on Ageing. Previously he chaired the European Commission's Observatory on Ageing and Older People. He has been researching and writing on ageing, social policy, and related issues for nearly 30 years and has published more than 20 books and 300 scientific papers. Recent books include *The New Generational Contract, Ageing Europe, Combating Age Barriers in Employment: The Politics of Old Age in Europe,* and *Growing Older: Quality of Life in Old Age.*

KEITH WHITFIELD is Associate Professor of Biobehavioral Health at Penn State University and is a faculty affiliate of the Center for Human Development and Family Research in Diverse Contexts. His research interests include the influence of culture on individual differences in aging with an emphasis on cognitive aging and health. Additionally, he is interested in quantitative genetic applications in the study of cognition and health in adult African Americans.

Index